MANNERS AND CUSTOMS

OF

ANCIENT GREECE.

———

VOL. II.

THE HISTORY

OF THE

MANNERS AND CUSTOMS

OF

ANCIENT GREECE.

BY J. A. ST. JOHN.

IN THREE VOLUMES.
VOL. II.

KENNIKAT PRESS
Port Washington, N. Y./London

THE HISTORY OF THE MANNERS AND
CUSTOMS OF ANCIENT GREECE

First published in 1842
Reissued in 1971 by Kennikat Press
Library of Congress Catalog Card No: 73-113303
ISBN 0-8046-1203-X

Manufactured by Taylor Publishing Company   Dallas, Texas

KENNIKAT CLASSICS SERIES

CONTENTS

OF THE SECOND VOLUME.

BOOK III.

BOOK IV.

CONTENTS.

BOOK V.

RURAL LIFE.

THE HISTORY

MANNERS AND CUSTOMS

OF

ANCIENT GREECE.

BOOK III.

CHAPTER IV.

MARRIAGE CEREMONIES.

WHEN marriage was determined on, whether love
or interest prompted to it, the business part of the
transaction, which in all countries is exceedingly
unromantic, was delegated, as in China, to a female
matchmaker,[1] whose professional duties appear to
have been considered important. She carried the
lover's proposals to the family of his mistress, or
rather, perhaps, broke the ice and paved the way
for him. In the earlier ages men, no doubt, performed this delicate office themselves, or entrusted
it to their parents; as in Homer we find Achilles
declaring, that his father Peleus shall choose a wife
for him. Earlier still, if we may credit certain prevalent traditions, men dispensed altogether with such

---

[1] Προμνηστρία. Aristoph. Nub. 41. et Schol. Poll. iii. 41.

preliminaries and lived " more pecudum" with the
first females who came in their way; a state of bar-
barism from which it is said they were reclaimed
by Cecrops.[1] But, to whomsoever this fable may
trace its origin, it is evidently unworthy of the
slightest credit. Of times sunk in such an abyss
of ignorance no record could remain, or even of
many succeeding revolutions of manners touching
close upon the orbit of civilisation. If, however,
the tradition arose originally out of any real innovation in manners, it may refer to the partial abo-
lition of polygamy, which, whether made by Cecrops
or not, was an important step in the progress of
the Greeks towards polished life.

But if Cecrops ever lived, and should not be regarded as a mere mythological creation, we must
still reject the comparatively modern tradition which
fetches him from Egypt. Coming from the East,
he would more probably have instituted polygamy
than the contrary. In every point of view the tradition is absurd ; for it at once represents the people
of Attica as savages, and as having made considerable advances in the science of civil government.
They have already emerged from the state of patriarchal rule, not by any means the lowest, and
have arrived at the monarchical period in the history
of society—for Cecrops marries the daughter of king
Actæos—yet have not made the first step in refine-

---

[1] Athen. xiii. 2. Mr. Mitford
defers too much to " the tradi-
" tions received in the polished
" ages " when, upon the authority of such traditions and of
such writers as Justin (ii. 6.), he
appears to conclude that, before
the time of Cecrops, the people
of Attica were in knowledge and
civilisation inferior to the wildest
savages. Hist. of Greece, i. 58.
Upon legends and authors of this
description no reliance can be
placed. If society existed, everything "indispensable " to society
also existed; therefore, if marriage
be so, it could not be unknown.
Besides, how happens it that this
same Cecrops who instituted marriage did not likewise teach them
to sow corn, which, if Egypt was,
when he left it, a civilised country,
must have been as familiar to him
as matrimony ? This most necessary acquisition, however, they
were left to make many ages
afterwards, during the reign of
Erechtheus. Justin, ii. 6.

ment,[1] have not passed the barrier dividing the rudest savage from even the barbarian,—had not made the discovery that, for the preservation of society, children must be cared for and maintained, which is impossible until they have other fathers than the community. We must, therefore, reject this Cecropian legend, and acknowledge that, from the earliest times of which any record remains, the people of Hellas married and were given in marriage.

Whatever the original practice of the Greeks may have been, traces of polygamy long continued discernible in their manners. Heracles maintained a seraglio worthy of an Ottoman sultan. His wives, indeed, like those of a wandering Brahmin, were scattered at convenient points over the country, that, whithersoever he roamed, he might find lodging and entertainment; but, as rumours of his different establishments travelled about, the jealousy of the ladies was at last excited and proved fatal to him. Ægeus, too, and his brother Pallas, old Priam, Agamemnon, Theseus, and nearly every public man in the heroic times, are represented as possessing a harem. Indeed, to judge by the practice of princes, it would seem

---

[1] Cf. Goguet, Origine des Loix. iv. 394, where the learned author contends most chivalrously for the received theory. Apollodorus, however, represents Cecrops as an Autochthon, συμφύες ἔχων σῶμα ἀνδρὸς καὶ δράκοντος. iii. 14. 1.—The reason why he was thus said to partake of two natures —half-man and half-snake—has been very variously and very fantastically explained. Diodorus Siculus, (i. p. 17,) derives his title to be considered half a man and half a beast, from his being, by choice a Greek, by nature a barbarian. Yet he conceives that it was the beast that civilised the man. Others explain διφυὴς somewhat differently

to mean that he was of gigantic stature and understood two languages: διὰ μῆκος σώματος οὕτω καλούμενος, ὥς φησιν ὁ Φιλόχορος, ἢ ὅτι Αἰγυπτίων τὰς δύο γλώσσας ἠπίστατο.—Euseb. No. 460.— Eustathius, familiar with the fables of the mythology, turns the tables upon Cecrops, and conceives that he may have civilised himself, not the Athenians, by settling in Attica. He supposes him ἀπὸ ὄφεως εἰς ἄνθρωπον ἐλθειν, ἐπειδὴ ἐκεῖνος ἐλθὼν εἰς Ἑλλάδα καὶ τὸν βάρβαρον Αἰγυπτιασμὸν ἀφεις, χρηστοὺς ἀναλάβετο τρόπους πολιτικοὺς. —In Dionys. Peneg. p. 56.

as if polygamy were the law of every land; so habitual is it with them to transgress, in this point, against public opinion.   A report, still current among certain writers, represents Socrates with two wives, the gentle nature of Xantippe encouraging him, perhaps, to venture on a second! But even that diligent retailer of scandal, Athenæus,[1] rejects this story, which, no doubt, originated with some sophist, who owed the philosopher a grudge. If not in the son of Sophroniscos, however, at least in Philip of Macedon, the kings of heroic times found an exact imitator.   This Pellæan fox, though he did not, like the Persian monarch, lead about with him an army of concubines in his military expeditions, yet, from policy or other motives, contracted numerous marriages, as many, perhaps, as Heracles. Satyros has bequeathed to us a curious account of his majesty's matrimonial exploits. During his long reign, of from twenty to four-and-twenty years, the dishes of one nuptial feast had scarcely time to cool before a new one was in preparation. It was nothing but truffles and rich soup from June till June. I am unable to furnish a list of all the ladies who claimed, through Philip's diffusive love, to be queens of Macedon; but it may be proper to name a few, to show how the morals of his subjects must have been improved by his example. The first lady whose landed attractions won Philip's heart was *Andatè*, an Illyrian, by whom he had a daughter, called Cynna.   To her succeeded *Phila*, sister of Derda and Macatè. His next wives were two Thessalian women, *Pherè* of Nikesipolis, mother of Thessalonia,

---

[1] Deipnosoph. xiii. 2. — Compare the account in Diogenes Laertius, ii. 5. 10.—The conduct of Socrates, who married Xantippe to prove the goodness of his temper, was imitated, we are told, by a Christian lady, who " desired of St. Athanasius to " procure for her, out of the widows fed from the ecclesiastical " corban, an old woman morose, " peevish, and impatient, that " she might by the society of " so ungentle a person have often " occasion to exercise her patience, her forgiveness, and " charity."—Jeremy Taylor's Life of Christ, i. 384.

and *Philinna* of Larissa, mother of Aridæos. Had
he sought merely the women these might have sufficed; but Philip had other views, and, finding marriage a still more expeditious method of extending
his dominions even than conquest, he forthwith added to the list *Olympias*, who brought him the
kingdom of Molossia in dowry, and, as every one
knows, was mother of Alexander. Had the crafty
prince stopped here, posterity, overlooking his immorality, might have applauded his prudence. But,
elated by success, he proceeded to augment the
number of his queens. To Olympias succeeded
Meda, daughter of Cithalas, king of Thrace; and,
lastly, *Cleopatra*, sister of Hippostratos, and niece
of Attalos. By this time he was somewhat advanced in years, for Alexander, son of Olympias,
approached manhood. At the feast given in honour of this new marriage, when the wine had
circulated, as was customary among Macedonians,
Attalos, who had probably drunk deep, observed,
" At length we shall have legitimate princes, not
bastards ! " Alexander, who was present, in resent-
ment of the affront, threw his goblet in the face
of Attalos, who saluted him in the same way. Upon
this, perceiving how matters were likely to proceed,
Olympias fled to Molossia, Alexander into Illyria.
Philip lived to have by Cleopatra one daughter,
Europa; but, shortly afterwards, at the instigation,
it is supposed of Olympias and Alexander, was
murdered by Pausanias.[1]

Ordinary individuals, however, were restrained
from the commission of such immoralities by the
laws, more particularly at Athens, where marriage
was contemplated with all the reverence due to
the great palladium of civilisation. As a necessary
consequence, celibacy could be no other than dis-
reputable, so that, to a man ambitious of public
honour, the possession of a wife and children was

---

[1] Athen. xiii. 5.

no less indispensable than the means of living.[1]
Among the Spartans, bachelors were delivered over
to the tender mercies of the women, and subjected
to very heavy penalties.   During the celebration of
certain festivals they were seized by a crowd of pe-
tulant viragoes, each able to strangle an ox,[2] and
dragged in derision round the altars of the gods,
receiving from the fists of their gentle tormentors
such blows as the regular practice of boxing had
taught the young ladies to inflict.[3]

> "And ladies sometimes hit exceeding hard."

But we shall be the less inclined to judge un-
charitably of this somewhat unfeminine custom, if
we consider that, in the ancient world, no less than
in the modern, unmarried and childless women were
held but in slight esteem.   And this feeling, which
never for a moment slumbers in society, teaches
better than the cant of a thousand sentimentalists
what the true origin of love is.

Of the impediments to marriage arising, among
ancient nations, from relationship or consanguinity,
very little is with certainty known.   In the heroic
ages, all unions excepting those of parents with
their children appear to have been lawful; for, in
the Odyssey, we find the six sons of Æolos joined
in marriage with their six sisters, the manners of
the olden times, abandoned on earth, still lingering
among the gods.

Iphidamos has to wife his mother's sister,[4] and
Alcinoös, by no means a profligate or immoral prince,
is united with his brother's daughter;[5] Deiphobos,
after Paris's death, takes possession of Helen,[6] and
Helenos, the seer, is united in wedlock with Andromache, the widow of his brother Hector.[7]   But
without alleging any further examples, we may, from

---

[1] Dinarch. in Demosth. §11. Cf.
Poll. viii. 40.   Comm. p. 644.

[2] Aristoph. Lysistrat. 78, seq.

[3] Athen. xiii. 2.

[4] Hom. Il. λ. 221, seq.

[5] Hom. Odyss. η. 55, seq.

[6] Keightley, Mythology, p. 490.

[7] Serv. ad Virg. Æn. iii. 297.

the practice imputed to the gods, among whom scarcely any degree of relationship was a bar to marriage, infer that, in very early ages, few scruples were entertained upon the subject. Later mythologists have even imputed to Zeus an illicit amour with his daughter Aphrodite,[1] but libellously, and in contradiction to the best ancient authorities.[2] Nature, indeed, has so peremptorily prohibited the union of parents with their own children, that positive laws forbidding connexions so nefarious, have in all ages been nearly unnecessary, though the superstition of the Magi [3] in ancient, and the profligacy of popes and princes in modern times, have been accused of transgressing these natural boundaries.

Could we credit the sophist of Naucratis, there was likewise one distinguished person [4] among the Athenians who coveted the reputation of equal guilt.

[1] Virg. Cir. 133.
Sed malus ille puer, quem nec
    sua flectere mater,
Iratum potuit, quem nec pater,
    atque avus idem
Jupiter.

[2] For Valckernaer's correction of Eurip. Hippol. 536, where for ὁ Δίος παῖς, he reads ὄλιγος παῖς, should, I think, be adopted. Diatrib. in Eurip. Perd. Dram. xv. p. 159, c. His whole defence of Zeus on this count is triumphant. Still the notes of Monk, Beck, Musgrave, and the Classical Journal, vi. 80, should be compared.

[3] Diog. Laert. Prœm. § 6. To this practice Euripides probably alludes in the Andromache, v. 173, sqq., where Hermione describes, with scorn, the profligate manners of the barbarians. Catullus, inveighing against the impious depravity of a contemporary, observes—

" Nam Magus ex matre et gnato
    gignatur oportet,
Si vera est Persarum *impia religio*."
Epig. lxxxiii. 3, seq. Pope Alexander VI. and the Emperor Shah Jehan have, in modern times, been accused of similar crimes. Bayle, Dict. Hist. et Crit. Art. Alexandre VI. and Bernier, Voyages, t. i. On the prohibited degrees of consanguinity, see Sepulveda, de Ritu Nupt. et Dispens. i. § 20, where he says, that the Pope could authorize all unions, save those between parents and children. " Et ideo hodiè non ligant, nisi quatenus ab ecclesia sunt assumptæ ; ac propterea Papa dispensare potest cum omnibus personis, nisi cum matre et patre, ut matrimonium contrahant." Card. Cajetan. ap. Sepulved. ub. sup.
[4] Alcibiades. Athen. xii. 48. xiii. 34. Lysias, fr. p. 640.

The marriage of brothers with their own sisters was, in later ages, considered illegal; not so with respect to half sisters by the fathers's side, whom no law forbade men to marry.[1] Still the recorded examples of those who availed themselves of this privilege are few; but among them we find the great Cimon, son of Miltiades, who, from affection, observes Cornelius Nepos, and in perfect conformity with the manners of his country, took to wife his sister Elpinice.[2] Plutarch, too, speaks of the union as public and legal, but Athenæus[3] characteristically insinuates that Elpinice was merely her brother's mistress. The Spartan law took a different view of what constitutes sisterhood. Here the father was everything, and therefore with an uterine sister, as no near relation, marriage might be contracted.[4] All connexions in the direct line of ascent or descent were prohibited; but the prohibition extended not to the collateral branches,[5] uncles being permitted to take to wife their nieces, and nephews their aunts.

The precise age at which an Athenian citizen might legally take upon him the burden of a family, is said, without proof, though not altogether without probability, to have been determined by Solon; for such matters were in those ages supposed to come within the legitimate scope of legislation.[6] They attributed to the season of youth a much greater duration than comports with our notions. It was, in

[1] Sch. Aristoph. Nub. 1353.

[2] Corn. Nep. Vit. Cim. i. Plut. Cim. § 4, where we find this lady accused of an amour with the painter Polygnotos, who introduced her portrait among the Trojan ladies in the Stoa Pœcile.

[3] Deipnosophist. xiii. 56. Muretus, Var. Lect. vii. i. discusses the question, but without throwing much new light upon it.—Andocides cont. Alcibiad. § 9, assigns

Cimon's amour with Elpinice as the cause of his banishment. We find, however, Archeptolis, son of Themistocles, marrying his half-sister Mnesiptolema. Plut. Themistocl. § 32.

[4] Meurs. Themis Attica. i. 14. Philo. De Leg. Spec. ii. Eurip. Orest. 545. sqq.

[5] Cf. Herod. v. 39. Pausan. iii. 3, 9.

[6] Censor. de Die Natal. 14.

fact, thought to extend to the age of thirty-five or thirty-seven, more or less : when entering upon the less flowery domain of manhood, men would need the aid and consolation of a helpmate. But if there ever existed such a law it was often broken,[1] for early marriages, though less common perhaps than in modern times, are constantly alluded to both by historians and poets. Apprehensions of the too great increase of population already led philosophers, even in those early ages, vainly to apply themselves to the discovery of checks, which the irresistible impulses of nature always render nugatory; and viewing in that light the regulation attributed to Solon,[2] they, with some variation, adopt it in their political works. Plato,[3] in accordance with Hesiod's notion, fixes for the male, the marriageable age at thirty; but Aristotle, who chose on most points to differ from his master, allows his citizens seven years more of liberty. For women the proper age, he thought, is about eighteen. His reasons are, that the husband and wife will thus flourish and decay together ; and, their offspring inheriting the bloom and highest vigour of their parents, be at once[4] healthy in body and energetic in mind.

Winter, more particularly the month of January, thence called Gamelion, or the " Nuptial Month," was regarded as the fittest season[5] of the year for the celebration of marriage; and if the north wind happened to blow, as at that time of the year it often does, the circumstance was supposed to be peculiarly auspicious. For this notion several physiological reasons are assigned ; as that, during the

---

[1] Thus Mantitheos, in Demosthenes, marries at the age of eighteen, in obedience to his father's wishes.—Contr. Bœot. ii. § 1.

[2] Aristot. Polit. ii. 7. vii. 14. Gœttling.—Cf. Malthus on Population, í. 9, 10.

[3] Repub. v. t. vi. p. 237. De

Legg. vi. t. vii. p. 452. Hesiod, Opp. et Dies, 696. Gœttling.

[4] Polit. vii. 16. Hist. Anim. vii. 5, 6. Cf. Tac. de Mor. Germ. 20. Just. Instit. t. x. Brisson. de Jur. Nupt. p. 99.

[5] Olympiod. in Meteor. c. 6. Meurs. Grec. Fer. v. 240.

prevalence of that wind, the human frame is peculiarly nervous and full of energy; that the spirits are consequently light, and the temper and disposition sweet, cheerful, and flexible. Lingering sparks of ancient superstition may also have had their share in establishing this persuasion : towards that quarter of the heavens, as towards an universal *Kebleh*, all the civilised nations of antiquity turned as the home of their gods; in that direction point all the openings of the Egyptian pyramids; thither to the present moment turn the Chinese and Brahmins when they pray, and in the holy tabernacle of the Jews the Table of Shewbread [1] likewise faced the north. Attention, too, was paid to the lunar influences; for, no other circumstance preventing it, it was usual to fix on the full of the moon, when the festival denominated *Theogamia*, or "Nuptials of the Gods" was celebrated, in order that religion itself, by its august and venerable ceremonies, might appear to sanctify the union of mortals effected under its auspices.

To this practice there are several allusions in ancient writers. Agamemnon, in Euripides, when questioned by his wife respecting the time of Iphigenia's marriage, replies, that it shall take place

"When the blest moon its silvery circle fills." [2]

And Themis, adjudging Thetis to Peleus, to terminate the contentions of the gods, selects the same season for the solemnization of the nuptial rites.

> " But when next that solemn eve
> Duly doth the moon divide,
> For the chieftain let her leave
> Her lovely virgin zone aside."[3]

Most ancient nations, as the Hebrews, Indians,

---

[1] Exod. xl. 22.
[2] Iphigen. in Aul. 717.
[3] Pindar, Isth. Od. viii. 44, seq.

Dissen.—Rev. H. F. Cary's translation, admirable for its closeness and spirit, p. 212.

Thracians, Germans, and Gauls, regarded women as
a marketable commodity; and, in this respect, the
Greeks of early times perfectly agreed with them,
buying and selling their females like cattle.[1] But,
by degrees, as manners grew more polished, this
barbarous custom was discontinued, though, in re-
membrance of it, presents were still made both to
the father and the bride, even in the most civilised
periods. We must, nevertheless, beware that we
infer not too much from these gifts; for equally
primitive and prevalent was the custom imposing
upon fathers the necessity of dowrying their daughters.[2] In the case, too, of the husband's death this
matrimonial portion devolved to the children, so that
if the widow chose,—as widows sometimes will,[3]—to
embark a second time on the connubial sea, her
father was called upon to furnish a fresh outfit.
But, if the husband grew tired of his better half,
and would insist on a divorce, or if, after his death,
the sons were sufficiently unnatural to chase their
mother from the paternal roof, the right over the
entire dowry reverted to her.[4]

Parties were usually betrothed before marriage
by their parents. And young women, whose parents
no longer survived, were settled in marriage by
their brothers, grandfathers, or guardians. Husbands
on their deathbeds sometimes disposed of the hands
of their wives, as in the case of Demosthenes' father, who bequeathed Cleobula to Aphobos, whom
he likewise appointed guardian of his children. In
this instance, the widow had better have chosen for

---

[1] Aristot. Polit. ii. 6. Tacit.
de Mor. Germ. 18. Heracl. Pont.
v. Θρακων. Leg. Salic. Art. 46.
Hist. Gen. des Voy. vi. 144. Cf.
Goguet, Orig. des Loix, i. 53.

[2] In cases where the fathers
were unable to dowry them, we
find daughters growing old in the
paternal mansion. Demosth. in
Steph. i. § 20. Dowries were

frequently considerable, amounting sometimes to a hundred minæ.
§ 18.

[3] On their anxiety to discover
the designs of the Fates in this
respect, see Schol. Aristoph. Lysist. 597.

[4] Goguet, Orig. des Loix, iii.
127, sqq.

herself. Aphobos possessed himself of the dowry, and consented to fulfil the office of guardian, that he might plunder the children; but the marriage he declined. Another example occurs in the case of Phormio who, having been slave[1] to an opulent citizen, and conducted himself with zeal and fidelity, received at once his freedom and the widow of his master. In all serious matters the Athenians were a very methodical people, and conducted everything, even to the betrothing or marrying of a wife, with an attention to form worthy the quaintest citizen of our own great city.

Potter observes, with great naïveté, that, before men married, it was customary to provide themselves with a house to live in. The custom was a good one, and the thrifty old poet of Ascra, undertaking to enlighten his countrymen in economics, is explicit on the point—

" First build your house and let the wife succeed : " [2]

which, no doubt, is better advice than if he had said "first marry a wife and next consider where you shall put her." And we find that, even among pastoral, young ladies who, in modern poets, make their meat and drink of love, and hang up a rag or two of it to preserve them from the elements, in antiquity posed their lovers with interrogations about comforts. " You are very pressing, my dear Daphnis, and swear you love me ; but that is not just now the question. Have you a house and harem to take me to ?" [3]

But prudent as they may be considered, the Athenians were still more pious than thrifty. Before the virgin quitted her childhood's home, and passed from the state she had tried, and in most cases, perhaps, found happy, to enter into one altogether unknown to her, custom demanded the performance, on

[1] Demosth. pro Phorm. § 8—
10.

[2] Opera et Dies, 405.

[3] Theocrit. Eidyll. xxvii. 36.

the day before the marriage, of several religious ceremonies eminently significant and beautiful. Hitherto,
in the poetical recesses of their thalamoi, they had
been reckoned as so many nymphs attached to the
train of the virgin goddess of the woods. About
to become members of a noviciate more conformable to nature than that of the Catholic church,
they deemed it incumbent on them to implore their
Divinity's permission to transfer their worship from
her to Hymen; and, the more readily to obtain it,
they approached her, in the simplicity of their hearts,
with baskets full of offerings such as it became them
to present and her to receive.[1] Nor was Artemis
the only deity sought, on this occasion, to be rendered auspicious by sacrifice and prayer. Offerings
were likewise made to the Nymphs, those lovely
creations with which the fancy of the Greeks peopled the streams and fountains of their native land.[2]
These rites performed, the future bride was conducted in pomp to the citadel, where solemn sacrifice was offered up to Athena, the tutelar goddess
of the state, with prayers for happiness, peculiarly the
gift of supreme wisdom.[3] To Hera, also, and the
Fates,[4] as to the goddesses that watched over the
connubial state and rigidly punished those who trans-
gressed its sacred laws, were gifts presented, and
vows preferred; and on one or all of their several
altars did the maiden deposit a lock of her own
hair, in remoter ages, perhaps, the whole of it, to
intimate that, having obtained a husband, she must
preserve him by other means than beauty, and the
arts of the toilette.[5] At Megara the young women

[1] Theocrit. Eidyll. ii. 66, ibique
Schol.
[2] Schol. Pind. Pyth. iv. ap.
Meurs. Græc. Fer. p. 238.
[3] Suid. v. προτέλεια. t. ii. p.
629. v. Æschyl. Eumen. 799.
Cf. Cœl. Rhodig. xxviii. 24.
[4] Poll. iii. 38. Schol. Pind.

Pyth. x. 31. Aristoph. Thesmoph. 982. Kust.
[5] Poll. iii. 38. ibique Comm. p.
529, seq. Cf. Spanh. Observ. in
Callim. 149, 507. The youth
usually cut off their hair on reaching the age of puberty. Athen.
xiii. 83.

devoted their severed locks to Iphinoë. Those of
Delos to Hecaerga and Ops,[1] while, like the Athenians, the maidens of Argos performed this rite in
honour of Athena.[2]

Having, by the performance of the above rites and
others of similar significance, discharged their instant
duties to the gods, and impressed on their own minds
a deep sense of the sacred engagements they were
about to contract, they proceeded to perform the
nuptial ceremonies themselves, still intermingling the
offices of religion with every portion of the transaction. An auspicious day having been fixed upon,
the relations and friends of both parties assembled
in magnificent apparel, at the house of the bride's
father, where all the ladies of the family were busily
engaged in the recitation of prayers and presenta-
tion of offerings. These domestic ceremonies concluded, the bride, accompanied by her paranymph or
bridesmaid, was led forth into the street by the
bridegroom and one of his most intimate friends,[3]
who placed her between them in an open carriage.[4]
Their dresses, as was fitting, were of the richest and
most splendid kind. Those of the bridegroom full,
flowing, and of the gayest and brightest colours,[5]
glittered with golden ornaments, and diffused around,
as he moved, a cloud of perfume. The bride herself,
gifted with that unerring taste which distinguished
her nation, appeared in a costume at once simple and
magnificent—simple in its contour, its masses, its
folds, magnificent from the brilliance of its hues
and the superb and costly style of its ornaments.
She was not, like some modern court dame, a blaze

[1] Pausan. i. 43. 4. Callim. in
Del. 292. Spanh. Observat. t. ii.
p. 503, sqq.

[2] Stat. Theb. ii. 255, with the
ancient commentary of Lutatius.

[3] Πάροχος. Suid. v. Ζεῦγος
ἡμιονικὸν. t. i. p. 1123, b.
Eurip. Helen. 722, sqq.

[4] This was the usual practice.
When the bride was led home on
foot she was called χαμαίπους a
term of disrespect not far removed
in meaning from our word tram-
per. Poll. iii. 40.

[5] Aristoph. Plut. 529, et Schol.
Suid. v. βαπτά. t. i. p. 533, b.

of precious stones tastelessly heaped upon each other ;
but through the snowy gauze of her veil flashed the
jewelled fillet and coronet-like sphendone which, with
a chaplet of flowers,[1] adorned her dark tresses; and
between the folds of her robe of gold-embroidered
purple, appeared her gloveless fingers, with many
rings glittering with gems. Strings of Red Sea
pearls encircled her neck and arms ; pendants, variously wrought and dropped with Indian jewels,
twinkled in her ears; and her feet, partly concealed
by the falling robe, displayed a portion of the golden
thonged sandal, crusted with emeralds, rubies, or
pearls. But all these ornaments often failed to dis-
tract the eye from those which she owed to nature.
Her luxuriant hair, which in Eastern women often
reaches the ground :

> Her hair in hyacinthine flow,
> When left to roll its folds below,
> As 'midst her maidens in the ball
> She stood superior to them all,
> Hath swept the marble, where her feet
> Gleamed whiter than the mountain sleet,
> Ere from the cloud that gave it birth
> It fell and caught one stain of earth ;

her hair, I say, perfumed with delicate unguents,[2]
such as nard from Tarsos, œranthe from Cypros,
essence of roses from Cyrene, of lilies from Ægina
or Cilicia, fell loosely in a profusion of ringlets
over her shoulders, while in front it was confined by
the fillet and grasshoppers of gold.[3] More perish-
able ornaments, in the shape of crowns of myrtle,
wild thyme,[4] poppy, white sesame, with other flowers

---

[1] Eurip. Iphig. in Aul. 905.
This chaplet was placed on the
bride's head by her mother.
Hopfn. in loc.—In Locrensibus
usu erat, ut matronæ ex lectis
floribus nectant coronas. Nam
emptagestare serta, vitio dabatur.
Alex. ab Alexand. p. 58. b.

[2] Aristoph, Plut. 529. id. Pac.
862.

[3] Thucyd. i. 60.

[4] Σισυμϐρία. Dioscor. ii. 155.

and plants sacred to Aphrodite, adorned the heads
of both bride and bridegroom.[1]

The relations and friends followed, forming, in most
cases, a long and stately procession, which, in the
midst of crowds of spectators, moved slowly towards
the temple, thousands strewing flowers or scattering perfume in their path, and in loud exclamations
comparing the happy pair to the most impassioned
and beautiful of their nymphs and gods.[2] Meanwhile, a number of the bride's friends, scattered
among the multitude, were looking out anxiously
for favourable omens, and desirous, in conjunction
with every person present, to avert all such as superstition taught them to consider inauspicious. A
crow appearing singly was supposed to betoken sorrow or separation, whereas, a couple of crows,[3] issuing from the proper quarter of the heavens,
presaged perfect union and happiness. A pair of
turtle doves, of all omens, was esteemed the best.[4]

On reaching the temple, the bride and bridegroom
were received at the door by a priest, who presented
them with a small branch of ivy, as an emblem of
the close ties by which they were about to be united for ever. They were then conducted to the
altar,[5] where the ceremonies commenced with the
sacrifice of a heifer,[6] after which Artemis, Athena,
and other virgin goddesses, were solemnly invoked.
Prayers were then addressed to Zeus and his con-
sort, the supreme divinities of Olympos;[7] nor, on this
occasion, would they overlook the ancient gods, Ou-
ranos and Gaia, whose union produces fertility and

---

[1] Schol. Aristoph. Av. 160.
In Bœotia the bride was crowned
with a reed of wild asparagus, a
prickly but sweet plant. Plut.
Conjug. Præcept. 2. Bion. Epitaph. Adon. 88. On Nuptial
Crowns vide Paschal. De Co-
ronis, lib. ii. c. 16. p. 126, sqq.

[2] Charit. Char. et Callir.
Amor. iii. 44.

[3] Orus Apollo Hieroglyph. viii.
p. 6. b.

[4] Meziriac sur les Epitres
d'Ovide, p. 190, sqq. Ælian de
Animal. Nat. iii. 9. Alex. ab
Alexand. ii. 5, p. 57, b.

[5] Theod. Prodrom. de Rhodanth.
et Dosicl. Amor. ix.

[6] Eurip. Iphig. in Aul. 1113.

[7] Poll. iii. 38.

abundance,[1]—the Graces, whose smile shed upon life
its sweetest charm, and the Fates, who shorten or
extend it at their pleasure, were next in order
adored ; and, lastly, Aphrodite, the mother of Love,
and of all the host of Heaven, the most beautiful
and beneficent to mortals.[2] The victim having been
opened, the gall was taken out and significantly
cast behind the altar.[3] Soothsayers skilled in divination then inspected the entrails, and if their appearance was alarming the nuptials were broken
off, or deferred. When favourable, the rites proceeded as if hallowed by the smile of the gods.
The bride now cut off one of her tresses, which,
twisting round a spindle, she placed as an offering
on the altar of Athena, while, in imitation of Theseus, the bridegroom made a similar oblation to
Apollo, bound, as an emblem of his out-door life,
round a handful of grass or herbs.[4] All the other
gods, protectors of marriage, were then, by the parents or friends, invoked in succession, and the rites
thus completed, the virgin's father, placing the hand
of the bridegroom in that of the bride, said, " I be-
" stow on thee my daughter, that thine eyes may
" be gladdened by legitimate offspring."[5] The oath
of inviolable fidelity was now taken by both, and
the ceremony concluded with fresh sacrifices.

The performance of rites so numerous generally
consumed the whole day, so that the shades of evening were falling before the bride could be conducted
to her future home. This hour, indeed, according
to some, was chosen to conceal the blushes of the
youthful wife.[6] And now commenced the secular
portion of the ceremony. Numerous attendants,

[1] Procl. in Tim. t. v. Meziriac. p. 155.
[2] Etym. Mag. 220, 53. sqq. Cf.
Plut. Conj. Præcept. prooem. t. i.
p. 321. Tauchnitz.
[3] Plut. Conj. Precept. 27. Cœl.
Rhodig. xxviii. 21.

[4] Meurs. Lect. Att. iii. 6, 106,
sqq. Herod. iv. 34.

[5] Menand. ap. Clem. Alexand.
Stromat. ii. p. 421, a. Heins.

[6] Potter, Arch. Græc. ii. 281.

bearing lighted torches,[1] ran in front of the procession, while bands of merry youths dancing, singing, or playing on musical instruments, surrounded the nuptial car. Similar in this respect was the practice throughout Greece, even so early as the time of Homer, who thus, in his description of the Shield, calls up before our imagination the lively picture of an heroic nuptial procession :

> " Here sacred pomp and genial feasts delight,
>   And solemn dance and Hymeneal rite.
> Along the streets the new-made brides are led,
>   With torches flaming, to the nuptial bed.
> The youthful dancers in a circle bound
> To the soft flute and cittern's silver sound.[2]
> Through the fair streets the matrons, in a row,
> Stand in their porches and enjoy the show." [3]

The song on this occasion sung received the name of the " Carriage Melody," from the carriage in which the married pair rode while it was chaunted.[4]

The house of the bridegroom, diligently prepared for their reception, was decorated profusely with garlands, and brilliantly lighted up. When, among the Bœotians, the lady, accompanied by her husband, had descended from the carriage, its axletree was burnt, to intimate that having found a home she would have no further use for it.[5] The celebration of nuptial rites generally puts people in good temper, at least

[1] Eurip. Helen. 722. Hesiod, Scut. Heracl. 275, seq. where the torches are said to be borne by Dmoës.

[2] In Hesiod a troop of blooming virgins, playing on the phorminx, lead the procession. αἱ δ' ὑπὸ φορ-μίγγων ἄναγον χορὸν ἱμερόεντα. A band of youths follow, playing on the syrinx. See the note of Gœttling on Scut. Heracl. 274, p. 117, sqq.

[3] Iliad. σ. 490, sqq. Pope's Translation.

[4] Ἁρμάτειον μέλος. Leisner, in his notes on Bos (Antiq. Græc. Pars. iv. c. ii. § 4.), observes, that in Suidas, Hesychius, and Eustathius (ad Il. χ. p. 1380. 5), these words have a different meaning from that which, with Bos and Potter (Antiq. Græc. ii. 282), I have adopted. But in the passage quoted by Henri de Valois (ad Harpocrat. p. 222), they would seem to bear the signification above given them.

[5] Plut. Quæst. Roman. xx. 19. Valckenaer ad Herodot. iv. 114.

for the first day; and new-married women at Athens
stood in full need of all they could muster to assist
them through the crowd of ceremonies which beset
the entrances to the houses of their husbands. Sym-
bols of domestic labours, pestles, sieves,[1] and so on,
met the young wife's eye on all sides. She herself,
in all her pomp of dress, bore in her hands an earthen
barley-parcher.[2] But, to comfort her, very nice cakes
of sesamum,[3] with wine and fruit and other dainties
innumerable, accompanied by gleeful and welcoming
faces, appeared in the background beyond the sieves
and pestles. The hymeneal lay,[4] with sundry other
songs, all redolent of "joy and youth," resounded
through halls now her own. Mirth and delight
ushered her into the banqueting-room, where appeared
a boy covered with thorn branches, and oaken boughs
laden with acorns, who, when the epithalamium
chaunters had ceased, recited an ancient hymn beginning with the words, "I have escaped the worse and
" found the better."[5] This hymn, constituting a portion of the divine service performed by the Athenians
during a festival instituted in commemoration of the
discovery of corn, by which men were delivered from
acorn-eating, they introduced among the nuptial ceremonies to intimate, that wedlock is as much superior
to celibacy as wheat is to mast. At the close of the
recitation, there entered a troop of dancing girls
crowned with myrtle-wreaths, and habited in light
tunics reaching very little below the knee, just as
we still behold them on antique gems and vases, who,
by their varied, free, and somewhat wanton, movements, vividly represented all the warmth and energy
of passion.

The feast which now ensued was, at Athens, to
prevent useless extravagance, made liable to the in-

---

[1] Poll. iii. 37.
[2] Poll. i. 246.
[3] Schol. Aristoph. Pac. 834.
[4] Athen. xiv. 10. Anac. Od.
xviii. Schol. Hom. Il. σ. 493.

Pind. Pyth. iii. 17. Dissen. Schol.
ad v. 27.
[5] Suid. v. ἔφυγον κακὸν. t. i.
p. 1113, d.

spection of certain magistrates. Both sexes partook
of it ; but, in conformity with the general spirit of their
manners and institutions, the ladies, as in Egypt, sat
at separate tables.¹ At these entertainments we may
infer that, among other good things, great quantities
of sweetmeats were consumed, since the woman employed in kneading and preparing them, and in officiating at the nuptial sacrifices, was deemed of sufficient importance to possess a distinct appellation,
(δημιουργὸς,)² while the bride-cake, which doubtless
was the crowning achievement of her art, received the
name of Gamelios. The general arrangement of the
banquet, however, they entrusted to the care of a sort
of major-domo, who received the appellation of Trape-
zopoios.³

Among the princes and grandees of Macedonia the
nuptial banquet differed very widely, as might be expected, from the frugal entertainments of the Athenians ; but as it may assist us in comprehending the
changes introduced into Hellenic manners by the
conquests of Alexander and his successors, I shall
crave the reader's permission to lay before him a description, bequeathed to us by antiquity, of the magnificent banquet⁴ given at the marriage of Caranos.

The guests, twenty in number, immediately on
entering the mansion of the bridegroom, were crowned
by his order with golden stlengides,⁵ each valued at
five pieces of gold. They were then introduced into
the banqueting-hall, where the first article set before
them on taking their places at the board was, no
doubt, exceedingly agreeable, consisting of a silver

---

¹ Luc. Conviv. § 8. In the se-
pulchral grottoes of Eilithyia, in
the Thebaid, we find a rough
fresco representing a marriage-
feast, at which the men and women sit as described in the text.

² Schol. Aristoph. Pac. 421.
Poll. iii. 41. The water of the
bath used on this occasion by the
bride was, according to ancient

custom, brought from the fountain of Enneakrounos. Etym.
Mag. 568, 57, seq.

³ Poll. iv. 41.

⁴ Athen. iv. 2, seq.

⁵ Cf. Schol. Aristoph. Eq. 578.
Ἔστι τι στλεγγὶς, δέρμα κεχρυ-
σωμένον, ὁ περὶ τὴν κεφαλὴν
φοροῦσι. — Poll. vii. 179.

beaker presented to each as a gift, which, when they had drained off, they delivered to their attendant slaves, who, according to the custom of the country, stood behind their seats with large baskets intended to contain the presents to be bestowed on them by the master of the feast.[1] There was then placed before every member of the company a bronze salver, of Corinthian workmanship, completely covered by a cake, on which were piled roast fowls and ducks and woodcocks, and a goose, together with other dainties in great abundance. These, likewise, followed the beakers into the corbels of the slaves, and were succeeded by numerous dishes, of which the guests were expected to partake on the spot. Next was brought in a capacious silver tray, also covered by a cake, whereon were heaped up geese, hares, kids, other cakes curiously wrought, pigeons, turtle-doves, partridges, with a variety of similar game, which, likewise, after they had been tasted, I presume, were handed to the servants.[2]

When the rage of hunger had been appeased, as it must soon have been, they washed their hands, after which crowns, wreathed from every kind of flower, were brought in, and along with them other golden stlengides, equal in weight to the former, were placed, for form's sake, on the heads of the company, before they found their way to the baskets in the rear.

While they were still in a sort of delirium of joy, occasioned by the munificence of the bridegroom, there entered to them a troop of female flute players,

---

[1] When the host happened to be less rich or generous, people sometimes, in the corruption of later ages, endeavoured to steal what they could not obtain as a gift. Thus the sophist Dionysodoros is detected in Lucian with a cup stuffed into the breast of his mantle. — Conviv. seu Lapith. § 46.

[2] This singular kind of liberality continued in fashion down to a very late period: — καὶ ἅμα εἰς ἐκικόμιστο ἡμῖν τὸ ἐντελὲς ὀνομαζόμενον δεῖπνον, μία ὄρνις ἑκάστῳ, καὶ κρέας ὑὸς, καὶ λαγῶα, καὶ ἰχθὺς ἐν ταγήνου, καὶ σησαμοῦντες, καὶ ὅσα ἐν τραγεῖν, καὶ ἐξῆν ἀποφέρεσθαι ταῦτα. Luc. Conviv. § 38.

singers, and Rhodian performers on the Sambukè,[1]
naked in the opinion of some, though others reported
them to have worn a slight tunic. When these
performers had given them a sufficient taste of their
art, they retired to make way for other female slaves,
bearing each a pair of perfume vases, containing
the measure of a cotyla, the one of gold, the other
of silver, and bound together by a golden thong.
Of these every guest received a pair. In fact, the
princely bridegroom, in order, as we suppose, that his
friends might share with him the joy of his nuptials, bestowed upon every one of them a fortune
instead of a supper; for immediately upon the heels
of the gift above described came a number of silver dishes, each of sufficient dimensions to contain
a large roast pig, laid upon its back, with its paunch
thrown open, and stuffed with all sorts of delicacies
which had been roasted with it, such as thrushes,
metræ, and becaficoes, with the yolk of eggs poured
around them, and oysters and cockles. Of these
dishes every person present received one, with its
contents, and, immediately afterwards, such another
dish containing a kid hissing hot. Upon this, Caranos observing that their corbils were crammed,
caused to be presented to them wicker panniers,
and elegant bread-baskets, plaited with slips of ivory.[2]
Delighted by his generosity, the company loudly
applauded the bridegroom, testifying their approbation by clapping their hands. Then followed other
gifts, and perfume vases of gold and silver, presented

---

[1] The Sambukè was a stringed
instrument of triangular form, invented by the poet Ibycos. It
was sometimes called Iambukè,
because used by chaunters of
Iambic verse.—Suid. in v. t. ii.
p. 709, c. d. Poll. iv. 59.

[2] Casaubon is particular in his
explanation of this passage, lest
any one should fall into the singular mistake of supposing these
nuptial bread-baskets to have
been made with plaited thongs
of elephant's hide: " *Lora ele-
phantina* fortasse aliquis capiat
de *corio elephanti:* sed ἱμάντας
arbitror appellare Hippolochum
virgas subtiles ex ebore, quibus
ceu vimine utebantur in contex-
endis panariis istis."—Animadv.
in Athen. t. vii. p. 392.

to the company in pairs as before. The bustle having subsided, there suddenly rushed in a troop of performers worthy to have figured in the feast of the Chytræ,[1] at Athens, and along with them ithyphalli, jugglers, and naked female wonder-workers, who danced upon their heads in circles of swords, and spouted fire from their mouths. These performances ended, they set themselves more earnestly and hotly to drink, from capacious golden goblets, their wines, now less mixed than before, being the Thasian, the Mendian, and the Lesbian. A glass dish, three feet in diameter, was next brought in upon a silver stand, on which were piled all kinds of fried fish. This was accompanied by silver bread-baskets, filled with Cappadocian rolls, some of which they ate, and delivered the rest to their slaves. They then washed their hands, and were crowned with golden crowns, double the weight of the former, and presented with a third pair of gold and silver vases filled with perfume. They by this time had become quite delirious with wine, and began a truly Macedonian contest, in which the winner was he who swallowed most; Proteas, grandson of him who was boon companion to Alexander the Great, drinking upwards of a gallon at a draught, and exclaiming—

> " Most joy is in his soul
> Who drains the largest bowl."

The immense goblet was then given him by Caranos, who declared, that every man should reckon as his own property the bowl whose contents he could despatch. Upon this, nine valiant bacchanals started up at once, and sought each to empty the goblet before the others, while one unhappy wight among the company, envying them their good fortune, sat down and burst into tears because he should go cupless away. The master of the house,

---

[1] Vid. Animadv. in Athen. t. vii. p. 393. Meurs. Græcia Feriata. i. p. 30, seq.

however, unwilling that any should be dissatisfied, presented him with an empty bowl.[1]

A chorus of a hundred men now entered to chaunt the epithalamium; and after them dancing girls, dressed in the character of nymphs and nereids.

The drinking still proceeding, and the darkness of evening coming on, the circle of the hall appeared suddenly to dilate, a succession of white curtains, which had extended all round, and disguised its dimensions, being drawn up, while from numerous recesses in the wall, thrown open by concealed machinery, a blaze of torches flashed upon the guests, seeming to be borne by a troop of gods and goddesses, Hermes, Pan, Artemis, and the Loves, with numerous other divinities, each holding a flambeau and administering light to the assembled mortals.

While every person was expressing his admiration of this contrivance, wild boars of true Erymanthean dimensions, transfixed with silver javelins, were brought in on square trays with golden rims, one of which was presented to each of the company. To the *bon vivants* themselves nothing appeared so worthy of commendation, as that, when anything wonderful was exhibited, they should all have been able to get upon their legs, and preserve the perpendicular, notwithstanding they were so top-heavy with wine.

" Our slaves," says one of the guests, " piled all the " gifts we had received in our baskets; and the trum- " pet, according to the custom of the Macedonians, " at length announced the termination of the repast." Caranos next began that part of the potations in which small cups alone figured, and commanded the slaves to circulate the wine briskly; what they drank in this second bout being regarded as an antidote against that which they had swallowed before.

[1] In like manner, Alexander, son of Philip, when he entertained nine thousand persons at a marriage feast at Susa, presented each of them with a golden goblet, and paid all their debts, amounting to nearly ten thousand talents. — Plut. Alexand. § 70.

They were now, as might be supposed, in the right trim to be amused, and there entered to them the buffoon Mandrogenes, a descendant, it was said, of Strato the Athenian. This professional gentleman for a long time shook their sides with laughter, and terminated his performances by dancing with his wife, an old woman, upwards of eighty.[1] This fit of merriment would appear to have restored the edge of their appetites, and made them ready for those supplementary dainties which closed the achievements of the day. These consisted of a variety of sweetmeats, rendered more tempting by the little ivory-plaited corbels in which they nestled, delicate cakes from Crete, and Samos, and Attica, in the boxes in which they were imported.

Hippolochos, to whose enthusiasm for descriptions of good cheer, the reader is indebted for the above picturesque details, concludes his important narrative by observing, that, when they rose to depart, their anxiety respecting the wealth they had acquired sobered them completely. He then adds, addressing himself to his correspondent Lynceus, " Meanwhile " you, my friend, remaining all alone at Athens, enjoy "the lectures of Theophrastus with your thyme, " rocket and delicate twists, mingling in the revels " of the Linnean and Chytrean festivals. For our " own part we are looking out, some for houses, others " for estates, others for slaves, to be purchased by " the riches which dropped into our baskets at the " supper of Caranos."

The marriage feast having been thus concluded,

---

[1] If octogenarian dancers were held in admiration in England, it would, according to Lord Bacon, be easy to form an army of them; since "there is, he says, scarce a village with us, if it be any whit populous, but it affords some man or woman of fourscore years of age; nay, a few years since there was, in the county of Hereford, a May-game, or morrice-dance, consisting of eight men, whose age computed together, made up eight hundred years, inasmuch as what some of them wanted of an hundred, others exceeded as much." History of Life and Death, p. 20.

the bride was conducted to the harem by the light
of flambeaux, round one of which, pre-eminently
denominated the "Hymeneal Torch," her mother,
who was principal among the torch-bearers, twisted
her hair-lace,[1] unbound at the moment from her head.
On retiring to the nuptial chamber the bride, in
obedience to the laws, ate a quince, together with
the bridegroom, to signify, we are told, that their
first conversation should be full of sweetness and
harmony.[2] The guests continued their revels with
music, dancing, and song, until far in the night.[3]

At daybreak on the following morning their friends
re-assembled and saluted them with a new epithalamium, exhorting them to descend from their bower
to enjoy the beauties of the dawn,[4] which in that
warm and genial climate are even in January equal
to those of a May morning with us. On appearing in
the presence of their congratulators, the wife, as a mark
of affection, presented her husband with a rich woollen cloak,[5] in part, at least, the production of her own
fair hands. On the same occasion the father of the
bride sent a number of costly gifts to the house of
his son-in-law, consisting of cups, goblets, or vases
of alabaster or gold, beds, couches, candelabra, or
boxes for perfumes or cosmetics, combs, jewel-cases,
costly sandals, or other articles of use or luxury.
And, that so striking an instance of his wealth and
generosity might not escape public observation, the
whole was conveyed to the bridegroom's house in
great pomp by female slaves, before whom marched
a boy clothed in white, and bearing a torch in
his hand, accompanied by a youthful basket-bearer

---

[1] Senec. Thebais, Act. iv. 2,
505.

[2] Plut. Conjug. Præcept. i. t.
i. p. 321. Meurs. Them. Att. i·
14, p. 39. Petit. Legg. Att. vi.
i. p. 449.

[3] See Douglas, Essay on certain
points of resemblance between
the ancient and modern Greeks,
p. 114, and Chandler, Travels, ii.
152.

[4] Theocrit. Eidyll. xviii. 9.

[5] Ἀπαυλιστηρία. Poll. iii. 40.

habited like a canephora in the sacred processions.[1]
Customs in spirit exactly similar still survive among
the primitive mountaineers of Wales, where the new-
ly-married couple, in the middle and lower ranks of
life, have their houses completely furnished by the
free-will offerings, not only of their parents but of
their friends. It is, however, incumbent on the re-
cipients to make proof in their turn of equal generosity when any member of the donor's family ven-
tures on the hazards of housekeeping.

[1] Etymol. Mag. 354. 1. sqq. Suid. v. ἐπαυλία, t. i. p. 964, e. sqq.

CHAPTER V.

CONDITION OF MARRIED WOMEN.

FROM the spirit pervading the foregoing ceremonies it will be seen, that married women enjoyed at Athens numerous external tokens of respect. We must now enter the harem, and observe how they lived there. Most, perhaps, of the misapprehensions which prevail on this subject arise out of one very obvious omission,—a neglect to distinguish between the exaggeration and satire of the comic poets, much of which, in all countries, has been levelled at women, and the sober truth of history, less startling, and therefore, less palatable. To comprehend the Athenians, however, we must be content to view them as they were, with many virtues and many vices, often sinning against their women, but never as a general rule treating them harshly. Indeed, according to no despicable testimony, their errors when they erred would appear to have lain in the contrary direction.[1]

Certainly the mistress of a family at Athens was not placed above the necessity of extending her solicitude to the government of her household, though too many even there neglected it, degenerating into the resemblance of those mawkish, insipid, useless things, without heart or head, who often in our times fill fashionable drawing-rooms, and have their reputations translated to Doctors' Commons. Of female education I have already spoken, together with the several acts and ceremonies, which conducted an

[1] For example, public opinion regarded it as more atrocious to kill a woman than a man.— Arist. Prob. xxix. 11.

Athenian woman to the highest and most honourable station her sex can fill on earth. In this new relation she shares with her husband that domestic patriarchal sovereignty, pictures of which abound in the Scriptures. How great soever might be the establishment, she was queen of every thing within doors. All the slaves, male and female, came under her control.[1] To every one she distributed his task, and issued her commands; and when there were no children who required her care, she might often be seen sitting in the recesses of the harem, at the loom, encircled, like an Homeric princess, by her maids,[2] laughing, chatting, or, along with them, exercising her sweet voice in songs,[3] those natural bursts of melody which came spontaneously to the lips of a people whose every-day speech resembled the music of the nightingale.

Xenophon, in that interesting work, the Œconomics, introduces an Athenian gentleman laying open to Socrates the internal regulations of his family. In this picture, the wife occupies an important position in the foreground. She is, indeed, the principal figure around which the various circumstances of the composition are grouped with infinite delicacy and effect. Young and beautiful she comes forth hesitating and blushing at being detected in some slight economical blunders. The husband takes her by the hand; they

---

[1] She wakes them in the morning.—Aristoph. Lysist. 18. This comic poet gives a concise sketch of an Athenian woman's morning work, which rendered their going out difficult at such an hour :—

Χαλεπή τε γυναικῶν ἔξοδος· ἡ μὲν γὰρ ἡμῶν περὶ τὸν ἀνδρ' ἐκύπτασεν· ἡ δ'οἰκέτην ἤγειρεν· ἡ δὲ παιδίον κατέκλινεν· ἡ δ'ἐλουσεν· ἡ δ' ἐψώμισεν.—Lysist. 16, sqq.

[2] Precisely the same picture is presented in the interior of Jason's palace at Pheræ, where we find the tyrant's mother at work in the midst of her handmaidens.—Polyæn. Stratag. vi. i. 5.

[3] Plat. de Legg. t. viii. p. 36. —Among the Thracians, and many other people, women were employed in agriculture, as they are in England and France, as herdswomen and shepherds, and every other laborious employment, like men.—Id. ib.

converse in our presence, and while the interior arrangements of a Greek house are unreservedly laid open, we discover the exact footing on which husband and wife lived at Athens, and a state of more complete confidence, of greater mutual affection, of more considerate tenderness on the one side, or feminine reliance and love on the other, it would be difficult to conceive.

Ischomachos, I admit, is to be regarded as a favourable specimen; he unites in his character the qualities of an enterprising and enlightened country gentleman, with those of a politician and orator of no mean order, and his probity as a citizen infuses an air of mingled grandeur and sweetness into his domestic manners. Describing a conversation which, soon after their marriage, took place between him and his youthful wife, he observes:— "When "we had together taken a view of our possessions "I remarked to her that, without her constant care "and superintendence, nothing of all she had seen "would greatly profit us. And taking my illustra- "tion from the science of politics, I showed that, in "well-regulated states, it is not deemed sufficient "that good laws are enacted, but that proper persons "are chosen to be guardians of those laws, who "not only reward with praise such as yield them "due obedience, but visit also their infraction with "punishment. Now, my love," said I, "you must "consider yourself the guardian of our domestic "commonwealth, and dispose of all its resources as "the commander of a garrison disposes of the sol- "diers under his orders. With you it entirely rests "to determine respecting the conduct of every in- "dividual in the household, and, like a queen, to "bestow praise and reward on the dutiful and obe- "dient, while you keep in check the refractory by "punishment and reproof. Nor should this high "charge appear burdensome to you; for though "the duties of your station may seem to involve "deeper solicitude and necessity for greater exertion

" than we require even from a domestic, these greater
" cares are rewarded by greater enjoyments; since,
" whatever ability they may display in the improving
" or protecting of their master's property, the mea-
" sure of their advantages still depends upon his
" will, while you, as its joint owner, enjoy the right
" of applying it to whatever use you please. It fol-
" lows, therefore, that as the person most interested
" in its preservation you should cheerfully encounter
" superior difficulties."

Having listened attentively to the somewhat quaint
discourse of the Economist, Socrates felt anxious,
as well he might, to learn the result ; for the lady,
expected thus wisely " to queen it," was as yet but
fifteen. His faith, however, in womanhood was great ;
and Xenophon, who but reflects from a less brilliant
mirror the Socratic wisdom, delivers, under the mask
of Ischomachos, the mingled convictions both of the
master and the pupil. The moral beauty of the dialogue, and its truth to nature, would have been lost
had the lady at all shrunk from the duties of her
high office. But her ambition was at once awakened.
The obscurity to which, in the time of Pericles, women
were, by the manners of the country, condemned,
now no longer seemed desirable, and the love of fame
was urged upon her as a motive to extraordinary
exertions.[1] Her reply is highly characteristic. Running, with the unerring tact of her sex, even in advance of her husband, she desired him to believe that
he would have formed an extremely erroneous opinion of her character, had he for a moment supposed
that the care of their common property could ever
have proved burdensome to her : on the contrary,
the really grievous thing would have been to require
her to be neglectful of it !

Men always conceive they are complimenting a

---

[1] That this passion led women to interfere too frequently with politics may be inferred from the remark of Theophrastus, that to be versed in the science of domestic economy was more honourable to them.— Stob. 85. 7. Gaisf.

woman when they attribute to her a masculine understanding, and they thus, in fact, do place her on the
highest intellectual level known to them. Socrates
adopted this style of compliment in speaking of the
wife of Ischomachos. And I may here remark, that
we need no other proof of how differently the Athenians felt on the subject of women from the Orientals
with whom they have been compared, than the mere
circumstance of their conversing openly with strangers
respecting their wives. In the East, a greater affront
could scarcely be offered a man than to inquire about
his female establishment. The most an old friend
does is to say, " Is your house well?" — whereas at
Athens, women formed a never-failing theme in all
companies; which proves them to have been there
contemplated in a different light. In fact, the sentiments of Ischomachos, every way worthy the most
chivalrous people of antiquity, could only have sprung
up in a society where just and exalted notions of
female virtue prevailed; for, under the word " high-
mindedness," we find him grouping every refined and
estimable quality which a gentlewoman can possess.

But, perhaps, the reader will not be displeased if
we introduce dramatically upon the scene an Athenian married pair discussing in his presence a question
closely connected with domestic happiness. There
is little risk of exaggeration. The picture is by Xenophon, a writer whose subdued and sober colouring
is calculated rather to diminish than otherwise the
poetical features of his subject.

By Heaven! exclaimed Socrates, according to this
account, your wife's understanding must be of a highly
masculine character.

Nay, but suffer me, answered the husband, to place
before you a convincing proof of her high-minded-
ness, by showing how, on a single representation, she
yielded to me on a subject extremely important.

Proceed, cried the philosopher, (who had not found
Xantippe thus manageable,) proceed ; for, believe
me, friend, I experience much greater delight in con-

templating the active virtues of a living woman, than
the most exquisite female form by the pencil of Zeuxis
would afford me.

Observing, said Ischomachos, that my wife sought
by cosmetics[1] and other arts of the toilette to render
herself fairer and ruddier than she had issued from
the hands of Nature, and that she wore high-heeled
shoes in order to add to her stature,— Tell me, wife,[2]
I began, would you now esteem me to be a worthy
participator of your fortunes if, concealing the true
state of my affairs, I aimed at appearing richer than
I am, by exhibiting to you heaps of false money,
necklaces of gilded wood for gold, and wardrobes of
spurious for genuine purple?

Nay, exclaimed my wife, interrupting me, put not
the injurious supposition: it is what you could not be
guilty of. For, were such your character I could
never love you from my soul.

Well, by entering together into the bonds of marriage are we not mutually invested with a property in
each other's persons?

People say so.

They say truly: and since this is the case shall I
not more sincerely evince my esteem for you by
watching sedulously over my own health and well-

---

[1] Xen. Œcon. x. ii. 60. Among
the Orientals we find there existed a peculiar collyrium for the
white of the eye. Bochart, Hieroz,
Pt. ii. p. 120.

[2] Γύναι, a term of greatest en-
dearment among the Greeks, as
with the French " ma femme."
On this point our language is
more sophisticated. The practice
reprehended by Ischomachos, in
the text, was generally prevalent
in Greece, where certain classes
of the community, who could
afford nothing better, used, when
they had painted the rest of their
skin white, to dye the cheeks
with mulberry-juice, and paint
the eyelids black at the edge. In
hot weather, therefore, dusky
streamlets sometimes flowed from
the corners of their eyes ; and the
roses melted from their cheeks,
and dropped into their bosoms.
They imitated old age, too, by
covering their hair with white
powder. (Athen. xiii. 6.) It was
likewise, at one time, the fashion
to bring forward their curls so as
to conceal the forehead, as was
the practice in France and England during a part of the eighteenth century. — Lucian, Dial.
Meret. i. t. iv. p. 123.

being, and displaying to your gaze the natural hues
of a manly complexion, than if, neglecting these, I
presented myself with rouged cheeks, eyes encircled
by paint, and my whole exterior false and hollow?

Indeed, she replied, I prefer the native colour of
your cheeks to any artificial bloom, and could never
gaze with so much delight into any eyes as into
yours—bright and sparkling with health.

Then believe no less of me, said I; but be well
persuaded that, in my judgment, there are no tints
so beautiful as those with which nature has adorned
your cheeks. The same rule indeed holds universally. For, even in the inferior creation, every living
thing delights most in individuals of its own species.
And so it is with man whom nothing so truly pleases
as to behold the image of his own nature mirrored
in another and a fairer form of humanity. Besides,
false beauties, though they may deceive the incu-
rious glance of strangers,[1] must inevitably be detected by persons living always together. Women
necessarily appear undisguised when first rising in
the morning, before they have undergone the reno-
vation of the toilette; and perspiration, or tears, or
the waters of the bath, will even at other times
float away their artificial complexions.

And what, in the name of all the gods, did she
say to that? inquired Socrates.

What? replied the husband. Why, that for the
future she would abjure all meretricious ornaments,
and consent to appear decked with that simple grace
and beauty which she owed to nature.

At Sparta married persons, as in France, occupied
separate beds; but among the Athenians and in
other parts of Greece a different custom prevailed.
The same remark may be applied to the Heroic
Ages. Odysseus and Penelope, Alcinoös and Arete,
Paris and Helen, occupy the same chamber and the
same couch. The women in the Lysistrata of Aristophanes appealed to this circumstance in justifica-

[1] Cf. Lucian, Amor. § 42. Aristoph. Nub. 49.

tion of their late appearance at the female assembly held before day, and Euphiletos in the oration of Lysias on Eratosthenes' murder, who admits us freely into the recesses of the harem, confirms this fact, except, that when the mother suckled her own child she usually slept with it in a separate bed. At Byzantium also the same practice prevailed, as we learn from a very amusing anecdote. Python an orator of that city who, like Falstaff, seems to have been somewhere about two yards in the waist, once quelled an insurrection by a jocular allusion to this part of domestic economy. " My dear fellow-citi- " zens," cried he to the enraged multitude, " you see " how fat I am. Well ! my wife is still fatter than " I, yet when we agree one small bed will contain " us both ; but, if we once begin to quarrel, the " whole house is too little to hold us."[1]

We have seen above how absolute was the authority of women over their household, and this authority likewise extended to their children. The father no doubt could exercise, when he chose, considerable influence; but as most of his time was spent abroad, in business or politics, the chief charge of their early education, the first training of their intellect, the first rooting of their morals and shaping of their principles devolved upon the mother.[2] There have been writers, indeed, to whom this has seemed a circumstance to be lamented. But their judgment probably was warped by theory. In the original discipline of the mind, great attainments and experience of the world are less needed than tact to discern, and patience to apply, those minute incentives to action which women discover with a truer sagacity than we do. In this task, ever pleas-

[1] Athen. xii. 74.

[2] Xenoph. Œcon. vii. 12. 24. Cf. A. Cramer. de Educ. Puer. ap. Athen. 9. This writer acutely remarks, (p. 13,) that the words καὶ αὐτὸς ὁ πατήρ in Plat. Protag. p. 325. d. show that it was seldom the father meddled with the matter. The mother, therefore, from early habit, was held in greater love and reverence than the father. Casaub. ad Theoph. Char. p. 187.

ing to a true mother, the aid of nurses, however, was
usually obtained; nor are we, as Cramer observes, on
this account to blame the Athenian ladies, so long
as they did not, as in after times was too much the
fashion, consider their whole duty performed when
they had delivered their children to the nurse.

It will be evident from what has been said, that
an Athenian lady who conscientiously discharged her
duties was very little exposed to ennui. She arose
in the morning with the lark, roused her slaves, distributed to all their tasks,[1] superintended the operations of the nursery, and, on days frequently recurring,
went abroad in the performance of rites specially al-
lotted to her sex. But, one effect of democracy is
to confer undue influence upon women.[2] And this
influence, where by education or otherwise they happen to be luxurious or vain, must infallibly prove
pernicious to the state. At Athens, the number of
this class of women, extremely limited in the beginning, augmented rapidly during the decline of
the republic, and the comic poets substituting a
part for the whole, invest their countrywomen generally with the qualities belonging exclusively to these.
—But, the success of such writers depending generally on ingenious extravagance and exaggeration, we
must be on our guard against their insinuations.
Their faith in the existence of virtue, male or female, has, in all ages, if we are to judge by their
works, been very lanksided. In their view, if there
has been one good woman since the world began, it
is as much as there has. Accordingly when these
lively caricaturists describe the female *demos* as addicted extravagantly to wine[3] and pawning their

---

[1] Aristoph. Lysist. 18. Plato,
who admired the practice, requires
his airy female citizens to go and
do likewise. Καὶ δὴ καὶ δέσποιναν
ἐν οἰκίᾳ ὑπὸ θεραπαινίδων ἐγεί-
ρεσθαί τινων καὶ μὴ πρώτην αὐτὴν
ἐγείρειν τὰς ἄλλας, αἰσχρὸν λέ-

γειν χρὴ πρὸς αὐτοὺς δοῦλόν τε
καὶ δούλην καὶ παῖδα, καὶ εἴ πως
ἦν οἷόν τε, ὅλην καὶ πᾶσαν τὴν
οἰκίαν. De Legg. vii. t. viii. p.
40. Bekk.

[2] Cf. Plat. de Rep. t. vi. p. 102.

[3] Arist. Lysist. 113, seq. 205.

wardrobe to purchase it—as compelling the men by
their intemperance to keep their cellars under lock
and key, and still defeating them by manufacturing
false ones—as forming illicit connexions, and having
recourse to the boldest stratagems in furtherance of
their intrigues, we must necessarily suppose them to
have amused themselves at the expense of truth;
though that, among the Athenians, there were examples enough of women of whom all this might
be said, it would be absurd to deny.

We know that where the minds of married dames
are fixed chiefly upon dress and show their anxiety
has often very little reference to their husbands.
And if it be their object to excite admiration out
of doors, it is simply as a means to an end, which
end, in too many cases, is intrigue. Proofs exist
that among the Athenian ladies there were numbers whose idle lives and luxurious habits produced
their natural results—loose principles and dissolute
manners. The beauty of Alcibiades drew them after
him in crowds,[1] though we do not read that, like
another very handsome personage in a modern republic, the son of Cleinias found it necessary to carry
about a club to defend himself from their impor-
tunities. They went abroad elaborately habited and
adorned merely to attract the gaze of men,[2] and
having thus sown the first seeds of intrigue, they
took care to cultivate and bring them to maturity.
The felicitous invention of Falstaff's friends, which

[1] Xenoph. Memor. i. 2. 24.
'Αλκιβιάδης δ' αὖ διὰ μὲν κάλλος
ὑπὸ πολλῶν καὶ σεμνῶν γυναικῶν
θηρώμενος. κ. τ. λ.

[2] Aristoph. Nub. 60. Married
ladies occasionally rode out in carriages with their husbands. Demosth. cont. Mid. § 44. Even
at Sparta we find young ladies
possessed of their carriages called
Canathra, resembling in form
griffins, or goat-stags, in which
they rode abroad during religious
processions. Plut. Ages. § 19.
Cf. Xenoph. Ages. p. 73. Hut-
chin. cum not. et add. p. 89.
Athen. iv. 16, cum annot. p. 449.
Scheffer. de Re Vehic. i. 7. p. 68.
The same custom prevailed in
Thessaly and elsewhere. Athen.
xii. 37. Luxurious ladies at
Athens used to perfume even the
soles of their feet. Their lapdogs
lived in great state, and slept on
carpets of Miletos. Athen. xii.
78.

got him safe out of Ford's house in a buck-basket, was not so new as Shakspeare, perhaps, imagined. His predecessors on the Athenian stage had already discovered stratagems equally happy among their countrywomen, whose lovers we find made their way into the harem wrapped up in straw, like carp— or crept through holes made purposely by fair hands in the eaves—or scaled the envious walls by the help of those vulgar contrivances called ladders.[1]

The laws of Athens, however, were more modest than its women. For, from the very interference of the laws, it is evident, that the example of the Spartan ladies, who enjoyed the privilege of exposing themselves indecently, found numerous imitators among the female democracy. To repress this unbecoming taste, it was enacted, that any woman detected in the streets in indecorous deshabille[2] should be fined a thousand drachmæ, and, to add disgrace to pecuniary considerations, the name of the offender, with the amount of the fine, was inscribed on a tablet and suspended on a certain platane tree in the Cerameicos. However, what constituted *indecorous deshabille* in the opinion of Philippides, who procured the enactment of the law, it might be difficult to determine. Possibly it may have consisted in the too great exposure of the bosom, for the covering of which ladies in remoter ages appear to have depended very much on their veils. Thus in the interview of Helen with Aphrodite she saw, says the

---

[1] Xenarch. ap. Athen. xiii. 24.

[2] Ἀκοσμοῦσαι. Harpocrat. v. ὅτι χιλίας. κ. τ. λ. Potter, Arch. Græc. ii. 309, understands his law to have meant, women who literally appeared *laconically* in the streets. " Undressed," is his word. But will ἀκοσμοῦσαι, which Meursius, Lect. Att. ii. 5, 62, renders by "inornatius," bear such a signification? Κόσμος γυναικῶν does not, as Kühn observes, signify *ornamentum mulierum*, nor ἀκοσμοῦσαι *inornatius prodeuntes feminæ*; but κόσμος is εὐταξία and ἀκοσμοῦσαι means ἀτακτοῦσαι, that is, women who acted in any way whatever contrary to decorum and good manners, which persons appearing indecently dressed in public unquestionably do.—Ad. Poll. viii. 112. p. 763. On the manners of the Tyrrhenian women, Cf. Athen. xii. 14. sqq.

poet, her beautiful neck, desire-inflaming bosom, and
eyes bright with liquid splendour. Her garments concealed the rest.[1] Now, as it was customary for ladies
to appear veiled in public, the object of the law of
Philippides may simply have been to enforce the ob-
servance of this ancient practice. The magistrates
who presided over this very delicate part of Athenian police were denominated "Regulators of the
women,"[2] an office which Sultan Mahmood in our
day took upon himself. They were chosen by the
twenty from among the wealthiest and most vir-
tuous of the citizens, and in their office resembled
the Roman Censors and similar magistrates in several other states.[3]

The evil influence of women of this description,[4]
who, as Milton expresses it, would fain at any
rate ride in their coach and six, was perceived and
lamented by the philosophers. To their vain and
frivolous notions might be traced, in part at least, the
love of power, of trifling distinctions, of unmanly
pleasures, which infected the Athenians towards the
decline of their republic. By them the springs of
education were poisoned, and the seeds sown of those
inordinate artificial desires which convulse and over-

[1] Il. γ. 396. sqq. Cf. 141.
[2] Γυναικόσμοι. Poll. viii. 112.
[3] Cf. Arist. Pol. iv. 15. 120.
[4] On the luxurious manners of
the Syracusan women see Athen.
xii. 20. In such disorders may
be discovered the first germs of
the decay of states; on which account prudent statesmen even in
oligarchies have sought to restrain
the licentious manners of women.
Thus Fra Paolo: "Let the wo-
"men be kept chaste, and in or-
"der to that, let them live retired
"from the world; it being certain
"that all open lewdness has had
"its first rise from a salutation,
"from a smile."—i. § 20. To this
let us add the opinion of the female Pythagorician Phintys : ἴδια
δὲ γυναικὸς, τὸ οἰκουρὲν, καὶ ἔνδον
μένεν καὶ ἐκδέχεσθαι καὶ θεραπεύεν
τὸν ἄνδρα. Stob. Florileg., 74. 61.
Both the philosophical lady, however, and the Venetian monk have
their views corroborated by the
authority of Pericles: τῆς τε γὰρ
ὑπαρχούσης φύσεως μὴ χείροσι
γενέσθαι, ὑμῖν μεγάλη ἡ δόξα, καὶ
οἷς ἂν ἐπ᾽ ἐλάχιστον ἀρετῆς ἢ
ψόγου ἐν τοῖς ἄρσεσι κλέος ᾖ.
Thucyd. ii. 45. Besides leading
a retired life, ladies were likewise
expected to cultivate the virtue of
silence. Soph.Ajax, 293. Hom.
Il. ζ. 410.

throw states. In vain did philosophers inculcate
temperance and moderation, while the youth were
imbued with different opinions by their mothers.
The lessons of the Academy were overgrown and
checked in the harem. Such dames no doubt would
grieve to find their husbands content with little[1] (as
was the case with Xantippe) and not numbered
with the rulers, since their consequence among their
own sex was thus lessened. They would have had
them keen worshipers of Mammon, eagerly squab-
bling and wrangling in the law-courts or the ec-
clesiæ, not cultivators of domestic habits or philosophical tranquillity and content: and in conversing with their sons would be careful to recommend
maxims the reverse of the father's, with all the cant
familiar to women of their character.[2]

Our review of female society at Athens would
be incomplete were we to overlook the Hetairæ
who exerted so powerful an influence over the morals and destinies of the state. They occupied
much the same position which the same class of
females still do in modern communities, cultivated
in mind, polished and elegant in manners, but scarcely deserving as a body to be viewed in the light
in which a very distinguished historian has placed
them.[3] Their position, however, was anomalous, resembling rather that of kings' mistresses in modern
times, whose vices are tolerated on account of their
rank, than that of plebeian sinners whose deficiencies
in birth and fortune exclude them from good society. There is much difficulty in rightly appre-
hending the notions of the ancients on the subject
of these women. At first sight we are shocked

[1] Which, according to Plato,
well-educated men generally are.
De Repub. t. vi. p. 173.

[2] Plat. De Repub. viii. 5. t. ii.
p. 182. Stallb.

[3] Mitford, Hist. of Greece, iii.
4. sqq. It appears not to have
been common for these women to
rear the children they bore, more
particularly when they were girls.
They flew to the practice of in-
fanticide that they might remain
at liberty. Lucian, Hetair. Diall.
ii. 5. iv. 124.

to find that, during one festival, they were permitted to enter the temples in company with modest ladies. But in what Christian country are they excluded from church?[1] Again, behold in our theatres the matron and the courtezan in the same box, while at Athens even foreign women were not suffered to approach the space set apart for the female citizens. Nevertheless, though on this point so rigid, they were in their own houses permitted occasionally to visit them[2] and receive instructions from their lips, as in Turkish harems ladies do from the Almè.

It is not permitted here to lift the curtain from the manners of these ladies. But their position, pregnant with evil to the state through its contaminating influences on the minds of youth, must be comprehensively explained before a correct idea can be formed of the internal structure of the Athenian commonwealth, of the germs of dissolution which it concealed within its own bosom, or the premature blight which an unspiritual system of morals was mainly instrumental in producing. No doubt the question whether the existence of such a class of persons should be tolerated at all, is environed by difficulties almost insurmountable. They have always existed and therefore, perhaps, it is allowable to infer that they always will exist; but this does not seem to justify Solon for sanctioning, by legislative enactments, a modification of moral turpitude debasing to the individual, and consequently detrimental to the state. To do evil that good may come, is as much a solecism in politics as in ethics. On this point I miss the habitual wisdom of the Athenian legislator. Lycurgus himself could have enacted nothing more at variance with just principles, or more subversive of heroic sentiments.

---

[1] Besides, from a passage in Lucian it appears that the ladies and the hetairæ frequented together the public baths.—Diall. Hetair. xii. 4.

[2] Cf. Antiphon. Nec. Venef. § 5.

The Hetairæ,[1] recognised by law and scarcely proscribed by public opinion, may be said to have constituted a sort of monarchical leaven in the very heart of the republic; they shared with the sophists, whom I have already depicted, the affections of the lax ambitious youths, panting at once for pleasure and distinction, fostered expensive tastes and luxurious habits, increased consequently their aptitude to indulge in peculation, shared with the unprincipled the spoils of the state, and vigorously paved the way for the battle of Chæronea. But if their existence was hurtful to the community, so was it often full of bitterness to themselves. In youth, no doubt, when beauty breathed its spell around them, they were puffed up and intoxicated with the incense of flattery[2]—their conversation at once sprightly and learned seemed full of charms—their houses spacious as palaces and splendidly adorned were the resort of the gay, the witty, the powerful, nay, even of the wise—for Socrates did not disdain to converse with Theodota or to imbibe the maxims of eloquence from Aspasia. But when old age came on, what were they? It then appeared, that the lively repartees and grotesque extravagancies which had pleased when proceeding from beautiful lips, seemed vapid and poor from an old woman. The wrinkles which deformed their features were equally fatal to their wisdom that flitted from their dwellings, and became domiciliated with the last beauti-

[1] Vice is generally superstitious; and these ladies accordingly when they lost a lover, instead of attributing it to the superior beauty or accomplishments of their rivals, or the common love of novelty of mankind, always supposed that enchantments had been employed.—Luc. Diall. Hetair. i. t. iv. 124.

[2] Statues, for example, were sometimes erected in their honour—Winkelm. iv. 3. 7. They were generally well educated, and there were none probably who could not read.—Drosè, in Lucian, complaining of the philosopher who kept away her lover, observes that his slave came in the evening bearing a note from his young master.—Diall. Hetair. x. 2. 3.

ful importation from Ionia. Thus deserted, the most
celebrated Hetairæ became a butt for the satire even
of the most clownish. The wit wont to set the
table in a roar scarcely served to defend them
against the jests of the agora.

" How do you sell your beef?" said Laïs to a
young butcher in the flesh-market.

" Three obels the *Hag*," answered the coxcomb.

" And how dare you, said the faded beauty, here
in Athens pretend to make use of barbarian weights?"
The word in the original signifying an old woman
and a Carian weight, it suited her purpose to understand him in the latter sense.[1]

Worshiped and slighted alternately they adopted
narrow and interested principles in self-defence. Besides, generally barbarians by birth, they brought along
with them from their original homes the creed best
suited to their calling—" Let us eat and drink for
to-morrow we die." They were often the lumber
of Asia and hence known under the appellation of
" strange women," though it is very certain, that
many female citizens were from time to time en-
rolled among their ranks, some through the pressure of adversity, others from a preference for that
kind of life. Their education it must be conceded,
however, was far more masculine than that of other
women. They cultivated all the sciences but that
of morals, and concealed their lack of modesty by
the dazzling splendour of their wit. Hence among
a people with whom intellect was almost everything

---

[1] Athen. xiii. 43. where the
word is κύϐδα. — The Turkish
practice of drowning female delinquents in sacks, is merely an
imitation of what was performed
by a tyrant of old, who disposed
of wicked old women in this
manner. — Idem. x. 60. In
France likewise formerly it was
customary to avoid the scandal
of a public trial, for noblemen and
gentlemen to be examined pri-
vately by the king who, when he
could satisfy his conscience that
they were guilty, ordered them to
be " without any fashion of judg-
" ment put in a sack and in the
" night season, by the Marshall's
" servants, hurled into a river and
" so drowned." Fortescue, Laud,
Legg. Angl. chap. 35. p. 82. b.

their company was much sought after and highly valued, not habitually perhaps by statesmen, but by wits, poets, sophists, and young men of fashion.

Many of the *bons mots* uttered by those ladies have been preserved. One day at table Stilpo the philosopher accused Glycera of corrupting the manners of youth.

"My friend," said she, "we are both to blame; for you, in your turn, corrupt their minds by innumerable forms of sophistry and error. And if men be rendered unhappy, what signifies it whether a philosopher or a courtezan be the cause?"

It is to her that a joke, somewhat hackneyed but seldom attributed to its real author, was originally due. A gentleman presenting her with a very small jar of wine sought to enhance its value by pretending it was sixteen years old. "Then," replied she, "it is extremely little for its age." Gnathena too, another member of the sisterhood, sprinkled her conversation with sparkling wit, but too redolent of the profession to be retailed. Some of her sayings, however, will bear transplantation, though they must suffer by it. To stop the mouth of a babbler who observed that he had just arrived from the Hellespont—"And yet," she remarked, "it is clear to me that you know nothing of one of its principal cities!" "Which city is that?"—"Sigeion,"[1] (in which there appears to be a reference to the word Silence) answered Gnathena. Several noisy gallants, who being in her debt sought to terrify her by menaces, once saying they would pull her house down, and had pickaxes and mattocks ready, "I disbelieve it," she replied, "for if you had, you would have pledged them to pay what you owe me." A comic poet remarking to one of these ladies that the water of her cistern was delightfully cold—"It has always been so," she replied, "since we have got into the habit of throwing your plays into it." The repartee of Melitta

[1] Athen. xiii. 47.

to a conceited person who was said to have fled ignominiously from the field of battle is exceedingly keen. Happening to be eating of a hare which she seemed much to enjoy, our soldier, desirous of directing attention to her, inquired if she knew what was the fleetest animal in the world. "The runaway," replied Melitta.

The same taste which induces many persons of rank in our own day to marry opera dancers and actresses, in antiquity favoured the ambition of the Hetairæ, many of whom rose from their state of humiliation to be the wives of satraps and princes. This was the case with Glycera, whom after the death of Pythionica, Harpalos sent for from Athens, and domiciliated within his royal palace at Tarsos. He required her to be saluted and considered as his queen, and refused to be crowned unless in conjunction with her. Nay, he had even the hardihood to erect in the city of Rossos, a brazen statue to her, beside his own.[1] Herpyllis, one of the same sisterhood, won the heart of Aristotle, and was the mother of Nicomachos. She survived the philosopher, and was carefully provided for by his will.[2] Even Plato, whose genius and virtue are still the admiration of mankind, succumbed to the charms of Archæanassa, an Hetaira of Colophon, whose beauty, which long survived her youth, he celebrated in an epigram still extant.[3]

Of all these ladies, however, not even excepting Phryne, or the Sicilian Laïs,[4] Aspasia[5] has obtained

[1] Athen. xiii. 50.

[2] Athen. xiii. 56.—Diog. Laert. v. 12.

[3] Diog. Laert. iii. 31.

[4] She was a native of Hyccara, but taken prisoner in childhood, and carried to Corinth, whence that city has generally the honor of being regarded as her birthplace. — Athen. xiii. 54. — Cf.

Thucyd. vi. 62. Sch. Aristoph. Lysist. 179.

[5] Of the younger Aspasia, who had the reputation of being the loveliest woman of her time, we have the following sketch in Ælian: — " Her hair was auburn, " and fell in slightly waving ring- " lets. She had large full eyes, a " nose inclined to aquiline, (ἐπί- "γρυπος) and small delicate ears.

the most widely extended fame. This illustrious
woman, endowed by nature with a mind still more
beautiful than her beautiful form, exercised over
the fortunes of Athens an influence beyond the
reach of the greatest queen. Her genius, unobserv-
ed for some time, by degrees drew around her all
those whom the love of letters or ambition induced
to cultivate their minds. Her house became a sort
of club-room, where eloquence, politics, philosophy,
mixed with badinage, were daily discussed, and
whither even ladies of the highest rank resorted
to acquire from Aspasia those accomplishments which
were already beginning to be in fashion. From her
Socrates professed to have in part acquired his knowledge of rhetoric, and it is extremely probable that
he could trace to the habit of conversing with one
so gifted by nature, so polished by rare society,
something of that exquisite facility and lightness of
manner which characterize his familiar dialectics.
No doubt, we may attribute something of the reputation she acquired to the desire to disparage Pericles.
It was thought that by appropriating many of his
harangues to her they could bring him down nearer
their own level. She was, in influence and celebri-

"Nothing could be softer than her
"skin, and her complexion was
"fresh as the rose; on which ac-
"count the Phoceans called her
"Milto, or 'the Blooming'. Her
"ruddy lips, opening, disclosed
"teeth whiter than snow. She,
"moreover, possessed the charm
"on which Homer so often dwells
"in his descriptions of beautiful
"women, of small, well-formed
"ankles. Her voice was so full of
"music and sweetness, that those
"to whom she spoke imagined
"they heard the songs of the
"Seirens. To crown all she was
"like Horace's Pyrrha, simplex
"munditiis, abhorring superfluous

"pomp of ornament."—Hist. Var.
xii. 1. Some persons, however,
would not have admired the nose
of Milto:—thus, the youth in Te-
rence (Heauton, v. 5. 17. seq.)
"What? must I marry"

" Rufamne illam virginem
Cæsiam, sparso ore, adunco na-
so? Non possum, pater."

Aristotle (Rhet. i. 2) does not un-
dervalue the slightly aquiline nose;
and Plato appears rather to have
admired it in men.—Repub. v. §
19. t. i. p. 392.—Stallb. where
the philosopher calls it the Royal
Nose.

ty, the Madame Roland of Athens, though living in times somewhat less troubled.

The name of Phryne, though not so celebrated, is still familiar to every one, partly, perhaps, through the accusation brought against her in the court of Heliæa,[1] by Euthios. She was a native of Thespiæ, but established at Athens, and beloved by the orator Hyperides, who undertook her defence. His pleading, it may therefore be presumed, was eloquent. Perceiving, however, he could make but little impression on the judges, he had her called into court, and, as if by accident, bared her bosom,[2] the fairness and beauty of which heaving with anguish and terror—for it was a matter of life and death—so wrought upon the august judges that her acquittal immediately followed. The Heliasts, renowned for their upright decisions, were suspected on this occasion of undue commiseration, though the charge was probably grounded on some frivolous pretence of impiety; and, to prevent the recurrence of similar partiality in future, a decree was passed, rendering it illegal thus to extort the pity of the court, or, on any account, to introduce the accused, whether man or woman, into the presence of the judges. It was on her figure that Apelles chiefly relied in painting his Aphrodite rising from the sea, as Phryne herself rose before all Greece on the beach at Eleusis; and Praxiteles also wrought from the same model his Cnidean Aphrodite.[3] This sculptor, who was the rival of Hyperides, and, indeed, of all Athens, in the affections of Phryne, permitted her one day to make choice for herself from two statues of his own workmanship — the Eros and the Satyr. Discovering, by a stratagem,

---

[1] Poseidip. ap. Athen. xiii. 60.

[2] Honest old Burton, whom few anecdotes of this description escaped, imagines this artifice to have been the only defence he made.—Anatomy of Melancholy. ii. 222.

[3] Athen. xiii. 59. seq.

that he himself preferred the former, she was guided
by his judgment, and dedicated the winged god in
a temple of her native city. In admiration of
her beauty, a number of gentlemen erected, by sub-
scription, in her honour, a golden statue at Delphi.
It was the work of Praxiteles, and stood on a
pillar of white marble of Pentelicos, between the
statues of Archidamos, king of Sparta, and Philip,
son of Amyntas. The inscription ran simply thus :—

<blockquote>" Phryne, of Thespiæ, daughter of Epicles."</blockquote>

On seeing this statue, Crates, the cynic, exclaimed,
" Behold a trophy of Hellenic wantonness ! "

It is not, of course, among women of this class,
that we should expect to discover proofs of female
truth or enduring attachment. But the human heart
sometimes triumphs over adverse circumstances.[1]
History has preserved the memory of more than
one act of heroism performed by an Hetaira, to
show that woman doth not always put off her other
virtues, though habitually trampling on the one which
constitutes for her the boundary between honour
and infamy.

Ptolemy, son of Philadelphos, while commanding
the garrison of Ephesos, had along with him the
courtezan, Irene, who, when his Thracian mer-
cenaries rose in revolt, fled along with him to
the temple of Artemis, where they fell together,
sprinkling the altar with their blood.[2] Alcibiades,
too, of all his friends, found none adhere to him in
his adversity but an Hetaira, who cheerfully exposed her life for his sake ; and, when the assassins
of Pharnabazos had achieved their task, performed,
like another Antigone, the last duties over the ashes

---

[1] Athen. xiii. 59.—In the apprehension of Lucian, too, they
were anything but mercenary ;
and stripped themselves cheerfully of all their personal ornaments to bestow them, like so
many sisters, on the person they
loved. — Diall. Hetair. vii. 1.

[2] Athen. xiii. 64.

of the man she loved.[1] Other anecdotes might be added equally honourable to their feelings and fidelity, but these will sufficiently illustrate their character and the estimation in which they were generally held.

[1] Plut. Alcib. § 39.

CHAPTER V.

TOILETTE, DRESS, AND ORNAMENTS.

HAVING now described the condition and influence of women, it will be necessary to institute some inquiry into one of the principal means by which they achieved and maintained their empire. At first sight, perhaps, the disquisition may appear scarcely to deserve all the pains I have bestowed upon it; but, as the dress of the ancients is connected on the one hand with the progress of the useful arts, as spinning, weaving, dyeing, &c., and on the other with the forms and developement of sculpture, it can scarcely, when well considered, be reckoned among matters of trifling moment. Besides, the costume and ornaments of a people often afford important aid towards comprehending the national character, constituting, in fact, a sort of practical commentary on the mental habits, and tone and principles of morals, prevailing at any given period among them.

The raiment of the Grecian women, of which the public generally obtain some idea from the remaining monuments of ancient art, may be said to have been regulated by the same laws of taste which presided over the developement of the national genius in sculpture and painting. Every article of their habiliment appeared to harmonise exactly with the rest. Nothing of that grotesque extravagance which in some of the fleeting vagaries of fashion transforms our modern ladies, with their inflated balloon sleeves and painfully deformed waists, into so many whalebone and muslin hobgoblins, was ever allowed to disfigure the rich contour of a

Greek woman. As she proceeded lovely from the hands of nature, her pride was to preserve that loveliness. Her garments, accordingly, were not fashioned with a view to disguise or conceal her form, but by graceful folds, flowing curves, ornaments rich and tastefully disposed, to afford as many indications of its matchless symmetry and perfection as might be compatible with her sex's delicacy and the severity of public morals. Consequently the art of dress, like every other conversant with taste and beauty, reached in Greece its highest perfection. A woman draped according to the prevalent fashion in the best ages of the Athenian commonwealth, was an object not to be equalled for elegance or grace. From the snow white veil which probably shaded her countenance and ringlets of auburn or hyacinth, to the sandals of white satin and gold that ornamented her small ankle, the eye could detect nothing gaudy, affected, or out of keeping. There was magnificence without ostentation, brilliance of colours, but a brilliance that harmonised with whatever was brought in contact with it; the splendour of numerous jewels and trinkets of gold, but no appearance of display, or of a wish to dazzle. Everything appeared to stand where it did, because it was its proper place.

But in Sparta where there existed little tendency towards art or refinement,[1] a costume the antipodes of all this prevailed. That of the virgins differed in some respects from that of the matrons, and the difference arose out of a peculiar feature of manners, in which, if in nothing else, they resembled the English. In several Ionic countries, as at present on the continent, girls were previously to marriage guarded with much strictness. At Sparta, on the contrary, and among the Dorians generally,[2] they were permitted, as in England, to

---

[1] Cf. Montaigne, Essais, t. iv. p. 214, seq.   [2] See above, chapter ii.

walk abroad in company with young men, and, of
course, to form attachments at their own discretion. In this, too, as in their dress, they only preserved the customs of antiquity; for in Homer we
find the Trojan ladies making anxious inquiries of
Hector respecting their relations and friends in the
field, and going forth from their houses attended
only by their maids. The married women led more
retired lives, and when they went abroad fashion
required that they should be veiled, as we learn
from the following apophthegm of Charillos, who
being asked why the maidens went abroad uncovered while the matrons concealed their faces, replied: "Because it is incumbent on the former to
"find themselves husbands, on the latter only to
"keep those they have."[1]

The principal, or, rather, the sole garment of the
Dorian maidens was the chiton, or himation,[2] made
of woollen stuff, and without sleeves, but fastened
on either shoulder by a large clasp, and gathered
on the breast by a kind of brooch. This sleeveless
robe, which seldom reached more than half way to
the knee, was moreover left open up to a certain
point on both sides,[3] so that the skirts or wings,
flying open as they walked, entirely exposed their
limbs, closely resembling the shift of the Bedouin
women,[4] slit up to the arm-pit, but gathered tight
by a girdle about the waist. When the girdle was
removed it reached to the calves of the legs,[5] and
would then, but for the side-slits, have been quite
as becoming as the blue chemise of the modern
Egyptian women, which is open in front from the

---

[1] Plut. Apophtheg. Lacon.
Charill. 2. t. i. p. 161.
[2] Herod. v. 87. Duris. ap.
Schol. Eurip. Hecub. 922. Æl.
Dionys. ap. Eustath. ad Il. p.
963. 17. ed. Basil. Æl. Var.
Hist. i. 18. Cf. Spanh. Observ.
in Hymn. in Apoll. 32. t. ii.

p. 63. Schol. Pind. Nem. i. 74.
[3] Poll. vii. 54. seq. Mus. Chiaramont. pl. 35. Antich. di Ercol.
t. iv. tav. 24.

[4] Castellan, Mœurs des Otto-
mans, vi. 47.

[5] Schol. Eurip. Hecub. 922.

neck to the waist.[1] When dressed in this single
robe, their whole form breathing health, and modesty
in their countenance, there was no doubt a simple
elegance in their appearance, little less attractive,
perhaps, than the exquisite and elaborate *mise* of
an Ionian or an Attic girl. In this costume Me-
lissa, daughter of Procles, of Epidaurus, was habited
when, as she poured out wine to her father's labourers, Periander, the Corinthian,[2] beheld and loved
her. The married women, however, did not make
their appearance in public *en chemise*, but when
going abroad donned a second garment which seems
to have resembled pretty closely their husbands'
himatia.[3]

Of the simple wardrobe of a Doric lady, which
in ancient times was that of all women of Hellenic
race, exceedingly little can be said. It is altogether
different with respect to that of the gentlewomen
of Attica, where, though inferior in personal beauty
to none, the women exhibited so much fertility in
the matter of dress, that they appeared to depend
on that alone for the establishment of their empire. For this reason it would be vain to pretend
to describe all their vestments and ornaments, or the
arts of the toilette by which they were adapted to

---

[1] Suidas, however, supposes
these garments to have been less
becoming when the girdle was
removed, and adds ἐν Σπάρτῃ
δὲ καὶ τὰς κόρας γυμνὰς φαίνεσ-
θαι. — v. δωριάζειν. t. i. p. 772.
Montaigne observes, that the ancient Gauls made little use of
clothing; and that the same thing
might be said of the Irish of his
time, t. iv. p. 214.—The French
ladies, also, of his own day,
affected a costume in no respect
less indelicate than that of the
Spartan girls : " nos dames, ainsi molles et delicates qu'elles sont,

elles s'en vont tantôt entre ou-
vertes jusques au nombril."—
Essais, II. xii. t. iv. p. 213.

[2] Athen. xiii. 56.

[3] Cf. Il. ε. 425.—In the life of
Pyrrhus, the difference between
the dress of married women and
that of the virgins is distinctly
pointed out : — ἀρχομένοις δὲ
ταῦτα πράττειν, ἧκον αὐτοῖς τῶν
παρθενῶν καὶ γυναικῶν, αἱ μὲν ἐν
ἱματίοις, καταζωσάμεναι τοὺς
χιτωνίσκους, αἱ δὲ μονοχίτωνες,
συναργασόμεναι τοῖς πρεσβυτέροις·
Plut. Pyrrh. § 27.

their purposes. To do so properly would, in fact, require a volume. But all that can be crowded into one short chapter shall be given, since I am not deterred by any such scruples as formerly arrested the pen of a very learned writer, who apprehended that, if he proceeded, he might be supposed to have been rummaging the boudoir notes of an Athenian lady![1]

The primary garment,[2] answering to the *chemise* of the moderns, was a white tunic reaching to the ground,[3] in some instances sleeveless, and fastened on the shoulders with buttons, in others furnished with loose hanging sleeves descending to the wrist, and brought together at intervals upon the arm by silver or golden agraffes.[4] It was gathered into close folds under the bosom by a girdle,[5] or riband, sometimes fastened in front by a knot, sometimes by a clasp.[6] This inner robe, made in the earlier ages of fine linen,[7] manufactured in Attica, or imported from Tyre, Egypt, or Sidon, came, in after times, to be of muslin from Tarentum, or woven at home from Egyptian cotton. The use of linen, however, for this purpose was not wholly superseded. A very beautiful kind, from the island of Amorgos,[8] one of the Cyclades, was often substituted down to a very late period in place of the byssos, or fine muslin of Egypt; and this insular fabric,[9] whether snow-white or purple, would have rivalled the finest cambric, being of the most delicate texture and semi-transparent,[10] like the Tarentine and Coan vests of the Roman ladies, the sandyx-coloured Lydian

---

[1] Taylor ad Demosth.

[2] Athen. xii. 5. 29. Boeckh. i. 141. Aristoph. Lysist. 43. sqq.

[3] Ἐκ δὲ λίνου, λινοῦς χιτὼν, ὂν Ἀθηναῖοι ἔφορουν ποδήρη.—Poll. vii. 71.

[4] Ælian. V. H. i. 8.

[5] On the ζώνη, Cf. Il. ξ. 181. Odyss. τ. 231. Damm. 988. On the Cestus Il. ξ. 214. Aris-

toph. Lysist. 72. βαθυζώνοι Æschyl. Pers. 155. et Schol. — Bœttig. Les Furies, p. 34.

[6] Achilles Tatius. ii. cap. xi. p. 33, seq. Jacobs

[7] Thucyd. i. 6.

[8] Aristoph. Lysist. 150. 735, et Schol. [9] Poll. vii. 75.

[10] Aristoph. Lysist. 48. Poll. vii. 57. 74.

robe, or the silken chemises of the Turkish sultanas,
described by Lady Montague.[1] It is in a tunic of
this linen that Lysistrata, in Aristophanes, advises
the Athenian ladies to appear before their husbands
in order to give full effect to the splendour of
their charms.[2]

Because the Amorginean linen was often, perhaps
commonly, dyed purple, it has been inferred, that
none purely white was produced; but this, as Bochart[3]
observes, is, probably, a mistake. At all events, it
was of extraordinary fineness, superior, in the opinion of Suidas,[4] even to the byssos and carbasos, or
lawn of Cyprus, and appears to have been of a thin,
gauze-like texture, like the drapery of "woven air"
which Petronius[5] throws around his female characters.

Over the chiton was worn a shorter robe not
reaching below the knee, and confined above the
loins by a broad riband. This also was, in some
instances, furnished with sleeves, and of a rich purple
or saffron colour, generally ornamented, like the
chiton, with a broad border of variegated embroidery. To these, in order to complete the walking-
dress, was added a magnificent mantle, generally
purple, embroidered with gold, which, being thrown
negligently over the shoulders,[6] floated airily about
the person, discovering the under garments exqui-
sitely disposed for the purpose of displaying all the
contours of the form, particularly of the waist and
bosom. The Athenian ladies being, like our own,
peculiarly jealous of possessing the reputation of a
fine figure, and nature sometimes failing them, had

[1] Works, ii. 191.
[2] Aristoph. Lysist. 48.
[3] Chanaan. I. 14. p. 449.
[4] Corrected by Bochart, who
reads ἔστι δὲ σφόδρα λεπτὸν ὑπὲρ
τὴν βύσσον ἢ τὴν κάρπασον.
Cf. Suid. v. 'Αμοργ. t. i. p. 204.
c. Etym. Mag. 85. 15.

[5] Satyricon. cap. 55. p. 273.
Burmann.
[6] We find, from ancient monuments, that persons likewise wore
over their shoulders an article of
dress exactly resembling the modern cape or tippet.—Mus. Cortonens. tab. 58.

recourse to art, and wore what, among milliners, I
believe, are called *bustles*.[1] I am sorry to be obliged
to add, that there were, also, mothers at Athens
who anticipated us in the absurdity of tight lacing,
and invented corsets for the purpose of compressing
the abdomen and otherwise reducing the figures of
their daughters to some artificial standard which
they had already begun to set up in defiance of
nature.[2] Some women, too, when apprehensive of
growing fat, would collect on fine wool a quantity
of summer dew, which they afterwards squeezed out
and drank, this liquid having been supposed to be
possessed of deleterious qualities, more particularly
the ascending dew.[3]

Like the eastern ladies of the present day, they
seldom went abroad without their veil, which was
a light fabric of transparent texture, white or purple,
from Cos, or Laconia. It was thrown tastefully over
the head, raised in front on the point of the sphendone,[4] as in modern Italy by the comb, and hung
waving on the shoulders and down the back in
glittering folds. But this was not the only covering
they made use of for their head. Those modern
writers who have so thought are mistaken, since it
is clear, both from contemporary testimony and numerous works of art still remaining, that very frequently they wore caps or bonnets. Several examples occur in Mr. Hope's work, on the Costumes of
the Ancients;[5] and Mnesilochos, in Aristophanes,
when putting on the disguise of a woman for the
purpose of being present at the Festival of Demeter, like Clodius at that of the Bona Dea, desires
to borrow from Agathon a net or mitre for the

[1] Athen. xiii. 23. Alex. Frag.
v. 13, seq.
[2] Victor. Var. Lect. ii. 6. 32.
[3] Plut. Quæst. Nat. § 6. t. v.
p. 321.—Coray sur Hippocrate,
t. II. p. 82, seq.
[4] See an exact representation
of it in the Mus. Chiaramont. pl.
8, where we likewise find an example of the sleeves closed with
agraffes.—Cf. pl. 16.

[5] Plates. Nos. 98. 108. 131.
162. 172.

head. " Will you have my night-cap ? " inquires the
poet. " Exactly," replies Euripides, " that is just
what we want." [1]

But we have hitherto scarcely entered upon the
list of their wardrobe, in enumerating some of the
articles of which, I must crave the reader's permission to employ the original terms, our language,
in most cases, furnishing us with no equivalent.
And, first, following the order of Pollux, who observes no principle of classification, we have the
Epomis, a robe with sleeves, opposed to the *Exomis*,
which had none. The *Diploïdion*, an ample cloak,
or mantle, capacious enough to be worn double.
The *Hemidiploïdion*, a more scanty mantle ; the
Katastiktos, adorned with flowers or figures of animals, or richly marked with spots, the *Katagogis*,
the *Epiblema*, or cloak, and the *Peplos*,[2] a word of
very equivocal character, used to signify a veil or
mantle, a sofa-carpet, or a covering for a chariot.
Generally, it seems to have designated a garment
of double the necessary size, that, at pleasure, it
might be put on, or cast, like a cloak, over the
whole body, as appears from the Peplos of Athena.[3]
That the word sometimes was used to signify a
tunic appears from Xenophon, who says " the peplos
being rent above, the bosom appeared." [4] He, how-

---

[1] Aristoph. Thesmoph. 256.

[2] Poll. vii. 49, seq.—The *pe-
ploma* of Pindar (Pyth. ix. 219)
is now paploma. Wordsworth,
Athens and Attica, p. 32. Cf.
Iliad. ε. 315. — The peplos was
sometimes embroidered with figures.—Il. ζ. 289—295.

[3] Sch. Aristoph. Eq. 564.
Poll. vii. 50.

[4] Poll. vii. 50. Cf. Cyrop. iii.
1. 13.—3. 67. In Homer, Iliad,
γ. 385, &c. the word, ἑανὸς, signifying a richly-wrought vest or
robe, is synonymous, as Pollux re-

marks, with πέπλος vii. 51. This
is, likewise, the opinion of Butt-
mann, who, however, supposes
it to mean a " flexibly soft garment."—Lexil. Art. 41. Others
draw a distinction between ἑανὸς
and πέπλος, the former, they say,
being employed to signify a veil
unwrought and purely white, the
latter, one which was variegated
with colours and embroidery.
Passow considers it to be a mere
adjective signifying " clear, light,"
and says, that εἷμα or ἱμάτιον is
always understood with it.

ever, considers it to have formed part of the male costume.

Another article of female dress was the *Zoma*, a short vest fitting close to the shape, and adorned at the bottom with fringe, as appears from a fragment of Æschylus in the Onomasticon. A character of Menander, too, exclaims,—" Don't you perceive the nurse habited in her Zoma?"—for, adds Pollux, it was generally worn by old women. An elegant woollen dress, called *Parapechu*, white, but with purple sleeves, was imported from Corinth, and would appear to have been much worn by the Hetairæ.[1] Other garments seem to have been affected by the middle class of citizens, who, being unable to dress in purple,[2] the distinguishing colour of the wealthy and the noble, brought into fashion the *Paruphes* and *Paralourges*, robes adorned on either side with a purple stripe. As much dignity is supposed to belong to ample drapery, our citizen ladies took care not to be sparing of stuff, their dresses trailing to the ground, and displaying numerous folds, produced purposely at the extremity by a band passing round the edge. These garments were generally of linen ; but when a lady, in Homer, is said to be wrapped in her shining mantle, the poet[3] is supposed to intend a fine, light, woollen cloak, like the white burnooses of the Tunisian and Egyptian ladies.[4]

Several sorts of dresses obtained their appellation from their colours ; as the *Crocotos*, a saffron robe of ceremony, the *Crocotion*, a diminutive of the same ; the *Omphakinon*, of the colour of unripe grapes, which, though prescriptively appropriated to women, was much affected by Alexander the Great. Modern ladies have delighted in flea-coloured dresses, and, in

---

[1] Poll. vii. 53. Jam παρά-πηχυ λήδιον vel ἱμάτιον, collatis Hesychii et Pollucis interpretationibus, intelligi videtur dictam fuisse vestem albam cui manicæ adpositæ essent purpureæ. — Schweig. ad Athen. xiii. 45. t. xii. p. 146.

[2] Athen. xiii. 45. Poll. *ubi supra*.

[3] Iliad, γ. 141.

[4] Poll. vii. 54.

like manner, the ancients had theirs of asinine hue,
called *Killios,* from a Doric name for the ass, and
afterwards *Onagrinos,*[1] which, if they really resembled
the wild ass in hue, must have been exceedingly beautiful. There was a scarlet robe, with the appellation
of *Coccobaphes,* the *Sisys,* a thick heavy cloak, likewise called *Hyphandron Himation,* resembling the
Amphimallos, which had a double warp, and was hairy
on both sides.[2]

Not to extend this list of dresses beyond the patience of a milliner, we will now pass on to the principal ornaments for the head,[3] in which the Greek
ladies evinced extraordinary taste and invention.[4]
Among these one of the most elegant was the *Ampyx,*
a fillet by which they confined their hair in front.
It sometimes consisted of a piece of gold embroidery,
the place of which was often supplied by a thin plate
of pure gold, studded with jewels. Another Homeric
ornament, the *Kekruphalos,*[5] can only be alluded to as
a critical puzzle which has baffled all the commentators, in which predicament the *Plekte anadesme*[6] also
stands; all that we know being, that it found its place

[1] Among the Dorians the ass
(ὄνος) was called κίλλος, and an
ass-driver (ὀνηλάτης) κιλλακτήρ.
Poll. vii. 56.

[2] Poll. vii. 56, seq.

[3] Cf. Winkelmann, iv. 2. 76.
Alex. Pædag. ii. 12.

[4] Theoc. Eidyll. i. 33. Æmil.
Port. Lex. Dor. in voce.

[5] Iliad. χ. 469. Heyne in loc.
Pollux. v. 95, enumerates the
ἄμπυξ among female ornaments,
but without giving any description of it. Cf. Pind. Olymp. vii.
118. Dissen. Comm. ad v. 64.
Bœttiger. Pictur. Vascul. i. 87.
— The κεκρύφαλος, or κροκύφαν-
τος, which occurs once in the Iliad,
was a female ornament for the
head, unknown to the later Greeks.
The scholiast describes it as κόσμος τὶς περὶ κεφαλήν; and Damm
observes that, it was " redimicu-
" lam *vel* reticulam quo mulieres
" crines coërcent."—1158. Heyne
is equally unsatisfactory. The
commentators on Pollux. v. 95,
avoid the subject altogether. Cf.
Foës. Œcon. Hippoc. p. 202.

[6] Iliad, χ. 469. Πλεκτὴ ἀνα-
δέσμη· οἱ μὲν διάδημα, says Apollonios, οἱ δὲ μίτραν. Πλὴν κοσ-
μου εἶδος περὶ τὴν κεφαλὴν. This
is the basis of Hesychius' article. The Leyden scholia say: —
ἀναδέσμη λέγεται, σειρά, ἥν περὶ
τοὺς κροτάφους ἀναδοῦνται· κα-
λεῖται δ' ὑπ' ἐνίων καλανδάκη.
(In which Heyne imagines we
may detect *calantica,* " a hood,
hurlet, or coif.") Κρήδεμνον δὲ
πάλιν τὸ μαφόριον.

in the female head-dress, though whether as a mitre
or a diadem Apollonios is unable to determine. It
may possibly have been, under another appellation,
that graceful wreath or garland, consisting of fragrant
flowers interwoven or bound together by their stems,
described among female ornaments by Pollux.[1]

Another article of the same ambiguous character
was the *Pylæon*, supposed to have derived its name
from φύλον, *a leaf.* Athenæus,[2] on a subject of this
kind, perhaps, one of the best authorities, describes it
as the crown which, during certain festivals, the Spartans placed upon the head of Hera. Doubtless, however, the most tasteful and elegant of this class of
female ornaments was the *Kalyx*, a golden syrinx or
reed, passed like a ring over each several tress to
keep it separate.[3] Eustathius describes it as a ring
resembling a full-blown, but not expanded, rose; and
this explanation will not be inconsistent with that of
Hesychius, if we suppose the golden tubes to have
terminated in the form of that flower. The *Strophion*
was a band or fillet[4] with which women confined
their hair, as we discover from many ancient statues.
Parrhasios the artist, who used to bind his luxuriant
locks with a white strophion, was therefore accused
of effeminacy.[5] The name, however, appears to have
been applied to any kind of band, even to the broad
belt worn to support the bosom: " My strophion
being untied the walnuts fell out," says the girl in
Aristophanes.[6] There was also an ornament of the
same name worn by priests.[7]

[1] Poll. v. 96. Iliad. σ. 595.
In Homer the epithet, however,
is not πλεκτὴ but καλὴ Hemsterhuis ad Poll. t. iv. p. 998.

[2] Deipnosoph. xv. 22. Cf. Poll.
v. 96.

[3] Cœl. Rhodig. xxvii. 27, imagines it to mean a female head-
dress, or a parasol. Jungermann.

ad Poll. v. 96. Eustath. ad Iliad.
ϛ. 401.

[4] On a mask, engraved among
the Gemm. Antich. of Agostini,
we find an exact representation of
the modern feronet, pl. 24.

[5] Athen. xii. 62. Pollux. v. 96.

[6] Poll. vii. 67. 95.

[7] Plut. Arat. § 58.

The *Opisthosphendone*,[1] one of the female ornaments enumerated in a fragment of Aristophanes, was worn only on the stage. Its proper name *sphendone* it derived from its resemblance to a sling, being broad and elevated in front,[2] and terminating in narrow points at the back of the head where it was tied. On the comic stage it was sometimes worn for sport with the fore part behind.[3] The *Anadesma*[4] was a gilded fillet or diadem of gold, used like the *strophion* for encircling the forehead. What was the precise use or form of the *Xanion*, another golden ornament fashionable in remote antiquity, could not be ascertained in the age of Pollux, who says that many writers supposed it to have been a comb Of this number are Hesychius, Suidas,[5] and Phavorinus. But a learned modern conjectures with more probability, that it was some talismanic idol worn as a spell against the evil eye.[6] In fact it is expressly observed in the Etymologicon Magnum,[7] that the Hellenic women reckoned it among their phylacteries.

Of the ear-rings worn by Grecian women the variety was very great. The most ancient kind were called *Hermata*, of which mention occurs both in the Iliad and the Odyssey.[8] They were usually

[1] Clem. Alexand. Pædag. ii. 12. Winkelmann, Histoire de l'Art. iv. 2. 75. note 6, and i. 2. 18. See also Cabinet Pio Clement, t. i pl. 2, with the observations of Visconti.

[2] Cf. Mus. Chiaramont, pl. 20.

[3] Poll. v. 96. vii. 95. Eustath. ad Dion. Perieg, v. 7. Comment. ad Poll. iv. 999. On the καλαμος, named but not described by Pollux, v. 96, see Eustath. ad Il. τ. p. 1248. Phavor. et Hesych. *in voce* καλαμις. What the ἔντροπον was, Jungermann confesses he does not know; nor do I, though it appears probable that

it may have been the golden or gilt ornament with which the hair when gathered on the top of the head was bound together.

[4] Damm. 444. Aristoph. Plut. 589. Poll. v. 96.

[5] This lexicographer speaks of it as follows:—κτένιον. ὁ φοροῦσιν αἱ γυναῖκες ἐν τοῖς ἀναδέμασιν, οἷς κόσμος χρυσοῦς ἐπὶ κεφαλῆς. t. ii. p. 252. b.

[6] 612, 23, seq.

[7] Hemsterhuis. ad Poll. t. iv. p. 1000.

[8] Il. ξ. 182. Odys. σ. 296. Ælian. Var. Hist. i. 18.

adorned with three emerald drops,[1] for which reason
they were by the Athenians denominated *Triopia*
or *Triopides*,[2] and by the other Greeks *Triopthalma*
or " the triple eye." By this word, as an ancient
grammarian informs us, some understood an animal
like the beetle, supposed to have three eyes, whence
a necklace with three hyaline or crystal eyes, depending from it in front, was likewise called by the
same name. Pollux[3] supposed the earrings of Hera
to have been adorned with three diminutive figures
in precious stones, or gold, probably of goddesses.
The *Diopos* seems to have been an earring with two
drops. The *Helix* appears in Homer[4] rather to mean
an earring than an armlet, and to have received its
name from its circular shape or curvature; but the
spiral gold rings round the walking-stick of Parrhasios
are also called *Helices* by Athenæus.[5] Another name
for this sort of earring was *Heliktes*.[6] In the Æolic
dialect earrings were called *Siglai*, in the Doric *Ar-
tiala*. A particular kind denominated *Enclastridia*
and *Strobelia*, by the comic poets, had gold drops in
the form of a pine cone.[7] Two very curious kinds
of earrings were the *Caryatides*, and the *Hippocam-
pia*, the former representing in miniature the architectural figures, so called, the latter little horses
with tails ending in a fish. There were earrings,
likewise, with drops in the forms of centaurs and
other fantastic creations.[8]

The names and figures of necklaces were scarcely
less numerous.[9] A jewelled collar fitting tight to
the throat formed, under the name of *Peritrachelion*,

[1] Fabri. Thes. v. auris.

[2] Damm. 2195, reads τριόττατα,
and τριοττίδες, in the passage of
Eustathius, which forms the basis
of my text; but Kuhn and Jungermann ad Poll. t. iv. p. 1003,
correct as above.

[3] Onomast. v. 97.

[4] Il. σ. 401. Cf. Eustath. ad
Odyss. ω. 49.

[5] Deipnosoph. xii. 62.

[6] Poll. v. 97.

[7] Jungermann ad Poll. t. iv.
1001.

[8] Poll. v. 95.

[9] Odyss. σ. 290. Hymn, in
Ven. ii. 11, seq. Necklaces of
gilded wood. Xen. Œcon. x. 3.
61.

the principal of these ornaments, of which another was the *Perideraion*.[1] The *Hypoderaion* was as its name imports a necklace that hung low on the bosom, and the same was the case with the *Hormos*.[2] On the *Tantheuristos Hormos* little information can be obtained, for which reason the commentators would alter the text; but the most probable conjecture is, that it obtained its appellation from the flashing and glancing of the jewels depending from it upon the breast.[3] The *Triopis* was a species of necklace distinguished for having three stars or eye-like gems depending from it as drops. This being the most fashionable necklace was known under a variety of names, as the *Kathema*, and *Katheter*, and *Mannos* or *Monnos*, among the Dorians.[4]

Of armlets and bracelets there was likewise a great variety. Some worn above the elbow were denominated *Brachionia*, others called *Pericarpia*, or *Echinoi* encircled the wrists and were often in the form of twisted snakes of gold, which the woman-hater in Lucian would have converted into real serpents.[5] The *Psellia* or chain bracelets were much worn; the *Clidones* adorned the rich and luxurious only. As stockings were not in common use, and shoes and sandals frequently dispensed with when within doors, fashion required that the feet and ankles should not remain unadorned. Ancient writers, accordingly, enumerate several kinds of anklets, or bangles, all of gold, and varying only in form, the distinction between which I have been unable to discover. The *Ægle* the *Pede* and the *Periscelides* were so many ornaments for the instep or ankle.[6]

---

[1] Plut. Mar. § 17. Bulenger, De Spoliis Bellicis, c. 12.

[2] Sch. Aristoph. Vesp. 677.

[3] Comment. ad Poll. v. 98 p. 1003.

[4] Theocrit. xi. 41. Casaub. Lect. Theocrit. c. 13.

[5] Amor. § 41.

[6] Poll. v. 100. Golden periscelides are enumerated by Longus l. i. among the possessions of the young Lesbian girl; and Horace, Epist. i. xvii. 56, speaks of the periscelis being snatched away

Among the ornaments for the bosom we find the
Ægis, evidently like the ægis of Athena, a sort of
rich covering with two hemispherical caps to receive the breasts, such as we find worn by the
Bayadères of the Dekkan. Extending from this
on either side, or passing over its lower edge was
the *Maschalister*, a broad belt which covered the
armpits, though in Herodotus the word merely signifies a sword-belt.[1]

Like all other delicate and luxurious women, the
Grecian ladies displayed upon their fingers a profusion
of rings, of which some were set with signets, others
with jewels remarkable for their colour and brilliance.
To each of these their copious language supplied a
distinct name.[2] Other female ornaments are spoken
of by the comic poets; but in their descriptions it is
difficult to distinguish satire from information. Among
these were the *Leroi*, golden drops attached to the
tunic ; the *Ochthoiboi*, which seem to have been a
sort of rich tassels; the *Helleboroi*, ornaments shaped
perhaps like the leaves or flowers of that plant; and
the *Pompholuges*, which, though left unexplained by
the commentators, probably signified a large clear
kind of bead, as the word originally meant a " water-
bubble," which a transparent bead resembles.[3]

The Athenian ladies, likewise, displayed their taste
for luxury and splendour in their shoes and sandals.[4]

from a courtezan. Here Dr.
Bentley understands the word to
mean *tibialia*, and observes, —
" delicatulæ fasciolis involve-
" bant sibi crura et femora."
But Gesner ad Horat. p. 503,
seq. rather supposes "compedes
" mulierum," to be intended, and
he is probably right. Cf. Petron.
Sat. c. 67.

[1] Cf. Mus. Chiaram. pl. 14.
pl. 18.

[2] Poll. v. 101. Rhodig. vi. 12.

[3] Poll. v. 101. Cf. Schol. Aristoph. Ran. 249. Bergler ad loc.

renders it by *bulla*, which, among
the Romans, signified " a golden
ornament worn about the neck,
or at the breast of children,
fashioned like a heart, and hollow
within, which they wore until
they were fourteen years old, and
then hung up to the household
gods."—Porphyr. in Horat. vid. et
Fab. Thes. in v.

[4] Diog. Laert. ii. 37. c. Sch.
Aristoph. Lysist. 417. Wooden
shoes were worn in Thessaly.
With these the women killed Lais
in the temple of Aphrodite —

Like our own fashionable dames, they seldom contented themselves with articles of home manufacture,
but imported whatever was considered most elegant
or tasteful from the neighbouring countries. Sometimes, perhaps, the fashion only and the name were
imported, as in the case of the Persian half-boot,
fitting tight to the ankle.[1] The same thing may
probably be said of the Sicyonian slipper. But there
was an elegant sandal, ornamented with gold, which,
down to a very late period, continued to be imported
from Patara, in Lycia,[2] Snow-white slippers of fine
linen, flowered with needlework, were occasionally
worn; and from many ancient statues it would seem,
that something very like stockings had been already
introduced. Short women, desirous of adding, if not
a cubit, at least a few inches to their stature, adopted
the use of *baukides* with high cork heels, and soles of
great thickness.[3]

An Athenian beauty usually spent the whole morning in the important business of the toilette.[4] The
crowd of maids who attended on these occasions appears to have exceeded in number the assistants at
similar rites in a modern dressing-room, the principle
of the division of labour having been pushed to its
greatest extent. Like Hera, who was said by mythologists to renew her virgin charms as often as she
bathed in the fountain of Canathos,[5] the Attic lady
appeared to undergo diurnal rejuvenescence under the
hands of her maids.[6] Her lovely face grew tenfold
more lovely by their arts. Clustering in interesting

Athen. xiii. 55. There was a
species of shoes peculiar to female
slaves called peribarides. — Poll.
vii. 87. Aristoph. Lysist. 47.

[1] Sch. Aristoph. Nub. 152. See
in Antich. di Ercol. t. vi. p. 11,
a representation of half-boots open
in front.

[2] Lucian, Diall. Meret. xiv. 3.
ἐκ Πατάρων σανδάλια ἐπίχρυσα.

[3] Athen. xiii. 23. Poll. vii.
94.

[4] Their perfumes and essences
were kept in alabaster boxes from
Phœnicia, some of which cost no
more than two drachmæ.—Lucian, Diall. Meret. xiv. 2.

[5] Paus. ii. 37, 38.

[6] Aristoph. Concion. 732, et
Schol.

groups around her, some held the silver basin and
ewer, others the boxes of tooth-powder, or black
paint for the eyebrows, the rouge pots or the blanching varnish, the essence-bottles or the powder for
the head, the jewel-cases or the mirrors.[1] But on
nothing was so much care bestowed as on the hair.[2]
Auburn, the colour of Aphrodite's tresses[3] in Homer,
being considered most beautiful,[4] drugs were invented in which the hair being dipped, and exposed
to the noon-day sun, it acquired the coveted hue,
and fell in golden curls over their shoulders.[5] Others,
contented with their own black hair, exhausted their
ingenuity in augmenting its rich gloss, steeping it in
oils and essences, till all the fragrance of Arabia
seemed to breathe around them. Those waving ringlets which we admire in their sculpture were often
the creation of art, being produced by curling-irons
heated in ashes;[6] after which, by the aid of jewelled
fillets and golden pins, they were brought forward
over the smooth white forehead,[7] which they sometimes shaded to the eyebrows, leaving a small ivory
space in the centre, while behind they floated in
shining profusion down the back. When decked in

[1] Pignor. de Serv. p. 195.
[2] Cf. Suid. v. κομᾷ. t. i. p.
1489. b.
[3] See Pashley, i. 247. Pignor.
de Serv. 193.
[4] " The beautiful colour we
" call auburn, and which the an-
" cients expressed by the term
" golden, is the most common
" among the Greeks; and they
" have gilt wire and various other
" ornaments (among which might
" yet perhaps be recognised the
" Athenian grasshopper) in ring-
" lets, which they allow to float
" over their shoulders, or bind
" their hair in long tresses that
" hang upon the back." — Douglas, Essay, &c. p. 147, seq.

[5] This is beautifully described
by Lucian:—Γυναικὶ δὲ ἀεὶ πάσῃ
ἡ τοῦ δαψιλεῖς μὲν ἀπὸ τῶν βοσ-
τρύχων τῆς κεφαλῆς ἕλικες, ὑα-
κίνθοις τὸ καλὸν ἀνθοῦσιν ὅμοια
πορφύροντες· οἱ μὲν, ἐπινώτιοι
κέχυνται μεταφρένων κόσμος, οἱ
δὲ παρ' ὦτα καὶ κροτάφους, πολὺ
τῶν ἐν λειμῶνι οὐλότερον σελί-
νων· τὸ δ' ἄλλο σῶμα, μηδ' ἀκαρῆ
τριχὸς αὐταῖς ὑποφυομένης ἠλέκ-
τρου, φάσιν, ἢ Σιδωνίας ὑέλου
διαφεγγέστιρον ἀπαστράπται. —
Amor. § 26.
[6] Pignor. de Serv. 194, seq.
[7] The young lady, in Lucian,
describes thin hair drawn back
so as to expose the forehead as a
great deformity.—Diall. Meret. i.

this manner, and dressed for the harem [1] in their light flowered sandals and semi-transparent robes already described, they were scarcely farther removed from the state of nature than the Spartan maids themselves.

Contrary to the fashion prevalent in modern times the bosom, however, was always closely covered, because being extremely full shaped it began very early to lose its firmness and beauty.[2] Earrings, set with Red-Sea pearls of great price, depended from their ears, and an orbicular crown studded with Indian jewels surmounted and contrasted strikingly with their dark locks. Add to these the jewelled throat bands, and costly and glittering necklaces. Their cheeks though sometimes pale by nature, blushed with rouge,[3]

---

[1] A taste not greatly dissimilar presides over the in-door dress of the modern Greek women. "In "the gynecæum," says Chandler, "the girl, like Thetis, treading on "a soft carpet, has her white and "delicate feet naked; the nails "tinged with red. Her trowsers, "which in winter are of red cloth, "and in summer of fine calico or "thin gauze, descend from the hip "to the ankle, hanging loosely "about her limbs, the lower por-"tion embroidered with flowers, "and appearing beneath the shift, "which has the sleeves wide and "open, and the seams and edges "curiously adorned with needle-"work. Her vest is of silk, ex-"actly fitted to the form of the "bosom and the shape of the "body, which it rather covers "than conceals, and is shorter "than the shift. The sleeves "button occasionally to the hand, "and are lined with red or yel-"low satin. A rich zone encom-"passes her waist, and is fasten-"ed before by clasps of silver "gilded, or of gold, set with pre-"cious stones. Over the vest is "a robe, in summer lined with "ermine, and in cold weather "with fur. The head-dress is a "skull-cap, red or green, with "pearls; a stay under the chin, "and a yellow fore-head cloth. "She has bracelets of gold on "her wrists; and, like Aurora, "is rosy-fingered, the tips being "stained. Her necklace is a "string of zechins, a species of "gold coin, or of the pieces called "Byzantines. At her cheeks is "a lock of hair made to curl to-"ward the face; and down her "back falls a profusion of tresses, "spreading over her shoulders." —ii. 140.

[2] Lucian. Amor. § 41. Homer in numerous passages celebrates the deep bosoms of his country women, and Anacreon, also, touches more than once on the same topic.

[3] Anchusa. Theoph. Hist. Plant. vii. 8. 3. Dion. Chrysost.

and they even possessed the art to superinduce over this artificial complexion that peach-like purple bloom which belongs to the very earliest, dewiest dawn of beauty. To the tint of the rose they could likewise add that of the lily. White paint was in common use,[1] not merely among unmarried women, and ladies of equivocal reputation, but with matrons the chastest and most prudent in Athens, for we find that pattern of an Attic gentlewoman, the wife of Ischomachos, practising after marriage every delusive art of the toilette.[2]

It by no means follows that all this attention[3] to dress had any other object than to please their husbands ; for the Turkish Sultanas who pass their lives in the most rigid seclusion are no less sumptuous in their apparel; but we know that at Athens, as in London, much of this care was designed to excite admiration out of doors. For it is highly erroneous to transfer to Athens the ideas of female seclusion acquired from travellers in the East, where no such rigid seclusion was ever known. Husbands, indeed, who had cause, or supposed they had, to be jealous, might be put on the rack by beholding the crowds of admirers who flocked around their wives the moment they issued into the streets. But there was no remedy. The laws and customs of the country often forced the women abroad to assist at processions and perform their devotions at the shrines of various goddesses.[4]

i. 262. Poll. vii. 95. Aristoph. Lysist. 46. et Schol. Muret. Not. in Xen. Cyrop. p. 743, seq. Xen. Cyrop. i. 3. 2.

[1] Poll. v. 101, vii. 95.

[3] Xenoph. Œconom. x. 2, 60.

[3] Cf. Xen. de Vect. iv. 8.

[4] Luc. Amor. § 41, seq. Cf. Casaub. ad Theoph. Char. p. 339. Aristoph. Plut. 1015, et schol. Plut. Vit. x. Orat. Lycurg. In the country, too, women went

often abroad, and evidently led a very comfortable life ; their habits, in fact, greatly resembled those of English country ladies ; the wives of men whose estates lay contiguous freely visiting and gossiping with each other. Thus in the action on the damage caused by the torrent, we find the wife of Tisias and the mother of Callicles discussing the spoiling of the barley and the

The dress of men included many of the garments
worn by women; for example, the chiton of which
there were several kinds, some with and some without sleeves. Among the latter was the *Exomis*,[1]
a short tunic worn by aged men and slaves, but
the name was sometimes applied to a garment
thrown loosely round the body, and to the chiton
with one sleeve.[2] Over this in Homeric times was
worn as a defence against the cold, the *Chlaina*[3] a
cloak strongly resembling a highlander's tartan, or
the burnoose of the Bedouin Arab. It was, in fact,
a square piece of cloth, occasionally with the corners
rounded off, which, passing over the left shoulder, and
under the right arm, was again thrown over the left
shoulder, leaving the spear arm free.[4] This is what
the poet means where he terms the *Chlaina* double.
It was wrapped twice round the breast, and fastened over the left shoulder by a brooch.[5] Even
this, however, was not deemed sufficient in very
cold weather, and a cloak of skins sown together
with thongs was wrapped about the body as a defence against the rain or snow. Some persons appear to have worn skin-cloaks all the year round,
for we find Anaxagoras, in the midst of summer at
Olympia, putting on his when he foresaw there
would be rain.[6] Rustics also appear to have considered a tunic and skin-cloak necessary to complete their costume.[7]

barley meal, and meeting, evidently, as often as they thought
proper. In fact, before the quarrel, the footpath across the field
was clearly well worn. — Demosth. in Call. § 7.

[1] Aristoph. Lysist. 662.

[2] Poll. vii. 49.

[3] If the appearance of a ghost
can be regarded as good testimony, it may be concluded that
the Thessalians wore the chlamys,
since Achilles when called up by
Apollonios of Tyana, presented
himself in that garment.—Philost. Vit. Apoll. iv. 16.

[4] Müll. Dor. ii. 283. Diog.
Laert. ii. 47. Clothes were sus-
pended in the house on pegs.—
Odyss. a. 440.

[5] Il. ω. 230. Poll. vii. 49.

[6] Diog. Laert. ii. iii. 5. Cum
not. Menag. t. ii. p. 49.

[7] Dion, Chrysost. i. 231.
Reiske. On the dress of the Arcadians, Polyæn. Stratagem. iv. 14.

The Dorian style of dress formed the point of transition from the simple elegance of the Homeric period to the elaborate splendour of the historic age at Athens. In this mode of clothing, a modern author remarks, a peculiar taste was displayed, an antique simplicity " equally removed from the splen-"dour of Asiatics, and the uncleanliness of barba-"rians."[1] They preserved the use of the Homeric chiton, or woollen shirt, and over this wore also the *Chlaina* or *Himation*, in the manner described above. To these was added the *Chlamys*, which, as the Spartan laws prohibited dyeing, was universally white, and denominated *Hololeukos*.[2]

It was of Thessalian or Macedonian origin, of an oblong form, the points meeting on the right shoulder, where they were fastened with a clasp. This garment was not in use in the heroic ages, and the earliest mention of it occurs in Sappho;[3] but when once introduced, it quickly grew fashionable, at first among the young men, afterwards as a military cloak. At Athens it was regarded as a mark of effeminacy, and was fastened with a gold or jewelled brooch on the breast.[4]

The men of Sparta, though less thinly clad than the women, still went abroad very scantily covered. Their *Tribon*, a variety of the himation,[5] like the cloak of the poor Spanish gentleman, was clipped so close that it would barely enclose their persons, like a case, but was thick and heavy, and calculated to last. Accordingly, the youth were allowed only one of these per annum, so that, in warm weather, it is probable that, with an eye to saving it for winter, they exchanged it for that more lasting coat with

[1] Müller. Hist. Dor. ii. 277. See the picturesque description which Hesiod gives of the rustic winter costume of Bœotia. Opp. et Dies, 534, sqq. Goettl.

[2] Poll. vii. 46.

[3] Σαπφὼ πρώτη γὰρ μέμνηται τῆς χλαμύδος.—Ammonius, p. 147. Valcken.

[4] Heliodor. i. and ii.

[5] Sch. Aristoph. Nub. 415. Cf. Vesp. 116, 475.

which nature had furnished them.[1] In the towns, however, and as often as they thought proper to put on the appearance of extreme modesty, the young Spartans drew close their cloaks around them so as to conceal their hands,[2] the exhibiting of which has always been regarded as a mark of vulgarity. Hence the use of gloves, and the affectation of soft white hands in modern times. The same notions prevail even among the Turks, who, like Laertes in Homer, wear long sleeves to their pelisses for the purpose of defending the hand, to have which white and well-shaped is among them a mark of noble blood.

The Spartans had the good taste to suffer their beards and hair to grow long, and were at much pains to render them glossy and shining. Even in the field, contrary to the practice at Athens, they preserved this natural ornament of their heads, and we find them busy in combing and putting it in order on the very eve of battle.[3] It was usually parted at the top, and was, in fact, the most becoming covering imaginable. But they set little value on cleanliness, and bathed and perfumed themselves seldom, being evidently of opinion,[4] that a brave man ought not to be too spruce. However, having no object to gain by aping the exterior of mendicants, they eschewed the wearing of ragged cloaks, which, indeed, was forbidden by law.

But the Athenians ran into the opposite extreme. Wealthy, and fond of show, they delighted in a style of dress in the highest degree curious and magnificent, appearing abroad in flowing robes of the finest linen, dyed with purple and other bril-

[1] Plut. Lyc. § 16. Inst. Lac. § 5.

[2] Xenoph. de Rep. Laced. iii. 4. Of Phocion, an imitator of Spartan manners, the same thing is related.—Plut Phoc. § 4.

[3] Herod. vii. 208, with the notes of Valckenaar and Wesseling.

[4] Plut. Instit. Lacon. § 5.

liant colours.[1] Beneath these they wore tunics of various kinds, which, though the fashion afterwards changed, were at first sleeveless, since we find the women, in Aristophanes, suffering the hair to grow under their arm-pits to avoid being discovered when, disguised as their husbands, they should hold up their hands to vote in the assembly.[2]

Like the women, they affected much variety and splendour in their rings, which were sometimes set with a stone with the portrait engraved thereon of some friend or benefactor, as Athenion wore on one of his the portrait of Mithridates.[3]

In his girdle and shoes,[4] too, the Athenian betrayed his love of splendour. The hair worn long like that of the ladies,[5] was curled or braided and built up in glossy masses on the crown of the head, or arranged artfully along the forehead by golden grasshoppers.[6] But as all this pile of ringlets could not be thrust into the helmet, it was customary in time of war to cut the hair short, which the fashionable young men reckoned among its most serious hardships. Hats[7] were not habitually worn, though

---

[1] Thucyd. i. 6. Plat. de Rep. t. vi. p. 167. Tim. Lex. 188. Aristoph. Eccles. 332. Sch. A-ristoph. Eq. 879. Lucian. Amor. § 3.

[2] Aristoph. Concion. 60, et Schol.

[3] Athen. v. 49.—Even slaves were in the habit of wearing rings set with precious stones, sometimes of three colours, of which several specimens are found in the British Museum. Thus, in Lucian, we find Parmenon, the servant of Polemon, with a ring of this kind on his little finger.— Diall. Meret. ix. 2. Cf. Hemster. ad Poll. ix. 96. t. vi. p. 1193.

[4] Poll. vii. 92, seq.

[5] Casaub. ad Theoph. Char. p. 329.

[6] Athen. xii. 5. Sch. Aristoph. Eq. 1328. Nub. 971.

[7] It is very clear from a passage in Demosthenes (De Fals. Leg. § 72), that hats or caps were sometimes worn in the city. There are those indeed who suppose the word to mean a wig; but Brodæus disposes of this by inquiring whether sick persons would be likely to go to bed with their wigs on as men did with their πιλίδια. Miscell. i. 13. However, I must confess their wearing hats in bed is still less likely. The Bœotians appeared in winter with caps which covered the ears. Hesiod. Opp. et Dies, 545. On the form of which, see Theoph. Hist. Plant. iii. 9. 6, with the note of Schneid. t. iii. p. 191.

on journeys or promenades undertaken during hot weather they formed a necessary part of the costume. Above all things the Athenian citizen affected extreme cleanliness and neatness in his person, and the same taste descended even to the slaves who in the streets could scarcely be distinguished by dress, hair, or ornaments, from their masters.[1]

Even the philosophers, after holding out a long time, yielded to the influence of fashion, and, lest their profession should suffer, became exquisites in its defence. Your truly wise man, says an unexceptionable witness in a matter of this kind, has his hair closely shaved, (this was an eastern innovation,) but suffers his magnificent beard to fall in wavy curls over his breast. His shoes, fitting tight as wax, are supported by a net-work of thongs, disposed at equal distances up the small of the leg. A chlamys puffed out effeminately at the breast conceals his figure, and like a foreigner he leans contemplatively upon his staff.[2]

But the art of dress appears to have received its greatest improvements in Ionia, where, according to Democritos, the Ephesian, both the garments, at one time in fashion, and the stuffs of which they consisted, were varied with a skill and fertility of invention worthy of a polished people. Some persons, he says, appeared in robes of a violet, others of a purple, others of a saffron colour, sprinkled with dusky lozenges. As at Athens, much attention was bestowed on the hair, which they adorned with small ornamental figures. Their vests were yellow, like a ripe quince, or purple, or crimson, or pure white. Even their tunics, imported from Corinth, were of the finest texture, and of the richest dyes, hyacinthine or violet, flame-coloured or deep sea-green. Others adopted the Persian *calasiris*,[3] of all tunics

[1] Xenoph. de Rep. Athen. i. 10.
[2] Athen. xi. 120. On the gorgeous dress of the painter Parrhasios. xii. 62.

[3] We find mention made of Persian dresses variegated with the figures of animals. Philost. Icon. ii. 32.

the most superb, and there were those among the
opulent who even affected the Persian *actœa*, a shawl-
mantle of the costliest and most gorgeous appearance.   It was formed of a close-woven, but light
stuff, bedropped with golden beads in the form of
millet-seed, which were connected with the tissue
by slender eyes passing through the stuff and fastened by a purple thread.[1]

Duris, on the authority of the poet Asios, draws
a scarcely less extravagant picture of the luxury
and magnificence of the Samians, who, on certain
festivals, appeared in public adorned, like women,
with glittering bracelets, their hair floating on their
shoulders, skilfully braided into tresses.   The words
of Asios preserved in the Deipnosophist are as follow: "Thus proceed they to the fane of Hera,
"clothed in magnificent robes, with snowy pelisses,
"trailing behind them on the ground.   Glistening
"ornaments of gold, like grasshoppers, surmount the
"crown of their heads, while their luxuriant tresses
"float behind in the wind, intermingled with golden
"chains.   Bracelets of variegated workmanship adorn
"their arms, as the warrior is adorned by his shield
"thongs."[2]   This excess of effeminate luxury, attended as everywhere else by enervating vices, terminated in the ruin of Samos.   Similar manners in
the Colophonians drew upon them a similar fate,
and so in every other Grecian community; for men
never learn wisdom by the example of others, but
hurry on in the career of indulgence as if in the
hope that Providence might overlook them, or set
aside, in their favour, its eternal laws.

---

[1] Athen. xii. 29.   [2] Athen. xii. 30.

BOOK IV.

CHAPTER I.

PRIVATE DWELLINGS.

THE opinion appears to prevail among certain writers, that the private dwellings of the Hellenes, or at least of the Athenians, were always mean and insignificant.[1] This imaginary fact they account for by supposing, that nobles and opulent citizens were deterred from indulging in the luxuries of architecture by the form of government and the envious jealousy of the common people. But such a view of the matter is inconsistent with the testimony of history. At Athens, as everywhere else, things followed their natural course. In the early ages of the commonwealth, when manners were simple, the houses of the greatest men in the state differed very little from those of their neighbours. As wealth, however, and luxury increased, together with the developement of the democratic principle, individuals erected themselves mansions vying in extent and splendour with the public edifices of the state;[2] and as the polity

---

[1] But even from a fragment of Bacchylides we may infer the magnificence of Grecian houses; for the poor man who drinks wine, he says, sees his house blazing with gold and ivory:

χρυσῷ δ' ἐλέφαντί τε
μαρμαίρουσιν οἶκοι.
Athen. ii. 10.

Men had by this time advanced considerably from the state in which they are supposed to have built their huts in imitation of the swallow's nest. Vitruv. ii. 1.

[2] Plat. Repub. iv. t. vi. p. 165. Dion Chrysost. i. 262. ii. 459. Dem. cont. Mid. § 44.—Lucian. Amor. § 34.

degenerated more and more into ochlocracy, the dwellings of the rich[1] increased in size and grandeur, until they at length outstripped the very temples of the gods. A similar process took place at Sparta, where shortly after the Peloponnesian war, the more distinguished citizens possessed suburban villas, which seem to have been of spacious dimensions and filled with costly furniture.[2]

Upon these points, however, I dwell, not from any belief that they are honourable to the Greek character, but because they are true. It would have been more satisfactory to find them preserving, in every period of their history, the stern and lofty simplicity of republican manners, far outshining in the eyes of the philosopher the palaces of Oriental kings glittering with gold and ivory and jewels, insomuch that the cottage of Socrates, erected in the humblest style of Athenian domestic architecture, would be an object, were it still in existence, of far deeper interest to the genuine lover of antiquity than the mansions of Meidias or Callias, or even than the imperial abodes of Semiramis, Darius, and Artaxerxes.

Nevertheless, wherever there exists opulence, it will exhibit itself in the erection of stately dwellings; and accordingly we find that, prior even to the Trojan war,[3] commerce and increasing luxury had already inspired the Greeks with a taste for splendour and magnificence, which displayed itself especially in the architecture and ornaments of their palaces and houses of the great.[4]

Homer, minute and graphic in his descriptions, delineates a very flattering picture of Greek domestic architecture in his time, when the chiefs and nobles had already begun to enshrine themselves in spacious edifices, elaborately ornamented

---

[1] Dem. Olynth. iii. § 9. De Rep. Ord. § 10.
[2] Xenoph. Hellen. vi. 5. 27.
[3] Cf. Athen. i. 28.
[4] Cf. Müll. Dor. ii. 272.

with, and surrounded by, all the circumstances of
pomp known to their age.[1]

In those days the greatest men did not disdain
to apply themselves to agriculture, to have their
dwellings surrounded by the signs and implements
of the pursuit in which they were engaged.[2] And
as in southern Italy the ancient nobles erected shops
in front of their palaces or villas, in which the produce of their land was disposed of, so in the Homeric houses the same space was occupied by the
farm-yard enclosed by strong and lofty walls, surrounded by battlements, within which were their
heaps of manure, harrows, ploughs, carts, and waggons, and stacks of hay and corn;[3] and hither, too,
in the evening were driven in their numerous flocks
and herds, to protect them from the nightly marau-
ders. The great entrance gates were in the heroic
ages guarded by ban dogs,[4] which afterwards made
way for porters,[5] and in still later times were succeeded by eunuchs.[6]

Occasionally for the canine doorkeepers were substituted in commercial states gold and silver representations, more likely to attract than repel thieves;
for example, at the entrance to Alcinoös's palace
were groups of this description, attributed to the
wonder-working Hephæstos.[7] A coarse imitation of
this practice prevailed among the Romans, for we find

---

[1] Il. ϵ. 657, sqq.

[2] A similar taste prevailed
among the Merovingian princes
of France: "The mansion of
"the long-haired kings was sur-
"rounded with convenient yards
"and stables for the cattle and
"the poultry; the garden was
"planted with useful vegetables;
"the various trades, the labours
"of agriculture, and even the
"arts of hunting and fishing were
"exercised by servile hands for
"the emolument of the sovereign;
"his magazines were filled with

"corn and wine, either for sale
"or consumption, and the whole
"administration was conducted
"by the strictest maxims of pri-
"vate economy."—Gibbon, Decline and Fall of the Roman Empire, ii. 356.

[3] Hesych. v. αὐλῆς.

[4] Feith. Antiq. Hom. iii. 10.
p. 242.

[5] Casaub. ad Theoph. Char.
p. 145.

[6] Plat. Protag. t. i. p. 159. Cf.
Aristid. t. i. p. 518. Jebb.

[7] Odyss. η. 93.

in Petronius that Trimalchio had his court guarded
by a painted mastiff, over which in good square characters were the words "Beware of the dog."[1]

Along the walls of this enclosure the cattle-sheds
would in remoter ages appear to have been ranged,
where afterwards stood suites of chambers for the
domestics, or piazzas, or colonades, to serve as covered walks in extremely hot or bad weather. Within,
on either side the gateway,[2] chiefly among the Dorians, rose a pillar of conical shape, sometimes an
obelisk, in honour of Apollo or of Dionysos, or,
according to others, of both, while in the centre
was an altar of Zeus Herceios, on which family sacrifices were offered up.[3] At its inner extremity
you beheld a spacious portico, adjoining the entrance
to the house, where in warm weather the young men
often slept. From the descriptions of the poet, however, it would appear to have been something more
than a common portico, resembling rather the porches
of our old English houses, roofed over and extending like a recess into the body of the house itself.
In the dwellings of the great, this part of the
building, adorned with numerous statues, was probably of marble finely polished if not sculptured,
and being merely a chamber open in front could
not in those fine climates be by any means an unpleasant bedroom, particularly as it usually faced
the south and caught the early rays of the sun.
Here Odysseus[4] slept during his stay with Alcinoös,
as did likewise Priam and the Trojan Herald while
guests of Achilles in his military hut.[5]

In this porch were seats of handsome polished

[1] Satyr. c. 29. p. 74. Hel-
lenop.

[2] Sch. Aristoph. Vesp. 875.
Here the Romans sacrificed to
Janus, the Greeks to Apollo.
Macrob. Saturn. l. i. c. 9. Poll.
iv. 123. Comm. p. 790.

[3] Eustath ad Od. χ. 376. p.

790. Cf. Poll. i. 22, seq. Muret.
in Plat. de Rep. p. 635. Soph.
Œdip. Tyr. 16.

[4] Odyss. η. 345. Cf. Il. ζ.
243. Hesych. v. πρόδομος.

[5] Il. ω. 673, sqq. Cf. Feith.
Antiq. Hom. iii. 10. p. 244.

stone, as in the palace of Nestor at Pylos, which,
to render them more shining, would appear to have
been rubbed with oil.[1]   Similar seats are found to
this day before the houses of the wealthy at Cairo
and other cities of the East, where in the cool of
the evening old men habitually take their station,
and are joined for the purpose of gossip by their
neighbours.   In the larger towns of Nubia an open
space planted with dates, palms, or the Egyptian
fig-tree, more shady and spreading than the oak,
and furnished with wooden seats, collects together
the elders, who there enjoy what the Englishman
seeks in his club, and the Greek found in his lesche
—the pleasure of comparing his opinions with those
of his neighbours.

When, in after times, this plain porch had been
succeeded by a magnificent peristyle or colonnade,
the primitive custom of sleeping in the open air was
abandoned ; but here the master of the house with
his guests took their early walk to enjoy the morning
sun.   It was customary among all ranks at Athens
to rise betimes, as it generally is still in the warm
countries of the South.   Socrates and his young
friend, the sophist-hunter,[2] coming to the house of
Callias, soon after day-break, find its owner taking
the air with several of his guests in the colonnade,
the young men moving in the train of their elders,
and making way for them as they turn round to re-
trace their steps.   There was usually at Athens a
similar peristyle on both sides of the house—one
for summer the other for winter, and a door generally opened from the women's apartment into that
communicating with the garden, where the ladies
enjoyed the cool air in the midst of laurel copses,
fountains, and patches of green sward,[3] interspersed
with rose-trees, violet-beds, and other sweet shrubs
and flowers.

[1] Odyss. γ. 406, sqq. Cf. π.
343, seq.
[2] Plat. Protag. t. i. p. 160.

[3] Plat. Epist. t. viii. p. 403.
Athen. v. 25.   Poll. ix. 466.

The town-houses of Homeric times had generally no aulè, but the porch opened directly into the street, since it is here that, in the description of the shield, we find the women standing to behold the dancers and enjoy the music of the nuptial procession.[1] Afterwards, as the taste for magnificence advanced, the whole façade of the corps de logis[2] was richly ornamented, while the outer gates were purposely left open, that the passers-by might witness the splendour of the owner. Occasionally, likewise, the great door, leading from the portico into the house, was concealed by costly purple hangings,[3] which, being passed, you entered a broad passage, having on either side, doors[4] leading into the apartments on the ground floor, and conducting to an inner court, surrounded by a peristyle, where the gynæconitis,[5] or harem, commenced.

The apartments of palaces displayed, even in very early times, the taste of the Greeks for splendour and magnificence. The walls were covered with wainscoting inlaid with gold and ivory, as we still find in the East whole chambers lined with mother-of-pearl.[6] At first, the gold was laid on in thin plates, which, in process of time, led to the idea of gilding.[7] Even Phocion, who affected great simplicity and plainness, had the walls of his house adorned with laminæ of copper,[8] probably in the same style as that subterraneous chamber discovered, during the last

---

[1] Il. σ. 496. Cf. Sch. Aristoph. Nub. 93.

[2] Hesych. v. ἐνώπια. Casaub. ad Theoph. Char. p. 330. Compare the whole character of the "Vain Man," pp. 57—59. Etym. Mag. 346. 10.

[3] Athen. v. 25. Hesych. v. αυλεία. Suid. in v. t. i. p. 491. d.

[4] "The doors (at Tanjeers) are "richly carved, and placed in "arches shaped like an ace of "spades, a form so completely "oriental, that there is no mis-

"taking its origin; these, when "they opened on the verandah, "were further ornamented with "curtains of rich crimson silk." —Napier, Excursions along the Shores of the Mediterranean, i. p. 264.

[5] Hesych. v. γυναικωνῖτις.

[6] Lady Montague's Works, ii. 234.

[7] Plin. xxxiii. 18. Cf. Dion. Chrysost. t. i. p. 262. t. ii. p 259. Pignor. de Serv. p. 214.

[8] Plut. Phoc. § 18.

century, in the excavations made at Rome. It appears, too, that, occasionally, the walls of the apartments at Athens, as at Herculaneum and Pompeii were decorated with paintings in bright colours,[1] probably in the same style, though as much superior in beauty and delicacy of execution, as art, in the age of Pericles, was superior to art in the days of Nero. Still the paintings discovered in the excavated Italian cities,—sometimes[2] grotesque and extravagant, as where we behold the pigmies making war upon the cranes, winged geniuses at work in a carpenter's or shoemaker's shop, or an ass laden with hampers of wine, rushing forward to engage a crocodile, whilst his master pulls him back by the tail —sometimes rural and elegant, consisting of a series of wild landscapes, mountains dotted with cottages, sea-shores, harbours, and baths, Nymphs and Cupids angling on the borders of lakes, beneath trees of the softest and most exquisite foliage,—may enable us to form some conception of the landscapes with which Agelarcos[3] adorned the house of Alcibiades.

The halls and saloons on the ground-floor were paved with marble or mosaic work,[4] which often, if we may judge from the specimens left us by their imitators, represented pictures of the greatest elegance, containing, among other things, likenesses of the loveliest divinities of Olympos.[5] These mosaics were wrought with minute shards of precious marbles of various colours, interspersed with pieces of amber,[6] and, probably, also, of glass, as was the fashion in Italy, where whole hyaline floors have been found consisting either of one piece or of squares so finely joined together, that the sutures

[1] As, *minium*, Dioscor. v. 109.

[2] Antich. di Ercol. t. i. tav. 34. p. 181. tav. 35. p. 187. tav. 36. p. 191. tav. 48. pp. 253, 257. t. ii. tav. 39. p. 273. Cf. Poll. x. 34.

[3] Andocid. cont. Alcib. § 7.

[4] Plin. xxxvi. 60. Poll. vii. 121. Cf. Sir W. Hamilton, Acc. of Discov. at Pomp. p. 7, seq. pl. 5.

[5] Galen. in Protrept, § 8. t. i. p. 19.

[6] Hom. Eires. 10. p. 199. Franke.

were invisible to the naked eye. No mention, I believe, is made in Greek authors of lining the walls
of apartments with glass, or even of glass windows,[1]
which, however, were common in the cities of Magna
Græcia in the age immediately succeeding that of
our Saviour. It is extremely probable, however,
that as the Greeks were as well acquainted as the
Romans with the properties of the lapis specularis;[2]
they likewise made use of thin plates of this stone,
or talc, or gypsum, as they still do in Egypt for
window-panes. So much, indeed, seems inferable
from a passage of Plutarch,[3] as, also, that transparent squares of horn were employed for the same
purpose, as oyster-shells and oiled paper still are
in China. Previously, however, the windows[4] (sometimes square and situated high in the wall, sometimes reaching from the ceiling to the floor) were
closed with lattice-work[5] in iron, bronze, or wood,
over which, in bad weather, blinds of hair-cloth or
prepared leather were usually drawn.

The ceilings at first consisted merely of the beams,
rafters, and planks, forming the roof, and supporting
the layers of earth or straw that covered it; but, by
degrees, the wood-work was carefully painted, and

---

[1] See the authorities collected
by Nixon, Phil. Trans. t. i. p.
126, sqq. Seneca speaks of glass
windows as a new invention,
Epist. 90. Sir William Hamilton, however, in his Account of
Discoveries made at Pompeii,
observes: — " Below stairs is a
" room with a large bow-window;
" fragments of large panes of
" glass were found here, shewing
" that the ancients knew well
" the use of glass for windows."
— p. 13. Cf. Caylus, Rec.
d'Ant. t. 2. p. 293. Mazois,
Pal. de Scaur. p. 97. Castell.
Villas of the Ancients, p. 4.
Vitruv. vii. 3.

[2] In lieu of the lapis specularis,
they make use in Persia of thin slabs
of Tabreez marble for the windows of baths, and other buildings
requiring a soft subdued light.
— See Fowler, Three Years in
Persia, where the growth of this
stone is curiously described.—i.
228, sqq.

[3] De Plac, Phil. iii. 5, ed. Cor-
sin. Flor. 1750, p. 81. Cf. Plin.
Hist. Nat. xi. 37.

[4] Sir W. Hamilt. Acc. of Discov. at Pomp. p. 7, seq. Antich. di Ercolano. t. i. tav. i. p. 1.
tav. 3. p. 11. Cf. Schol. Aristoph. Eq. 996.

[5] Mazois, Pal. de Scaur. p. 98.

arranged so as to form a succession of coffers and
deep sunken panels.   Sometimes the whole ceiling
consisted of chamfered, or fretted cedar work,[1] or
of cypress wood, or was covered with paintings in
blue and gold, and supported on columns[2] lofty and
deeply fluted for the purpose, as has been ingeniously
conjectured,[3] of receiving spears into the semi-cylin-
drical cavities thus formed.   If this idea be well
founded, we have a very satisfactory reason of the
origin of fluting columns, and it appears to be perfectly consistent with Homer's account of Odysseus's
chamber, where a number of lances are spoken of
standing round a pillar.[4]

The principal apartments, according to the fashion
still prevailing in the East, were furnished with
divans,[5] or broad immovable seats, running along the
walls, which are now stuffed soft atop with cotton,
and covered with scarlet or purple, bordered by gold
fringe a foot deep.   In the Homeric age they would
appear to have been of carved wood, inlaid with
ivory and gold, and studded with silver nails.[6]   For
these divans they had a variety of coverings, sometimes skins, at others purple carpets, in addition to
which they, as now, piled up, as a rest for the back
or elbow, heaps of cushions, purple above, and of
white linen beneath.[7]   By degrees, these seats became movable and were converted into couches or
sofas, manufactured of bronze, or silver, or precious
woods, veneered with tortoiseshell.[8]   In the palaces
of oriental sultans they are sometimes made of
alabaster, encrusted with jewels.   Somewhere in the

---

[1] Athen. ix. 67.   Plat. de Rep.
t. vi. p. 353.   Cf. Gog. Origine
des Loix, t. v. p. 443.   Poll.
Onom. x. 84.   Comm. p. 1552.
Maz. Pal. de Scau. p. 102.   Ti-
bull. iii. 3. 16.   Luc. de Dea
Syr. § 30. Cynic, § 9.   Eurip.
Orest. 1361.

[2] Odyss. δ. 45, seq.   Luc.
Somn. seu Gall. § 29.

[3] By Payne Knight, Prolegg.
ad Hom. § 47.   Cf. Feith. Antiq. Homer, iii. 11. 6.

[4] Odyss. α. 127, seq.

[5] Id. η. 95, seq.

[6] Id. θ. 65. π. 32.

[7] Id. κ. 352, seq.

[8] Lucian, Luc. siv. Asin. § 53.

more retired parts of the Domos were the picture-gallery and library, of neither of which have we any exact description. The former, however, faced the north, and the latter the west. If the libraries of the Greeks at all resembled in form and dimensions those found at Pompeii, they were by no means spacious; neither, in fact, was a great deal of room necessary, as the manuscripts of the ancients stowed away much closer than our modern books,[1] and were sometimes kept in circular boxes, of elegant form, with covers of turned wood. The volumes consisted of rolls of parchment, sometimes purple at the back,[2] or papyrus, about twelve or fourteen inches in breadth, and as many feet long as the subject required. The pages formed a number of transverse compartments, commencing at the left, and proceeding in order to the other extremity, and the reader, holding in either hand one end of the manuscript, unrolled and rolled it up[3] as he read. Occasionally these books were placed on shelves, in piles, with the ends outwards, adorned with golden bosses,[4] the titles of the various treatises being written on pendant labels.

If we proceed now to the court[5] dividing the Domos from the Thalamos we shall perceive, on both sides of the door leading out of the Andron, flights of steps ascending to the upper chambers where, in the heroic ages, the young men and strangers of distinction usually slept. Thus, in the palace of Ithaca, Telemachos had a bed-chamber on the second story, whence the poet is careful to observe he enjoyed a good prospect.[6] In later times, however,

[1] Antich. di Ercol. t. ii. tav. 2. p. 13.—Books were preserved from the moth by cedar-oil.—Geopon. v. 9.

[2] Luc. de Merced. Conduct. § 41.

[3] Luc. Imag. § 9.

[4] Luc. de Merced. Conduct. 41.

[5] Similar courts in the houses of Magna Græcia are described as having had in the middle a square tank where the rain-water was collected, and ran into a reservoir beneath.—Sir W. Hamilt. Acc. of Discov. at Pomp. p. 13.

[6] Odyss. a. 425. seq.

there were, on the ground floor, suites of apartments, denominated Xenon, appropriated to the use of guests, who there lived freely and at ease as in their own houses.

At the further extremity of the interior court a steep flight of steps led to an elevated basement and doorway, which formed the entrance into the thalamos.[1] This part of the house would appear to have been laid out in a peculiar manner, consisting, first, of a lofty and spacious apartment,[2] where all the females of the family usually sat while engaged in embroidery or other needlework.[3] It likewise formed the nursery, and, at its inner extremity, in a deep recess, the bed of the mistress of the family appears to have stood, on either side of which were doors leading to flights of steps into the garden, set apart for the use of the women.

It has by many been supposed, that the Thalamos was a chamber particularly appropriated to the use of young unmarried ladies; but, since we find Helen and Penelope inhabiting the Thalamos, it may be presumed that it was common to all the females of the house. Hector, in his visit to Paris, finds him in the Thalamos, turning about and polishing his arms, as if he meant to use them, while, close at hand, are Helen and her maids engaged in weaving or embroidery. The word was often used in the same signification as Gynæconitis,[4] or "the harem;" and,

---

[1] Eustath. ad Odyss. χ. p. 776. —These female apartments were sometimes hired out and inhabited by men. — Antiph. Nec. Venef. § 3.—Mr. Fosbroke's account is curious: — " The thalamos was an apartment where " the *mothers of families* worked " in embroidery, in tapestry, and " other works, *with their wives,* " or their friends." — Encyclop. of Ant. i. 50.

[2] Sometimes, at least, roofed with cypress-wood, as we learn from Mnesimachos, in his Horsebreeder: βαίν' ἐκ ϑαλάμων κυπαρισσορόφων ἔξω, Μάνη. — Athen. ix. 67.

[3] We find ladies, however, sometimes dining with their children in the Aulè.—Demosth. in Ev. et Mnes. § 16.

[4] Hesych, v. γυναίκ. p. 866. Cyrill. Lex. Ms. Bren. Bret. ad Hesych. l. c.

therefore, when Theocritus [1] speaks of a " maiden
from the Thalamos," and Phocylides, with the suspicious caution of a more vicious age, advises that young
women be kept in " well-locked Thalamoi," it is clear
that the female apartments generally are meant.
These were, in Sparta, called *oä* (which, as is well
known, in the common language of Greece, signi-
nifies eggs), whence, according to Clearchos, [2] the
fable which describes Helen proceeding from an egg,
because born and educated in the chambers so called.
Throughout the Iliad and the Odyssey we find the
poet speaking of this part of the house as inhabited
by women. Here lived Penelope, [3] far from the
brawls of the suitors who crowded the halls of the
Domos; and here Ares pressed his suit with success
to Astyoche and Polymela, who both became the
mothers of valiant sons. [4] From which, among many
other circumstances, it is manifest that, in those
ages, the sexes met easily, even the entrance to the
harem not being impracticable to a lover.

The bedchambers of the young unmarried women
appear to have flanked the great central hall of the
Thalamos, and here the female slaves likewise slept,
apparently in recesses, near the chamber-doors of
their mistresses, as we find particularly remarked
in the case of Nausicaa and her maids. At Athens,
the door of communication between the Andron [5] and
the Gynæconitis was kept carefully barred and locked
to prevent all intercourse between the male and
female slaves, the keys being entrusted solely to
the mistress of the house.

As these apartments were less exposed than any
other portion of the building, and far more carefully guarded, it became customary, as in the East
it still is, to lay up in the Thalamos, more especially in the dark basement story, much valuable

---

[1] Eidyll. ii. 136. Phocyl. v.
198.
[2] Athen. ii. 50. Cf. Sch. Aristoph. Vesp. 68.

[3] Odyss. *o.* 516.
[4] Il. ε. 514. π. 184.
[5] Cf. Poll. vi. 7. Cœl. Rhodig.
xvii. 24.

property, such as arms, gold, silver, the wardrobe of both sexes, and even oil and wine. Among the Romans, or, indeed, among the Greeks, of a later age,[1] this step would scarcely have been taken, lest the ladies should have grown too assiduous in their attention to the skins. But in remoter ages these sordid fears had no existence. Accordingly, we find the prudent Odysseus, who apprehended, perhaps, the tricks of his domestics, stowing away his casks of choice old wine in the Thalamos, doubtless, considering it safer there, under the keeping of Euryclea, than it would have been anywhere else in the palace.[2]

In later and more civilized ages, the Thalamos was still used for the same purposes; for, in the establishment of Ischomachos, a pattern of Attic economy, we find that the more valuable portion of the family wardrobe, with the plate and other costly utensils, was there deposited. Corn, according to the suggestions of common sense, they laid up in the driest rooms, wine in the coolest. The apartments into which most sunshine found its way were appropriated to such employments and to the display of such furniture as required much light.[3] Their dining-rooms, where, also, the men usually sat when at home, they carefully contrived so as to be cool in summer and warm in winter, though, in severe weather, a good fire was often found necessary.[4] The same judicious principle commonly regulated the erection of their habitations, which were divided

[1] Plut. Paral. Vit. § 3.
[2] Odyss. ε. 337, 345. χ. 442. Schol. 459. 466. Poll. vii. 397.
[3] Xen. Memorab. iii. 8, 9.
[4] Anaxand. ap. Athen. ii. 29. —So also thought Socrates, who observes, that in winter every one will have a fire who can get wood. And, though he himself wore the same garments all the year round, he considered it, apparently, a judicious practice in others to put on warm clothing. —Xen. Œcon. xvii. 3. Sch. Aristoph. Acharn. 716. When the dining-room was not furnished with a chimney, braziers were kindled outside the door, and carried in when the worst fumes of the charcoal had evaporated.—Plut. Symp. vi. 7.

into two sets of apartments, suited to the two great divisions of the year. As we have already remarked, the principal front looked towards the south, that it might catch the rays of the wintry sun, whose more vertical summer beams were excluded by broad verandahs, or colonnades.

In what part of the edifice stood the bathing-room (βαλανεῖον, so called from its having, in remoter ages, been heated with acorns, βάλανοι)[1] I have been unable to discover, though it appears certain that, even so far back as the heroic ages, a chamber was always set apart for the bath. At first, doubtless, they were content with cold water; but that this was soon succeeded by warm water[2] may be conjectured from the tradition ascribing the first use of it to Heracles, whence warm baths were ever afterwards called the Baths of Heracles.

The form of the Puelos,[3] or vessel in which they bathed, appears occasionally to have resembled an Egyptian sarcophagus, and to have been sometimes round, and constructed of white or green marble, or glass, or bronze, or common stone, or wood,[4] in which case it would seem to have been portable. In the baths of Pompeii the marble basins, whether parallelogramatic or circular, were of spacious dimensions, and raised two or three feet above the pavement. A step for the convenience of the bathers extends round it on the inside, and at the bottom are marble cushions upon which they rested. In the labra of the Grecian female baths rose a smooth cippus in the form of a truncated cone, denominated omphalos, on which the ladies sat while chatting with their female companions.[5]

When once the warm bath came into use, people

---

[1] Etym. Mag. 186, 8. Athen. i. 18. Phot. Bib. 60. b. Hesiod. Frag. 53. Baths, at Sparta, were common to both sexes.—Goguet, v. 428. Cf. Pashley, Travels. i. 183.

[2] Baccius, de Thermis, p. 365. Schol. Aristoph. Nub. 1034.

[3] Cf. Etymol. Mag. 151, 52, seq. Schol. Aristoph. Eq. 1055.

[4] Baccius, de Therm. p. 399.

[5] Athen. xi. 104.

employed it to excess, bathing as frequently as five or six times a day, and in water so hot as to half scald themselves.[1] Immediately afterwards, to prevent the skin from chapping, they anointed their bodies with oils and perfumed unguents.[2] Occasionally, instead of plunging into the water, they sat upright, as is still the custom in the hammāms of the East, while the water was poured with a sort of ladle on their head and shoulders.

The public baths, of which no full description referring to very ancient times remains, were numerous in all Hellenic cities, more particularly at Athens, where they were surmounted with domes,[3] and received their light from above. These establishments were frequented by all classes of women who could afford to pay for such luxury, rich, poor, honourable, and dishonourable.

The attendants, in later and more corrupt times at least, were men, whose sole clothing consisted of a leathern apron about the loins, while the ladies, who undressed in the Apodyterion, went through the various processes of the bath in the same primitive clothing. It was, however, customary for them to enter the water together in crowds,[4] so that they kept each other in countenance. Here the matrons who had sons to marry studied the form and character of the young ladies who frequented the baths; and as all the defects both of person and features were necessarily revealed, it was next to impossible for any lady, not sufficiently opulent to keep up a bathing establishment in her own house, to retain for any length of time an undeserved celebrity for beauty. In the baths of the East, the bodies of the bathers are cleansed by small bags of camel-hair, woven rough,

[1] Schol. Aristoph. Nub. 1034.
[2] Plut. Alexand. § 40.
[3] Athen. xi. 104.
[4] Victor. ad Aristot. Ethic. p. 214. There was a set of vicious fellows, called τρίβαλλοι, who passed their lives disorderly in the baths.—Etym. Mag. 765. 55. Aristophanes bestows the name on certain barbarian divinities.—Aves. 1528.

and passed over the hand of the attendant; or with a handful of the fine fibres of the Mekka palm-tree combed soft, and filled with fragrant and saponaceous earths, which are rubbed on the skin till the whole body is covered with froth. Similar means were employed in the baths of Greece, and the whole was afterwards cleansed off the skin by gold or silver stlengides, or blunt scrapers somewhat curved towards the point.[1]

The architectural arrangements of these baths,[2] if we may draw any analogy from similar establishments in a later age, were nearly as follows:—Entering the building by a lofty and spacious portico, you found yourself in a large hall, paved with marble and adorned with columns, from which, through a side-door, you passed into the Apodyterion, or undressing-room; next, into a chamber where was the cold water in basins of porphyry or green jasper; immediately contiguous lay the Tepidarium, to which succeeded the Sudarium, a vaulted apartment furnished with basins of warm water, and where the heat was excessive; from this, moving forward, you successively traversed saloons of various degrees of temperature and dimensions, until you found yourself in the dressing-room, whither your garments had been carried by your domestic, or the attendants on the baths.[3] These establishments were likewise provided with water-closets,[4] placed in a retired part of the building, and furnished with wooden seats, basin and water-pipe, as in modern times.

To diminish the chances of being robbed, stealing from a bath was at Athens made a capital offence;[5] so that the persons who frequented them

---

[1] Xenoph. Anab. i. 2. 10. See one of these stlengides in Zoëga, Bassi Rilievi, tav. 29.

[2] Cf. Etymol. Mag. 384. 10. Poll. vii. 166, and Plut. Alexand. § 20, where he describes the luxurious baths of Darius.

[3] Lucian. Hippias. § 5, sqq.

[4] Sir W. Hamilton's Acc. of Discov. at Pompeii, p. 41. Cf. Casaub. ad Theoph. Char. p. 269.

[5] Aristot. Problem. xix. 14. Casaub. ad Theoph. Char. p. 215.

ran very little risk. The price was usually moderate, though in some cities, as for example at Pha-
selis, they were in the habit of doubling their
charges to foreigners, which drew from a witty sophist a very cutting remark; for his slave disputing
with the keeper of the bath, and contending that
his master ought not to be charged more than
other persons, the sophist, who overheard the dispute, exclaimed, "Wretch, would you make me a
"Phaselitan for a farthing?"[1]

The roofs of the more ancient Greek houses were
generally flat,[2] not sloping upwards to a point, as
was afterwards the fashion.[3] In Egypt and Syria,
and almost throughout the East, the same taste
still obtains; and as palm trees, loftier than the
buildings, often grow beside the walls, and extend
their beautiful pendulous branches over a great part
of the roof, nothing can be more delightful on a
mild serene evening than to sit aloft on those
breezy eminences sipping coffee, gazing over the
green rice fields, or watching the stars as they put
forth their golden lamps through the violet skirts
of day. But there a parapet usually preserves him
who enjoys the scene from falling. It was otherwise of old in Greece. The roof consisted simply
of a number of beams laid close together and covered with cement, so that, as was proved by the fate
of Elpenor,[4] the practice of sleeping there in warm
weather, quite common throughout the country, was
not wholly without danger.

On the construction of the kitchen,[5] which in
Greek houses was sometimes a separate little building erected in the court-yard, our information is
extremely imperfect. It is certain, however, con-

[1] Athen. viii. 45.

[2] Æsch. Agam. 3, sqq. We
find, however, an allusion to the
pointed roof in Iliad. ψ. 712,
seq.

[3] Antich. di Erc. tav. 3,
p. 11.

[4] Odyss κ. 559. Eustath. ad
loc. p. 1669, l. 15. Feith. Ant.
Hom. iii. 10, p. 249.

[5] Cf. Athen. ix. 22. iii. 60.

trary to the common opinion, that it was furnished
with a chimney,[1] and that the smoke was not permitted to find its way through an aperture in the
roof. Thus much might be inferred from a passage in the Wasps, when the old dicast, in love
with the courts of law, is endeavouring to escape
from the restraint imposed on him by his son, by
climbing out through the chimney. It is clear that
he has got into some aperture, where he is hidden
from sight, for hearing a noise in the wall, his son
Bdelycleon, cries out, " What is that?" upon which
the old man replies, " I am only the smoke." It
is plain, that he would not, like a Hindù Yoghi,
be balancing himself in the air, otherwise the young
man must have beheld him sailing up towards the
roof. But the matter is set entirely at rest by the
Scholiast, who observes, that the καπνοδόχη was a
narrow channel like a pipe through which the smoke
ascended from the kitchen. This explanation has
been confirmed by the discoveries of Colonel Leake,[2]
who on the rocky slopes of the hill of the Museion and Pnyx, found the remains of a house
partly excavated in the rock, in which the chimney
still remained.

The same convenience, also, existed in the Roman
kitchens,[3] though they would appear to have been
unskilfully constructed in both countries, since the
cooks complain of the smoke being borne hither
and thither by the wind, and interfering with their
operations. However, this may have arisen from
the numerous small furnaces which, as in France,
were ranged along the wall for the purpose of cooking several dishes at once. The chimneys having
been perpendicular, as in our old farm-houses, were

[1] Cf. Sch. Aristoph. Nub. 91.
Vesp. 139, 147.
[2] Topog. of Athens, p. 361.
[3] Cf. Perrault, sur Vitruv. vi.
9. Mazois, Pal. de Scaur. p.
178. On the interior of a Roman house, see Pet. Bellori,
Frag. Vet. Rom, p. 31.

furnished with stoppers to keep out the rain in bad weather.[1]

That the kitchens were sometimes not sufficiently airy and comfortable may be inferred from the practice of a philosophical cook in Damoxenos, who used to take his station immediately outside the door, and from thence give his orders to the inferior operatives. Great care was nevertheless taken that it should be well lighted, and that the door should be so situated as to be as little exposed as possible to whirling gusts of wind.[2] From a passage in the Scholiast on the Wasps, and the existence of drains in the excavations on the hill of the Museion, it is clear that the Athenian houses were furnished with sinks,[3] though in the Italian kitchens there seem merely to have been little channels running along the walls to carry off the water. The floor, too, was constructed in both countries with a view at once to dryness and elegance,[4] being formed of several layers of various materials all porous though binding, so that it allowed whatever water was spilt to sink through instantaneously. The upper layer, about six inches thick, consisted of a cement composed of lime, sand, and pounded charcoal or ashes, the surface of which, being polished with pumice-stone, presented to the eye the appearance of a fine black marble. The roof in early times was no doubt of wood,[5] though afterwards it came to be vaulted or run up in the form of a cupola. The walls were sometimes decorated with rude paintings.[6]

The street-door of a Grecian house, usually, when single, opened outwards, but when there were fold-

---

[1] Schol. Aristoph. Vesp. 148.
[2] Athen. iii. 60 ix. 22.
[3] Leake, Topog. of Ath. p. 361. Yet we find them sometimes throwing the water out of the window, crying, Stand out of the way. Schol. Aristoph. Acharn. 592.

[4] Vitruv. viii. 4.

[5] Mazois, Palais de Scaurus, p. 177.

[6] Representing, for example, a sacrifice to Fornax. Mazois, p. 177.

ing doors they opened inwards as with us.[1] In the
former case it was customary when any one happened to be going forth, to knock, or call, or ring
a bell, in order to warn passengers to make way.[2]
These doors were constructed of various materials,[3]
according to the taste and circumstances of the
owner, sometimes of oak, or fir, or maple, or elm;
and afterwards as luxury advanced they were made
of cedar, cyprus, or even of citron wood, inlaid as
in the East, with plates of brass or gold.[4] Mention is likewise made of doors entirely composed of
the precious metals; of iron also, and bronze and
ivory.

The jambs were generally of wood;[5] but likewise
sometimes of brass or marble. The doors were fastened at first by long bars passing into the wall on both
sides;[6] and by degrees smaller bolts, hasps, latches,
and locks and keys succeeded. For example the
outer door of the Thalamos in Homer was secured
by a silver hasp, and a leathern thong passed round
the handle and tied, perhaps, in a curious knot.[7]
Doors were not usually suspended on hinges, but
turned, as they still do in the East, upon pivots
inserted above into the lintel and below into the
threshhold.[8] In many houses there were in addition small half-doors of open wood-work,[9] which
alone were commonly closed by day, in order to

[1] Cf. Antich. di Ercol. t. i. tav. 34. pp. 175. 181. Sagittar. de Januis Veterum. p. 23.

[2] Plut. Poplic. § 20.

[3] Sagitt. de Jan. Vet. p. 152, seq. Plin. xvi. 40. Theoph. Hist. Plant. v. 4. 2. iii. 14. 1. Martial. xiv. 89, ii. 43. Lucian. l. ix. Tertull. de Pall. c. 5. Plin. xiii. 15. Ovid. Metamorph. iv. 487.

[4] Aristoph. Acharn. 1072.

[5] Sagitt. de Jan. Vet. p. 29, sqq.

[6] Sagitt. de Jan. p. 67.

[7] Odyss. α. 441. Schol. et Eustath. ad loc.—δ. 862. ρ. 186. Cf. Schol. Aristoph. Vesp. 155.

[8] Sagitt. de Jan. Vet. p. 41.

[9] Antich. di Ercol. t. i. tav. 3. p. 11. It should perhaps be re-marked, that when houses were built on a solid basement the door was sometimes approached by a movable pair of steps. Id. ibid. tav. 8. p. 39. tav. 43. p. 228.

keep the children from running out, or dogs or pigs from entering. The doors usually consisted of a frame-work, with four or six sunken panels, as with us; but at Sparta, so long as the laws of Lycurgus prevailed, they were made of simple planks fashioned with the hatchet.[1] In the great Dorian capital the custom was for persons desirous of entering a house to shout aloud at the door,[2] which, at Athens,[3] was always furnished with an elegant knocker.[4] Door-handles, too, of costly materials and curious work-manship,[5] bespoke even in that trifling matter the taste of the Greeks.

The materials commonly used in the erection of a house were stones and bricks. In the manufacture of the latter[6] the ancients exhibited more skill and care than we; they had bricks of a very large size, and half bricks for filling up spaces, which prevented the necessity of shortening them with the trowel. Of these some were simply dried in the sun, used chiefly in building the dwellings of the poor.[7] At Utica in Africa there were public inspectors of brick-kilns,[8] to prevent any from being used which had not been made five years. In several cities on the Mediterranean bricks were manufactured of a porous earth, which when baked and painted, as it may be conjectured, on the outside, were so light that they would swim in water.[9] To

---

[1] Plut. Lycurg. § 13. Agesil. § 19.

[2] Plut. Inst. Lac. § 30. Cf. Theocrit. Eidyll. xxix. 39.

[3] Schol. Aristoph. Nub. 133.

[4] Sometimes in form of a crow. Poll. i. 77.

[5] See Donaldson's Collection of Doorways. pl. 8.

[6] Winkelm. Hist. de l'Art. ii. 544. Cf. Xen. Memor. iii. 17. Cyropæd. vi. 3. 25. Plin. xxxv. 14. Polyb. x. 22. Plat. de Repub. t. vi. p. 15.

[7] Sanchon. ap. Euseb. Præp. Evang. i. 10. p. 35.

[8] Vitruv. ii. 3.

[9] Id. ibid. 3. In lieu of these light bricks, pumice stones are now frequently used on the shores of the Mediterranean, more particularly in turning arches. They are, consequently, cut into parallelopipeds, and exported in great quantities from the Lipari islands. —Spallanzani, Travels in the Two Sicilies, &c. vol. ii. pp. 298, 302, sqq.

diminish the weight of bricks, straw was introduced into them in Syria and Egypt, which was altogether consumed in the baking. In roofing such of their houses as were not terraced they employed slates, tiles, and reed-thatch.[1] Possibly, also, the wealthy may have tiled their houses with those elegant thin flakes of marble, with which the roofs of temples were occasionally covered.

[1] Poll. x. 170.   Luc. Contemplant. § 6.   Schol. Aristoph. Nub. 174.

CHAPTER II.

HOUSEHOLD FURNITURE.

THE movables in a Grecian house were divided into classes after a very characteristic manner. First, as a mark of the national piety, everything used in domestic sacrifices was set apart. The second division, placing women immediately after the gods, comprehended the whole apparatus of female ornaments [1] worn on solemn festivals. Next were classed the sacred robes and military uniforms of the men; then came the hangings, bed-furniture, and ornaments of the harem; afterwards those of the men's apartments. Another division consisted of the shoes, sandals, slippers, &c., of the family, from which we pass to the arms and implements of war, mixed up familiarly in a Greek house with looms, cards, spinning-wheels, and embroidery-frames, just, as Homer describes them in the Thalamos of Paris at Troy. Even yet we have not reached the end of our inventory in mere classification. The baking, cooking, washing, and bathing vessels formed a separate class, and so did the breakfast and dinner services, the porcelain, the plate of silver and gold, the mirrors, the candelabra, and all those curious articles made use of in the toilette of the ladies. [2]

In well-regulated families a second division took place, a separation being made of such articles as

---

[1] This profusion of wearing apparel was laid up in trunks and *mallekins* of wickerwork. The former were called κιϐωτοὶ, the latter κίσται. — Casaub. ad Theoph. Char. p. 233. Clem.

Alexand. Pæd. iii. Hesych. v. v. κιϐωτὸς — κίστη. Mention is also made of presses.—Mazois, Pal. de Scaur. p. 120.

[2] Xenoph. Œconom. ix. 6, sqq. Aristot. Œconom. i. 6.

might be required for daily use, from those brought
forward only when routs and large parties were
given.   The movables of all kinds having been
thus arranged in their classes, the next step was
to deposit every thing in its proper place.[1]   The
more ordinary utensils were generally laid up in a
spacious store-room, called *tholos*,[2] a circular building detached from the house, and usually terminating in a pointed roof, whence in after ages a
sharp-crowned hat obtained among the people the
name of Tholos.   When a gentleman first commenced housekeeping, or got a new set of domestics, he delivered into the care of the proper individuals his kneading troughs, his kitchen utensils,
his cards, looms, spinning wheels, and so on; and,
pointing out the places where all these, when not
in use, should be placed, committed them to their
custody.

Of the holiday, or show articles, more account
was made.   These, being brought forward only on
solemn festivals, or in honour of some foreign guest,
were entrusted to the immediate care of the house-
keeper, a complete list of everything having first been
taken; and it was part of her duty, when she delivered any of these articles to the inferior domestics,
to make a note of what she gave out, and take care
they were duly returned into her keeping.[3]

But the above comprehensive glance over the articles of furniture made use of in an Athenian gentleman's establishment, though it may give some notion
of the careful and economical habits of the people,
affords no conception of the splendour and magnificence often found in a Grecian house : for, as we
have already seen, their opinions are highly erroneous
who imagine that in the Attic democracy the rich
were by any prudential or political considerations

---

[1] Cicero ap. Columell. De Re
Rust. xii. 3.

[2] Odysseus had a storehouse
of this kind in his palace at

Ithaca. —Odyss. χ. 442, 459,
466.

[3] Xen. Œconom. ix. 10. 57.

restrained from indulging their love of ostentation by the utmost display they could make of wealth.[1] In fact, not content with outstripping their neighbours in the grandeur of their dwellings, furniture, and dress, these persons had often the ludicrous vanity, when they gave a large party, to excite the envy of such dinnerless rogues as might pass, by throwing out the feathers of game and poultry before their doors.[2] Indeed, since the Athenians exactly resembled other men, the exhibition of magnificence tended but too strongly to dazzle them; so that, among the arts of designing politicians, one generally was, to create a popular persuasion that they possessed the means of conferring important favours on all who obliged them.

To proceed, however, with the furniture. Though the principal value of many articles arose from the exquisite taste displayed in the design and workmanship, the materials themselves, too, were often extremely rare and costly. Porcelain, glass, crystal, ivory, amber,[3] gold, silver, and bronze, with numerous varieties of precious woods, were wrought up with inimitable taste and fancy into various articles of use or luxury. Among the decorations of the dining-room was the side-board, which, though sometimes of iron, was more frequently of carved wood, bronze, or wrought silver, ornamented with the heads of satyrs and oxen.[4] Their tables, in the Homeric age, were generally of wood, of variegated colours, finely polished, and with ornamented feet. Myrleanos, an obscure writer in Athen-

---

[1] That the sycophants were sometimes troublesome, however, is certain; that is to say, in later ages. Speaking of the time of his youth, Isocrates says: — Οὐδεὶς οὔτ' ἀπεκρύπτετο τὴν οὐσίαν οὔτ' ὤκνει συμϐάλλειν. κ. τ. λ.— Areop. § 12. Cf. Bergmann. in loc. p. 362. But their persecution must always have been confined to a very few individuals, as people generally continued to display whatever they possessed down to the final overthrow of the state.

[2] Aristoph. Acharn. 398. — Mitchell. The learned editor fails to remark how little this custom harmonizes with the fears which he imagines rich people felt at Athens.

[3] On the attractive power of this substance, see Plat. Tim. t. vii. p. 118.

[4] Athen. v. 45. Lys. Frag. 46. Orat. Att. t. ii. p. 647.

æus, imagines[1] they were round, that they might resemble the disc of the sun and moon; but from the passage in the Odyssey,[2] and the interpretation of Eustathius, they may be inferred to have been narrow parallelograms,[3] like our own dining-tables. The luxury of table-cloths being unknown, the wine spilled, &c., was cleansed away with sponges.[4] But the poet had witnessed a superior degree of magnificence, for he already, in the Odyssey,[5] makes mention of tables of silver. The poor were, of course, content with the commonest wood. But as civilisation proceeded, the tables of the wealthy became more and more costly in materials, and more elegant in form.

It grew to be an object of commerce, to import from foreign countries the most curious kinds of wood,[6] to be wrought into tables, which originally supported on four legs, rested afterwards on three, fancifully formed, or on a pillar and claws of ivory, or silver, as with us. There was a celebrated species of table manufactured in the island of Rhenea;[7] the great, among the Persians, delighted in maple tables with ivory feet, and, in fact, the knotted maple appears at one time to have been regarded as the most rare and beautiful of woods.[8] But the rage for sumptuous articles of furniture of this kind did not reach its full height until Roman times, when a single table of citron wood

(Gorgeous feasts
On citron tables or Atlantic stone)[9]

---

[1] Deipnosoph. xi. 78.

[2] a. 111. 138.

[3] This is also the opinion of Potter, ii. 376, 377; and Damm. in v. τράπεζα, col. 1822.

[4] Odyss. τ. 259. Pind. Olymp. i. 26.

[5] κ. 354, seq. 361, seq. In the letters attributed to Plato we find mention made of silver tables.

t. viii. p. 397. Sometimes, also, of brass. Athen. ix. 75.

[6] Plin. Nat. Hist. xvi. 27.

[7] Athen. xi. 27.

[8] Athen. ii. 31.

[9] Paradise Regained, iv. 114, seq. where see Mitford's curious and learned note. ii. 350, seq. and cf. Plin. v. 1. t. ii. p. 259. Hard. not. a. 261. xiii. 29. t. iv. p. 746,

sometimes cost six or seven thousand pounds sterling. Already, however, in the best ages of Greece,
their tables were inlaid with silver, brass, or ivory,
with feet in the form of lions, leopards, or other
wild beasts.[1]

In more early times, before the effeminate Oriental habit of reclining at meals obtained,[2] the
Greeks made use of chairs which were of various
kinds, some being formed of more, others of less
costly materials, but all beautiful and elegant in
form, as we may judge from those which adorn our
own drawing-rooms, entirely fashioned after Grecian
models. The thrones of the gods represented in
works of art, however richly ornamented, are simply
arm-chairs with upright backs, an example of which
occurs in a carnelian in the Orleans Collection,[3]
where Apollo is represented playing on the seven-
stringed lyre. This chair has four legs with tigers'
feet, a very high upright back, and is ornamented
with a sculptured car and horses. They had no
Epicurean notions of their deities, and never presented them to the eye of the public lounging in
an easy chair, which would have suggested the idea
of infirmity. On the contrary, they are full of force
and energy, and sit erect on their thrones, as ready
to succour their worshipers at a moment's warning.
In the Homeric age these were richly carved, like
the divans, adorned with silver studs, and so high
that they required a footstool.[4] The throne of the
Persian kings was of massive gold, and stood beneath a purple canopy, supported by four slender
golden columns thickly crusted with jewels.

sqq. Petronius speaks of the
"citrea mensa," p. 157. Erhard.
Symbol. ad Petron. 709, seq.
shows that Numidian marble was
in use at Rome.

[1] Potter, ii. 377.

[2] In the Antichita di Ercolano,
we have the representation of a
very handsome armed chair, with

upright back, beautifully turned
legs, and thick and soft cushions,
with low footstool. t. i. tav. 29.
p. 155. Athen. xi. 72.

[3] Pierres Gravées, du Cabinet
du Duc d'Orleans, t. i. No. 46.
Cf. No. 7, representing Zeus thus
seated.

[4] Odyss. η. 162. Il. σ. 390, 422.

Bedsteads were generally of common wood such as deal,[1] bottomed sometimes with planks, pierced to admit air, sometimes with ox-hide thongs,[2] which in traversing each other left numerous open spaces between them. Odysseus's bedstead, which the hero was sufficient joiner to manufacture with his own hands, was made of olive-wood, inlaid with silver, gold, and ivory. Sometimes the bed was supported by a sort of netting of strong cord, stretched across the bedstead, and made fast all round.[3] Later ages witnessed far greater luxury,—bedsteads of solid silver,[4] or ivory embossed with figures wrought with infinite art and delicacy,[5] or of precious woods carved, with feet of ivory or amber.[6] Occasionally, also, they were veneered with Indian tortoiseshell, inlaid with gold.[7] This taste would appear to have flowed from the East, where among the kings of Persia still greater magnificence was witnessed even in very early times. Thus, speaking of the royal feast celebrated at Susa, the Scripture says, there were in the court of the garden of the king's palace "white, green, and blue hangings, fastened "with cords of fine linen and purple to silver "rings, and pillars of marble. The beds were of "gold and silver, upon a pavement of red, and "blue, and white, and black marble." A similar style of grandeur is attributed by Hellenic writers to the Persian king, who, according to Chares,[8] reclined in his palace on a couch shaded by a spread-

---

[1] Athen. xi. 48. i. 60. ii. 29. Plat. de Rep. t. vi. p. 468. Cf. Xenoph. Memor. ii. 1, 30.

[2] This bedstead was called δέμνιον; (Odyss. η. 336, seq.) when heaped with soft mattresses it was πυκινὸν λέχος (345); εὐνή was the term applied to the whole, bed and bedstead. Iliad. ω. 644. Odyss. δ. 297, &c. Pind. Nem. i. 3.

[3] Odyss. ψ. 189, seq. Schol. ad Il. γ. 448.

[4] Plat. de Legg, t. viii. p. 397.

[5] Athen. vi. 67. ii. 30.

[6] Schol. Aristoph. Eq. 530.

[7] Lucian. Luc., sive Asin. § 53. Bedsteads of solid gold are spoken of in scripture.—Esther i. 6. Bochart. Geog. Sac. i. 6. 30.

[8] Athen. xii. 9, 55.

ing golden vine, the grape clusters of which were imitated by jewels of various colours.

Four-post bedsteads were in use in remoter ages, as appears from a white sardonyx in the Orleans Collection,[1] representing the surprisal of Ares and Aphrodite, by Hephæstos. There is a low floating vallance fastened up in festoons, the tester is roof-shaped, and the pillars terminate in fanciful capitals. The figure of an eagle adorns the corners of the bedstead below. From a painting on the walls of Pompeii we discover, that the peculiar sort of bedstead at present found almost universally in France was likewise familiar to the ancients, made exactly after the same fashion, and raised about the same height above the floor. With regard to the beds themselves they were at different times manufactured from very different materials, and those of some parts of Greece enjoyed a peculiar reputation. From a phrase in Homer,[2] it would appear that, in his times, beds were stuffed in Thessaly with very fine grass. Those of Chios and Miletos were famous[3] throughout Greece. In other parts of the country, persons of peculiar effeminacy slept on beds of sponge.[4] Sicily was famous for its pillows, as were also several other Doric countries. At Athens the rich were accustomed to sleep upon very soft beds, placed on bedsteads considerably above the floor;[5] and sometimes, it has been supposed, adorned with coverlets of dressed peacocks' skins with the feathers on.[6]

But the Greeks appear to have consulted their ease, and sunk more completely into softness and effeminacy, in proportion as they approached the East. Among the Peloponnesians most persons lived hard and lay hard; greater refinement and luxury

[1] No. 34.

[2] Il. ε. 697. δ. 383.

[3] Athen. xi. 72.

[4] Athen. i. 32.

[5] Xen. Mem. ii. 1. 30.

[6] Palm. Exercit. in Auct. Græc. p. 191. We find mention in ancient authors of certain tribes who went clad in garments covered with the feathers of birds. Senec. Epist. 90.

prevailed in Attica; but in Ionia and many of the
Ægæan isles the great—although there were excep-
tions as in the case of Attalos—fell little short in
self-indulgence of Median or Persian satraps. Some
idea may be formed of their habits in this respect
from the description of a Paphian prince's bed by
Clearchos of Soli.[1] Over the soft mattresses supported by a silver-footed bedstead, was flung a short
grained Sardian carpet of the most expensive kind.
A coverlet of downy texture succeeded, and upon
this was cast a costly counterpane of Amorginian
purple. Cushions, striped or variegated with the
richest purple, supported his head, while two soft
Dorian pillows[2] of pale pink gently raised his feet.
In this manner habited in a milk-white chlamys the
prince reclined. Their bolsters in form resembled
our own;[3] but the pillows were usually square, as
in France, though occasionally rounded off at both
ends, and covered with richly chequered or variegated muslins. To prevent the fine wool or whatever else they were stuffed with from getting into
heaps, mattresses were sewn through as now, and
carefully tufted that the packthread might not break
through the ticking.[4]

Among the Orientals it is common at present for
persons to sleep in their day apparel; but even in
the heroic ages it was already customary in Greece
to undress on going to bed. When Agamemnon
is roused before dawn by the delusive dream, the
whole process of the morning toilette is described.
First, says the poet, he donned his soft chiton which
was new and very handsome; next his pelisse; after
which he bound on his elegant sandals and suspended his silver-hilted sword from his shoulder. Thus
accoutred he issued forth, sceptre in hand, towards
the ships.[5]

---

[1] Athen. vi. 37.
[2] Athen. ii. 29, sqq.
[3] Gitone, Nozze di Ulisse è Penelope, Il Costume, &c. tav. 67.

[4] See the mattress on which the
statue of Hermaphroditos reclines
in the Louvre.
[5] Il. ε. 42, seq.

In Syria, children luxuriously educated are said to have been rocked in their cradles wrapped in coverlets of Milesian wool.[1] The sheep of Miletos were, in fact, the Merinos of antiquity; and their wool being celebrated for its fineness and softness, it was not only employed in manufacturing the best cloths, but also in stuffing the mattresses of kings and other great personages who thought much of their ease. And as the vulgar imagine they become great by habiting themselves in garments similar to those of their princes, like the honest man who sought wisdom through reading by Epictetus' lamp, the stuffs, couches, and coverlets of Miletos got into great vogue among the ancients. Virgil, Cicero, Servius, Columella, and many other writers speak accordingly of their excellence, and their testimonies have, with wonderful industry, been collected by the learned Bochart.[2]

But though Miletos had a reputation for this kind of manufacture, it by no means enjoyed a monopoly. The scarlet coverings of Sardis, and the variegated stuffs of Cyprus, produced by the famous weaver Akesas and his son Helicon,[3] appear in many instances to have obtained a preference over all others. Pathymias, too, the Egyptian, distinguished himself in the same line.[4]

All these bed-coverings were commonly perfumed with fragrant essences,[5] for which reason the voluptuous poets of antiquity dwell with a sort of rapture on the pleasure of rolling about in bed. Ephippos exclaims:—

> " How I delight
> To spring upon the dainty coverlets ;
> Breathing the perfume of the rose, and steeped
> In tears of myrrh !"

---

[1] Esther i. 6. Lament. iv. 5. Bochart. Geograph. Sac. i. 6. 30.
[2] Geog. Sac. i. 6. 28, seq.
[3] Eustath. ad Odyss. α. p. 32. 30.
[4] Athen. ii. 30.
[5] In old times the whole bedroom was sometimes perfumed. —Iliad, γ. 382.

Aristophanes, likewise, and Sophron, the mimographer, make mention of these fragrant counterpanes, which were extremely costly, and inwrought, according to the latter, with figures of birds.[1] Elsewhere Athenæus relates that the Persian carpets contained representations of men, animals, and monsters.[2] Their blankets, like our own, were plain white; but even so far back as the heroic ages, the upper coverings, as being partly designed for show, were of rich and various colours.[3]

There seems to be good ground for believing, that if the Greeks did not borrow their philosophy from the East, they at least derived from them many of the vain and luxurious habits which at length rendered that philosophy of none effect. No one appears to have paid a single visit to Persia, or Syria, or Egypt, without bringing back along with him some pestilent new freak in the matter of dress or furniture, wholly at variance with republican simplicity. We might adduce numerous anecdotes in proof of this. For the present we confine ourselves to the following. Among the Persians, renowned in all ages for sensual indulgences, it was judged of so much importance to enjoy soft and elegantly arranged beds, that in great houses persons were employed who attended only to this. An anecdote in illustration has been preserved by Athenæus. Timagoras, or, according to Phanias, Entimos of Gortyna, envying Themistocles his reception at the court of Persia, undertook himself a toadeating expedition to that country. Artaxerxes, whose ear could tolerate more flatterers than one, took the Cretan into favour, and made him a present of a superb marquee, a silver-footed bedstead, with costly furniture, and, along with them, sent a slave, as a Turkish pasha would send a cook or a pipe-lighter, because, in his opinion, the Greeks who prepared

---

[1] Athen. ii. 30. Aristoph. aub. ad Theoph. Char. p. 172.
Frag. incert. 2. Brunck. [3] Feith. Antiq. Homer, iii. 8.
[2] Deipnosoph. xi. 55. Cas- 4.

sleeping-places for so many Persians at Marathon and Platæa, understood nothing of bed-making.

Entimos evidently excelled the great Athenian in the arts of a courtier. In fact, he was the very prototype of Hajji Baba, and enjoyed even still greater influence over the Shah than the illustrious barber's son of Ispahan. Charmed by his cajolery, Artaxerxes invited him to his private table, where, usually, none but princes of the blood were admitted,[1] an honour, as Phanias assures us, which no other Greek ever enjoyed. For, though Timagoras of Athens performed *kou-tou* before the throne,[2] whereby he obtained great consideration among a nation of slaves, and was hanged when he got home, he was not invited to hob-and-nob with his majesty, but only enjoyed the distinction of having certain dishes sent him from the king's table. To Antalcidas, the Spartan, Artaxerxes sent his crown dipped in liquid perfume, an agreeable compliment, but which he more than once paid to Entimos, whose extraordinary favour at court in the long run, however, awakened the envy of the Persians. The canopy of the marquee presented to this Cretan was spangled with bright flowers, and, among the other articles of which the imperial gift consisted, were a throne of massive silver, a gilded parasol, several golden cups crusted with jewels, a hundred maple-tables with ivory feet,

[1] Very nearly the same customs prevail in Persia at the present day, except that the rules of etiquette seem to be still more rigidly observed. " It is a gene-" ral custom with the kings of " Persia to eat in solitary gran-" deur. The late Shah, how-" ever, would sometimes have " select portions of his family to " breakfast with him." On which occasion, " they used to squat " round him in the form of a " crescent, of which he was the " centre, and were all placed " scrupulously according to rank." —Fowler, i. 48.

[2] Athen. vi. 58. Vales. not. in Maussac. p. 282, where he corrects the old reading of the text. Cf. Xenoph. Hellen. vii. 1. 38. Plut. Pelop. § 30. Artax. § 22. Valer. Max. vi. 3. extern. 2. Demosth. de Fals. Leg. § 42, where the orator accuses Timagoras of having received a bribe of forty talents.

a hundred goblets of silver, several vases of the same
precious metal, a hundred female slaves, an equal
number of youths, with six thousand pieces of gold,
besides what was furnished him for his daily ex-
penditure.[1]

A gentleman travelling in Ireland witnessed the
ingenuity of that ready-witted people in applying the
same thing to various uses: first, he saw the table-
cloth, on which he had eaten a good supper, transferred as a sheet to his bed, and, next morning, his
kind hostess, offering her services to put him in the
right way, converted the same article into a mantle,
which she wrapped about her shoulders. The Greeks
were almost equally ingenious. With them what
was a cloak by day became sometimes a counterpane at night,[2] in addition, perhaps, to the ordinary bed-clothes; for it is clear they loved to be
warm, from the somewhat reproachful allusion of
Strepsiades in the " Clouds " to the five *sisyræ*,[3] rolled
snugly up in which, his son, Pheidippides, could
sleep while thoughts of his debts bit the old man
like so many bugs, and roused him hours before
day to consult his ledgers. All kinds of stromata
were, in Plato's time, divided into two classes, first,
coverings for the body, such as cloaks, mantles, and
so on ; secondly, bed-clothes, properly so called.

The walls of their chambers were frequently hung
with Milesian tapestry, a custom to which Amphis
alludes in his Odysseus :

  A. Milesian hangings line your walls, you scent
      Your limbs with sweetest perfume, royal myndax [4]
      Piled on the burning censor, fills the air
      With costly fragrance.
  B. Mark you that, my friend !
      Knew you before of such a fumigation ? [5]

---

[1] Athen. ii. 31.

[2] Xen. Anab. i. 5. 5.

[3] Nub. 10.   Cf. Av. 122.
Concionat. 838. ibique not. Pollux, vii. 382, seq. x. 542.

[4] Cf. Poll. vi. 105.

[5] Athen. xv. 42. Cf. Meineke.
Curæ Crit. in Com. Frag. p. 7.

Mention is likewise made among the ancients of purple tapestry, inwrought with pearls and gold.[1]

Carthage enjoyed celebrity for its manufacture of carpets and variegated pillows,[2] a piece of luxury which, as we have seen above, had already been introduced in the heroic ages; for Homer, in innumerable passages, speaks of rare and costly carpets, and these were not only spread over couches and seats, but over the floor likewise.[3] Rolled up, they would occasionally appear to have served for pillows. The manufacture of carpets had, moreover, been carried to considerable perfection, for the poet speaks of some with a soft pile on both sides, which were evidently very splendid.[4] Theocritus,[5] too, in his Adoniazusæ, enumerates, among the luxuries of the youthful God,

> Carpets of purple, *softer far than sleep,*[6]
> Woven in Milesian looms.

But in nothing did the Greeks display a more gorgeous or costly taste than in what may be termed their *plate*, which was not only fabricated of the rarest materials, but wrought likewise with all the elaborateness and delicacy and richness of design within the reach of art. Among the Macedonians, after

---

[1] Mazois, Pal. de Scaur. p. 103. Tibull. iii. 3, 17, seq. Athen. iv. 29.

[2] Athen. i. 49.

[3] Il. ι. 200.—The use of mats first prevailed, (Festus, in v. Scirpus.) but, as luxury increased, superb carpets were substituted. —Æschyl. Agam. 842. Tryphiod. "Αλωσις "Ιλιου. 343, seq. Hemster. Comm. in Poll. viii. 133. p. 287. Cf. Klausen. Comm. in Æschyl. Agam. p. 197, sqq.

[4] Il. π. 224. Poll. vi. 2. Synes. Epist. 61.

[5] Eidyll. xv. 125.

[6] A beautiful simile, which Virgil has imitated—

" Muscosi fontes, et *somno mollior herba.*"—Eclog. vii. 45.

Shakespeare, too, has, without imitation, struck upon a similar thought, where the amorous Troilus thus describes himself:—

" But I am weaker than a woman's tear,
Tamer than sleep, fonder than ignorance."
Troilus & Cressida, i. 1.

their Eastern conquests, gold plate appears not to
have been uncommon; for at the grand supper described by Hippolochos in his letter to Lynceus, every
guest is said to have used it.[1]   The predilection for
this sort of magnificence they acquired in Asia, where,
at a banquet given to Alexander, the whole dessert
was brought in tastefully covered with gold-leaf.[2]   In
the reign of his father, Philip, the precious metals
were rare in Macedonia.   Indeed, that crafty old
monarch, possessing but one gold cup in the world,
had so good an opinion of his courtiers that, to prevent their thieving it, he slept every night with it
under his pillow.[3]   Gold was, more early, plentiful in
Attica.   Alcibiades, with tastes and habits unsuited
to a democracy, carried so far his love of display as
to make use of thuribles, or censers, and wash-hand
basins of pure gold.[4]   But the ostentatious son of
Clinias, though extravagant, was in this respect only
a type of his nation.   Every rich citizen of Athens
aimed at the same degree of splendour; and, in describing his town-house or favourite villa, might, with
little alteration, have adopted the language of the
poet : —

> —— " My house within the city
> Is richly furnished with plate and gold,
> Basins and ewers to lave her dainty hands:
> My hangings all of Tyrian tapestry.
> In ivory coffers have I stuffed my crowns ;
> In cypress chests my arras, counterpanes,
> Costly apparel, tents, and canopies,
> Fine linen, Turkey cushions bossed with pearl,
> Vallance of Venice, gold in needle-work,
> Pewter and brass, and all things that belong
> To house or housekeeping."

Socrates, in the Republic, speaking of what the
prevailing fashion required to be found in a city,
makes out a list of good things, not much inferior
upon the whole to Shakspeare's, — beds, tables, and

---

[1] Athen. iv. 2, sqq. Cf. iii. 100.   [3] Deipnosoph. *ut sup.*
[2] Athen. iv. 42.   [4] Athen. ix. 75.

other furniture; dainties of all kinds; perfumes, unguents, sauces, &c.; to which the philosopher adds apparel, shoes, pictures, tapestry, ivory, and gold:[1] and these rare materials, as farther on he observes, were wrought into utensils for domestic purposes.

One of the most plentifully furnished departments of a Greek house was the *Kulikeion,* or " cupboard," usually closed in front with a curtain,[2] where they kept their goblets, cups, and drinking-horns, under the protection of a statue of Hermes, who, as god of thieves, would, it was supposed, be respected by his children. The form and workmanship of these materials varied, no doubt, according to the taste and means of the possessor; but they were in general distinguished for the elegance of their outline, the grace and originality of the sculpture, the fineness, delicacy, and minute finish of the execution. It is well known, as an able antiquarian[3] has remarked, to what an excess the luxury of the table was carried among the ancients, and how much they surpassed us in the dimensions, the massiveness, the workmanship, the quality, and the variety of their drinking apparatus.

Many persons, however, seem chiefly to have valued their plate as a mark of their wealth and magnificence; among whom may be reckoned Pythias of Phigaleia, who, when dying, commanded the following epitaph to be inscribed upon his tomb: —

> Here jolly Pythias lies,
> A right honest man, and wise,
> Who of goblets had very great store,
> Of amber, silver, gold,
> All glorious to behold,
> In number ne'er equalled before.[4]

Amber goblets not being, I believe, in fashion among the modern nations of Europe, some doubt

---

[1] Plat. De Rep. i. t. vi. p. 86. Cf. Tim. t. vii. p. 77.

[2] Athen. xi. 3. Poll. x. 122.

[3] Le Comte de Caylus, Mem.

de l'Acad. des Inscrip. t. xxiii. p. 353.

[4] Athen. xi. 14. Among the Egyptians were vases of papyrus. Bochart. Geog. Sac. i. 240.

may be experienced respecting the veracity of our friend of Phigaleia; but the ancients had other gobletary legends to bring forward in support of it. Helen,[1] it is said, justly proud of her beautiful bosom, dedicated in one of the temples of Rhodes, as a votive offering, an amber goblet, exactly of the size and shape of one of her breasts, which, had it come down to posterity, might have furnished artists with a perfect model of that part of the female form. However this may be, the ancients, in remote ages, set a great value on their cups, particularly such as were considered heir-looms in the family, and laid apart to be used only on extraordinary occasions. Hence Œdipos, in the old Cyclic poet, is seized with fierce anger at his son, who had, contrary to his will, brought forth his old hereditary goblets to be used at an ordinary entertainment.

[1] Bruyerin, De Re Cibaria, l. iii. c. 9. This goblet could by no means have been a diminutive one, if Helen resembled her countrywomen generally, who were celebrated for their large bosoms: βαθύκολποι. — Anacr. v. 14. Bruyerin's authority is Plin. Hist. Nat. xxxii. 23. " Minervæ templum habet Lindos, insula Rhodiorum, in quo Helena sacravit calycem ex electro. Adjicit historia, mammæ suæ mensura." This, I suppose, is what Rousseau calls " Cette coupe célèbre à qui le plus beau sein du monde servit de moule."—Nouv. Heloise, 1re partie. Lett. 23. t. i. p. 144, —though, I confess, I am not acquainted with the authors by whom it has been celebrated. Several votive offerings, representing the female breast, may be seen in the British Museum, among the Elgin Marbles. But the most curious relic of the ancient female form is mentioned in the following passage : " In the street just " out of the gate of this villa I " lately saw a skeleton dug out ; " and by desiring the labourers " to remove the skull and bones " gently, I perceived distinctly " the perfect mould of every fea- " ture of the face, and that the " eyes had been shut. I also saw " distinctly the impression of the " large folds of the drapery of the " toga, and some of the cloth it- " self sticking to the earth. The " city was first covered by a " shower of hot pumice-stones and " ashes, and then by a shower of " small ashes mixed with water. " It was in the latter stratum " that the skeleton above de- " scribed was found. In the Mu- " seum at Portici a piece of this " sort of hardened mud is pre- " served ; it is stamped with " the impression of the breast " of a woman, with a thin dra- " pery over it. The skeleton I " saw dug out was not above five " feet from the surface. It is " very extraordinary that the im-

Then Polyneices of the golden locks,
Sprung from the Gods, before his father placed
A table all of silver, which had once
Been Cadmus's, next filled the golden bowl
With richest wine.   At this old Œdipos,
Seeing the honoured relics of his sire
Profaned to vulgar uses, roused to anger,
Pronounced fierce imprecations, wished his sons
Might live no more in amity together,
But plunge in feuds and slaughters, and contend
For their inheritance : and the Furies heard.[1]

Agathocles, tyrant of Sicily, appears to have been an amateur of cups, and would sometimes while exhibiting his collection to his friends make a good-humoured allusion to his original occupation. " These golden vessels," said he, " have been made out of those earthenware ones which I formerly manufactured."[2] Drinking-bowls in fact made no inconsiderable figure in ancient times. They were bestowed as the prizes in gymnastic contests, and in Greece men boxed and wrestled for the cup as horses run for it in England. Parasites, like the jester of Louis XIV., used sometimes to carry home the cups and dishes set before them at dinner; but the tables were often turned when the subject gave and the prince pocketed the dole.

A curious legend has been preserved to us connected with the subject of cups. Several princes uniting, in remote times, to send a colony to Lesbos, were commanded by an oracle to cast a virgin, during their voyage, into the sea, as a sacrifice to Poseidon. Obedience, in those superstitious ages, was seldom refused to such injunctions. The maiden was precipitated into the waves, but Enallos, one of the chiefs, in whom love had quenched the reverence

" pression of the body and face
" should have remained from the
" year 79 to this day, especially
" as I found the earth so little
" hardened that it separated upon
" the least touch." — Sir W. Hamilton, Acc. of Discov. at Pompeii, p. 15.

[1] Athen. xi. 14.

[2] Athen. xi. 15.   Polyb. xii. 15. 6. xv. 35. 2.

for oracles, immediately plunged in to save her.   Neither the chief, however, nor the virgin appeared again, and the fleet proceeded.   The remainder of the tradition may be illustrated by an event said to have taken place in the Tonga islands.[1]   They were probably near some uninhabited isle, and instead of rising to the surface of the sea, emerged into a cavern elevated considerably above its level, and opening perhaps upon the land.   " God tempers the wind to the shorn lamb," says a modern writer, and so Enallos found it.   By means unrevealed in the ancient narrative, the hero and his bride continued to subsist on the rock, and many years afterwards, when the colony was already flourishing, he one day presented himself before his old friends at Methymna, and entertained them with a very romantic account of his residence among the Nereids at the bottom of the sea, where he was honoured with the care of Poseidon's horses when sent out to grass. At length, however, getting on the back of a large wave it bore him upwards and he escaped from the deep, bearing in his hand a golden cup, the metal of which was so marvellously beautiful that in comparison ordinary gold appeared no better than brass.[2]

Even the loftiest and least worldly-minded of the Homeric heroes, Achilles, set great value on a favourite drinking-cup, which he preserved for his own particular use, and for pouring out libations to Zeus alone.   Priam[3] was careful to include a rare goblet in the ransom of Hector's body, and a similar gift aided in alluring Alcmena from the paths of virtue.[4] But the most famous bowl of antiquity was that of Heracles, which, more capacious than the barber's basin in Don Quixote, served its illustrious owner in the double capacity of a drinking-cup and a canoe ; for when he had quenched his thirst, he could set

---

[1] See Mariner's Account, chap. 9.   [3] Iliad. ω. 234.
[2] Athen. xi. 15.   [4] Athen. xi. 16.

his bowl afloat, and, leaping into it, steer to any part
of the world he pleased. Some, indeed, speak of it
as a borrowed article, belonging originally to the
Sun, and in which the god used nightly to traverse
the ocean from West to East.[1]

To pass, however, over the goblets of mythology.
It was fashionable to possess plate of this kind finely
sculptured with historical arguments; and history has
preserved the names of Cimon and Athenocles, two
artists who excelled in this style of engraving. These
cups were sometimes of silver gilt, sometimes of massive gold crusted with jewels.[2] In addition to the
two artists named above, we may enumerate Crates,
Stratonicos, Myrmecides of Miletos, Callicrates the
Lacedemonian, and Mys, whose "Cup of Heracles,"
celebrated in antiquity, had represented upon it the
storming of Ilion, with this inscription,

> Troy's lofty towers by Grecians sacked behold !
> Parrhasios' draught, by Mys engraved in gold.[3]

The names by which the ancients distinguished
their several kinds of goblets are too numerous to
be here given. Some were curious—" Amalthea's
Horn," "The Year," &c. Rustics made use of two-
handled wooden bowls in which, when thirsty, they
drew fresh milk from the cow in the fields.[4] There
was a big-bellied cup with a narrow neck which
being shaped like a purse, participated with this
very necessary article in the name of Aryballos.[5]

Glass cups of much beauty were manufactured in
great abundance at Alexandria. Among these was
the *Baucalis*, mentioned by Sopater the parodist, who
says :—

[1] Bentley, Dissert. on Phal. i. 175, sqq.
[2] Plin. xxxiii. 2. Juven. v. 42. Athen. iv. 29.
[3] Athen. xi. 19.
[4] Athen. xi. 25, states this from Philetas : but Kayser, in his edition of that author's fragments, seems to have overlooked this passage.
[5] Athen. xi. 36. On the Can-tharos, see § 48.

'Tis sweet in early morn to cool the lips
With pure fresh water from the gushing fount,
Mingled with honey in the Baucalis,
When one o'er night has made too free with wine,
And feels sharp thirst.[1]

The glass-workers of Alexandria procured earthen-ware vessels from all parts of the world, which they used as models for their cups. Even the great sculptor Lysippos did not disdain to employ his genius in the invention of a new kind of vase. Having made a collection of vessels of many various shapes, and diligently studied the whole, he hit upon a form entirely new, and presented the model to Cassander, who having just then founded the city of Cassandria, was ambitious of originating an invention of this kind. He was desirous, perhaps, of recommending by the elegance of his drinking-cups the Mendæan wine exported in great quantities from his city.[2]

There was a peculiar kind of cup called Grammateion, from the letters of gold chased upon its exterior.[3] Alexis mentions one of this sort in the following lines:

A. But let me first describe the cup; 'twas round,
    Old, broken-eared, and precious small besides,
    Having indeed some letters on't.
B.   Yes letters;
    Eleven, and all of gold, forming the name
    Of Saviour Zeus.
A.   Tush! no, some other god.[4]

A very handsome sort of cup was imported from Sidon. It had two handles, and was ornamented with small figures in relief. Drinking-vases were also formed from the large horns of the Molossian and Pœonian oxen; and these articles were commonly rimmed with silver or gold.[5] Small cups were made

[1] Athen. xi. 28.
[2] Athen. xi. 28.
[3] We find in Winkelmann, Hist. de l'Art t. i. p. 23, the representation of a glass grammateion, on which are the words:

Bibe Vivas Multis Annis. See a detailed description of this vase by the Marquis Trivulsi, p. 46.
[4] Athen. xi. 30.
[5] Theopomp. ap. Athen. xi. 34. 51.

little account of. There was even one kind of bowl which, for its enormous capacity, was called the Elephant.

> A. If this hold not enough, see the boy comes
>   Bearing the Elephant !
> B.   Immortal gods !
>   What thing is that ?
> A.   A double-fountained cup,
>   The workmanship of Alcon ; it contains
>   Only three gallons.[1]

A very celebrated cup among the Athenians was the Thericlean,[2] originally invented by Thericles, a Corinthian potter, contemporary with Aristophanes. This ware was black, highly varnished, with gilt edges;[3] but the name came afterwards to be applied to any vessel of the same form from whatever materials manufactured. There were accordingly Thericlea of gold with wooden stands. The cups of this kind, made at Athens, being very expensive, an inferior sort, in imitation, was produced at Rhodes, which, as far more economical, had a great run among the humbler classes. The Thericlean was a species of deep chalice with two handles, and bulging but little at the sides. Theophrastus[4] speaks of Thericlea turned from the Syrian Turpentine tree, the wood of which being black and taking a fine polish, it was impossible at a glance to distinguish them from those of earthenware. The paintings on these utensils appear to have been various. Sometimes a single wreath of ivy encircled them immediately beneath the golden rim ; but it seems occasionally to have been covered with representations of animals, which gave rise to a forced and false etymology of the name.[5]

---

[1] Athen. xi. 35.

[2] Cf. Bentley on the Epist. of Phalaris i. 169—189.

[3] Alexis, ap. Athen. xi. 42.

[4] Hist. Plant. v. 4. 2. cum not. Schnei. t. iii. p. 426.

[5] Athen. xi. 41. ἄλλοι δὲ ἱστοροῦσι, θηρίκλειον ὀνομασθῆναι τὸ ποτήριον διὰ τὸ δορὰς θηρίων αὐτῷ ἐντετυπῶσθαι.

We have already observed, that the use of drinking-horns[1] was not unknown to the ancients. In fact,
it seems, in very remote ages, to have been customary to convert bulls' horns into cups with very little
preparation; and the practice of quaffing wine from
this rude kind of goblet had by some been supposed
to have suggested the idea to artists of representing
Bacchos with horns, and to poets the epithet of the
Bull Dionysos. He was moreover worshiped at
Cyzicos under the form of a bull. Afterwards, as
taste and luxury advanced, these simple vessels were
exchanged for horns of silver, which Pindar attributes to the Centaurs.[2] Xenophon[3] found drinking-
horns among the Paphlagonians, and afterwards even
in the palace of the Thracian king Seuthes. Æschylus speaks of silver horns, with lids of gold, in use
among the Perrhæbians, and Sophocles, in his Pan-
dora, makes mention of drinking-horns of massive
gold. Philip of Macedon was accustomed among
his friends to drink from the common horn. Golden
horns were found among the inhabitants of Cythera.
Horns of silver were in use at Athens; and, among
the articles enumerated as sold at a public auction,
mention is made of one of these vessels of a twisted
form.

Mirrors constituted another article of Hellenic
luxury. These were sometimes of brass,[4] whence
the proverb:

As forms by brass, so minds by wine are mirrored.[5]

The best, however, until those of glass came into
use, were made of silver or of a mixed metal, the exact

[1] Bœckh. Pub. Econ. of Athens,
ii. 254.
[2] Pind. Frag. Incert. 44. i. 244.
Dissen. Comm. ii. 659. Jacob.
Anthol. vii. 336. Athen. xi. 51.
Cf. Damm. v. κέρας.
[3] Anab. vi. 1. 4. vii. 3. 24, seq.
[4] Xen. Conv. vii. 4. They were
sometimes square and washed
with silver. Caylus, Rec. d'Antiq.
t. vi. p. 398. Cf. Cœl. Rhodig.
xv. 12, 13. Plat. Tim. t. vii. 52,
seq. 61. Lucian. Amor. § 39. Ter.
Adelph. ii. 3. 61. Cicero in Pison.
c. 29. Poll. vii. 95. x. 126, 164.
[5] Athen. x. 31.

composition of which is not now known. Another kind was fashioned from a species of carbuncle found near the city of Orchomenos,[1] in Arcadia. Glass mirrors[2] also came early into use, chiefly manufactured, at the outset, by the Phœnicians of Sidon. The hand-mirrors were usually circular,[3] and set in costly frames. To prevent their being speedily tarnished they were, when not in use, carefully enclosed in cases.[4]

There were mirrors, too, of polished silver, fashioned so as to magnify immensely the objects they reflected.[5] They invented also large cups containing within many diminutive mirrors, so that when any one looked into them, his eye was met by a multitude of faces all resembling his own.[6] In a temple of Hera in Arcadia, was a mirror fixed in the wall, wherein the spectator could at first scarcely, if at all, discern his own image, while the throne of the goddess and the statues of the other deities ranged around were most brilliantly reflected,[7] Many sorts of mirrors appear to have been made for the purpose of playing off practical jokes. For example, looking in one of these, a handsome woman would find her visage transformed into that of a Gorgon, so as to appear terrible even to herself. Others again were so very flattering, that a half-starved barber, viewing his figure therein, appeared to be gifted with the thewes of a Heracles. Another sort distorted the countenance, or inverted it, or showed merely the half.

Religion was the nurse of the fine arts, and first gave rise, not only to sculpture and painting, but

[1] Theoph. de Lapid. §. 33.

[2] It is to be observed, that before the application of quicksilver in the construction of these glasses (which I presume is of no great antiquity) the reflection of images by such specula must have been effected by their being besmeared behind, or tinged through with some dark colour, especially black, which would obstruct the refraction of the rays of light. Nixon in Philosoph. Trans. t. iv. p. 602. Cf. Plin. xxxvi. 26. § 67.

[3] Sch. Aristoph. Nub. 742.

[4] Sch. Aristoph. Nub. 741.

[5] Plaut. in Mostell. i. 3. 101.

[6] Plin. xxxiii. 45. Senec. Quæst. Nat. i. 4.

[7] Paus. viii. 37. 7.

also to those private collections of statues and pictures[1] in which we discover the germs of our modern galleries[2] and museums. The first step was made towards these when the Greek set up the images of his household gods upon his hearth. Thence, step by step, he proceeded, improving the appearance, enriching the materials, increasing the number of his domestic deities, with which niche after niche was filled, till his private dwelling became in some sort a temple. The religious feeling, no doubt, made way, in many cases, for a passion for show, or a nascent taste for the beautiful; so that rude figures in terra-cotta, wood, or stone, were gradually replaced by exquisite statues in ivory, gold, or silver,[3] or the fairest marble, breathing beauty and life, with eyes of gems, and clothed with majesty as with a garment. Hence flowed the passion for mimetic representations and all the plastic arts. The gods were transferred from the fireside to the temple, to the agora, to the senate-house, to the innumerable porticoes everywhere abounding in Greece.[4]

On their superb candelabra,[5] &c., matter for a curious volume might be collected. The lamps in common use,[6] though sometimes very beautiful in shape, were of course fictile,[7] such as we find in great numbers among the ruins of Greek cities, both in the mother-country, and in their Egyptian and other colonies. Sometimes, however, they were of bronze, silver, or massive gold. A very beautiful

[1] Plat. de Rep. t. vi. p. 86. Plin. Hist. Nat. vii. 39. xxxv. 36. xxxiii. 56.

[2] Athen. xi. 3. Menage, Observat. in Diog. Laert. vi. 32. p. 138. a. b.

[3] Poll. i. 28.

[4] Plat. de Rep. t. vi. p. 86.

[5] An elegant candelabrum, ornamented with the figure of a twisted serpent, and a flight of birds resting here and there on the branches, is found in the Mus. Cortonens. tab. 80.—They were sometimes of gilt wood.— Winkelmann, i. 34.

[6] Poll ii. 72. vi. 103. x. 115. Soph. Ajax. 285, sqq.

[7] Poll. x. 192.—On the brazen ladle (ἀρύταινα) for filling lamps with oil, see Sch. Aristoph. Eq. 1087.

specimen in this last metal was found, by Lord Belmore, among the ruins of an Egyptian temple, a short time before my visit to the Nile. In many houses were magnificent chandeliers, suspended from the ceiling, with numerous branches, which filled the apartments[1] with a flood of light. The most remarkable article of this kind which I remember was that set up as a votive offering to Hestia, in the Prytaneion of Tarentum, by Dionysios the Younger, which held as many lamps as there are days in the year.[2] Among people of humble condition wooden chandeliers, or candlesticks, were in use.[3] In remoter ages they burned slips of pine-branches, the bark of various trees, &c., instead of lamps. They were acquainted with the use of horn and wicker lanterns.[4]

Another kind of decoration of Greek houses we must not overlook,—their armour and implements of war,[5] with which the poet Alcæos[6] loved to adorn his chambers, though, like Paris, he cared little to make any other use of them. " My spacious man-
" sion," exclaims he, " gleams throughout with bra-
" zen arms. Even along the ceiling are ranged
" the ornaments of Ares, glittering helmets, sur-
" mounted by white nodding plumes; greaves of po-
" lished brass are suspended on the walls, with cui-
" rasses of linen, while, here and there, about my
" apartments, are scattered hollow shields. Else-
" where, you behold scimitars of Chalcis, and bald-
" ricks, and the short vest which we wear beneath our
" armour." [7] Besides the articles enumerated by the poet, there were shield-cases, sheaths for their spears,

---

[1] Athen. xi. 48. [2] Id. xv. 60.
[3] Id xv. 61. [4] Id. xv. 59.
[5] The custom, also, in Lydia. Herod. i. 34.
[6] Alcæi Frag. vi. p. 95. Anacr. ed. Glasg.
[7] Κύπασσις of which Pollux furnishes us with an exact description: ὁ δὲ κύπασσις, λίνου πεποίη-το, σμικρὸς χιτωνίσκος, ἄχρι μέσου μηροῦ, ὡς "Ιων φησὶ, βραχὺς λίνου κύπασσις, ἐς μηρὸν μέσον ἐσταλμένος. (vii. 60) That is, " the ku-passis is a small linen chiton, reaching mid-thigh, according to Ion, who says, ' a short linen kupassis, descending to the middle of the thigh.' "

quivers curiously adorned, feathered arrows, and bows
of polished horn, tipped at either end with gold.

From these gorgeous and costly commodities the
reader, we fear, will be reluctant to accompany us
into the kitchen, where we must pick our way among
kneading-troughs, pots and pans, Delphian cutlery[1]
and honey-jars.[2] But as without these the warriors,
as Homer himself acknowledges, could make but
little use of their weapons, it is absolutely necessary
we should inquire into their cooking conveniences.
To commence, however, we must allow[3] Clearchos
of Soli, to enumerate a few of the articles found
among the furniture of this important part of the
house. There was, first, says he, a three-legged
table, then a chytra, or earthen pot, which, as in
France, was always preferred for making soup. It
was not, however, of coarse brown ware, as with
us; for, Socrates, in his conversation with Hippias
on the Beautiful, observes that, when properly made,
round, smooth, and well-baked, the chytra was very
handsome, particularly that large sort which contained upwards of seven gallons. It had two
handles, and was evidently glazed.[4] In stirring the
chytra while boiling, the Attic cook made choice
of a ladle turned from the wood of the fig-tree,
which, it is said, communicated an agreeable flavour
to the soup, and, in Socrates's opinion, was preferable to one of gold which, being very weighty,
might chance to crack the pot, spill the broth, and
extinguish the fire.[5]

There was used in the kitchen a sort of candelabrum, or lamp-stand, which Clearchos merely names.
Then followed the mortar, the stool, the sponge,
the cauldron, the kneading-trough, the mug, the oil-

[1] Hesych. v. Δελφικὴ μάχαιρα.
[2] Athen. xi. 50, ὀξίνη, a vinegar cruet.—Sch. Aristoph. Eq.
1301. ὕρχη, a pickle-jar.—Vesp.
676.

[3] Athen. xiv. 60.
[4] Plat. Hipp. Maj. t. v. p. 425,
sqq.
[5] Plat. Opp. t. v. p. 429. seq.
Schol. Aristoph. Acharn. 244.

flask, the rush-basket, the large knife, the cleaver,[1]
the wooden platter, the bowl, and the larding-pin.[2]
Pollux, who had, doubtless, served an apprentice-
ship to Marcus Aurelius's cook, gives a formidable
list of culinary utensils, from which we must be content to select the most remarkable. First, however,
we shall show how important a piece of sponge was
to an Athenian cook. It often saved him his dinner; for, if any of his stewpans, crocks, or kettles,
had suffered from the embraces of Hephæstos,
in other words, had got a hole burnt in them, a
bit of sponge was drawn into the aperture, and on
went the cooking operations as before.[3] In some
houses culinary utensils were regarded as a nuisance,
the presence of which was not to be constantly en-
dured, and, accordingly, when the master desired to
treat his friends, cookey was despatched early in
the morning to hire pots and kettles of a broker.
To this custom Alexis alludes in his Exile :

How fertile in new tricks is Chæriphon,
To sup scot-free and everywhere find welcome !
Spies he a broker's door with pots to let ?
There from the earliest dawn he takes his stand,
To see whose cook arrives ; from him he learns
Who 'tis that gives the feast,—flies to the house,
Watches his time, and, when the yawning door
Gapes for the guests, glides in among the first.[4]

But we must not pass over the Pyreion or Try-
panon,[5] the clumsy contrivance which supplied the
place of our lucifers, phosphorus, and tinder-boxes.
This was a hollow piece of wood, in which another

---

[1] See a figure, probably, of that
instrument in Mus. Chiaramont.
tav. 21.

[2] Athen. xiv. 60. Poll. x. 95,
sqq.—We find mention, also, of
the cheese-rasp.—Schol. Aristoph.
Pac. 251.

[3] Aristoph. Acharn. 439. Brunck
is vastly scandalised at the idea
of the Scholiast, that any man
should have been so poor in At-

tica as to be driven to mend his
pots in the way commemorated
in the text ; but a German commentator, who had looked more
into kitchens, is satisfied that
the practice prevailed, and was
perfectly rational. In fact, similar contrivances are still resorted
to, even in England.

[4] Athen. iv. 58.

[5] Theoph. Histor. Plant. v. 9. 7.

piece was turned rapidly till sparks of fire flew out.[1]
Soldiers carried these fire-kindlers along with them
as a necessary part of their kit.

The ordinary fuel of the Greeks consisted chiefly
of wood and charcoal,[2] (kept in rush or wicker baskets,)
though the use of mineral coal was not altogether
unknown to them.[3] In Attica, where wood was always scarce, they economically made use of vine-cut-
tings,[4] and even the green branches of the fig tree
with the leaves on.[5] The charcoal of Acharnæ, the
best probably in the country, was sometimes prepared from the scarlet oak.[6] To prevent the wood,
used in their saloons, halls, and drawing-rooms from
smoking, it was often boiled[7] in water or steeped in
dregs of oil. The use of the bellows[8] was known
in Hellas from the remotest antiquity. They had
likewise a kind of osier flap, with a handle, and
shaped like a fan, which at times supplied the place
of a pair of bellows.

There were chopping-blocks[9] both of wood and
stone, mortars,[10] fish-kettles, frying-pans, and spits of
all dimensions,[11] some being so diminutive that thrushes and other small birds could be roasted on them.
Their ends in the heroic ages rested on stone hobs,
but afterwards andirons were invented, probably of
fanciful shape as in modern France. Occasionally
they would appear to have been manufactured of
lead. To these we may add the ovens, the bean
and barley-roasters, the sieves of bronze and other
materials, the wine-strainers in the form of colanders,
the crate for earthern-ware, and the chafing-dish.[12]

---

[1] Plat. de Rep. iv. t. vi. p. 194.
Pollux. x. 146. vii. 113.

[2] Cf. Schol. Aristoph. Acharn.
34, 302, 314. Plat. de Legg. t.
viii. 116.

[3] Theoph. de Lap. § 16.

[4] Schol. Aristoph. Lysist. 308.

[5] Schol. Aristoph. Acharn. 312.
Cf. Schol. Vesp. 145, 326.

[6] Sch. Aristoph. Acharn. 587.

[7] Plin. Hist. Nat. xv. 8.

[8] Schol. Aristoph. Acharn. 853.
Athen. ii. 71.

[9] Schol. Aristoph. Acharn. 319.
Vesp. 238. κρεάγρα a flesh-hook.
Sch. Eq. 769.

[10] Schol. Aristoph. Vesp. 924.

[11] Schol. Aristoph. Nub. 179.

[12] Aristoph. Acharn. 34. Cooks'
tables were made of wicker-work
or olive-wood. Etym. Mag. 298.
36, seq.

CHAPTER III.

FOOD OF HOMERIC TIMES — MEAT, FISH, ETC.

HAVING described the implements with which a
Greek meal was prepared, let us next inquire of
what materials it consisted, and how it was eaten.
There will be no occasion in pursuing this investigation to adhere to any very strict method. It will probably be sufficient to make a few broad divisions and
a flexible outline which we can fill up as the materials
fall in our way.

What the original inhabitants of Hellas ate might
no doubt be satisfactorily inferred from the accounts
we possess of nations still existing in the same state
of civilisation. -But it is nevertheless curious to ex-
amine their traditions relating to the subject. Ælian,
who has preserved many notices of remote antiquity, gives a list of various kinds of food, which, as
he would appear to think, constituted the chief, if
not the whole, sustenance of several ancient nations.
The Arcadians lived, he says, upon acorns; the Argives upon pears, the Athenians upon figs ;[1] the wild
pear-tree furnished the Tirynthians with their favourite food; a sort of cane was the chief dainty of the
Indians; of the Karamanians[2] the date; millet of
the Mæotæ and Sauromatæ; while the Persians[3] delighted chiefly in cardamums and pistachio nuts.[4]

[1] Cf. Plut. Quæst. Græc. 51.
[2] Cf. Dion. Perieg. 1082.
[3] These people were great ea-
ters, and held none in estimation
but those who resembled them.
Aristoph. Acharn, 74. sqq.
[4] Ælian. Var. Hist. iii. 39.

Perizonius in his note on this
passage observes, that ἄπιος and
ἀχράς are but different names
for the same thing, both signifying "the pear," the former term
prevailing among the Argives, the
latter among the Tirynthians and

The tradition that while some degree of civilisation already existed in the East, many tribes of Hellas still subsisted upon acorns, has given rise to much curious disquisition. It is abundantly clear, however, that the fruit of our English oak is not what is meant; for, upon this, no one who has made the experiment will for one moment imagine that man could subsist; but every kind of production comprehended by the Greeks under the term "acorn," (βάλανος). Gerard, an old English botanist, enumerates chestnuts among acorns, and Xenophon calls dates "the acorns of the palm-tree." The mast, however, of a tree common in Greece, would, as Mitford thinks, afford a not unwholesome nourishment, though he is quite right in supposing that it could not have been a favourite food in more civilised times.[1] While upon the subject of acorns, this ingenious and able writer appears disposed to make somewhat merry with a certain project of Socrates. If we rightly comprehend him, which very possibly we do not, he means to accuse the philosopher of reducing the citizens of his airy republic to very short commons indeed,[2] nothing but a little beech-mast, and a few myrtle-berries. This borders strongly on the notion of the comic writer, who describes the Athenians as living on air and hope. But though abstemious enough, Socrates was not so unreasonable as to require even his Utopians to fight and philosophise upon a diet so scanty.

Laconians. By the other Greeks both words were used promiscuously, though ἄπιος was the more common. This able commentator objects to the assertion of his author, that the Hindoos lived on cane, since they also ate millet, rice, &c. But Ælian could really have intended nothing more than that the articles he enumerates were in common use among the nations spoken of. Otherwise the whole must be regarded as a mere fable. The canes, mentioned by Ælian, are those from which sugar has been from very remote antiquity extracted.

Quique bibunt tenerâ dulces ab arundine succos.
Lucan. Pharsal. iii. 237.

[1] See Goguet, i. 160, seq.

[2] Hist. of Greece, i. 9, note. Cf. Anab. ii. 3.

Before he comes to the mast and the myrtle-berries, we find him enumerating wheaten and barley bread, salt, olives, cheese, and truffles, together with pulse and all such herbs as the fields spontaneously produce. For a dessert he would indulge them with figs, chickpeas, and beans, myrtle-berries, and beech-mast, or chestnuts roasted in the fire. Plato was aware how the luxurious wits of his time would turn up their noses at such primitive diet, and therefore brings in Glaucon inquiring, — "If you were "founding a polity of swine, what other food would "you provide for them?"[1] Pausanias remarks, however, that acorns long continued to be a common article of food in Arcadia,[2] but only those of the fagus.[3]

If we may credit some writers the ancient inhabitants of Hellas made use of food much more revolting than acorns, having been, in fact, cannibals who devoured each other. There, no doubt, existed among the Greeks of later times traditions of a state of society in which human flesh was eaten by certain fierce and lawless individuals, such as Polyphemos, but nothing in their literature can authorise us to infer that the practice was ever general. Superstition seems on very extraordinary occasions to have impelled them into the guilt of human sacrifice, when the officiating priests, and, perhaps, some few others, probably tasted of the entrails, and Galen had conversed with individuals

[1] Plat. de Rep. t. vi. p. 85.
[2] Cf. Polluc. i. 234.
[3] Paus. viii. 1. 6. Pliny observes that the fruit of the fagus is sweet "dulcissima omnium glans fagi." Hist. Nat. xvii. 6. Cf. Lucian. Amor. § 33. Theophrast. Hist. Plant. iii. 8, 2. This Arcadian dainty is still eaten in Spain. "In some parts (of Navarre) the mountains are girt at their base by forests of chestnut trees or of the Spanish oak called *encina*, whose acorn roasted, is as palatable as the chestnut." (A Campaign with Zumalacarregui, i. 40.) The same writer observes, that the fruit of the ever-green arbutus, in shape like a cherry, though insipid and intoxicating in its effects, is also eaten by the omniverous Spaniards, p. 51. See also Laborde's Itinerary of Spain, iv. 80, and Capell Brooke's Travels, ii. 72.

who had been led by mere curiosity to sup on man's flesh, and found its flavour to resemble that of tender beef.[1] But instances of this kind prove nothing; for how often does it not happen that mariners are even now driven by distressful circumstances to slaughter and eat their companions at sea! And yet shall we on this account pass for anthropophagi with posterity?

The Greeks, however, were not content with one set of traditions, or upon the whole inclined to give currency to the most gloomy. On the contrary, their poets casting backward the light of their imagination, and kindling up the landscapes of the far past, called up the vision of the golden age, when neither the domestic hearth[2] nor the altars of the gods were stained with blood, and the fruits of the field,—milk, honey, cheese, and butter sufficed to sustain life. But we must escape from these shadowy times, and come down to the age of beef and mutton.

Food is, with great precision, divided by Aristotle into moist and dry, that is, into meat and drink.[3] A classification, the credit of which, as Feith contends, belongs to Homer.[4] In this poet, bread ($\sigma\hat{\iota}\tau o\varsigma$), the principal article of provision, is made indiscriminately both from wheat and barley, though the latter grain is thought to have been first in use.[5] Herodotus found, in the matter of bread, a peculiar taste among the Egyptians; barley and wheat they despised, though in no country are finer produced

[1] See Bochart. Geog. Sac. i. 309.

[2] Cf. Plat. De Legg. vi. t. vii. p. 471.

[3] Problem. x. 56, 58.

[4] Iliad. α. 496. β. 432, seq.

[5] Iliad. ε. 196, et 341. The scholiast on this verse, observes that, before the invention of mills, men used to eat the raw grain. (Cf. on Iliad. α. 449, and Etym. Magn. v. οὐλόχυται, 641, 29.) But this is merely an absurd conjecture; for they could, at least, have roasted the young ear as in the East they still do, while it is full of juice, and have eaten it thus with salt, when it is both pleasant and nutritive. Besides, some means of reducing the grain to meal appears to have been known almost from the beginning.

than in Egypt; giving, very strangely, the preference to the *olyra,* by some supposed to be the
spelt, but more probably Syrian *dhourra,* ears of
which I observed sculptured on the interior of
the pronaos of Leto's temple at Esneh. Bread, in
the Homeric age, was brought to table in a reed
basket, the use of silver bread-baskets, or trays, not
having been then, as Donatus thinks, introduced.
But in this the learned commentator is mistaken;
or, if they had no silver trays, at least they had
them of brass and gold, to match their tables of
massive silver.[1]

Next to bread, flesh, in the heroic ages, was the
greatest stay-stomach, particularly beef, kid, mutton,
and pork. They had not, however, as yet discovered many ways of cooking it. Nearly all their
culinary ingenuity reduced itself in fact to roasting
and boiling, a circumstance which led Athenæus,[2]
and the president Goguet to look back with great
pity and concern on these unhappy ages when even
princes, generally gourmands, were deprived of the
supreme felicity of dining on ragouts, soups, and
boiled brains. Servius,[3] too, and Varro are inclined
to participate in this feeling of commiseration, and

---

[1] Iliad. λ. 629. Odyss. κ. 355.
See, too, Theocrit. Eidyll. xxiv.
135, sqq. Virgil. Æneid. i. 705.

[2] Deipnosoph. i. 15. Origine
des Loix, ii. 306. " J'ai dit que
la simplicité faisoit le caractère
distinctif de ses premiers âges. La
manière dont on se nourissoit
alors en fait preuve. On ne voit
paroître ni sauce ni ragoût, ni
même de gibier, dans la description que l'Ecriture fait du repas
donné par Abraham aux trois anges qui lui apparurent dans la
vallée de Membré. Ce Patriarche
leur sert un veau roti, ou, pour
mieux dire, grillé ; du lait de
beurre, et du pain frais cuit sous

la cendre. Voilà tout le festin.
Ce fait montre que les repas alors
étoient plus solides que délicats.
Abraham avoit certainement intention de traiter ses hôtes du
mieux qu'il lui étoit possible, et il
faut observer que ce Patriarche
possédoit de très-grandes richesses
en or, en argent, en troupeaux et
en esclaves. On peut donc re-
garder le repas qu'il donne aux
trois anges, comme le modèle
d'un festin magnifique, et juger
en conséquence quelle étoit de
son tems la manière de traiter
splendidement."

[3] Comm. ad Æneid. i. 710.

the latter observes, that among their own ancestors
people were originally compelled to dine on roast
meat, though in the course of time the arts of boiling and soup-making were introduced.[1]   With regard to Homer's heroes, however, our sympathies
are somewhat relieved by finding, that learned men
have overrated the extent of their misfortunes.
They were not altogether ignorant of the art of
boiling, as Athenæus himself admits, where he mentions the boiled shin of beef which one of the
drunken suitors flung at Odysseus's head.

The flesh of young animals was not habitually
eaten in those early ages, so that in denominating
them public devourers of kids and lambs, Priam
accuses his sons of scandalous luxury.[2]   In fact,
with the design of preventing a scarcity of animal
food, a law was enacted at Athens prohibiting the
slaughter of an unshorn lamb, and from the same
motive the Emperor Valens forbade the use of
veal.[3]

But there was nothing beyond the difficulty of
catching it, to prevent the Homeric heroes from
making free with game, such as venison, and the
flesh of the wild goat;[4] and from a passage in
the Iliad, Feith infers, that even birds were not
spared.[5]   We trust, however, that they feathered
and cooked them, and did not devour them *au na-
turel*, as certain Hindùs do their sheep, wool and
all.   The Egyptians had a very peculiar taste in
ornithophagy, and actually ate some kinds of birds
quite raw, as they likewise did several species of
fish; and this not in those early ages when Isis
and Osiris had not reclaimed the bogs of the Nile,
but in times quite modern, when Herodotus travelled in their country, and heard their vain priests

[1] Feith, Antiq. Homer, iii. 1, 3.   Schweigh, Animad. in Athen. t.
[2] Il. ω. 262.   vi. p. 96, seq.
[3] Hieron adv. Jovian. ii. 75.
a.   Diosc. ap. Athen. ix. 17. Eus-   [4] Od. ι. 185. κ. 180.
tath. ad Il. ω. p. 1481. 12.   [5] Iliad. ψ. 852, seq.

lay claim to having civilised Hellas. Both birds
and fish, indeed, underwent a certain sort of preparation. Of the latter some were dried in the sun,
others preserved in pickle, and the same process
was applied to ducks, quails, and many other species
of birds, after which they were eaten raw. We
recommend the practice to our gourmands, and have
no doubt they would find a pickled owl or jackdaw,
devoured in the Egyptian style, altogether as wholesome as diseased goose's liver. It must not, however, be dissembled, that many critics, concerned
for the gastronomic reputation of the Egyptians,
contend that, by the word which we translate "to
pickle," [1] Herodotus must have meant some kind
of cookery ; to which Wesseling replies, that, without designing to impugn the taste of those gentlemen, he must yet refuse to accept of their interpretation, since by observing that they roasted or
boiled all other species of birds and fish, such as
were sacred excepted, the historian evidently in-
tends to say, that these were eaten raw. The
learned editor might have added, that Herodotus
uses the same term in treating of the process of
embalming,[2] and we nowhere learn that the mum-
mies were cooked before they were deposited in
the tombs.

But to return to the Homeric warriors ; it seems
extremely[3] probable, notwithstanding the opinions
of several writers of great authority, both ancient
and modern, that the demi-gods, and heroes before
Troy, admitted that effeminate dainty called *fish*
to their warlike tables. At all events the common people understood the value of this kind of
food,[4] and it may safely be inferred that their betters, never slow in appropriating delicacies to their

---

[1] Προταριχεύειν. Herod. ii.
77, edit. Wessel.

[2] Herod. i. 77, seq. ii. 15. ix.
80.

[3] Plato, among others, remarks

that, in the military messes of his
heroes, Homer introduces neither
fish nor boiled meat. De Rep.
iii. t. vi. p. 141.

[4] Odyss. τ. 113.

own use, soon perceived that fish is no bad eating.
Hunger would at least reconcile them to the flavour
of broiled salmon, as we find by the example of
Odysseus's companions, who devoured both fish and
fowl.[1] This is acknowledged by Athenæus;[2] but
Plutarch contends, that they could have been driven to it only by extreme necessity. At all
other times he imagines they temperately abstained
from food of so exciting a kind,[3] though Homer
describes the Hellespont as abounding in fish,[4] and
more than once alludes to the practice of drawing
it thence with hook and line.[5] Thus we find that
angling can trace back its pedigree to the heroic
ages; and the disciple of the rod as he trudges
with Izaak in his pocket through bog and mire in
search of a good bite, may solace his imagination
with reminiscences of Troy and the Hellespont. But
the good people of those days did not wholly rely
for a supply of fish on this very tedious and ineffi-
cient process; they had discovered the use of nets,
which Homer describes the fisherman casting on
the sea shore.[6] Though the poet, however, had
omitted all allusion to this kind of food, its use
might, nevertheless, have been confidently inferred,
as may that of milk, common to all nations, though
Homer mentions it only, I believe, in the case of
the Hippomolgians,[7] and the cannibal Polyphemus,
who understood also the luxury of cheese.[8] Circe,
too, who being a goddess may be supposed to have
been a connoisseur in dainties, presents her para-
mour Odysseus with a curious mixture, consisting
of cheese, honey, flour, and wine,[9] very savoury, no

[1] Odyss. μ. 330. sqq.
[2] Deipnosoph. i. 47.
[3] Plut. Sympos. viii. 8.
[4] Il. ι. 360.
[5] Il. π. 407.
[6] Od. χ. 364, sqq. Eustathius, however, on this passage
observes, that though nets are
spoken of in the Iliad, (ε. 487,)
this is the only place where the
poet distinctly mentions their
being used in taking fish.
[7] Il. o. 6.
[8] Od. ι. 236, 246. Theoc.
Eidyll. xi. 35.
[9] Od. κ. 234, seq.

doubt, and by old Nestor considered of salutary nature, since Hecamedè, at his order, prepares a plentiful supply of it for the wounded Machaon. Along with this posset, garlic was eaten as a relish.[1]

Fruits and potherbs, as may be supposed, were already in use.[2] Garlic we have mentioned above; and Odysseus, after all his wars and wanderings, recals to mind with a quite natural pleasure the apple and pear trees which his father, Laertes, had given him when a boy.[3] Alcinoös possessed a fine orchard, where, though the process of grafting is supposed to have been then unknown, we find a variety of beautiful fruits, as pears, apples, pomegranates, delicious figs, olives, and grapes; and in his kitchen-garden were all kinds of vegetables.[4] And the shadowy boughs of a similar orchard, covered with golden fruit, wave over Tantalos in Hades, but are blown back by the wind whenever the wretched old sinner stretches forth his hand towards them.[5] From this circumstance Athenæus, with much ingenuity, infers that fruit was actually in use before the Trojan war! Apples seem then, as now, to have constituted a favourite portion of the dessert, though among the Homeric warriors they seem sometimes to have formed a principal part of the meal; for Servius[6] describes the primitive repasts as consisting of two courses, of which the first was animal food, and apples the second.

Salt was in great use in the Homeric age, and by the poet sometimes called divine.[7] Plato, also, in the Timæos,[8] speaks of salt as a thing acceptable to the gods, an expression which Plutarch quotes with mani-

---

[1] Il. λ. 623, sqq. This mixture called κυκεών, is more than once mentioned by Plato — De Rep. iii. t. vi. p. 148.

[2] Cf. Hom. Il. λ. 629, seq.

[3] Od. ω. 339.

[4] Od. η. 115, sqq. Plut. Sympos. v. 8.

[5] Od. λ. 587, sqq.

[6] Ad Æneid. i. 727.

[7] Il. ι. 214. In later times it was customary to bruise thyme small, and mingle it with salt to give it a finer flavour. Aristoph. Acharn. 772. Suid. v. θυμιτίδων ἁλῶν. t. i. p. 1336. b.

[8] Opera, t. vii. p. 80.

fest approbation in a passage where he grows quite
eloquent in praise of this article, which he denominates the condiment of condiments, adding, that of
some it was numbered among the Graces.[1] By the
most ancient Greeks salt was, for this reason, always
spoken of in conjunction with the table, as in the old
proverb, where men were advised " never to pass by salt
or a table," that is, not to neglect a good dinner.[2] Poor
men, who probably had no other seasoning for their
food, were contemptuously denominated " salt-lickers."[3]
But, in Homer's time, there existed certain Hellenic
tribes who had not yet arrived at a knowledge of this
luxury; among whom, accordingly, even the most aristocratic personages were compelled to go without salt
to their porridge.[4] The poet has, indeed, omitted to
mention their names; but Pausanias supposes him to
have alluded to the more inland clans of Epeirots,
many of which had not yet, in those ages, acquired
a knowledge of salt, or even of the sea.[5]

It appears to be agreed on all hands, that the primitive races of men were mere water-drinkers. Accordingly they had neither poets nor inn-keepers, nor
excisemen, — three classes of persons who never flourish but where wine, or at least beer, is found.
Homer more than once alludes to this vicious habit
of the old world, where, with a sly insinuation of
contempt, — for he was himself partial to the blood-
red wine, — he tells us that this or that nation drank,
like so many oxen or crocodiles, of the waters of
such or such a river. Thus, when enumerating the
allies of Ilion, he describes the Zeleians as those who
sipped the black waters of the Æsepos.[6] Pindar, too,
in the hope of obtaining a reputation for sobriety,
says, he was accustomed to drink the waters of

[1] Sympos. v. 9.
[2] Erasm. Adag. Chil. i. Cent.
vi. Adag. 10.
[3] Ἀλαλείχειν. Erasm. Adag.
iii. vi. 33, or, as Persius expresses

it, " digito terebrare salinum."
Sat. v. 138.
[4] Od. λ. 122.
[5] Paus. i. 1. 12.
[6] Il. β. 824, seq.

Thebes, which, in his opinion, were very delicious,[1] though Hippocrates would unquestionably have been of a totally different way of thinking. The Persian, and afterwards the Parthian kings, appear in many cases to have entertained a temperate predilection for the water of certain streams, of which Milton has given eternal celebrity to one :—

> " Choaspes, amber stream,
> The drink of none but kings." [2]

But evidently through mistake; for though historians pretend that the Parthian monarchs would drink of no water save that of the Choaspes, to which Pliny[3] adds the Eulæus, it is by no means said that they enjoyed a monopoly of those streams. Perhaps our great poet confounded the Choaspes with those Golden Waters which, in Athenæus, are said to have been wholly reserved for the use of the king and his eldest son.[4]

Wine, however, was invented very early in the history of the world; and the virtue of sobriety was born along with it; for, until then, it had been no merit to be sober. With whomsoever its use began, wine was well known to Homer's heroes, one of whom speaks of it, in conjunction with bread, as the chief root of man's strength and vigour.[5] Yet the warriors of those ages by no means exhibited that selfish par-

[1] Pind. Olymp. vi. 85.

[2] Paradise Regained, iii. 288, seq.

[3] Hist. Nat. xxxi. 21. " Parthorum reges," says this writer, " ex Choaspe et Eulæo tantum " bibunt; et eæ quamvis in lon- " ginqua comitatur eos." Hence Tibullus has the following verses in his Panegyric of Messala, iv. 1. 142 :

" Nec quâ vel Nilus vel *regia lympha* Choaspes
" Profluit.

Herod. i. 188. Æl. Var. Hist. xii. 40. Cf. Strabo. l. xv. c. 3. t. iii. p. 318.

[4] Athen. xii. 9. Ἀγαθοκλῆς δ᾽, ἐν τρίτῳ Περὶ Κυζίκου, ἐν Πέρσαις φησὶν εἶναι καὶ χρυσοῦν καλούμενον ὕδωρ. εἶναι δὲ τοῦτο λιβάδας ἑβδομήκοντα, καὶ μηδένα πίνειν ἀπ᾽ αὐτοῦ ἢ μόνον βασιλέα, καὶ τὸν πρεσβύτατον αὐτοῦ τῶν παίδων. τῶν δ᾽ ἄλλων ἐάν τις πίῃ, θάνατος ἡ ζημία.

[5] Iliad. ι. 702. τ. 161.

simony which led the Romans to debar their matrons the use of wine.[1] In Homer we find women, even while very young, permitted the enjoyment of it: for example, Nausicaa and her companions, who, in setting forth on their washing excursion, are furnished by the queen herself with a plentiful supply of provisions, and a skin of wine.[2] Boys, likewise, in the heroic ages, met with similar indulgence; for Phœnix is represented permitting Achilles to join him in his potations before the little urchin knew how to drink without spilling it over himself.[3] This practice, however, is very properly condemned by Plato, who considered that no person under eighteen should be allowed to taste of wine, and even then but sparingly.[4] After thirty, more discretion might, he thought, be granted them; though he recommended sobriety at all times, save, perhaps, on the anniversary festival of Dionysos, and certain other divinities, when a merry bowl was judged in keeping with the other ceremonies of the day.[5]

We shall now pass from the primitive aliments of the heroic times to those almost infinite varieties of good things which the ingenuity of later ages brought into use. The reader, not already familiar with the gastronomic fragments of ancient literature, will probably be surprised at the omniverous character of the Greeks, to whom nothing seems to have come amiss, from the nettle-top to the peach, from the sow's metra to the most delicate bird, from the shark to the small semi-transparent aphyæ, caught along the shores of Attica.[6] Through this ocean of dain-

---

[1] Athen. x. 33.
[2] Od. ζ. 77, seq.
[3] Iliad. ι. 487.
[4] Montaigne, whom few things of this kind had escaped, reads *forty*, and thinks that men might lawfully get drunk after that age. Essais, ii. 2. t. iii. p. 278.
[5] De Legg. ii. t. vii. p. 258, sqq.

[6] Ass's flesh was commonly eaten by the Athenians. Poll. ix. 48, et Comment. t. vi. p. 938, seq. Their neighbours the Persians, however, enjoyed one dainty not known, I believe, to the Greeks; that is to say, a camel, which, we are told, they sometimes roasted whole. Herod. i. 123. Athen. iv. 6. In the opi-

ties we shall endeavour to make our way on the following plan : — first, it will be our " hint to speak "
of the more solid kinds of food, as beef, mutton, pork,
veal ; we shall then make a transition to the soups,
fowls, and fish ; next the fruit will claim our attention ; and, lastly, the several varieties of wines.

It has already been observed, that in the earliest
ages men wholly abstained from animal food.[1] Afterwards when they began to cast " wolfish eyes " upon
their mute companions on the globe, the hog is said
to have been the first creature whose character em-
boldened them to make free with him. They saw
it endued with less intelligence than other animals ;
and, from its stupidity, inferred that it ought to be
eaten, its soul merely serving during life, as salt, to
keep the flesh from putrefying.[2] The determining
reason, however, appears to have been, that they
could make no other use of him, since he would
neither plough like the ox, nor be saddled and mounted like the horse or ass, nor become a pleasant companion, or guard the house, like the dog.

It was long before men in any country slew the
ox for food ; his great utility was his protection,
and in some parts of the East the well-meaning
priesthood at length compassed him round with the
armour of superstition, which outlasted the occasion, and in India has come down in nearly all its
strength to our own day. It was otherwise in
Greece. There common sense quickly dissipated
the illusion, which, while it was necessary, had
guarded the ox, and beef became the favourite food

nion of Aristotle the flesh of this
animal was singularly good : ἔχει
δὲ καὶ τὰ κρέα καὶ τὸ γάλα ἥδιστα
πάντων.—Hist. Anim. vi. 26. It
was this passage, perhaps, that
first induced Heliogabalus to try
a camel's foot, which he appears
afterwards to have much affected.
Lamprid. Vit. Anton. Heliogab.
§ 19.   Hist. Aug. Script. p. 195.

The same emperor also tried the
taste of an ostrich, whose eggs anciently constituted an article of
food among certain nations of Africa.   Lucian. de Dipsad. § 7.
[1] Plato, De Legg. vi. t. vii. p.
471.
[2] Cicero, De Natura Deorum,
ii. 64. Dion. Chrysost. i. 280,
cum not. Reisk.

of its hardy and active inhabitants, who likewise fed indiscriminately on sheep, goats, deer, hares, and almost every other animal, wild or tame.

It has been seen that in remote ages fish did not constitute any great part of the sustenance of the Greeks. But public opinion afterwards underwent a very considerable change. From having been held in so little estimation as to be left chiefly to the use of the poor, in the historical ages it became their greatest luxury.[1] And there arose among gourmands, those ancient St. Simonians, whose god was their belly, a kind of enthusiastic rivalry as to who should be first in the morning at the fish-market, and bear away, as in triumph, the largest Copaic eels, the finest pair of soles, or the freshest *anthias*.[2] On this subject, therefore, our details must be somewhat more elaborate than on beef and mutton. And first, we shall take the reader along with us to the market, whither it will be advisable that he carry as little money as possible, since, according to the comic poets, your Athenian fishmonger, not content with being a mere rogue, dealt a little also in the assassin's trade.[3]

The first thing which a rich gourmand inquired in the morning was, which way the wind blew. If from the north, and there was anything like a sea, he remained sullenly at home, for no fishing smacks could in that case make the Peiræeus;[4] but if the wind sat in any other quarter, out he

---

[1] The Pythagoreans, however, must be excluded from this category since they abstained from fish because they kept perpetual silence like themselves.—Athen. vii. 80. Another and a better reason, perhaps, may be discovered in a passage of Archestratos, who, observing that the sea-dog is delicious eating, proceeds to dispose of the objection that it feeds on human flesh, by saying, that all fish do the same. Id. vii. 85. From this fact the Pythagoreans esteemed fish-eaters no better than cannibals at second-hand.

[2] Cf. Schol. Aristoph. Acharn. 525.

[3] Amphis ap. Athen. vi. 5.

[4] Athen. viii. 81. Cf. Xenoph. Hellen. v. i. 23.

went eagerly and stealthily with a slave and basket[1]
at his heels, casting about anxious looks to discover
whether any other impassioned fish-eater had got
the start of him on his way to the Agora, who
might clear the stalls of the best anthias or thunny
before he could reach the spot.

The unmoneyed rogue, however, whose ambitious
taste soared to these expensive dainties, approached
the market with a rueful countenance. Thus we
find a poor fellow describing, in Antiphanes, his
morning's pilgrimage in search of a pair of soles:

> I once believed the Gorgons fabulous:
> But in the agora quickly changed my creed,
> And turned almost to stone, the pests beholding
> Standing behind the fish stalls. Forced I am
> To look another way when I accost them,
> Lest if I saw the fish they ask so much for,
> I should at once grow marble.[2]

Amphis, another comic poet, supplies us with
further details respecting the hardships encountered
by those who had to deal with fishmongers at
Athens. Much of his wit is, I fear, intransferable,
depending in a great measure on the vernacular clip-
ping of Greek common in the market-place. But
the sense, at least, may perhaps be given:

> " Ten thousand times more easy 'tis to gain
> Admission to a haughty general's tent,
> And have discourse of him, than in the market
> Audience to get of a cursed fishmonger.
> If you draw near and say, How much my, friend,
> Costs *this* or *that?*—No answer. Deaf you think
> The rogue must be, or stupid; for he heeds not
> A syllable you say, but o'er his fish
> Bends silently like Telephos (and with good reason,
> For his whole race he knows are cut-throats all).
> Another minding not, or else not hearing,

---

[1] This basket was usually of
rushes, in form like a basin, and
with a handle passing over the
top.—Antich. di Ercol. tav. 21.
tom. i. p. 111.

[2] Athen. vi. 4.

> Pulls by the legs a polypus.[1] A third
> With saucy carelessness replies, ' Four oboli,
> That 's just the price.   For this no less than eight.
> Take it or leave it !' "[2]

Alexis, too, that most comic of comic writers, seems to have imagined, that the humour of his pieces would be incomplete without a spice of the fishmonger.   Commencing, like Amphis, with an allusion to the haughty airs of military men, he glides into his subject as follows :—

> However, this is still endurable.
> But when a paltry fishfag will look big,
> Cast down his eyes affectedly, or bend
> His eyebrows upwards like a fullstrained bow,
> I burst with rage.   Demand what price he asks
> For—say two mullets ; and he answers straight
> " Ten obols "—" Ten ?   That 's dear : will you take eight ? "
> " Yes, if one fish will serve you."—" Friend, no jokes ;
> I am no subject for your mirth."—" Pass on, Sir !
> And buy elsewhere."—Now tell me is not this
> Bitterer than gall ?[3]

But if the reader should be disposed to infer from these testimonies that the fishmongering race were saucy only at Athens, he will be in danger of falling into error.   Throughout the ancient world they were the same, and we fear that should any poor devil from Grub-street, or the *Quartier Latin*, presume to dispute respecting the price of salmon with one of their cockney or Parisian descendants, he would meet with little more politeness.   At all events their manners had not improved in the Eternal city,[4] for it is *a propos* of the Roman fishfags that Athenæus brings forward his examples of like insolence elsewhere.   The poet Diphilos would appear, like Archestratos, to have travelled in search of good fish and civil fishmongers, but his labours

---

[1] Cf. Chandler, ii. 143.   Plin.
Hist. Nat. ix. 45, seq.
[2] Athen. vi. 5.

[3] Athen. vi. 5.

[4] Deipnosoph. vi. 4.

were fruitless; he might as well have peregrinated
the world in the hope of finding that island where
soles are caught ready-fried in the sea. Such at
least is the tenour of his own complaint:

> Troth, in my greener days I had some notion
> That here at Athens only, rogues sold fish;
> But everywhere, it seems, like wolf or fox,
> The race is treacherous by nature found.
> However, we have one scamp in the agora
> Who beats all others hollow. On his head
> A most portentous fell of hair nods thick
> And shades his brow. Observing your surprise,
> He has his reasons pat; it grows forsooth
> To form, when shorn, an offering to some god!
> But that's a feint, 'tis but to hide the scars
> Left by the branding iron upon his forehead.
> But, passing that, you ask perchance the price
> Of a sea-wolf—" Ten oboli"—very good.
> You count the money. " Oh not those," he cries,
> "Æginetan I meant." Still you comply.
> But if you trust him with a larger piece,
> And there be change to give; mark how the knave
> Now counts in Attic coin, and thus achieves
> A two-fold robbery in the same transaction! [1]

Xenarchos paints a little scene of ingenious roguery
with a comic extravagance altogether Shakespearian,
and incidentally throws light on a curious law of
Athens, enacted to protect the citizens against stink-
ing fish.[2] The power of invention, he observes—
willing to kill two birds with one stone—had totally deserted the poets in order to take up with
the fishmongers; for while the former merely hashed
up old ideas, the latter were always hitting upon
new contrivances to poison the Demos:

> Commend me for invention to the rogue
> Who sells fish in the agora. He knows

---

[1] Athen. vi. 6.

[2] The longer to preserve fish
fresh, the Orientals sometimes
cover them with a coating of wax.
Mullets, caught at Damietta, are
sent, thus preserved, throughout
the Turkish Empire, as well as to
different parts of Europe. Pococke's Description of the East.

In fact there's no mistaking,—that the law
Clearly and formally forbids the trick
Of reconciling stale fish to the nose
By constant watering. But if some poor wight
Detect him in the fact, forthwith he picks
A quarrel, and provokes his man to blows.
He wheels meanwhile about his fish, looks sharp
To catch the nick of time, reels, feigns a hurt :
And prostrate falls, just in the right position.
A friend placed there on purpose, snatches up
A pot of water, sprinkles a drop or two,
For form's sake on his face, but by mistake,
As you must sure believe, pours all the rest
Full on the fish, so that almost you might
Consider them fresh caught.[1]

By a law passed at the instance of the wealthy
Aristonicos, himself no doubt an ichthyophagos, the
penalty of imprisonment was decreed against all
those who, having named a price for their fish,
should take less, in order that they might at once
demand what was just and no more. In consequence of this enactment, an old woman or a child
might be sent to the fish-market, without danger
of being cheated. According to another provision
of this Golden Law, as it is termed by Alexis, fishmongers were compelled to stand at their stalls and
not to sit as had previously been the custom. The
comic poet, in the fulness of his charity, expresses
a hope that they might be all *suspended* aloft on
the following year, by which means, he says, they
would get a quicker sight of their customers, and

[1] Our readers will probably remember the good old Italian mar-
chioness, who having, perhaps,
been cajoled, by the blarney of
some Hibernian peripatetic, into
the purchase of a pair of strong-
odoured soles, recommended to
our magistrates the adoption of
an ordinance passed, as she affirmed, by his grace of Tuscany.
In that prince's territories, she
assured their worships, the man
who has fish to sell, must transact business standing on one leg in
a bucket of hot water, a practice
undoubtedly calculated to induce
despatch and prevent haggling.
This Tuscan enactment might
evidently have been adopted with
great advantage at Athens, where,
however, legislation proceeded on
exactly the same principles, and
attained in this point an almost
equal degree of perfection.

carry on their dealings with mankind from a machine like the gods of tragedy.[1]

In consequence no doubt of the perpetually increasing demand, fish was extremely dear at Athens. Accordingly Diphilos, addressing himself to Poseidon, who, as god of the sea, was god also of its inhabitants, informs him that, could he but secure the tithe of fish, he would soon become the wealthiest divinity in Olympos. Among those who distinguished themselves in this business in the agora, and apparently became rich, it is probable that many were metoiki, such as Hermæos, the Egyptian, and Mikion, who, though his country is not mentioned, was probably not an Athenian. In proportion as they grew opulent, the gourmands on whom they preyed became poor, and doubtless there was too much truth in the satire which represented men dissipating their whole fortunes in the frying-pan. There were those also it seems who spent their evenings on the highway, in order to furnish their daily table with such dainties. For this fact we have the satisfactory testimony of Alexis in his Heiress:

> Mark you a fellow who, however scant
> In all things else, hath still wherewith to purchase
> Cod, eel, or anchovies, be sure i' the dark
> He lies about the road in wait for travellers.
> If therefore you 've been robbed o'ernight, just go
> At peep of dawn to th' agora and seize
> The first athletic, ragged vagabond
> Who cheapens eels of Mikion. He, be sure,
> And none but he 's the thief: to prison with him![2]

They had at Corinth a pretty strict police regulation on this subject. When any person was observed habitually to purchase fish, he was interrogated by the authorities respecting his means. If found to be a man of property they suffered him to do what he pleased with his own; but, in the contrary event, he received a gentle hint that the

---

[1] Athen. vi. 8.   [2] Athen. vi. 10. 12.

state had its eye upon him. The neglect of this admonition was followed, in the first place, by a fine, and ultimately, if persevered in, by a punishment equivalent to the treadmill.[1] These matters were in Athens submitted to the cognizance of two or three magistrates, called Opsonomoi, nominated by the Senate.[2] With respect to the purchase of this class of viands, everywhere attended with peculiar difficulties, it may be said, that the ancients had considerably the advantage of us; since in Lynceus of Samos's " Fish-buyer's Manual," they possessed a sure guide through all the intricacies of bargaining in the agora.

But before we proceed further with this part of our subject, we will demand permission of Lynceus to hear what Hesiod has to say of saltfish, on which Euthydemos, the Athenian, composed a separate treatise. According to this poet, who boldly speaks of cities erected long after his death, immense quantities of fish were salted on the Bosporos, sometimes entire, as in modern times,[3] sometimes cut into gobbets of a moderate size. Among these were the oxyrinchos whose taste proved often fatal, the thunny, and the mackerel. The little city of Parion furnished the best kolias (a kind of mackerel), and the Tarentine merchants brought to Athens pickled orcynos from Cadiz, cut into small triangular pieces, in jars.[4] Physicians, indeed, inveighed against these relishes; but the gourmands would consult only their palates and preferred a short life with pickled thunny to that of Saturn himself on beef and mutton.

But the Hesiod of Euthydemos (a creation probably of his own) is but very poor authority compared with Archestratos, who made the pilgrimage of the world in search of good cheer, and afterwards, for the benefit of posterity, treasured up his experience in a grand culinary epic. In his opinion a

[1] Diphilos apud Athen. vi. 12.   [3] Herod. iv. 53.
[2] Athen. vi. 72.   [4] Athen. iii. 84.

slice of Sicilian thunny was a rare delicacy, while
the saperda, though brought from the Pontos Euxinos, he held as cheap as those who boasted of it.[1]
The scombros, by some supposed to be a species of
thunny, though others understand by it the common
mackerel, stood high in the estimation of this connoisseur. He directs that it be left in salt three
days, and eaten before it begins to melt into brine.[2]
In his estimation the horaion[3] of Byzantium was
likewise a great delicacy, which he advises the traveller, who might pass through that city, to taste
by all means. It seems to have been there what
macaroni is at Naples.

Alexis, in one of his comedies, introduces the Symposiarch of an Eranos (president of a picnic) accounting with one of the subscribers who comes to demand back his ring, and in the course of the dialogue, where something like Falstaff's tavern-bill is
discussed, we find the prices of several kinds of salt-fish. An omotarichos (shoulder piece of thunny) is
charged at five chalci; a dish of sea-mussels, seven
chalci, of sea-urchins, an obol, a slice of kybion,
three obols, a conger eel, ten, and another plate of
broiled fish, a drachma. This comic writer[4] rates
the fish of the Nile very low, and he is quite right,
for they are generally muddy and ill-tasted, though
the Copts, who have considerable experience during
Lent, contrive, by the application of much Archestratic skill, to render some kinds of them palatable.
Sophocles, in a fragment of his lost drama of Phineus, speaks of salt-fish embalmed like an Egyptian mummy.[5] Stock-fish, as I know to my cost,

---

[1] Athen. iii. 85.

[2] Athen. iii. 85. The Scomber Pelamys or mackerel of Pallas, caught in the Black Sea, is
pickled in casks and not eaten
for a twelvemonth. Travels in
Southern Russia, iv. 242.

[3] Poterant ὡραῖα nominari, ut
vere vel initio æstatis salita, quo

tempore minus pinguis totus piscis esset. Schweigh. Animadv.
in Athen. iii. 85. t. vii. 313. Cf.
Plin. Nat. Hist. xxxii. 53. Gesner, De Salsamentis.

[4] Ap. Athen. iii. 86. Cf. Herod. ii. 77.

[5] Athen. iii. 86.

is still a fashionable dish in the Mediterranean, especially on board ship, and from a proverb preserved by Athenæus we find it was likewise in use among the Athenians.[1]

The passion of this refined people for salt-fish furnished them with an occasion of showing their gratitude publicly. They bestowed the rights of citizenship on the sons of Chæriphilos, a metoikos who first introduced among them a knowledge of this sort of food.[2] A similar feeling prompted the Dutch to erect a statue to G. Bukel, the man who taught them to salt herrings.[3]

Without enumerating a tenth part of the other species eaten among the Greeks, we pass to the shell-fish, of which they were likewise great amateurs. Epicharmos, in his marriage of Hebe, supplies a curious list, which, however, might be extended almost ad infinitum. Among these were immense limpets, the buccinum, the cecibalos, the tethynakion, the sea-acorn, the purple fish, oysters hard to open but easy to swallow, mussels, sea-snails or periwinkles, skiphydria sweet to taste but prickly to touch, large shelled razor-fish, the black conch, and the amathitis. The conch was also called tellinè as the same poet in his Muses observes. Alcæos wrote a song to the limpet beginning with

" Child of the rock and hoary sea." [4]

Boys used to make a sort of whistle of tortoise and mussel shells. These mussels were usually broiled on the coals, and Aristophanes, very ingenious in his similes, compares a gaping silly fellow to a mussel in the act of being cooked.[5]

Like the sepia, of which excellent pilaus are made at Alexandria, the porphyra or purple fish was very good eating, and thickened the liquor in which it

[1] Deipnosoph. iii. 89.
[2] Athen. iii. 90.
[3] Goguet, Origine des Loix, i. 254.
[4] Athen. iii. 30, 31. Cf. Scheigh. Animadv. t. vii. p. 68, sqq.
[5] Fragm. Babylon. 2. Brunck. Athen. iii. 33.

was boiled.[1] There was a small delicate shell-fish
caught on the island of Pharos and adjacent coasts
of Egypt, which they called Aphrodite's ear,[2] and
there is still found on the same coast near Canopos
a diminutive and beautiful rose-coloured conch
called Venus's nipple. On the same shore, about
the rise of the Nile, that species of mussel called
tellinè was caught in great abundance, but the best-
tasted were said to be found in the river itself. A
still finer kind were in season about autumn in the
vicinity of Ephesos. The echinos, or sea-chestnut,[3]
cooked with oxymel, parsley, and mint, was esteemed good and wholesome eating. Those caught about
Cephalonia, Icaria, and Achaia were bitterish, those
of Sicily laxative; the best were the red and the
quince coloured. A laughable anecdote is told of
a Spartan, who being invited to dine where sea-chest-
nuts were brought to table, took one upon his plate,
and not knowing how they were eaten put it into
his mouth, shell and all. Finding it exceedingly
unmanageable, he turned it about for some time,
seeking slowly and cautiously to discover the knack
of eating it. But the rough and prickly shell still
resisting his efforts, his temper grew ruffled; crunch-
ing it fiercely he exclaimed, " Detestable beast!
Well! I will not let thee go now, after having
thus ground thee to pieces; but assuredly I will
never touch thee again."

Oysters were esteemed good when boiled with
mallows, or monks' rhubarb.[4] In general, however,

[1] Athen. iii. 30. During their
long fasts the modern Greeks also
eat the cuttle-fish, snails, &c.
Chandler, ii. 143.

[2] Athen. iii. 35.

[3] Athen. iii. 40. The taking
of this fish at Sunium is thus described by Chandler: " Meanwhile
" our sailors, except two or three
" who accompanied us, stripped
" to their drawers to bathe, all
" of them swimming and diving

" remarkably well; some running
" about on the sharp rocks with
" their naked feet, as if devoid of
" feeling, and some examining the
" bottom of the clear water for
" the Echinus or sea-chestnut, a
" species of shell-fish common on
" this coast, and now in perfec-
" tion, the moon being nearly
" at the full." Vol. ii. p. 8.

[4] Demet. Scep. ap. Athen. iii.
41.

the physicians of antiquity considered them hard of
digestion.   But lest the shelled-fish should usurp
more space than is their due, we shall conclude
with Archestratos' list, in which he couples with
each the name of the place where the best were
caught:

> For mussels you must go to Ænos ; oysters
> You 'll find best at Abydos.   Parion
> Rejoices in its urchins ; but if cockles
> Gigantic and sweet-tasted you would eat,
> A voyage must be made to Mitylene,
> Or the Ambracian Gulf, where they abound
> With many other dainties.   At Messina,
> Near to the Faro, are pelorian conchs,
> Nor are those bad you find near Ephesos ;
> For Tethyan oysters, go to Chalcedon ;
> But for the Heralds,[1] may Zeus overwhelm them
> Both in the sea and in the agora !
> Aye, all except my old friend Agathon,
> Who in the midst of Lesbian vineyards dwells.[2]

We have already mentioned the magnificent eels
of Lake Copais,[3] in Bœotia, a longing for which
appears to have been Aristophanes's chief motive
for desiring an end to the Peloponnesian war.
Next in excellence were those caught in the river
Strymon, and the Faro of Messina.[4] The ellops, by
some supposed to be the sword-fish,[5] was found
in greatest perfection near Syracuse; at least, in

---

[1] The κῆρυξ, ceryx, so called
because the Heralds (κήρυκες)
used its shell instead of a trum-
pet, when making proclamation
of any decree in the agora.

[2] Athen. iii. 44. Cf. Polluc.
vi. 47. The ancients made the
most of their fish in every way.
They were hawked about the
streets in rush-baskets, as with
us.—Athen. vii. 72.

[3] Sch. Aristoph. Acharn, 845.
Lysist. 36. There were in the
fountain at Arethusa, as we are
told by the philosophical Plutarch,

eels that understood their own
names.—Solert. Anim. § 23.

[4] Archestratos gives the preference over all other eels to those
caught in the Faro of Messina.
Athen. vii. 53. Very excellent
and large eels are taken in the
lake of Korion, in Crete, according to the testimony of Buondel-
monte. Pashley, i. 72.

[5] On the sword-fish fishery in
the Strait of Messina, see Spallanzani's Travels in the Two Sicilies,
vol. iv. p. 331, sqq.

the opinion of Archestratos; but Varro and Pliny give the preference to that of Rhodes, and others to that of the Pamphylian sea.[1] The red mullet, the hepsetos, the hepatos, the elacaten, the thunny, the hippouros, the hippos, or sea-horse, found in perfection on the shores[2] of Phœnicia, the ioulis, the kichlè, or sea-thrush, the sea-boar, the citharos, the kordylos, the river cray-fish, the shark, which was eaten when young, the mullet, the coracinos, the carp, the gudgeon, the sea-cuckoo, the sea-wolf, the latos, the leobatos, or smooth ray, the lamprey,[3] the myræna, the anchovy,[4] the black tail, the torpedo, the mormyros, the orphos, the onos, the polypus, the crab, the sea-perch, the physa, or sea-tench, the raphis, the sea-dog,[5] the scaros, the sparos, the scorpios, the salpe, or stock-fish, the synodon, the sauros, the scepinos, or halibut, the sciaina, the syagris, the sphyræna, the sepia, the tœnia, the skate, the cuttle-fish, the hyca, the phagros, the perca cabrilla, the chromis, the gilt-head, the trichidon, the thratta, and the turbot;[6] such is a list of the fish in common use among the Greeks. The species it will be seen has not in many cases been ascertained.

[1] Athen. vii. 57. Animadv. t. ix. p. 220.

[2] The finest prawns were taken at Minturnæ, on the coast of Campania, exceeding in size those of Smyrna, and the crabs (ἀστακοὶ) of Alexandria.—Athen. i. 12.

[3] See on Crassus's lamprey. Plut. Solert. Animal. § 23.

[4] Esteemed a delicacy cooked with leeks. Aristoph. Vesp. 494. Cf. Acharn. 901. Av. 76.

[5] See Spallanzani's Travels in the Two Sicilies, vol. iv. p. 343, sqq.

[6] Athen. vii. 16—39. Aristot. Hist. Anim. iv. 2—6. viii. 3, 4, 5, 16.

CHAPTER IV.

POULTRY, FRUIT, WINE, ETC.

THE reader by this time will, probably, be willing to escape from fish, though it would be easy
to treat him to many new kinds, and along with
us take a slice of Greek pheasant, or the breast
of an Egyptian quail. In other words, he will
hear what we have to say on Hellenic poultry.
Chrysippos, in his treatise on things desirable in
themselves, appears to have reckoned Athenian cocks
and hens among the number, and reprehends the
people of Attica for importing, at great expense,
barn-door fowls from the shores of the Adriatic,
though of smaller size, and much inferior to their
own; while the inhabitants of those countries, on
the other hand, were anxious to possess Attic poultry.[1] Matron, the parodist, who furnishes an amusing description of an Athenian repast, observes,
that excellent wild ducks were brought to town
from Salamis, where they grew fat in great numbers on the borders of the sacred Lake.[2]

The thrush,[3] reckoned among the greatest deli-

[1] Athen. vii. 23.
[2] Athen. iv. 23.
[3] The solitary sparrow inhabits
the cliffs of Delphi, and the song-
thrush is heard in the pine woods
of Parnassus. Above these, when
the heights of the mountain are
covered with snow, is seen the
Emberiza Nivalis, inhabitant alike
of the frozen Spitzbergen, and of
the Grecian Alp.—Sibthorpe in

Walp. Mem. i. 76, seq. Homer
is said to have written a poem
called Ἐπικιχλίδες, because when
he sung it to the boys they rewarded him with thrushes. In
consequence of the estimation in
which these birds were held
κιχλίζω " to feed on thrushes,"
came to signify " to live luxuriously."—Payne Knight, Prolegg. ad Hom. p. 8.

cacies of the ancients, generally at grand entertainments formed part of the propoma, or first
course, and was eaten with little cakes, called
ametiskoi.   If we may credit Epicharmos, a decided preference was given to such as fed on the
olive.   Aristotle divides the thrush into three species, the first and largest of which he denominates
Ixophagos, or the "mistletoe-eater;" it was of the
size of a magpie.   The second, equal in bigness
to the black bird, he calls Trichas,[1] and the third,
and smallest kind, which was named Ilas or Tulas,
according to Alexander, the Myndian, went in
flocks, and built its nest like the swallow.[2]   Next
in excellence to the thrush was a bird known by
a variety of names, elaios, pirias, sycalis,[3] the bec-
cafico of the moderns, which was thought to be
in season when the figs were ripe.   They likewise
ate the turtle and the ringdove,[4] which are excellent in Egypt ; the chaffinch, to whose qualities
I cannot bear testimony ; and the blackbird.   Nor
did they spare the starling, the jackdaw, or the
strouthanion, a small bird for which modern languages cannot afford a name.   Brains were thought
by the ancient philosophers an odious and canni-
bal-like food, because they are the fountain of all
sensation ; but this did not prevent the gourmands
from converting pigs' brains into a dainty dish,[5] and
their taste has maintained its ground in Italy.   Partridges, wood-pigeons, geese, quails, jays, are also
enumerated among the materials of an Hellenic
banquet.

[1] The red-winged thrush, well
known to sportsmen in hard
weather.

[2] Athen. ii. 68.

[3] Arist. Hist. Anim. viii. 3. p.
221. ix. 49. p. 305. Bekk.

[4] The turtle and the wood-
pigeon are found in the woods and
thickets.   Among the larks, I
observed the crested lark to be
the most frequent species, with a
small sort, probably the alauda
campestris of Linnæus.   Black-
birds frequent the olive grounds
of Pendeli. — Sibth. in Walp.
Mem. i. 76.

[5] Athen. ii. 69—72.

Goose's liver was in extreme request both at Rome and Athens.[1]   Another dainty was a cock served up with a rich sauce, containing much vinegar.   Aristophanes speaks of the pheasant in his comedy of the Birds; and, again, in the Clouds, Athenæus rightly supposes him to mean this bird, where others imagine he alludes to the horses of the Phasis.   Mnesilochos, a writer of the middle comedy, classes a plucked pheasant with *hen's milk*, among things equally difficult to be met with, which shows that the bird had not then become common. It obtained its name from being found in immense numbers about the embouchure of the Phasis, and the bird was evidently propagated very slowly in Greece and Egypt, since we find Ptolemy Philadelphos, in a grand public festival at Alexandria, exhibiting it, among other rarities, such as parroquets, peacocks, guinea-fowl, and Ethiopian birds in cages.[2]

Among the favourite game of the Athenian gourmands was the Attagas,[3] or francolin, a little larger than the partridge, variegated with numerous spots, and of common tile colour, somewhat inclining to red.   It is said to have been introduced from Lydia into Greece, and was found in extraordinary abun-

---

[1] See the fragment of Eubulos's Garland-Seller, in Athen. ix. 33.

[2] Athen. ix. 38.

[3] No bird appears to have puzzled commentators more than the *attagas*, some supposing it to be the *francolin*, or grouse, which is Schneider's opinion; others, as Passow, the *hazel-hen*; others, again, as Ainsworth, consider it to have been a delicious bird, resembling our wood-cock, or snipe. Mr. Mitchell's edit. of the Acharnæ of Aristophanes, 783.—This learned writer professes not to understand what Schneider means by *francolin*. The word in Ita-

lian is *francolino*, as appears from Bellon. v. 6: Les Italiens ont nommé cet oiseau Francolin, que parcequ'il est franc dans ce pays, c'est-à-dire, qu'il est defendu au peuple d'en tuer : il n'y a que les princes qui aient cette prérogative. — Valmont de Bomare, ii. 739.—Hardouin thinks, that the Attagas is the *gallina rustica*, or *gelinotte de bois*, which Laveaux explains to be a sort of partridge. —Çf. Dict. Franç. in voce, and Plin. Hist. Nat. xi. 68. ed. Franz. Cf. Schol. Aristoph. Vesp. 257. This bird was plentiful about Marathon, Pac. 249.

dance in the Megaris. Another of their favourites
was the porphyrion, a bird which might with great
advantage be introduced into many countries of modern Europe, since it was exceedingly domestic, and
kept strict watch over the married women, whose
faux pas it immediately detected and revealed to
their husbands, after which, knowing the revengeful
spirit of ladies so situated, it very prudently hung
itself. It is no wonder, therefore, that the breed
has long been extinct, or that the remnant surviving
has taken refuge in some remote region, where wives
require no such vigilant guardians. In the matter
of eating it agreed exactly with Lord Byron, loving
to feast alone, and in retired nooks, where none
could observe. Aristotle describes this half fabulous
bird as unwebfooted, of blue colour, with long legs,
and red beak. The porphyrion was about the size
of a cock, and originally a native of Libya, where
it was esteemed sacred.[1]

Another bird common in Greece, but now no
longer known, was the porphyris, by some confounded with the foregoing. Of the partridge, common throughout Europe, we need merely remark,
that both the gray and the red (the *bartavelle* of
the French) were common in Greece.

If we pass from the poultry to puddings and
soups,[2] we shall find that the Athenians were not ill-
provided with these dainties. They even converted
gruel into a delicacy,[3] and it is said, that the best
was made at Megara. They had bean soup, flour
soup, ptisans made with pearl-barley or groats.[4]
We hear, also, of a delicately-powdered dish or soup

[1] Athen. ix. 40. Aristoph. Hist. Anim. i. 17. viii. 6.
[2] Schol. Aristoph. Eq. 103.
[3] Schol. Aristoph. Eq. 803.— It was thought, also, to deserve a place among the offerings to Asclepios, especially by pious old women, who, having lost their teeth, could eat nothing else. In lieu of the classical name of ἀθάρα, this gruel obtained, in the dialect of the common people, the more homely designation of κυρκούτη. Schol. Plut. 673.
[4] Athen. iii, 101. iv. 30.

which was sprinkled over with fine flour and olives.
The polphos, evidently *soupe à la julienne*, is said,
by some, to have been composed of scraped roots,
vegetables, and flour.   Others take it to mean a
sort of made-dish, resembling macaroni or vermi-
celli.   Another kind of soup was the *kidron*, which,
according to Pollux,[1] they made of green wheat,
roasted and reduced to powder.

There was one dish fashionable among the ancient Greeks mistaken by our neighbours, the French,
for plum-pudding, which is still found in perfection
in the Levant, where I have many times eaten of
it.   Julius Pollux[2] has preserved the recipe for
making it, and we can assure our gourmands, that
nothing more exquisite was ever tasted, even in
the best café of the Palais Royal.   They took a certain quantity of the finest clarified lard, and, mixing it up with milk until it was quite thick, added
an equal portion of new cheese, yolks of eggs, and
the finest flour.   The whole rolled up tight in a
fragrant fig-leaf, was then cooked in chicken-broth,
or soup made with kid's flesh.   When they considered it well done, the leaf was removed and the
pudding soused in boiling honey.   It was then served
up hissing-hot.   All the ingredients were used in
equal proportions, excepting the yolks of eggs, of
which there was somewhat more than of anything
else, in order to give firmness and consistency to
the whole.[3]

Black puddings, made with blood, suet, and the
other materials now used were also common at
Athens.[4]   Mushrooms and snails were great favourites ; and Poliochos speaks of going out in the
dewy mornings in search of these luxuries.[5]   In
spring, before the arrival of the swallow, the nettle

[1] Onomast. vi. 62.—Made usually from panic seed in Caria.—
Schol. Aristoph. Pac. 580, et Eq.
803. Cf. Goguet, Origine des
Loix, i. 212.

[2] Onomast. i. 237. vi. 57, 69.
[3] Vid. Schol. Arist. Eq. 949.
Acharn. 1066.
[4] Aristoph. Eq. 208.
[5] Athen. ii. 19.

was collected and eaten, it being then young and tender.[1] Leeks, onions, garlic, were in much request, the last particularly, which grew in great plenty in the Megarean territory, and hence, perhaps, the inhabitants were accounted hot and quarrelsome, garlic being supposed to inspire game, even in fighting cocks, to which it was accordingly given in great quantities.[2]

Among the herbs eaten by his countrymen, Hesiod enumerates the mallow,[3] and the asphodel, which are likewise said by Aristophanes to have constituted a great part of the food of the early Greeks. Gœttling, therefore, not without reason, wonders that Pythagoras should have prohibited the use of the mallow. Lupines, pomegranates, horse-radish, the dregs of grapes and olives, all of which entered into the material of an Attic entertainment, were commonly cried about the streets of Athens.[4] But these edible lupines, ($\theta \acute{\epsilon} \rho \mu o \iota$) still eaten by the Egyptian peasantry and the poor generally throughout the Levant, must be distinguished from the common species. An anecdote of Zeno, of Cittion, will illustrate the character of this kind of pulse, with which the philosopher was evidently familiar. Being one day asked why, though naturally morose, he became quite affable when half-seas-over : " I am like the lupine," he replied, " which, when dry, is very bitter, but perfectly sweet and agreeable after it has been well soaked." [5] Kidney-beans, too, were in much request, and pickled olives, slightly flavoured with fennel.

The radish[6] was esteemed a great delicacy, par-

[1] Aristoph. Eq. 422. Brunck.

[2] Aristoph. Pac. 503.

[3] Cf. Lucian. Amor. § 33.

[4] Cf. Arist. Acharn. 166. Eq. 493. Athen. xiii. 22.

[5] This is as good as the reply of an English labourer who, being reproached for babbling in his drink, replied, " Sir, I am like a " hedgehog—when I 'm wet I " open."

[6] Hesiod. Oper. et Dies, 41. ed. Gœttling. Aristoph. Plut. 543. Brunck. — Lobeck. Aglaoph. p. 899.

ticularly that of Thasos and Bœotia. And the seeds
of the ground-pine,[1] still eaten as a dessert in Italy,
entered, in Greece, also into the list of edible fruits.[2]
The tree, I am informed, has been introduced into
England, but I have nowhere seen its fruit brought
among pears, walnuts, and apples, to table. Hen's
milk has already been spoken of among the good
things of Hellas;[3] but lest the reader should suspect us of amusing him with fables, it should be
explained, that the white of an egg was so called
by Anaxagoras.[4] Eggs of all kinds were much esteemed. Sometimes they were boiled hard, and cut
in two with a hair; but, many writers, confounding
ὄα, the berries of the service-tree, with ὠὰ, eggs,
have imagined that the Athenians, in the capri-
ciousness of their culinary taste, actually ate pickled
eggs, an idea which stirs to the bottom the erudite
bile of David Ruhnken.[5] Generally, eggs were eaten
soft, as with us, or swallowed quite raw. Those
of the pea-hen were considered the most delicate;
next to these, the eggs of the chenalopex bergander,
or Egyptian goose, and, lastly, those of the hen.
This, at least, is the opinion of Epicrates and He-
racleides, of Syracuse, in their treatises on cookery.[6]

As when an entertainment was given the host necessarily expected his guests to make a good dinner,
they usually commenced the business of the day with
an antecœnium or whet, consisting of herbs of the
sharpest taste. At Athens, the articles which generally composed this course were colewort, eggs, oysters,
œnomel — a mixture of honey and wine—all supposed to create appetite.[7] To these even in later

[1] The kernels of the stone-pine
are brought to table in Turkey.
They are very common in the
kitchens of Aleppo.—Russell ap.
Walp. Mem. i. 236.

[2] Tim. Lex. Platon. v. στέμ-
φυλα, p. 239. Ruhnken. Athen.
ii. 45.

[3] Schol. Aristoph. Vesp. 505.

[4] Athen. ix. 37.

[5] Not. ad Timæi Lex. Plat.
p. 189. Cf. Platon. Conviv.
Oper. iv. 404. Bekk. Athen.
ii. 50.

[6] Athen. ii. 50.

[7] Potter, Archæol. Græc. iv.
20. Stuck. Antiq. Conviv. iii. 11.
Petron. Satyr. § 31. 33.

times were added the mallow and the asphodel, king's-spear or day-lily, gourds,[1] melons, cucumbers. The melons of Greece are still delicious, and famous as ever in the Levant. Antioch was celebrated for its cucumbers, Smyrna for its lettuces. Mushrooms were always a favourite dish;[2] and they had receipts for producing them, which even now, perhaps, may not be wholly unworthy of attention.

The use, however, of this kind of food was always attended with great danger, there being comparatively few species that could be safely eaten. Persons were frequently poisoned by them, and a pretty epigram of Euripides has been preserved, commemorating a mother and three children who had been thus cut off, in the island of Icaros:

> Bright wanderer through the eternal way,
> Has sight so sad as that which now
> Bedims the splendour of thy ray,
> E'er bid the streams of sorrow flow?
> Here, side by side, in death are laid
> Two darling boys, their mother's care;
> And here their sister, youthful maid,
> Near her who nursed and thought them fair.[3]

Diocles, of Carystos, enumerates among wholesome vegetables the red beet, the mallow, the dock, the nettle, orach, the bolbos, or truffle, and the mushroom, of which the best kinds were supposed to grow at the foot of elm and pine trees.[4]

The sion[5] (sium latifolium), another of their vegetables, is a plant found in marshes and meadows, with the smallage.[6]

Another plant, of far greater celebrity, was the Silphion,[7] once extremely plentiful in Cyrenaica, as

---

[1] The σίκυα, or long Indian gourd, so called because the seed was first brought from India to Greece. Athen. ii. 53.

[2] Schol. Aristoph. Nub. 189. 191. Eccles. 1092. Theoph. Hist. Plant. vii. 13. 8. Dioscor. ii.

200, seq. Athen. xii. 44. 70. Plin. Hist. Nat. xix. 11.

[3] Athen. ii. 57.

[4] Athen. ii. 57. 59.

[5] Plin. Hist. Nat. xix. 11. Schol. Aristoph. Nub. 191. 199.

[6] Dioscorid. ii. 154.

[7] Sch. Aristoph. Eq. 891.

also, though of an inferior quality, in Syria, Armenia, and Media, but afterwards so rare as to be thought extinct. Besides being used in seasoning soups and sauces, and mixed with salt for giving a superior flavour to meat, its juice occupied a high place among the materia medica.[1] A single plant was discovered in the reign of Nero, and sent to Rome as a present to the Emperor. Its seed, according to Pollux,[2] was called magudaris, its root silphion, the stem caulos, and the leaf maspeton. Be this as it may, it communicated to the sauces in which it was infused a pungent and somewhat bitter taste, and was in no favour with Archestratos.[3]

We come now to the fruit,[4] and shall begin with that which was the pride of Attica, the fig.[5] According to traditions fully credited in Athens, figs were first produced on a spot near the city, on the road to Eleusis, thence called *Hiera Sukè*, " the sacred fig-tree."[6] Like its men, the figs of Attica were esteemed the best in the world, and to secure an abundant supply for the use of the inhabitants it was forbidden to export them. As might have been expected, however, this decree was habitually contravened, and the informers against the delinquents were called sycophants, that is, " revealers of figs,"[7] a word which has been adopted by most modern languages to signify mean-souled, dastardly persons, such as informers always are. The fig-tree of Laconia was a dwarfed species, and its fruit, according to Aristophanes,[8] sa-

---

[1] It is called *laser*, Plin. Hist. Nat. xix. 15. Hard. But Philoxenos, in his Glossary, writes λάσαριον. Idem. See Dioscorid. iii. 76 ; and Strabo, xi. 13. t. ii. p. 452. Cf. Ezek. Spanh. Diss. iv. De Usu et Præstant. Numism. p. 253, sqq. Brotier, in his notes on Pliny, observes, on the authority of Le Maire, that the Silphion is still found in the neighbourhood of Derné, where it is called *cefie* or *zerra*.

[2] Onomast. vi. 67.
[3] Ap. Athen. ii. 64.
[4] Plat. Tim. t. vii. p. 119. Bruyerin. de Re Cib. l. xi. p. 447, sqq.
[5] At present the green fig is esteemed insipid in Greece. Hobhouse, Travels, i. 227.
[6] Athen. iii. 6. Meurs. Lect. Att. v. 16. p. 274.
[7] Athen. iii. 6.
[8] Fragm. Γεωργ. iv. t. ii. p. 268. Bekk.

voured of hatred and tyranny, like the people themselves.

> There is no kind of fig,
> Whether little or big,
> Save the Spartan, which here does not grow ;
> But this, though quite small,
> Swells with hatred and gall,
> A stern foe to the Demos, I trow.[1]

Aristophanes, in Athenæus, speaking of fruit, couples
myrtle-berries with Phibaleian figs.[2]

According to the ancients, there were certain sorts
of fig-trees that bore twice, thrice, and even four times,
in the year. Sosibios, the Laconian, attributing the
discovery of the fig to Bacchos, observes, that for this
reason the god was, at Sparta, worshiped under the
name of *Sukites.* Andriscos, however, and Agasthe-
nes, relate that this divinity obtained the name of
Meilichios, " the gracious," among the Naxians because he taught them the use of figs. To eat figs
at noon was regarded as unwholesome; and they were
at all times supposed to be highly prejudicial to the
voice, for which reason singers should carefully eschew
them.[3]

The apples of Delphi enjoyed great celebrity, and
probably, therefore, were mild, since these were thought
superior, or at least more wholesome, than sharp ones.
Quinces they esteemed still more salubrious than apples, and, during certain public rejoicings, this fruit,
handfuls of myrtle-leaves, crowns of roses and violets,
were cast before the cars of their princes and other
great men.[4] The Greeks loved to connect something
of the marvellous with whatever they admired. To
the quince they attributed the honour of being a
powerful antidote, observing that even the Phariac
poison, though of extremely rapid operation, lost its
virulence if poured into any vessel which had held
quinces and retained their odour.[5] According to

[1] Athen. iii. 7.
[2] See Schol. Aristoph. Acharn.
707.

[3] Athen. iii. 19.
[4] Stesich. ap. Athen. iii. 20.
[5] Athen. iii. 21.

Hermon, in his Cretic Glossaries, the quince was called Kodumala, in Crete. Sidoüs, a village of Corin-
thia, was famous for its fine apples; and even Corinth
itself, the " windy Ephyrè" of Homer, produced them
in great perfection.

> " O where is the maiden, sweeter far
>   Than the ruddy fruits of Ephyrè are?
>   When the winds of summer have o'er them blown,
>   And their cheeks with autumn's gold have been strown!" [1]

Another favourite fruit was the peach, introduced
from Persia into Greece.[2] The citron, too, though
supposed by some not to have been known to the
ancient inhabitants of Hellas, perfumed in later
ages the tables of the Greeks with its delicious
fragrance. This is the fruit which, according to
King Juba, was called in Africa "the apple of the
Hesperides," a name bestowed by Timachidas on
a rich and fragrant kind of pear called *epimelis*.
The oldest Greek writer who has described the citron tree is Theophrastus,[3] who says it was found
in Persia and Media. Its leaf, he observes, resembled that of the laurel, the strawberry tree, or
the walnut. Like the wild pear tree, and the oxy-
acanthos, it has sharp, smooth, and very strong
prickles. The fruit is not eaten, but together with
the leaves exhales a sweet odour, and laid with
cloths in coffers protects them from the moth. The
citron tree, is always covered with fruit, some ripe
and fit to be gathered, others green, with patches
of gold; and, in the midst of these, are other
branches covered thick with blossoms. It now
forms the fairest ornaments of the gardens of He-
liopolis, where it shades the Fountain of the Sun.

[1] Antigonos Carystios, ap. Athen. iii. 22.

[2] Vict. Var. Lect. p. 892.

[3] Hist. Plantarum, iv. 4. 2. The orange attains great perfection in Crete. Mr. Pashley speaks of twelve different kinds, and nearly as many sorts of lemons. Travels, i. 96, seq.

Antiphanes observes, in his Bœotian, that it had only recently been introduced into Attica :

> A. 'Twould be absurd to speak of what 's to eat,
>   As if you thought of such things ; but, fair maid,
>   Take of these apples.
> B.   Oh, how beautiful !
> A. They are, indeed, since hither they but lately
>   Have come from the great king.
> B.   By Phosphoros !
>   I could have thought them from the Hesperian bowers,
>   Where th' apples are of gold.
> A.   There are but three.
> B. The beautiful is no where plentiful.[1]

Athenæus, after quoting the testimony of poets, relates a curious anecdote *à propos* of citrons, which I shall here repeat : it has, probably, some reference to the secret of the Psylli. An opinion, it seems, prevailed in Egypt, that a citron eaten the first thing in the morning was an antidote against all kinds of poison, whether taken into the stomach, or introduced by puncture into the blood, and the notion arose out of the following circumstance. A governor of Egypt, in the time of the Emperors, had condemned two criminals to be executed, in obedience to custom, by the bite of an asp. They were, accordingly, led in the morning towards the place of execution, and on the way the landlady of an inn, who happened to be eating citrons, compassionating their condition, gave them some which they ate. Shortly afterwards they were exposed to the hungry serpents, which immediately bit them, but instead of exhibiting the usual symptoms followed by death, they remained uninjured. At this the governor marvelled much,

[1] Ap. Athen. iii. 27. Mitford, Hist. Greece, i. 154, note 59, misled by Barthelemy (Anacharsis, ch. 59) confounds Antiphanes, the comic poet, born B. C. 407 (Clinton, Fast. Hellen. ii. 81) with Antiphon, the master of Thucydides, born B.C. 479, and who died in the year 411, four years before the birth of Antiphanes.— Clinton, ii. 31, 37.

and at length demanded of the soldier who guarded them, whether they had taken anything previously to their arrival. Learning what had happened
he put off the execution to the following day, and
ordering a citron to be given to one and not
to the other, they were once more exposed to the
bite of the asp. The wretch who had eaten nothing died soon after he was bitten, but the other
experienced no inconvenience. Similar experiments
were several times afterwards made by others, until
it was at length ascertained that this exquisite
fruit is really an antidote against poisons.[1]

Another fruit of which great use was made, was
the damascene plum, sometimes confounded with
the brabylon. The cherry,[2] introduced into Italy
by Lucullus, was known to the Greeks[3] at a much
earlier period, and is described by Theophrastus.
The wild service berry,[4] the dwarf cherry, the arbutus fruit, and the mulberry, formed part of their
dessert. Even the blackberry, when perfectly ripe,
was not disdained.[5] In fact, both the mulberry
and blackberry were esteemed a preventive of gout,
and an ancient writer relates, that this kind of
fruit having failed during a period of twenty years,
that disease prevailed like an epidemic, attacking
persons of both sexes and all ages, and extending
its ravages even to the sheep and cattle.

Filberts, walnuts, and almonds,[6] deservedly held

---

[1] Athen. iii. 28.

[2] Theoph. Hist. Plant. iii. 13, 1.

[3] It was spoken of by Xeno-
phanes in his treatise περὶ φύσεως.
Poll. vi. 46.   Now this philo-
sopher was born about the 40th
Olympiad, 620 B. C.—Clinton,
Fast. Hellen. ii. sub an. 477.

[4] The berry of the cedar, about
the same size as that of the
myrtle, had a pleasant taste, and
was commonly eaten.—Theoph.
Hist. Plant. iii. 12. 3.

[5] Athen. ii. 33—37. A dainty
of a very peculiar character is
sometimes seen on the tables of
the modern Greeks. " We were
served also with some φασκο-
μῆλια, or sage apples, the inflated
tumours formed upon a species of
sage, and the effect of the puncture of a cynops."—Sibth. in
Walp. Mem. t. i. p. 62. Cf. Sibth.
Flor. Græc. t. i. pl. 15.

[6] Theoph. Hist. Plant. i. 11. 2.

a high place in the estimation of the ancients. Of
almonds, the island of Naxos had the reputation of
producing very excellent ones, and those of Cypros
also enjoyed considerable reputation. These latter
were longer in form than the former; like pickled
olives they were eaten at the commencement of a
repast, for the purpose of producing thirst; and
bitter almonds were considered a preservative against
intoxication, as we learn from an anecdote of Tibe-
rius's physician, who could encounter three bottles
when thus fortified, but easily succumbed if deprived of his almonds. This fruit being extremely
common in Greece, they had their almond-crackers,
as we have our nut-crackers, which at Sparta were
called *moucerobatos* but *amygdalocatactes* in the rest
of Greece.[1]

The larger kind of chestnut, sometimes denominated the "acorns of Zeus," appears to have been
introduced into Greece from the countries round the
Pontos Euxinos, where they were produced in
great abundance, particularly in the environs of Heraclea. There was, likewise, a sort of chestnut imported from Persia, and another from the neighbourhood of Sardes, in Lydia. Both these and the
walnut were considered indigestible; but not so the
almond, of which it was thought great quantities
might be eaten with impunity.[2] The best kinds
were produced in Thasos and Cypros, and, when
freshly gathered, the almonds of the south are, undoubtedly, of all fruit, the most delicate. The
walnuts aud chestnuts of Euboea, in the opinion
of Mnestheos, were difficult of digestion, but fattening; and no one can have frequented the eastern
shores of the Mediterranean without observing what
an important article of food, and how nourishing,
they are.[3] The pistachio nut, produced from a tree

[1] Athen. ii. 40.

[2] Dioscorid. i. 176.   Athen. ii.

42.   Cf. Hippocrat. de Morb. ii.
p. 484.   Foës.

[3] Athen. ii. 43.

resembling the almond-tree, was imported from Syria and Arabia.[1]   The *persea*, now no longer known, but supposed to be represented on the walls of the Memnonium,[2] at Thebes, is, also, said, by Poseidonios, the stoic, to have grown in Arabia and Syria, and I brought home a quantity of leaves, preserved in an Egyptian coffin, which are, probably, those of this tree.   Pears, which were brought to table floating in water,[3] and service-berries, were grown in great perfection in the island of Ceos, and Bœotia was famous for its pomegranates.[4]

Speaking of this fruit, which the Bœotians call *sidè*, Agatharchides relates the following anecdote: A dispute arising between the Athenians and Bœotians, respecting a spot called *Sidè*, situated on the borders, Epaminondas, in order to decide the question, took out a pomegranate from under his robe, and demanded of the Athenians, what they called it.   "*Rhoa*," they replied.   "Very good," said Epa-"minondas; but we call it *Sidè*, and, as the place "derives its name from the fruit which grows there "in abundance, it is clear the land must belong to "us."   And it was decided in favour of the Bœotians.[5]

[1] Athen. xiv. 61.

[2] We find that the Persea grew, likewise, in the island of Rhodes, but there, though flowers came, it produced no fruit.—Theoph. Hist. Plant. iii. 3, 5. For a full description of the tree see iv. 2, 5, and Cf. Caus. Plant. ii. 3, 7.—In its original country, Persia, the fruit of this tree is said to have been poisonous, for which reason the companions of Cambyses carried along with them numerous young trees, which they planted in various parts of Egypt, that the inhabitants, eating of the fruit, might perish.   But, through the influence of soil and climate, the nature of the Persea was wholly changed, and, instead of a harsh and fatal berry, produced delicious fruit.—Ælian. de Nat. Animal. ap. Schneid. ad Theoph. Hist. Plant. iv. 2, 5. t. iii. p. 284. — Cf. Athen. xiv. 61. — Schweigh. Animadv. t. xii. p. 585. Plin. xv. 13. xvi. 46.

[3] Athen. xiv. 63.

[4] The best pomegranates, however, were grown in Egypt and Cilicia. — Theoph. Caus. Plant. ii. 13. 4.

[5] Athen. xiv. 64.

We have already observed, that the palm-tree flourished and produced dates in Greece, particularly in Attica and Delos;[1] but it is clear, from a remark of Xenophon, that these dates were small and of an inferior quality; for, speaking of the productions of Mesopotamia, he says, that they set aside for the slaves such dates as resembled those produced in Greece, while the larger and finer kinds,[2] which were like amber in colour, they selected for their own use. They were also dried, as they still are in the East, to be eaten as a dessert, at other seasons of the year. From which we learn, that the black date, which is larger and finer than the yellow, was not then cultivated in Persia. But neither dates, nor any other fruit, could compare with the grape, which is found in perfection in almost every part of Greece, where, as in Burgundy and, I presume, in the rest of France, the law regulated the period of the vintage, prohibiting individuals from gathering their grapes earlier under a heavy penalty.[3] The best kind of grape in Attica, like that of the *Clos Vougeot* in Burgundy, was the *Nikostrateios*, supposed to be unrivalled for excellence, though the Rhodians pretended, in their *Hipponion*, to possess its equal.[4]

From the grape we pass naturally to wine, which has of itself formed the subject of many treatises. It will not, therefore, be expected that we should enter into very minute details; though, if we are sparing, it will certainly not be for want of materials. D'Herbelot[5] relates an oriental tradition which at-

[1] Theoph. Char. pp. *33, 233.* Casaub. A very fine palm-tree is at present growing in one of the principal streets of Athens. —Blackwood's Magazine, April, 1838.

[2] Pollux. i. 73. Herod. i. 28, 172, 193. ii. 156. iv. 172, 183.

[3] Plato de Legg. t. viii. p. 106. Bekk. Athen. xiv. 68.

[4] Athen. xiv. 68. Cf. Bruyerin. de Re Cibaria, xi. 447, sqq.

[5] Biliothèque Orientale, Article Giamschid.

tributes the invention of wine to the ancient Persian monarch Giamshid; and Bochart, with some
show of ingenuity, attributes to Bacchos, the Grecian inventor and god of wine, an origin which
would confound him with the founder of Babylon.[1]
A very celebrated wine, called *nectar*, is said to
have been produced in the neighbourhood of that
city.[2] But, according to Theopompos, it was the
inhabitants of Chios who first planted and cultivated
the vine, and from them the knowledge was transmitted to the other Greeks.[3]

Theophrastus[4] relates that, in the territory of
Heraclea, in Arcadia, there was a wine which rendered men insane and women prolific.[5] In the
environs of Cerynia, in Achaia, grew a vine, the
wine of which blasted the fruit of the womb, nay,
the very grapes were said to possess a similar quality.[6] At Thasos were two kinds of wine, of which
the one caused stupefaction, while the other was in
the highest degree exhilarating.[7] The wine called
anthosmias,[8] according to Phanias of Eresos, was
produced by mixing one part of salt-water with
fifty parts of wine, and it was considered best when
made with the grapes of young vines. The comic
poets are eloquent in praise of the wines of Thasos,
particularly of that mixed sort, of most agreeable
flavour, which was drunk in their Prytaneion. Theophrastus[9] gives the recipe for making it. They threw,
he says, into the jars, a small quantity of flour
kneaded with honey, the latter to impart a sweet
odour to the wine, the former mildness. A similar

[1] Geog. Sacr. I. ii. 13.
[2] Chæreas. ap. Athen. i. 58.
[3] Athen. i. 47.
[4] Hist. Plant. ix. 18. 10, seq.
In Athenæus, instead of Heraclea, we find Heræa, i. 57. Cf.
Ælian. Var. Hist. xiii. 6.
[5] The same effect was attributed to the waters of a fountain
flowing near a temple of Aphro-

dite upon Mount Hymettos.—
Chandler, ii. 164.
[6] Plin. Hist. Nat. xiv. 18.
[7] Athen. i. 57.
[8] Ὁ ἀνθέων ὀσμὴν ἔχων οἶνος.
— Etym. Mag. 108. 41. Cf.
Suid. v. ἀνθοσμίας. t. i. p. 289.
b. Aristoph. Plut. 808. Ran.
1181.
[9] De Odor. 51.

effect was produced by mixing up hard inodorous wine with one which was oily and fragrant.[1]

The wines of Cos, Myndos, and Halicarnassos, being thought to temper the crudity of rain and well-water, were, therefore, like all others containing a quantity of salt-water, in great request at Athens and Sicyon, where the springs were harsh. The Mareotic wine[2] was made from vineyards on the banks of the lake Mareotis, where the present Pasha has his gardens, in the vicinity of Marea, once a place of considerable importance, but now a small village. Attempts, however, have been made by M. Abro, an Armenian, once more to cover the ancient sites with vineyards, several acres of ground being planted with cuttings imported from the great nursery grounds at Chambéry, in Savoy.

The town of Marea derived its name, according to tradition, from Maron,[3] a person who accompanied Bacchos in his military expedition, and, in honour of its founder, surrounded itself with the fruit-tree most agreeable to that god. The grapes here produced were delicious, and the wine, slightly astringent and aromatic, had an exquisite flavour. The Mareotic was white, of delicate taste, light, sparkling, and by no means heady. The best sort was the Tæniotic, so called from the *tænia*, " sandy eminences," on which the vineyards were situated. This wine, in its pure state, had a greenish tinge, like the Johanisberg, and was rich and unctuous; but, mingled with water, it assumed the colour of Attic honey. By degrees the vine grew to be cultivated along the whole course of the Nile,[4] but its produce differed greatly in different places, both in colour and quality. Among the best was that of Antylla, a city near Alexandria,

[1] Athen. i. 56. — Cydonia, in Crete, is conjectured, by Mr. Pashley, to have produced a good wine.—Travels in Crete, i. 23, seq.   [2] Athen. i. 59.
[3] Idem, i. 60.   Horat. Carm. i. 37. 14.
[4] The cultivation of the vine appears to have flourished in Egypt down to the reign of the Caliph Beamrillah, who commanded all the vineyards both in the valley of the Nile and in Syria to be utterly destroyed. Maured Allatafet Jemaleddini, p. 7.

the revenues arising from which the ancient kings of
Egypt, and afterwards those of Persia, settled on their
queens for their girdle. The wines of the Thebaid,
particularly those made about Koptos, were so extremely light as to be given even in fevers, as, moreover, they passed quickly, and greatly promoted digestion.[1]

According to Nicander of Colophon, the word οἶνος,
"wine," was derived from the name of *Oineus*, who
having squeezed out the juice of the grape into vases,
called it, after his own name, *wine*. Diphilos,[2] the
comic poet, gives us, however, something better than
etymologies in that burst of Bacchic enthusiasm in
which, in verses fragrant as Burgundy, he celebrates
the praises of the gift of Dionysos :

" Oh ! friend to the wise, to the children of song,
    Take me with thee, thou wisest and sweetest, along ;
    To the humble, the lowly, proud thoughts dost thou bring,
    For the wretch who has thee is as blythe as a king :
    From the brows of the sage, in thy humorous play,
    Thou dost smooth every furrow, every wrinkle away ;
    To the weak thou giv'st strength, to the mendicant gold,
    And a slave warmed by thee as a lion is bold."

Nectar, the poetical drink of the gods, was a
sort of wine made near Olympos in Lydia, by mingling with the juice of the grape a little pure
honey and flowers of delicate fragrance. Anaxan-
drides, indeed, regards the nectar as the food of
the immortals, and ambrosia as their wine; in which
opinion he is upheld by Alcman and Sappho. But
Homer and Ibycos take an opposite view of the
matter.[3]

Alexis speaks of those who are half-seas-over
as much addicted to reasoning. Nicænetus[4] considers wine as the Pegasus of a poet, mounted on
the wings of which like Trygæos on his beetle he
soars " to the bright heaven of invention." At the

---

[1] Athen. i. 60.

[2] Idem, ii. 1, where are collected many other etymologies
and curious fables.

[3] Athen. ii. 8.

[4] Or Nicarchos. Anthol. Græc.
xiii. 29. Athen. ii. 9.

port of Munychia, too, good wine was held in high
estimation ; indeed, the honest folks of this borough, with small respect for the water nymphs,
paid particular honour to the hero *Acratopotes*, that
is, in plain English, "one who drinks unmixed
wine." Even among the Spartans,[1] in spite of their
cothons, and black broth, certain culinary *artistes*
set up in the Phydition, or common dining-hall,
statues in honour of the heroes *Matton* and *Keraon*,
that is, the genii of eating and drinking. In
Achaia, too, much reverence was paid to *Deipneus*,
or the god who presides over good suppers.[2]

As the Greeks had a marvellous respect for wine
they, like the German paper enthusiast, almost appeared to imagine it could be made out of a stone.
They had, accordingly, fig wine,[3] root wine, palm
wine, and so on ; and their made or mixed wines
were without number. There was scarcely an
island or city in the Mediterranean that did not
export its wines to Athens : they had the Lesbian,
the Eubœan, the Peparethian, the Chalybonian, the
Thasian, the Pramnian, and the Port wine. We
have already observed, that wine was drunk mixed
with flour,[4] and in the island of Theræ it was
thickened with the yolk of an egg. In the Megaris they prepared with raisins or dried grapes [5]
a wine called *passon*, in taste resembling the Ægos-
thenic sweet wine, or the Cretan malmsey. But,
however exquisite the wines themselves, it was not
thought enough in the summer months unless they
were brought to table cooled with ice or snow,[6]
which was accordingly the practice.

[1] Athen. ii. 9.
[2] Athen. ii. 9. Cf. x. 9.
[3] Damm. 2224. βρύτον. Athen.
x. 67. Plato de Rep. t. vi. p.
144. Xenoph. Anab. p. 54. 138.
Cyrop. p. 522. Plin. Hist. Nat.
xiii. 4. Diod. Sic. ii. 136. On
the οἶνος συκίτης vid. Foës. Œ-
con. Hip. in v. Dioscorid. v.

40. Lotus wine. Theoph. Hist.
Plant. iv. 3. 1. Herod. iv. 177.
Athen. vii. 9—13.

[4] Plato de Repub. t. vi. p.
144. Bekk. Athen. viii. 1. On
the Pramnian cf. Athen. 1, 17.

[5] Athen. x. 41.

[6] Athen. x. 56.

CHAPTER V.

ENTERTAINMENTS.

HAVING now gone rapidly through the materials of which Grecian repasts consisted, it will next be necessary to describe the manner in which all these good things were disposed of, first to maintain the energy of the frame, and secondly, for mere pleasure and pastime. Locke, with many other modern philosophers, erroneously supposes the Greeks of remote antiquity to have been so abstemious as to content themselves with one meal per diem. But experience appears to have led all mankind on this point to much the same conclusion ; viz., that health and comfort require men to eat at least thrice in the day,[1] which accordingly was the practice of the ancient Greeks, though Philemon and others enumerate four repasts. Our own ancestors, before the introduction of tea and coffee, appear to have been very well content with beer or ale for their morning's meal, so that we could not pity the Greeks even though it should be found that they had nothing better[2] than hot rolls, muffins, or crumpets, with strawberries, grapes, pears, and a flask of Chian or Falernian. But they soon found the necessity of some warm beverage ; and though it does not appear how it was prepared, they had a substitute for tea,[3] in use at Athens, in Eu-

[1] Æschyl. Palamed. fr. 168. Klausen. Comm. in Agamemnon. p. 136.

[2] In modern times a breakfast in the Troad often consists of grapes, figs, white honey in the comb, and coffee.—Chandler, i. p. 37.

[3] Athen. xi. 26, 50. Pollux. ix. 67, sqq. Schol. Aristoph. Acharn. 643. Cf. Bœckh. Pub. Econ. of Athens, i. 140.

bœa, in Crete, and, no doubt, in all other parts
of Greece. This meal, of whatever it consisted,
was called *acratisma*, or *ariston*, and eaten at break
of day.[1] Homer's heroes, whose business was fighting, just snatched a hasty meal, and hurried to the
field; but at Athens, where people had other employments, they breakfasted early, to allow themselves ample time for despatching their affairs in
the city, if they had any, and afterwards at their
neighbouring farms or villas.[2] The second repast,
deipnon, or dinner, seems to have been eaten about
eleven or twelve o'clock: the *hesperisma*,[3] equivalent to our tea, late in the afternoon, and the
dorpon, or supper, the last thing in the evening.
But of these meals two only were serious affairs,
and the *hesperisma* was often dispensed with altogether. In fact, Athenæus, a great authority
on this subject, considers it perfectly absurd to
suppose, that the frugal ancients could have
thought of eating so often as three times in one
day.[4]

As the greater includes the less, instead of con-
fining ourselves to the ordinary daily dinner of a
Greek, we shall in preference describe their grand
entertainments, introducing remarks on the former
by the way. These repasts were divided into three
classes, the public dinner, the pic-nic, and the mar-

---

[1] Which we may infer from a
passage of Aristotle, Hist. Anim.
vi. 8. where describing the habits
of birds, he says, τῶν δὲ φαβῶν
ἡ μὲν θήλεια ἀπὸ δείλης ἀρξαμένη
τήν τε νύχθ' ὅλην ἐπῳάζει καὶ
ἕως ἀκρατίσματος ὥρας, ὁ δ'
ἄρρην τὸ λοιπὸν τοῦ χρόνου.—
One of the Homeric scholiasts is
more explicit:—καὶ τὴν μὲν
πρώτην ἐκάλουν ἄριστον, ἣν ἐλάμ-
βανον πρωΐας σχεδὸν ἔτι σκοτίας
οὔσης.—In Iliad β. 381. Cf.
Athen. i. 19.

[2] Xenoph. Œcon. xi. 14.
[3] Philemon, ap. Athen. i. 19.
Suid. v. δεῖπνον t. i. p. 671. a. b.
[4] Deipnosoph v. 20.—τρισὶ δὲ
οὐδέποτε οὔτε μνηστῆρες οὔτε μὴν
κύκλωψ ἐχρῶντο τροφαῖς.—Schol.
Il. β. 381. Yet Athenæus i. 19.
speaks in one place of a fourth
repast in Homeric times.— τῆς δὲ
τετάρτης τροφῆς οὕτως "Ομηρος
μέμνηται—" σὺ δ' ἔρχεο δειελιή-
σας." ὃ καλοῦσί τινες δειλινόν, ὁ
ἐστι μεταξὺ τοῦ ὑφ' ἡμῶν λεγομέ-
νου ἀρίστου καὶ δείπνου.

riage feast. The last, so far as it had any peculiar features, has been described among the circumstances attending matrimony. We have, therefore, for the present, to do with two only; and, as the Greek contrived to throw much of his ingenuity into all matters connected with feasting and merry-making, the discussion of this part of our subject should savour strongly of mirth and jollity.

The grand dinner,[1] which they called *eilapinè*, was generally given at the expense of an individual, and its sumptuousness knew no limit but the means of the host. Other kinds of feasts there were at which all the members of a tribe, a borough, or a fraternity, were entertained, not to speak for the present of the common tables of the Cretans, Spartans, or Prytanes of Athens. We now confine ourselves to those jovial assemblages of private citizens whose object in meeting was not so much the dinner, though that was not overlooked, as the elevation of animal spirits and flow of soul produced by the union of a thousand different circumstances.

When a rich man desired to see his friends around him at his board, he delivered to his *deipnocletor*,[2] a domestic kept for this purpose, a tablet, or as we should say, a card, whereon the names of the persons to be invited, with the day and hour fixed upon for the banquet, were inscribed. With brothers and other very near relations this ceremony was thought unnecessary.[3] They came without invitation. So likewise did another class of men, who, living at large upon the public and lighting unbidden upon any sport to which they were attracted by the savour of a good dinner, were denominated[4] Flies,

[1] On the subject of dining see Pollux, vi. 9, seq. with the notes of Jungermann, Kuhn, Hemsterhuis. &c.

[2] Athen. iv. 70. Aristoph. Concion. 648, et Schol.

[3] For a further account of the persons usually invited, see Athen. v. 4.

[4] Plut. Sympos. vii. 6. Each guest was also followed by a footman who stood behind his master's chair and waited on him. Casaub. ad Theoph. Char. p. 219.

and occasionally SHADES or PARASITES. There was at one time a law at Athens, which a good deal nonplussed these gentlemen. It was decreed, that not more than thirty persons should meet at a marriage feast, and a wealthy citizen, desirous of "going the whole hog," had invited the full complement. An honest Fly, however, who respected no law that interfered with his stomach, contrived to introduce himself, and took his station at the lower end of the table. Presently the magistrate appointed for the purpose, entered, and espying his man at a glance, began counting the guests, commencing on the other side and ending with the parasite. "Friend," said he, "you must retire. I find there is one person "more than the law allows." "It is quite a mis- "take, sir," replied the Fly, "as you will find if you "will have the goodness to count again, beginning "*on this side.*"[1] Among the Egyptians, who shrouded all their poetry in hieroglyphics, *a fly* was the emblem of impudence, which necessarily formed the principal qualification of a Parasite, and in Hume's[2] opinion is no bad possession to any man who would make his way in the world.

Archbishop Potter,[3] in his account of Grecian entertainments, observes, upon the authority of Cicero

To persons of this description the guests delivered the presents that were made them, or if they happened to be bad characters, what they stole. Athen. iv. 2. Plut. Anton. § 28. Lucian. Conviv. seu Lapith. § 46. Rich men then as now were usually haunted by flatterers who would pluck off the burrs from their cloaks or the chaff which the wind wafted into their beards, and try to screw a joke out of the circum-stance by saying, they were grown grey! Theoph. Char. c. ii. p. 7. If the patron joked, they would stuff their chlamys into their mouths as if they were dying of laughter. In the street they would say to the person they met, "Stand aside, friend, and allow "this gentleman to pass!" They would bring apples and pears in their pocket for his little ones and be sure to give them in his sight, with great praise both of father and children.

[1] Athen. vi. 45, seq.

[2] Nothing, says this philosopher, carries a man through the world like a true genuine natural impudence. Essays, p. 9, quarto.

[3] Antiq. iv. 19.

and Cornelius Nepos, that women were never invited with the men.[1] But in this, as has been shown in the proper place, he was misled by those learned Romans; for, in many cities and colonies of Greece, no banquet was given at which they were not present. Even at Athens, where women of character thought it unbecoming to mingle in the convivial revelries of the men,[2] in which wine constantly overleaps the boundaries of decorum, their place was supplied by hetairæ, whose polished manners, ready wit, and enlarged and enlightened understandings, recommended them to their companions, and caused the laxity of their morals to be forgotten.[3] To proceed, however, with our feast: it will readily be supposed, that gentlemen invited out to dinner were careful to apparel themselves elegantly, to shave clean, and arrange their beards and moustachios after the most approved fashion of the day. Even Socrates, who cared as little as most people for external appearances, bathed, put on a pair of new shoes, brushed his chlamys, and otherwise spruced himself up when going to sup at Agathon's with Phædros, Aristophanes, Eryximachos, and other exquisites. Even in Homeric times the bath was

---

[1] Plato giving directions for a marriage feast, observes, that five male and five female friends should be invited; along with these, five male and five female relations, who with the bride and bridegroom, with their parents, grandfathers, &c., would amount to 28. De Legg. vi. t. vii. Schweigh. ad Athen. t. vi. p. 60. Among the ancient Etruscans, who, if not Greeks, had many Greek customs, the women reclined at table with the men, under the same cover. Athen. i. 42.

[2] Isæus, De Pyrrh. Hered. § 2. That among the more simple and old-fashioned citizens of Athens,

however, men and women, when of the same family or clan, dined together, we have the testimony of Menander to prove. He introduces one of his characters, apparently a fop, observing that it was a bore to be at a family party, where the father, holding the goblet in his hand, first made a speech, abounding with exhortations: the mother followed, and then the grandmother prated a little. Afterwards stood up her father, hoarse with age, and his wife, calling him her dearest; while he mean time nodded to all present. Athen. ii. 86.

[3] Athen. v. 6.

among the preliminaries to dinner, and guests arriving from a distance were attended through all the operations of the toilette by female slaves.[1] But this general ablution was not considered sufficient. On sitting down to table water was again presented to every guest in silver[2] lavers or ewers of gold. And since they ate with their fingers, as still is the practice in the Levant, it was moreover customary to wash the hands between every course,[3] and wipe them,[4] in remoter ages, with soft bread, which was thrown to the dogs, and in aftertimes with napkins. The Arcadians, however, about whose mountains all the old superstitions of Hellas clung like bats, found a very different use for the cakes with which they wiped their fingers. They supposed them to acquire some mystic powers by the operation, and preserved them as a charm against ghosts.[5]

But we are proceeding too fast, for the guests are scarcely within doors, and our imagination has jumped to the conclusion. To return then. Immediately on entering, and when the host had welcomed and shaken hands with all, such gentlemen as possessed beards[6] had them perfumed over burning censers of frankincense, as ladies have their tresses on visiting a Turkish harem. The hands, too, after each lavation, were scented.[7] Before sitting down to table,

[1] Odyss. δ. 48, sqq.
[2] Athen. ix. 27. In some luxurious houses wine mingled with spices was presented to the guests in lavers for the purpose of washing their feet. Plut. Phoc. § 20. In the palace of Trimalchio we find Egyptian servants pouring water, cooled with snow, on the hands of the guests. Petron. Satyr. p. 76.
[3] Schol. Aristoph. Eq. 412.
[4] Rich purple napkins were sometimes used. Sappho in Deipnosoph. ix. 79. These articles are still in the Levant elaborately embroidered.

[5] Athen. iv. 31.
[6] Hom. Odyss. γ. 33, seq. Athen. xv. 23. Similar customs still prevail in the Levant : " When we visited the Turks " we were received with cordiality " and treated with distinction. " Sweet gums were burned in the " middle of the room to scent the " air, or scattered on coals before " us while sitting on the sofa, to " perfume our moustachios and " garments, and at the door, at " our departure, we were sprink- " led with rose-water." Chandler, ii. 150. [7] Athen. ix. 77.

and while the cooks were peppering the soup, fry-
ing the fish, or giving the roast-meat another turn,
politeness required the guests to take a stroll [1] in
the picture-gallery and admire the exquisite taste
of their entertainer in articles of *virtu*.[2] Here while
the scent of the savoury viands found its way through
every apartment, and set the bowels of the hungry
parasites croaking, the rogues who had lunched well
at home leisurely discussed the merits of Zeuxis or
Parrhasios, of Pheidias or Polygnotos, or opened
wide their eyes at the microscopic creations of
that Spartan artist whose chisel produced a chariot
and four that could be hidden under the wing of
a fly. At length, however, the connoisseurs were interrupted in their learned disquisitions by the entrance
of Xanthos, Davos, or Lydos, with the welcome intelligence that dinner was on the table.

But the appetites of the gourmands had still to
encounter another trial.[3] The Greeks were above
all things a pious people, and regarded every banquet, nay, every meal, in the light of a sacrifice, at
which the first and best portion should be offered
as an oblation to the gods,[4] with invocations and
prayer, after which it was considered lawful to attend to their own appetites. An altar, accordingly,
of Zeus stood in the midst of every dining-room,
on which these ceremonies were performed, and libations of pure wine poured.[5] This done, the guests

---

[1] Cf. Hom. Odyss. δ. 43, sqq.

[2] Aristoph. Vesp. 1208. Athen.
v. 6, where the splendid roofs
and ornaments of the court are
mentioned. These ornaments,
κρεκάδια, whatever they were,
must have been worth looking at.
See the note of Casaubon, Animadv. in Athen. t. viii. p. 27, seq.
Consult likewise the note on
Aristophanes in Bekker's edition,
t. iii. p. 606.

[3] Athen. v. 7. Cf. Plat. Symp.
t. iv. p. 376, et Xenoph. Conviv.

ii. 1. Schweigh. Animadv. in
Athen. viii. p. 26, seq.

[4] Casaubon mentions this as a
thing *nota eruditis*. Ad Theoph.
Charact. p. 232 ; but we must not
on that account pass it over.
Alexis poetically deplores the
miseries of the half-hour before
dinner. Athen. i. 42.

[5] There was in great houses
a person whose duty it was to
assign each guest his place at
table, ὀνομακλήτωρ, or nomencla-
tor. Athen. ii. 29.

took their places, in the earlier ages on chairs, but
afterwards, when they had become familiar with the
East, on rich sofas, arranged round the board.[1] Occasionally, however, even so late as the age of Alexander,[2] princes and other great men chose to adopt
the ancient custom, and, on one occasion, that conqueror himself entertained four hundred of his offi-
cers, when seats of wrought silver, covered with
purple carpets, were provided for all.

The manner of reclining on the divans was not
a little ludicrous. For, at the outset, while the appetite was keen, they stretched themselves flat upon
their stomachs, in order, I presume, to command
the use of both hands, and putting forward their
mouths towards the table looked like so many spar-
rows with their open bills projecting over the nest.
But this they could conveniently do only when they
had a large space to themselves. When packed
close, as usually they were, one man, the chief in
dignity, throwing off his shoes,[3] placed himself on
the upper end of the divan, that is, next the host,
reclining on one elbow supported by soft cushions.
The head of the next man reached nearly to his
breast,—whence in Scripture, the beloved disciple
is said to recline on the bosom of Christ,[4]—while
the feet of the first extended down behind him.
The third guest occupied the same position with
respect to the second, and so on until five individuals sometimes crowded each other on the same
sofa.

As the heaven of the poets was but a colossal

---

[1] Plin. xxxiii. 51. xxxiv. 8.

[2] At most sumptuous entertainments *tasters* were employed
who, as in the East, made trial
of the dishes before the guests,
lest they should be poisoned.
These persons were called ἐδέα-
τροι and προτένθαι. Athen. iv.
71.

[3] Schol. Aristoph. Eq. 825.

[4] John, xiii. 23. On the cushions, of which there was a great
variety, see Pollux, vi. 9, where
he reckons among them the ὑπηρ-
έσιον, which Mitford confounds
with the ἄσκωμα, or leathern
bags which closed the row-port of
war-galleys round the oar, to prevent the influx of sea-water.

picture of earth, we may, from the practice of the gods, infer what took place among mortals, even where supported by no direct testimony. Now, in Homer, we find gods and goddesses mingling freely together at the feast. Zeus takes the head of the table, next him sits his daughter Athena, while the imperial Hera, as Queen of Heaven, takes precedence of all the she Olympians, by placing herself at the head of the secondary divinities, directly opposite her husband. On one occasion we find Athena, the type of hospitality and politeness, yielding up her seat of honour to Thetis, because, as an Oceanid, she was somewhat of a stranger in Olympos.[1] Potter has discussed, with more learning than perspicuity, the question of precedence at table. To render the matter perfectly intelligible would require a plan of the dining-room; but wanting this, it may be observed, that in Persia the king, or host of whatever rank, sat in the middle, while the guests ranged themselves equally on both sides of him.

In Greece, the bottom of the table was the end next the door. Here no one sat, it being left open for the servants to bring in and remove the dishes. From this point, on either side, the seats augmented in value, and consequently the post of greatest honour was the middle of the other extremity.[2] There were those, however, who made no account of these matters, but suffered their guests to seat themselves as they pleased. This was the case with Timon, who, having invited a very miscellaneous party, would not be at the pains to settle the question of precedence between them; but a pompous individual of aristocratic pretensions, dressed like an actor, arriving late with a large retinue, and surveying the company from the door, went away again, observing, there was no fit place left for him. Upon which the guests, who, as Plutarch remarks, were

---

[1] Iliad. ω. 100.

[2] Cf. Plut. Conv. Quæst. i. 3. Pet. Ciacon, De Triclin. p. 44.

far gone in their cups, burst into shouts of laughter, and bade him make the best of his way home.[1]

Some persons observed a very different order in arranging their guests, grouping those together whom they considered suited by age or temper to each other, in order by this contrivance to produce general harmony, — the vehement and impetuous being placed beside the meek and gentle, the silent beside the talkative, the ripe and full and expansive minds beside those who were ready to receive instruction. But very often, as at Agathon's, those sat next each other, who were most intimately acquainted or united together by friendship; for thus the greatest freedom of intercourse with the brightest sallies of convivial wit were likely to be produced.

At length, however, we must imagine the guests in their places and every thing in proper train. The servants bring in first one well-covered table, then a second, then a third, till the whole room is filled with dainties. Brilliant lamps and chandeliers poured a flood of light over the crowned heads of the guests, over the piled sweetmeats, over the shining dishes, and all the baits with which the appetite is caught. Then, on silver pateræ, cakes whiter than snow were served round. To these succeeded eggs, pungent herbs, oysters, and thrushes.[2] Next several dishes of rich eels, brown and crisp, sprinkled thickly with salt, followed by a delicious conger dressed with every rare device of cookery, calculated to delight the palate of the gods. Then came the belly of a large ray, round as a hoop; dishes, containing, one some slices of a sea-dog, another garnished with a sparos, a third with a cuttle-fish, or smoking polypus whose legs were tender as a chicken. While the sight of these dainties was feasting the eyes of the

[1] Sympos. i. 2. 1.

[2] Probably also the myttotos, a dish flavoured with garlic and rich spices, formed a part of this course. Schol. Aristoph. Acharn. 173. Vesp. 62.

guests, the noses of the experienced informed them of the approach of a synodon,[1] which perfumed the passages all the way from the kitchen, and, flanked with calamaries, covered the whole table. Shrimps too were there in their yellow cuirasses, sweet in flavour as honey, with delicious varieties of puff pastry bordered with fresh green foliage.[2] The teeth of the parasites watered at the sight. But while deeply engaged in the discussion of these good things, in came some smoking slices of broiled thunny, a mullet fresh from the fish-kettle, with the teats of a young sow cooked *en ragoût*.

Pleasure of all kinds being supposed to promote digestion, female singers, flute-players and dancers, were meanwhile exercising their several arts for the entertainment of the guests. But as they paid very little attention to them till the rage of hunger was appeased, we shall imitate their example, and proceed with the gourmandize. One of the greatest accomplishments a boon companion could possess, was the power to seize with the fingers, and swallow hissing-hot, slices of grilled fish or morsels of lamb or veal broiled like kabobs, so as to be slightly burnt and cracking externally, while all the juice and flavour of the meat remained within. And the acquirement being highly important, great pains were taken to become masters of it. For this purpose some accustomed themselves daily to play with hot pokers, others case-hardened their fingers by repeatedly dipping them in water as hot as they could bear, and gargled their throats with the same, while one famous gourmand, more inventive than the rest, hit upon the ingenious device of wearing metallic fingerlings with which he could have seized a kabob even from the gridiron. These proficients in the art of eating, an art practised indeed by all, but possessed in perfection by very few, enjoyed great advantages over the ignorant and uninitiated. And

[1] Athen. i. 8. vii. 46. 68. 119.   [2] Pollux, vi. 77.
Arist. Hist. Anim. v. 5.

accordingly, when invited out, they generally succeeded in bribing the cook to send in all his dishes hot as Phlegethon, that, while the more modest and inexperienced guests sat gazing on, they might secure the best cuts, and come again before the others could venture on a mouthful.

Among the articles served up in this scorching state were calf's pluck, pig's harslet, with the chine, the kidneys, and a variety of small hors-d'œuvre. To these may be added the head of a sucking-kid which had tasted nothing but milk, baked between two dishes well luted together; giblets boiled; small, delicate hams with their white sward unbroken; pigs' snouts and feet swimming in white sauce, which the gourmand Philoxenos thought a rare invention. Roast kid and lamb's chitterlings, or the same viands boiled, formed a supplement to the dishes above enumerated, and were usually done so exactly to a turn, that even the gods, Bacchos for example, and Hermes, the parasites of Olympos, might have descended expressly to wag their beards over them. But the Levantines have always been enamoured of variety in cookery. Lady Wortley Montague counted fifty dishes served up in succession at the Sultana Hafiten's table; and this she-barbarian, with all her wealth, could never rival the variety of invention of an ancient Eleian or Sicilian cook, who usually closed the list of his dainties with hare, chickens roasted to the gold-colour celebrated by Aristophanes, partridges, pheasants, wood-pigeons or turtle-doves, which your true gourmand should eat in the Thebaid, immediately after the close of harvest. But the dinner was not yet over. There still remained the dessert to be disposed of, consisting of pure honey from the district of the silver mines, curdled cream, cheese-tarts, and all that profusion of southern fruit of which we have already spoken.[1]

It is a well-known rule among modern gourmands,

[1] Athen. iv. 28. There was a kind of cheese, apparently much in use, imported from Gythion, in Laconia. Lucian. Diall. Hetair. xiv. 2.

that no man should utter a syllable at table till the first course is removed, and precisely the same regulation prevailed among the ancients. Silence, however, was sometimes interrupted by the arrival of some wandering buffoon, who, after long roaming about in search of a dinner, happened, perhaps, to be attracted thither by the wings and feathers ostentatiously scattered before the door. This sort of gentry required no introduction: they had only to knock and announce themselves to ensure a ready welcome; for most men would willingly part with a share of their supper to be made merry over the remainder. The Athenian demos was pre-eminently of this humour. No king, in fact, ever kept up so large an establishment of fools by profession, or, which is much the same thing, of wits, — fellows who grind their understandings into pointed jests to tickle the risible muscles and expand the mouths of sleek junketters, who esteem nothing ·beyond eating and grinning.

At a feast given by Callias, the famous jester, Philip, a-kin in spirit, I trow, to him of Macedon, presented himself in this way, and, on being admitted, — " Gentlemen," said he, " you know my profession and " its privileges, relying on which I, am come unin- " vited, being a foe to all ceremony, and desiring to " spare you the trouble of a formal invitation." — " Take your place," replied the host; " your company " was much needed, for our friends appear to be " plunged up to the chin in gravity, and would be " greatly benefited by a hearty laugh." [1]

In fact, the heads of the honest people were filled with very serious meditations, being all in love, and endeavouring to discover how each might excel the other in absurdity. Philip began to fear, therefore, that he had carried his jests to a bad market, and, in reality, made many vain attempts to kindle the spirit of mirth, and call home the imaginations of persons who had evidently suffered them to stray as far as the clouds. Aware that success on this point was indis-

[2] Xenoph. Conv. i. 13, 14.

pensable to his subsistence, the jester grew piqued at the indifference of his hearers, and breaking off in the midst of his supper, wrapped up his head in his chlamys, and lay down like one about to die. "What, now!" cried Callias. "Has any sudden panic "seized on thee, friend?"—"The worst possible, by "Zeus!" replied Philip; "for, since laughter, like "justice, has taken its leave of earth, my occupation "is gone. Hitherto I have enjoyed some celebrity "in this way, living at the public expense, like the "guests of the Prytaneion, because my drollery was "effective, and could set the table in a roar. But it "is all over, I see, with me now, for I might as soon "hope to render myself immortal as acquire serious "habits." All this he uttered in a pouting, desponding tone, as if about to shed tears. The company, to humour the joke, undertook to comfort him, and the effect of their mock condolences, and assurances that they would laugh if he continued his supper, was so irresistibly ludicrous, that Autolychos, a youthful friend of Callias, was at length unable to restrain his merriment; upon which the jester took courage, and apostrophising his soul, informed it very gravely, that there would be no necessity for them to part company yet.[1]

The Greeks had, properly speaking, no drawing-rooms, so that, instead of retreating to another part of the house, they had the tables themselves removed immediately after dinner. Libations were then poured out to Zeus Teleios, and having sung a hymn to Phœbos Apollo, the amusements of the evening commenced. Professional singers and musicians were always hired on these occasions. They were female slaves, selected in childhood for their beauty and budding talents, and carefully educated by their owners.[2] When not already engaged, they stood in blooming bevies in the agora, waiting, like the Labourers of Scripture, until some one should

[1] Xenoph. Conviv. i. 15. 16. [2] Cf. Luc. Amor. § 10. Schol. Aristoph. Acharn. 1058.

hire them, upon which they proceeded, dressed and
ornamented with great elegance, to the house of
feasting.   But, besides these, there were other *artistes* who contributed to the entertainment of the
demos, persons that, like our Indian jugglers, performed wonderful feats by way of interlude between
the regular exhibitions of the damsels from the agora.[1]

Xenophon introduces into that living picture of
Greek manners called the Banquet, a company of
this kind.   Finding Philip's jokes dull things, he
brings upon the scene a strolling Syracusan, with
a beautiful female flute-player, a dancing girl who
could perform surpassing feats of activity, and a
handsome boy, who, besides performing on the cithara,
was likewise able, on occasion, to sport the toe like
his female companions.

But, where philosophers were present, amusements
of this kind were not allowed to occupy their whole
attention.   Every thing that occurred was made a
handle for conversation, so that discussions, more or
less lively, according to the temperament or ability
of the interlocutors, formed the solid ground-work
upon which the flowers of gaiety and laughter were
spread.   It was usual, immediately after supper, to
perfume the guests, and great was the variety of
unguents, essences, and odorous oils, made use of
by the rich and vain upon these occasions; but when
Callias proposed conforming to the mode in this
particular, Socrates objected, observing, that the
odour of honourable toil was perfume enough for a
man.[2]   Women, indeed, to whom every thing sweet
and beautiful naturally belongs, might, he admitted,
make use of perfume, and they did so most lavishly
as we have already shown, when we entered their
dressing-room and assisted at their toilette.

The Greeks, however, were careful not to convert

---

[1] The Indian jugglers themselves became known to the
Greeks in the age of Alexander.
Ælian. Var. Hist. viii. 7.
[2] Xen. Conv. ii. 4.

their pleasure-parties into a mere arena for the exhibition of dialectic power. They from time to time glanced at philosophy, but only by the way, in the moments of transition from one variety of recreation to another. Their conversation was now and then brought to a pause by the rising of dancing girls,[1] robed elegantly, as we behold them still on vases and on bas-reliefs, in drapery adapted to display all the beauty of their forms. Hoops were brought them, and while musicians of their own sex called forth thrilling harmonies from the flute, they executed a variety of graceful movements, in part pantomimic,—now casting up the hoops, now catching them as they fell, keeping time exactly with the cadences of the flute. Their skill in this accomplishment was so great, that many were enabled to keep up twelve hoops in the air at the same time, while others made use of poniards.[2]

When the novelty of this exhibition was worn off a little, other different feats followed. A hoop stuck all round with upright swords was placed in the midst of the apartment, into which one of the dancing girls threw herself head foremost, and while standing on her head balanced the lower part of her body round over the naked points, to the infinite terror of the spectators. She would then dart forth between the swords, and, with a single bound, regain her footing without the circle.[3] To add to the entertainment of the company, some parasitical buffoon would at times undertake to exhibit his awkwardness as a foil to the grace of the dancers, frisking about with the clumsy heaviness of a bear, and exaggerating his own ignorance of orchestics to excite a laugh. Sometimes the female dancer, like our own fair tumblers, would throw back her head till it reached her heels, and then putting herself in motion, roll about the room like a hoop,[4] To

[1] Lucian. Amor. § 10.   [3] Poll. iii. 134.
[2] Artemid. Oneirocrit. i. 68.
Xen. Conviv. ii. 8.   [4] Xen. Conviv. ii. 22.

these, as a relief and a change, would succeed, perhaps, a youth with fine rich voice, who accompanied himself on the lyre with a song.

But nothing could entirely restrain the Greeks from indulging in the pleasure of listening to their own voices. The buzz of conversation would soon be heard in different parts of the room, which, when Socrates was present, sometimes provoked from him a sarcastic reproof. For example, at Callias's dinner, observing the company broken up into knots, each labouring at some particular question in dialectics, and filling the apartment with a babel of confused murmurs; " As we talk all at " once," said he, " we may as well sing all at " once; " and without further ceremony he pitched his voice and began a song.[1]

But when professed jugglers happened to be present, gentlemen were not long abandoned to their own resources for amusement. Trick followed trick in rapid succession. To the pantomimic dances, and the sword circle, succeeded the exhibition of the potter's wheel, in which a young girl seated on this machine, like a little Nubian at a cow's-tail in a *sakia*, was whirled round with great velocity,[2] but retained so much self-possession as to be able both to write and to read. These, however, were merely sources of momentary wonder. Other amusements succeeded capable of exciting superior delight, such for example, as the mimetic dance, which, like that of the ghawazi, could tell a whole story of love, of adventure, of war, of religious frenzy and enthusiasm, transporting by vivid representations the fancy of the spectators to warmer or wilder scenes, calling up images and reminiscences of times long past, or steeping the thoughts in poetical dreams, filled with the caverned nymphs, the merry Seileni, the frisking satyrs, Bacchos, Pan, the Hours, the Graces, sporting by moonlit fountains, through antique woods,

[1] Xen. Conviv. vii. 1. [2] Xen. Conviv. vii. 3.

or on the shelled and sand-ribbed margin of the ocean.[1]

On some occasions a slight dramatic scene was represented. Clearing the centre of the banqueting hall, the guests ranged themselves in order as at the theatre. A throne was then set up in the open space, and a female actor, representing Ariadne, entering, took her seat upon it, decked and habited like a bride, and supposed to be in her Thalamos at Naxos. Dionysos, who has been dining with Zeus, comes flushed with Olympian nectar into the harem to the sound of the Bacchic flute, while the nymph who has heard his approaching footsteps makes it manifest by her behaviour that her soul is filled with joy, though she neither advances nor rises to meet him, but restrains her feelings with difficulty, and remains apparently tranquil. The god, drawing near with impassioned looks, and dancing all the while, now seats himself, and places the fair one on his knee. Then, in imitation of mortal lovers, he embraces and kisses her, nothing loth; for, though she hangs down her head, and would wish to appear out of countenance, her arms find their way round his neck and return his embrace. At this the company, we may be sure, clapped and shouted. The god, encouraged by their plaudits, then stood up with his bride, and going through the whole pantomime of courtship, not coldly and insipidly, but as one whose heart was touched, at length demanded of Ariadne if in truth she loved him. Sometimes the mimic scene concealed beneath it all the reality of passion. From personating enamoured characters, the youthful actor and his partner learned in reality to love; and what was amusement to others contained a deep and serious meaning for them. This, Xenophon says, was the case with the youth and maiden who enlivened the banquet of Callias. Absorbed in the earnestness of their

[1] Plat. de Legg. vii. t. viii. p. 55. Bekk. Xen. Conv. vii. 5.

feelings, they seem to have forgotten the presence
of spectators, and instead of a stage representation,
gave them a scene from real life, where every impassioned look and gesture were genuine, and every
fiery glance was kindled at the heart.[1]

This, however, may be considered a serious amusement, and something like broad farce was necessary
to awaken the guests from the reverie into which
the love scene had plunged them.   Jesters were,
therefore, put in requisition; and, as even they
sometimes failed to raise a laugh, their more humorous brethren the wits and jesters of the forests,
or, in the language of mortals, monkeys were called
upon to dissipate the clouds of seriousness.   These
were the favourite buffoons of the Scythian Anacharsis,—not the Abbé Barthélemy's,—who said,
he could laugh at a monkey's tricks, because his
tricks were natural, but that he found no amusement in a man who made a trade of it.[2]   Nor
could Euripides at all relish punsters and manu-
facturers of jokes, whom he considered, with some
reason, as a species of animal distinct from mankind.

> Many there be who exercise their wits
> In giving birth, by cutting jests, to laughter.
> I hate the knaves whose rude unbridled tongues
> Sport with the wise; and cannot for my life
> Think they are men, though laughter doth become them,
> And they have houses filled with treasured stores
> From distant lands.[3]

But if Euripides found nothing desirable in laughter,
there were those who had a clean contrary creed,
and lamented nothing so much as the loss of their
risible faculties.   On this subject Semos has a story
quite *à propos*.   Parmeniscos, the Metapontine, having descended, he says, into the cave of Trophonios,
became so extremely grave, that with all the ap-

---

[1] Xen. Conviv. ix. 1—7.   [3] Eurip. Fragm. Melanipp. 20.
[2] Athen. xiv. 2.

pliances, and means to boot, furnished by wealth, and they were not a few, he thereafter found himself quite unable to screw up his muscles into a smile; which taking much to heart, as was natural, he made a pilgrimage to Delphi, to inquire by what means he might rid himself of the blue devils. Somewhat puzzled at the strangeness of the inquiry, the Pythoness replied, —

> Poor mortal unmerry, who seekest to know
> What will bid thy brow soften, thy quips and cranks flow,
> To the house of the mother I bid thee repair—
> Thou wilt find, if she's pleased, what thy heart covets, there.

Upon this, Parmeniscos hastened homeward, hoping soon to enjoy a good laugh as the reward of his industry; but, finding his features remain fixed as cast-iron, he began to suspect the oracle had deceived him. Some time after, being at Delos, he beheld with admiration the several wonders of the island, and, lastly, proceeded to the temple of Leto, expecting to find in the mother of Apollo something worthy of so great a divinity. But, on entering and perceiving, instead, a grotesque and smoky old figure in wood, he burst into an immoderate fit of laughter, whereupon the response of the oracle recurred to his mind, and he understood it; and, being thus delivered from his infirmity, he ever after held the goddess in extremest reverence.[1]

Even from this story, therefore, it will be seen how highly " broad grins " were estimated in antiquity, particularly at Athens, where there was a regular " Wits' Club," consisting of threescore members, who assembled during the Diomeia,[2] in the temple of Heracles. The names of several of these jovial mortals have come down to us; Mandrogenes, for example, and Strato, Callimedon, who, for some particular quality of mind or body, ob-

[1] Athen. xiv. 2.   53. Etym. Mag. 277. 24.
[2] Eustath. ad Iliad. δ. p. 337.   Meurs. Græc. Feriat. ii. 96.

tained the *sobriquet* of the *Lobster*, Deinias, Mna-
sigeiton, and Menæchmos. The reputation of these
gentlemen spread rapidly through the city, and,
when a good thing had a run among the small wits,
it was remarked, that "the Sixty had said *that*."
Or, if a man of talent were asked, whence he came,
he would answer, "From the Sixty." This was in
the time of Demosthenes, when, unhappily, jesters
were in more request in Athens than soldiers; and
Philip of Macedon, himself no mean buffoon, learning
the excellent quality of their *bon mots*, sent them
a present of a talent of gold, with a request that,
as public business prevented his joining the sittings
of the club, they would make for his use a collection in writing of all their smart sayings, which
was, probably, the first step towards those reposi-
tories for stray wit, called "Joe Millers," that form
so indispensable a portion of a bon vivant's library.[1]

But we are all this while detaining the company
from their wine, and those other recreations which
the fertile genius of the Greeks invented to make
the wheels of life move smoothly. Though the tables,
according to the fashion of the times, were removed
with the solid viands, others were brought in to re-
place them, on which the censers, the goblets, the
silver or golden ladles for filling the smaller cups,
were arranged in order.[2] The chairman, or, as he
was then called, the king of the feast,[3] enjoyed absolute power over his subjects, and could determine better than their own palates, how much and
how often each man should drink. This important
functionary was not always identical with the entertainer, but sometimes his substitute, sometimes

[1] Athen. xiv. 3.
[2] Among the Etruscans these
ladles were of bronze, and of extremely elegant form, the point
ending in a swan's or duck's
head.
[3] The proceedings of this person were governed by a code of
laws, the making and reformation
of which employed the wits of no
less personages than Xenophanes,
Spensippos, and Aristotle. Athen.
i. 5.

a person chosen by lot.[1] Capacious bowls of wine,[2]
mingled with water, were placed on a sideboard,
whence cup-bearers, sometimes of one, sometimes
of the other sex, but always selected for their youth
and beauty, filled, with ladles,[3] the goblets of the
guests, which, when the froth rose above the brim,
were, by an obvious metaphor, said to be crowned.[4]
Among the Doric Greeks, female cup-bearers seem
to have been always preferred ; the Ptolemies of
Egypt cherished the same taste ; and the people
of Tarentum, themselves of Doric race, passing
successively through every stage of luxury, came,
at length, to be served at table by beautiful young
women without a vestige of clothing. In most
cases, these maidens were slaves, but, in some countries, and everywhere, in remoter ages, the performance of such offices was not regarded as any way
derogatory to persons of noble or princely blood.
But, whatever might be their birth, beauty of form
and countenance constituted their chief recommen-
dation. For there is a language in looks and gestures, there is a fountain of joy and delight concealed deep in the physical structure, and its waters
laugh to the eye of intellect, and reflect into the
hearts of those who behold it a sunniness and ex-
hilaration greater than we derive from gazing on the
summer sea. Hence, Hebe and Ganymede were
chosen to minister at the tables of the gods, even
Zeus himself[5] not disdaining to taste of the pleasures to be derived from basking in the irradiations
of beauty.

When the goblets were all crowned with the

<hr/>

[1] Horat. Od. ii. 7. 25.
[2] Schol. Aristoph. Eq. 1183.
Vesp. 1005.
[3] Eustath. ad Iliad. γ. p. 333.
Schol. Aristoph. Vesp. 855.—
A specimen of these ladles (ἀρύ-
ταιναι) occurs in Mus. Chiaramont. pl. 2.
[4] Virgil actually wreaths the

bowls with garlands. — Æneid.
iii. 525. — Homer, however,
crowns his bowls only with
wine.—Il. ε. 471.
[5] Homer. Iliad. δ. 2. γ. 232.
β. 813. Odyss. o. 327. Juven.
Sat. v. 60. Cf. Philo. Jud. de
Vit. Contempl. t. ii. p. 479.
Mangey.

nectar of earth, the Master of the Feast[1] set the
example of good-fellowship by drinking to his guests,
beginning with the most distinguished.[2] Originally,
custom required him who drank to the health of
another to drain off his cup while his comrade did
the same; but, in after ages, they sipped only a portion of the wine, and, as they still do in the East,
presented the remainder to their friend. The latter,
by the rules of politeness, was bound to finish the
goblet, or, where the antique fashion prevailed, to
drink one of equal size.[3] The Macedonians, who,
probably, excelled the Greeks in drinking, if in nothing else, disdained small cups as supplying a very
roundabout way to intoxication, and . plunged into
Lethe at once by the aid of most capacious bowls.
It was customary, when the practice of passing round
the goblet had been introduced, for the king of the
feast to drink to the next man on his right hand,
who, in his turn, drank to the next, and so on till
the bowl had circulated round the board. But different customs prevailed in the different parts of
Greece. At Athens, small cups, like our wine-
glasses, were in use; among the Chians, Thracians,
and Thessalians, nations more prone to sensual indulgences, the goblets were of larger dimensions;
but, at Sparta, where sobriety and frugality long
flourished, the practice was to drink from diminutive vessels, which, as often as required, were re-
plenished by the attendants.[4]

Isocrates, in his exhortation to Demonicos, marks
the distinction between the true and false friend,
by observing, that, while the latter thinks only of
those around him, the former remembers the absent,
and makes his affection triumph over time and distance. And the Greeks generally had this merit.

[1] There were certain barbarians, who, to cement their
friendships, drank wine tinged
with each other's blood.—Athen.
xv. 47.

[2] Plut. Symp. i. 2. 2. The first

cup was drunk to the Agathode-
mon.—Schol. Aristoph. Eq. 85.
Athen. xv. 47.

[3] Athen. v. 20.

[4] Athen. x. 39. Plut. Cleom.
§ 13.

Amid the enjoyments of the festive board, they re-called to mind the friends of other days; and, having first performed libations to the gods, those best and purest of friends, drank to the health and prosperity of former associates, now far removed by circum-stances,[1] and this they did not in the mixed beve-rage which formed their habitual potations, but in pure wine.[2] There was something extremely deli-cate in this idea, for tacitly it intimated, that their love placed the objects of it almost on a level with their divinities, in whose honour, also, on these oc-casions, a small portion of the wine was spilt in libations[3] upon the earth. The young, in whose hearts a mistress held the first place,[4] drank deeply in honour of their beloved, sometimes equalling the number of cups to that of the letters forming her name,[5] which, if the custom prevailed so early, would account for Ægisthos's being a sot. Sometimes, however, taking the hint from the number of the Graces, they were satisfied with three goblets; but, when an excuse for drinking " pottle deep " was sought, they chose the Muses for their patrons, and honoured their mistresses' names with three times three.[6] This is the number of cheers with which favourite political toasts are received at our public dinners, though every one who fills his bumper, and cries " hip, hip, hip, hurrah ! " on these occasions, is, probably, not conscious that he is keeping up an old pagan custom in honour of the Muses.

The number four was in no favour at the drinking-table, not because it was an even number, for they sometimes drank ten, but because some old super-stition had brought discredit on it. Our very fox-hunters, however, exhibit an inferior capacity to many

---

[1] Theoc. Eidyll. vii. 69.

[2] Cicero in Verr. Act. ii. Orat. i. § 26, and Ascon. Pedan. in loc.

[3] Antiphon. Acc. Nec. Ven. § 3.—The third libation was in honour of Zeus.—Scol. Pind. Isth. vi. 22.

[4] Theocrit. Eidyll. xiv. 18, et Schol.

[5] Mart. Epig. i. 78.

[6] Horat. Od. iii. 19. 11, sqq. Lambinus in loc. p. 143.

of the ancients in affairs of the bottle, though when
it is the poets who perform the feat, we may safely
consider them to be simply regaling their fancies on
" air-drawn " goblets, which cost nothing, and leave
no head-aches behind them. On this subject there
is a very pretty song in the Anthology, which Potter,
following some old edition, completely misrepresents.[1]
It deserves to be well translated, and I would translate it well if I could. The following at least preserves the meaning :

> Pour out ten cups of the purple wine,
> To crown Lycidicè's charms divine;
> One for Euphrantè, young and fair,
> With the sparkling eye and the raven hair.
> Then I love Lycidicè more, you say ?
> By this foaming goblet I say ye nay.
> More valued than ten is Euphrantè to me,
> For, as when the heavens unclouded be,
> And the stars are crowding far and nigh
> On the deep deep blue of the midnight sky,
> The moon is still brighter and lovelier far
> Than the loveliest planet or brightest star;
> So, ' mid the stars of this earthly sphere,
> None are so lovely or half so dear
> As to me is Euphrantè young and fair,
> With the sparkling eye and the raven hair.[2]

But the Macedonians entertained no respect for
poetical goblets : they loved to scent their moustachios
with the aroma of the real rosy wine when it sparkled
in the cup, — when it moved itself aright, as the wise
king of Judah expresses it. Plutarch describes briefly
one of their drinking-bouts which took place on the
evening of the day wherein old Kalanos, the Hindù
Yoghi, burnt himself alive to escape the colic.
Alexander, on returning from the funeral pile, invited a number of his friends and generals to sup
with him, and, proposing a drinking contest, appointed
a crown for the victor. Prodigious efforts were made
by all present to achieve so enviable a triumph; but
the man who proved himself to possess the most
capacious interior was Promachos, who is said to have

[1] Antiq. ii. 394, seq.   [2] Marc. Argent. ap. Anthol. Græc. v. 110.

swallowed upwards of two gallons. He obtained
the prize, which was a golden crown, valued at a
talent, but died within three days.[1] Chares, the Mity-
lenian, relates the matter somewhat differently. According to him, Alexander celebrated funeral games
in honour of Kalanos, at his barrow, where horse-
races and gymnastic contests took place,[2] and a poetical encomium was pronounced upon the Yoghi, who,
like the rest of his countrymen, was, doubtless, a
great toper, and thence the drinking-match instituted
in the evening. Chares says there were three prizes ;
the first, in value, a talent ; the second, thirty minæ,
or about a hundred and twenty pounds sterling ; the
third, three minæ. The number of aspirants is not
stated, but thirty-five (Plutarch says forty-one) perished in cold shiverings on the spot, and six more died
shortly after in the tents.[3]

Numbers have celebrated the military genius of
Alexander; but Athenæus alone has given him due
credit for his truly royal power of drinking. Like
his father, Philip, who, in his jolly humour, ruffled
the Athenian dead at Chæronea, where he could
safely beard the fallen republicans, Alexander delighted to spend his evenings among drunken roysterers,
whose chief ambition consisted in making a butt of
their bowels. One of these worthies was Proteas,
the Macedonian mentioned by Ephippos, in his work
on the sepulture of Alexander and Hephæstion. He
was a man of iron constitution, on which wine, whatever quantity he drank, appeared to make no impression. Alexander, knowing this, loved to pledge
him in huge bowls, such as none, perhaps, but themselves could cope with. This he did even at Babylon, where the climate suffers few excesses to be
indulged in with impunity. Taking a goblet more
like a pail than a drinking-cup, Alexander caused it
to be crowned with wine, which, having tasted, he
presented the bowl to Proteas. The veteran imme-

[1] Plut. Alexand. Magn. §§ 69, 70.　　[3] Athen. x. 49.
[2] Ælian. Var. Hist. ii. 41. Periz.

diately drained it off, to the great amusement of the company, and presently afterwards, desiring to pledge the king, he filled it up again, and sipping a little, according to custom, passed the bowl to Alexander, who, not to be outdone by a subject, forthwith drank the whole. But if he possessed the courage, he wanted the physical strength of Proteas: the goblet dropped from his hand, his head sank on a pillow, and a fever ensued of which the conqueror of Persia, and the rival of Proteas in drinking, died in a few days.[1]

But to return from these barbarians: as the presence of sober persons must always be felt by hard drinkers to be a tacit reproach, it was one of the rules of good fellowship, that all such as joined not in the common potations should depart. " Drink, or begone ! " said the law, and a good one in Cicero's opinion it was, for if men experienced no disposition to join in the mirth and enjoyment of the company, what had they to do there ? [2]

From the existence of these rules, however, an inference has been drawn unfavourable to the Greek character, as if, because some were merry, the nation generally must of necessity have been wine-bibbers.[3] But this is scarcely more logical than the reasoning of a writer, who, because the comic poets speak chiefly of the mirth and lighter enjoyments of the Athenians, very gravely concludes that they busied themselves about little else. The truth is, that like all ardent and energetic people, they threw their whole souls into the affair, whether serious or otherwise, in which they happened to be engaged ; and besides, while the careful and industrious applied themselves to business, there was always an abundance of light and trifling people to whom eating and drinking constituted a serious occupation.

[1] Athen. x. 44.   [2] Tuscul. Quæst. ii. 41.   [3] Potter, ii. 396.

CHAPTER VI.

ENTERTAINMENTS.

THE man upon the creations of whose art the principal enjoyments of Greek gourmands were based was the cook,[1] whose character and achievements ought not perhaps to be entirely passed over. We are, indeed, chiefly indebted for our information to the comic poets; but, in spite of some little exaggeration, the likeness they have bequeathed to us is probably upon the whole pretty exact.

The Athenian cook was a singularly heterogeneous being, something between the parasite and the professed jester; he was usually a poor citizen, with all the pride of autochthoneïty about him, who considered it indispensable to acquire, besides his culinary lore, a smattering of many other kinds of knowledge, not only for the purpose of improving his soups or ragouts, but in order, by the orations he pronounced in praise of himself, to dazzle and allure such persons as came to the agora in search of an artist of his class. Of course the principal source of his oratory lay among pots and frying-pans, and the wonders effected by his art. Philemon hits off with great felicity one of these worthies, who desires to convey a lofty opinion of himself,—

" How strong is my desire 'fore earth and heaven,
    To tell how daintily I cooked his dinner
    'Gainst his return! By all Athena's owls!

---

[1] On famous Cooks see Max. Tyr. Dissert. v. 60. 83. Pollux, vi. 70, seq. Athen. iii. 60.

'Tis no unpleasant thing to hit the mark
On all occasions. What a fish had I—
And ah! how nicely fried! Not all bedevilled
With cheese, or browned atop, but though well done,
Looking alive, in its rare beauty dressed.
With skill so exquisite the fire I tempered,
It seemed a joke to say that it was cooked.
And then, just fancy now you see a hen
Gobbling a morsel much too big to swallow ;
With bill uplifted round and round she runs
Half choking; while the rest are at her heels
Clucking for shares. Just so 'twas with my soldiers;
The first who touched the dish upstarted he
Whirling round in a circle like the hen,
Eating and running ; but his jolly comrades,
Each a fish worshiper, soon joined the dance,
Laughing and shouting, snatching some a bit,
Some missing, till like smoke the whole had vanished.
Yet were they merely mud-fed river dabs :
But had some splendid scaros graced my pan,
Or Attic glaucisk, or, O saviour Zeus !
Kapros from Argos, or the conger eel,
Which old Poseidon exports to Olympos,
To be the food of gods, why then my guests
Had rivalled those above. I have, in fact,
The power to lavish immortality
On whom I please, or, by my potent art,
To raise the dead, if they but snuff my dishes ! "[1]

This honest fellow, in the opinion of Athenæus, exceeded in boasting even that Menecrates of Syracuse, who for his pride obtained the surname of Zeus ; he was a physician, and used vauntingly to call himself the arbiter of life to mankind. He is supposed to have possessed some specific against epilepsy ; but being afflicted with a vanity at least equal to his skill, he would undertake no one's cure unless he first entered into an agreement to follow him round the country ever after as his slave, which great numbers actually did. Nicostratos, of Argos, one of the persons so restored, travelled in his train habited and equipped like Heracles ; others personated Asclepios, and Apollo, while Menecrates himself enacted in this fantastic

----

[1] Athen. vii. 32.

masquerade the part of Zeus; and, as the actors
say, he dressed the character well, wearing a purple
robe, a golden crown upon his head, sandals of the
most magnificent description, and bearing a sceptre
in his hand.[1]

But whatever might have been the conceit of
our Syracusan physician, there were those among
the cooking race, who certainly lagged not far behind him. They usually stunned such as came to
hire them with reciting their own praises, laying
claim to as much science and philosophy as would
have sufficed to set up two or three sophists. In
fact, to take them at their word, there was nothing which they did not know, nothing which they
could not do. Painting they professed to comprehend as profound connoisseurs, and, no doubt, the
soles they fried tasted all the better for the accomplishment. In astronomy, medicine, and geometry,
they appear to have made a still greater profi-
ciency than Hudibras, notwithstanding that—

> " In mathematics he was greater
> Than Tycho Brahe, or Erra Pater ;
> For he by geometric scale
> Could take the size of pots of ale ;
> Discern by sines and tangents strait
> If bread and butter wanted weight ;
> And wisely tell what hour o' the day
> The clock does strike by algebra."

In all this he was a fool to the Athenian cooks;
for, by the help of astronomy, they could tell when
mackerel was in season, and at what time of the
year a haddock is better than a salmon. From
geometry they borrowed the art of laying out a
kitchen to the best advantage, and how to hang
up the gridiron in one place, and the porridge-pot
in another. To medicine it is easy to see how
deeply they must have been indebted, since it not
only taught them what meats are wholesome, and

[1] Athen. vii. 33.

what not, but also enabled them by some sleight of
art to diminish the appetite of those voracious parasites, who when they dined out appeared to have
stomachs equal in capacity to the great tun of
Heidelberg.[1]

Many individuals, half guests, half parasites, used
to extract considerable matter for merriment out
of the dinner materials, that they might render
themselves agreeable, and be invited again. Thus
Charmos, the Syracusan, used to convert every dish
served at table into an occasion for reciting poetical quotations or old proverbs, and sometimes, perhaps, suffered the fish to cool while he was displaying his erudition. He had always civil things to
say both to shell-fish and tripe, so that a person
fond of flattery might have coveted to be roasted,
in order that his shade might be soothed with this
kind of incense, which even Socrates allowed was
not an illiberal enjoyment. It was, however, a
common custom among parasites to make extracts
from the poets and carry them in portfolios to the
tables of their patrons, where they recited all such
as appeared to be *à propos*. In this way the above
Charmos obtained among the people of Messina the
reputation of a learned man, and Calliphanes,[2] son
of Parabrycon,[3] succeeded no less ingeniously by
copying out the first verses of various poems, and
reciting them, so that it might be supposed he
knew the whole.

Cleanthes, of Tarentum, always spoke at table
in verse, so likewise did the Sicilian Pamphilos ;
and these parasites, travelling about with wallets
of poetry on their backs, were everywhere welcomed and entertained, which might with great

[1] Athen. vii. 37.
[2] Suidas in v. t. i. p. 1361. c.
[3] Athen. i. 6. "Sic ut παρά-
" σιτος, et παραμασήτης vel παρα-
" μασύντης convivam denotat in-
" vocatum, qui absque symbola

" ad convivium venit ; sic nomen
" παραβρύκων (à verbo βρύκω,
" mordeo, rodo, deglutio) eum-
" dem habet significatum." —
Scheigh. Animadv. t. vi. p. 54.

propriety have been adduced by Ilgen [1] among
his other proofs of the imaginative character of the
Greeks.

Archestratos, the Syracusan, belonged no doubt to
this class. He composed an epic poem on good eating,
which commenced with recommending that no company, assembled for convivial enjoyment, should ever
exceed four,[2] or at most five, otherwise he said
they would rather resemble a troop of banditti than
gentlemen. It had probably escaped him, that there
were twenty-eight guests at Plato's banquet. Antiphanes, after observing that the parasites had lynx's
eyes to discover a good dinner though never invited,
immediately adds, that the republic ought to get up
an entertainment for them, upon the same principle
that during the games an ox [3] was slaughtered some
distance from the course at Olympia, to feast the
flies, and prevent them from devouring the spectators.

Besides Archestratos, there were several other celebrated gastronomers among the ancients. Of these
the principal were Timachidas, of Rhodes, who wrote
a poem in eleven books on good eating,[4] Noume-
nios, of Heraclea, pupil to the physician Dieuches,
Metreas, of Pitana, the parodist Hegemon, of Thasos,
surnamed the *Lentil*, by some reckoned among the
poets of the old comedy, Philoxenos, of Leucadia,
and a second Philoxenos, of Cythera, who composed
his work in hexameter verse. The former, after
chaunting the eulogium of the kettle, comes nevertheless to the conclusion at last, that superior merit
belongs to the fryingpan. He earnestly recommended
truffles to lovers, but would not have them touch the

[1] De Scol. Poes. p. 8.
[2] Athen. i. 7.
[3] Athen. i. 7. This ox was
sacrificed to Zeus the Fly-Chaser,
in order to prevail on him to drive
the swarms of insects, by which
the spectators were incommoded,

beyond the Alpheios. Cf. Plin.
Nat. Hist. x. 40. ix. 34. Pausan. v. 14. i. viii. 26. 7. Ælian. De Nat. Animal. v. 17. xi.
8.

[4] Athen. i. 8. Suidas. v. Τιμα-
χίδας. t. i. p. 899, seq.

barbel. His anger burst forth with great vehemence against those who cut in pieces fish which should be served up whole; and, though he admits that a polypus may occasionally be boiled, it was much better, he says, to fry it. From this man the Philoxenian cakes derived their name; and he it is whom Chrysippos reproaches with half scalding his fingers in the warm bath and gargling his throat with hot water, in order that he might be able to swallow kabobs hissing from the coals.[1] He likewise used, at the houses of his friends, to bribe the cooks to bring up everything fiery hot, that he might help himself before any one else could touch them. A kindred gourmand, in the poet Krobylos, exclaims: " My fingers are insensible to fire like the Dactyls " of Mount Ida. And ah! how delightful it is to "refresh my throat with the crackling flakes of " broiled fish! Oh I am in fact an oven, not a " man! "

According to Clearchos it was this same Philoxenos, who used to maraud about rich men's houses, followed by a number of slaves laden with wine, vinegar, oil, and other seasonings. Wherever he smelled the best dinner he dropped in unasked, and slipping slily among the cooks, obtained their permission to season the dishes they were preparing, after which he took his place among the guests where he fed like a Cyclops. Arriving once at Ephesos, by sea, he found, upon inquiry in the market, that all the best fish had been secured for a wedding feast. Forthwith he bathed, and repairing to the house of the bridegroom, demanded permission to sing the Epithalamium. Every one was delighted; they could do no less than invite him to dinner. And " Will you come again to-morrow? " inquired the generous host. " If there be no fish in the market," replied Philoxenos. It was this gourmand who wished nature had bestowed on man the neck of the

---

[1] Athen. i. 9.

crane that the pleasure of swallowing might be prolonged.[1]

Pithyllos, another parasite, surnamed "the Dainty," not content with the membrane which nature has spread over the tongue, superinduced artificially a sort of mucous covering, which retained for a considerable time the flavour of what he ate.[2] To prolong his luxurious enjoyment as much as possible, he afterwards scraped away this curious coating with a fish. Of all ancient gourmands he alone is said to have made use of artificial finger-points, that he might be enabled to seize upon the hottest morsels. An anecdote so good as to have given rise to many modern imitations, is related of Philoxenos, of Cythera. Dining one day with Dionysios, of Syracuse, he observed a large barbel served up to the prince, while a very diminutive one was placed before him. Upon this, taking up the little fish, he held it to his ear and appeared to be listening attentively. Dionysios, expecting some humorous extravagance, made a point of inquiring the meaning of this movement, and Philoxenos replied, that happening just then to think of his Galatea,[3] he was questioning the barbel respecting her. But as it makes no answer, said he, I imagine they have taken him too young and that he does not understand me. I am persuaded, however, that the old fellow they have placed before your majesty must know all about it. The king, amused by his ingenuity, immediately sent him the larger fish which he soon questioned effectually.[4]

But the Athenians were not reduced to depend for amusement at table upon the invention of these

---

[1] Suid. in v. Φιλοξ. t. ii. p. 1058. c. Athen. i. 10.

[2] Athen. i. 10. Suid. v. Πιθυλλ. t. ii. p. 526. c.

[3] Making allusion perhaps to his love for Galatea, the mistress

of Dionysios. Athen. i. 11. Ælian. Var. Hist. xii. 44. Schol. Aristoph. Plut. 290.

[4] Athen. i. 11. See another anecdote of this gourmand in Ælian. Var. Hist. x. 9.

humble companions. They knew how, when occasion required, to entertain themselves, and, in the
exuberance of their hilarity, descended for this purpose to contrivances almost infantine. They posed
each other with charades, enigmas, conundrums, and,
sometimes, in the lower classes of society, related
stories of witches, lamias, mormos, and other hobgoblins believed in by the vulgar of all nations.
Among persons engaged in public affairs the ex-
citement of political discussion was often, of course,
intermingled with their more quiet pleasures.[1] But
with this we have, just now, nothing to do, nor
with the enigmas which we shall describe anon.
There was another and more elegant practice observed by the Greeks at convivial meetings, which,
though not peculiar to them, has nowhere else, perhaps, prevailed to the same extent,—I mean the introduction of music and the singing of songs,[2] light,
graceful, and instinct with wit and gaiety, to the
barbitos or the lyre.

Among the Greeks, generally, the love of music
and poetry seemed to be a spontaneous impulse of
nature. Almost every act of life was accompanied
by a song,—the weaver at his loom, the baker at
his kneading-trough, the reaper, the " spinners and the
knitters in the sun," the drawer of water, even the
hard-working wight who toiled at the mill, had his
peculiar song, by the chaunting of which he lightened
his labour. The mariner, too, like the Venetian
gondolier, sang at the oar, and the shepherd and
the herdsman, the day-labourer and the swineherd,
the vintager and the husbandman, the attendant
in the baths, and the nurse beside the cradle. It
might, in fact, be said, that from an Hellenic village music arose as from a brake in spring. Their
sensibilities were tremblingly alive to pleasure.
There was elasticity, there was balm in their atmo-

---

[1] Aristoph. Aves. 1189, sqq.   [2] Sch. Aristoph. Eq. 403.

sphere, and joy and freedom in their souls.—How could they do other than sing?

But, if music and poetry thus diffused their delights over the industry of the laborious, it was quite natural that where men met solely for enjoyment, these best handmaids of enjoyment should not be absent. Accordingly, we find that while the goblet circulated, kindling the imagination, and unbending the mind, the lyre was brought in and a song called for. Nor was the custom of recent date. It prevailed equally in the heroic ages, and, like many other features of Greek manners, derived its origin from religion. For, in early times, men rarely met at a numerous banquet, except on occasion of some sacrifice, when hymns in honour of the gods constituted an important part of the ceremonies. Thus Homer, describing the grand expiatory rites by which the Achæan host sought to avert the wrath of Apollo, observes, that they made great feasts, and celebrated the praises of the god amid their flowing goblets.[1]

Yet, though the theme of those primitive songs may have been at first serious, it was, probably, not long before topics better adapted to festive meetings obtained the preference. At all events, they soon came to be in fashion. The first step appears to have been from the gods to the heroes, whose achievements, being sometimes tinged with the ludicrous, opened the door to much gay and lively description. And these convivial pleasures,' so highly valued on earth, were, with great consistency, transferred to Olympos, where the immortals themselves were thought to heighten their enjoyments by songs and merriment.

In the ages following, the art of enhancing thus the delights of social intercourse, so far from falling into

[1] Iliad. α. 492, sqq. Ilgen, Disq. de Scol. Poes. p. 55.　　[2] Conf. Odyss. θ. 72, sqq. α. 154. 350.

neglect, grew to be more than ever cultivated. Even the greatest men, beginning from the Homeric Achilles, disdained not to sing. They did not, says a judicious and learned writer, consider it sufficient to perform deeds worthy of immortality, or to be the theme of poets and musicians, or so far to cultivate their minds as to be able to relish and appreciate the songs of others, but included music within the circle of their own studies, as an accomplishment without which no man could pretend to be liberally educated. For this reason it was objected by Stesimbrotos, as a reproach to Cimon, that he was ignorant of music, and every other gentlemanly accomplishment held in estimation among the Greeks;[1] and even Themistocles himself incurred the charge of rusticity, because, when challenged at a party, he refused to play on the cithara.[2]

A different theory of manners prevailed among the Romans, who, like the modern Turks, considered it unbecoming a gentleman to sing. But to the Greeks, a people replete with gaiety and ardour, and whose amusements always partook largely of poetry, music presented itself under a wholly different aspect, and was so far from appearing a mean or sordid study, that no branch of education was held in higher honour, or esteemed more efficacious in promoting tranquillity of mind, or polish and refinement of manners. The lyre is accordingly said, by Homer, to be a divine gift, designed to be the companion and friend of feasts, where it proved the source of numerous advantages. In the first place, persons too much addicted to the bottle found in this instrument an ally against their own failing, for, whether playing or listening, a cessation from drinking was necessarily effected. Rudeness also and violence, and that unbridled audacity commonly inspired by wine, were checked by music, which, in their stead, inspired a pleasing exalt-

---

[1] Plut. Cim. § 4. Afterwards, however, we find Cimon represented as singing with great skill. § 9.

[2] Cicero, Tuscul. Quæst. i. 2. Cf. Ilgen. De Scol. Poes. p. 62.

ation of mind, and joy free from all admixture of passion.[1]

It has already been observed that the convivial song soon divested itself of its religious and sombre character; for, as parties are made up of persons differing extremely in taste and temperament, it necessarily happened that when each was required to sing, much variety would be found in the lays, which generally assumed a festive and jocund air. Hymns in honour of the gods were more sparingly introduced,[2] nor was much stress laid on the praises of heroes;[3] the spirit of joviality moulded itself into

> Quips and cranks, and wanton wiles ;
> Nods and becks, and wreathed smiles.

Every one poured forth what the whim of the moment inspired, — jokes, love-songs, or biting satires, with the freedom and fertility of an improvisatore.[4]

These convivial songs were divided by the ancients into several kinds, with reference sometimes to their nature, sometimes to the manner in which they were chaunted : the most remarkable they denominated Scolia, or zig-zag songs,[5] for a reason somewhat difficult of explanation. Several of the later Greek writers appear to have been greatly at a loss to account for the appellation, which is, no doubt, a singular one; but the learning and diligence of Ilgen[6] may be said to have fully resolved this curious question. After determining the antiquity of the Scolion, which Pindar[7] supposes to have been an invention of Ter-

[1] Athen. xiv. 24. Ilgen, Disq. De Scol. Poes. p. 64.

[2] The hymn, for example, in honour of Pallas was, in all ages, sung. Sch. Aristoph. Nub. 954.

[3] Of Harmodios, for example, and Aristogeiton. Sch. Aristoph. Acharn. 942. See Ilgen, Disq. de Scol. Poes. p. 69.

[4] Conf. Hom. Hymn. in Herm. 52, sqq. Pind. Olymp. i. 24.

[5] Poll. vi. 108, with the notes of Seber and Jungermann, t. v. p. 142.

[6] Who has published a collection of these songs, accompanied by very interesting and instructive notes. Σκολία· hoc est, Carmina Convivalia Græcorum. Jenæ, 1798.

[7] Apud Plut. de Musica, § 28.

pander, or, at least, the verses of the song, but which
Ilgen dates as far back as the heroic period, he observes, that the name itself was known in very remote
ages, since they formed a separate class among the
works of Pindar, and are mentioned by Aristophanes
and Plato,[1] and that, like the Cyclic chorus, it arose
out of the circumstances under which it was sung.
For as this chorus was called Cyclic, or circular, because chaunted by persons moving in a circle round
the altar of Bacchos, so the Scolion, or zig-zag song,[2]
received its name from the myrtle branch, or the
cithara, to which it was sung, being passed from one
guest to another in a zig-zag[3] fashion, just as those
who possessed the requisite skill happened to sit at table.

To render this explanation perfectly intelligible,
it will, perhaps, be necessary to describe succinctly
the whole process of singing in company. At first,
it has been conjectured, when manners were rude,
and the language still in its infancy, singing, like
dancing, required no great art, and was little more
than those wild bursts of melody still common among
the improvisatori of Arabia and other Eastern countries, but that from these humble beginnings lyrical
poetry took its rise, preserving still the freedom of
its original state, and rising, unshackled by the rigid
laws of metre, to heights of sublimity and grandeur
beyond which no human composition ever soared.
By degrees some complex forms of verse obtained
the preference,—such, for example, as those of Sappho
and Alcæos, — and fixed and definite laws of metre
were established.

[1] Pind. Fragm. Dissen. t. i. p.
234, with the Commentary, t. ii.
p. 639, sqq. Aristoph. Vesp. 1222,
1240. Acharn. 532. Pac. 1302.
Plat. Gorg. t. iii. p. 13. Bekk.

[2] Suidas, v. σκολίον, t. ii. p.
759, e. sqq. Etym. Mag. 718,
35, sqq. Eustath. ad Odyss. η.
276, 49.

[3] Mr. Müller, however, disap-

proves of this etymology. " It
" is much more likely," he says,
" that in the melody to which
" the scolia were sung, certain
" liberties and irregularities were
" permitted, by which the ex-
" tempore execution of the song
" was facilitated." — History of
Greek Literature, pt. i. chap. xiii.
§ 16, seq.

The Scolion, however, always preserved something of its original spontaneous character, at least in appearance, and the same thing may be predicated of all their festive lays. But before they gave loose to their gaiety, the deep religious sentiment which pervaded the whole nation required a pæan, or hymn, to be sung in honour of the gods, and in this every person present joined.[1] While thus engaged, each guest, it is supposed, held in his hand a branch of laurel, the tree sacred to Apollo.[2] To the pæan succeeded another air, which all present sang in their turn, holding this time a branch of myrtle,[3] which, like the laurel bough mentioned above, was called æsakos, or the " branch of song."[4] The singing commenced with the principal guest, to whom the symposiarch or host delivered the Cithara[5] and æsakos, demanding a song, which, according to the laws of the table, no one could refuse. Having performed his part, the singer was, in turn, entitled to call upon his neighbour, beginning on the right hand, and delivering to him the Cithara and the myrtle branch. The second, when he had sung, handed it then to the third, the third to the fourth, and so on until the whole circle of the company had been made. It sometimes happened, though not often, that among the guests an individual, unskilled in instrumental music, was found, and, in this case, he sang without accompaniment, holding the æsakos in his hand.[6]

The poets who had the honour thus to cheer the convivial hours of the Greeks were, in remoter times, Simonides and Stesichoros, and, probably, Anacreon, with others of the same grade;[7] and, if we may credit Aristophanes, songs were also selected from the plays of Æschylus, Sophocles, and Euripides, as

[1] Plut. Symp. i. 1. Athen. xiv. 24.

[2] Hesych. v. ᾇσακος, ap. Ilgen. De Scol. Poes. p. 154.

[3] Sch. Aristoph. Nub. 1339, 1346.

[4] Potter, Antiq. ii. 403.

[5] Scol. Aristoph. Nub. 1337, seq.

[6] Ilgen, De Schol. Poes. p. 156.

[7] Aristoph. Nub. 1358. Conf. Schol. ad Vesp. 1222.

among ourselves from Shakespeare, Beaumont and Fletcher, or Ben Jonson. It may even be inferred that passages from Homer himself [1] were sung on these occasions; or, if not sung, they were certainly recited by rhapsodists introduced for the purpose into the assembly, who, holding a laurel branch while thus engaged, probably gave rise to the practice of passing round the myrtle bough. This branch, therefore, whether of myrtle or laurel, [2] constituted a part of a singer's apparatus. The latter was originally chosen as sacred to Apollo, the patron of music, and because it was also believed to be endowed with something of prophetic power, the Pythoness eating its leaves before she ascended the tripod, while it was the symbol of ever-during song. Instead of the laurel, myrtle was afterwards introduced, on account, probably, of its being sacred to Aphrodite, whose praises were celebrated in those amatory songs common at feasts. It may, likewise, have been considered an emblem of republican virtue, since Harmodios and Aristogeiton concealed their swords in a myrtle wreath. [3]

To proceed, however, with the Scolia. These lays, like the rest, made the circle of the company, though not by passing in an unbroken series from man to man, but, as has already been said, from one skilful singer to another. In fact, the chanting of the scolia was a kind of contest which took place when all the other songs were concluded. [4] The person who occupied the seat of honour chanted to the Cithara a song containing the praises of some mortal or immortal, or the developement of some moral precept or erotic subject, which was comprehended in a small number of verses. When he had finished, he handed the Cithara and myrtle, at his own discretion, to some other among the guests, and the

[1] Schol. Aristoph. Nub. 1367.
[2] Dresig. de Rhapsodis. p. 7. sqq. ap. Ilgen, De Scol. Poes. p. 157. Pind. Isthm. iv. 63.
[3] Ilgen, De Scol. Poes. p. 159.
[4] Athen. xv. 49.

person thus challenged, who could not refuse without passing for an illiterate clown, must at once take
up the same subject, and, without delay or premedi-
tation, break forth into a song in the same metre
and number of verses, if possible ; and if unfamiliar
with the Cithara, he could sing to the myrtle. The
second singer now exercised his privilege and called
upon a third, who was expected to do as he had
done; so that very often the same idea underwent
five or six transformations in the course of the evening. When the first argument had thus made the
circle of the company, he who concluded had the
right to start a new theme, which received the same
treatment as the first; so that sometimes, when people were in a singing humour, air followed air, until
eight or ten subjects had received all the poetical
ornaments which the invention of those present could
bestow upon them.

But to sing without wine would have been insipid. I have said the chanting of the scolia
was a sort of contest, and, as he who contends and
obtains the victory looks naturally for a reward, so
the successful performer aspired to his, which, it
must be owned, was not inappropriate, consisting
of a brimming bowl, called *odos*, or the "cup of
song," at once a mark of honour and a reward of
skill.[1] All these particulars are inferable from the
examples of the scolion, which still remain; and
Aristophanes in the "Wasps," presents something
like an outline, though dim and obscure, both of
the argument and the mode of execution. He imagines a company of jolly fellows,[2] such as Theoros,
Æschines, Phanos, Cleon, Acestor, and a foreigner
of the same kidney, and represents them as engaged in
performing certain scolia for their own entertainment.

But the idea we should form of this kind of song
from the very comic passage in the "Wasps" differs
materially from the theoretic view of Ilgen, since
Philocleon constantly interrupts his son, terminat-

---

[1] Athen. xi. 110.   [2] Vesp. 1220.

ing each sentence for him in a manner wholly unexpected, and of course calculated to excite laughter.

But though musical, the Greeks would not imitate the grasshoppers,[1] who are said to sing till they starve; but, having accomplished the circle abovementioned, proceeded to other amusements which, though too numerous to be described at length, must not be altogether passed over. In the heroic ages the discovery had not been made that rest after meals is necessary to digestion, which in later times was a received maxim, and accordingly we find from the practice of the Phæacians,[2] who, if an afterdinner nap had been customary, would certainly have taken it, that the men of those times, instead of indulging in indolent repose out of compliment to their stomachs, sallied forth to leap, to run, to wrestle, and engage in other athletic sports, which by no means appear to have impaired their health or their prowess. As civilisation advances, however, excuses are found for laying aside the habits of violent exercise. Science, in too many cases, fosters indolence and pronounces what is fashionable to be wise. But to the race-course and the wrestling-ring, sedentary, or at least indoor, pastimes succeed, and, instead of overthrowing their antagonists on the palæstra-floor or the greensward, men seek to subdue them at Kottabos, or on the chess-board, or to ruin them at the card-table or in the billiard-room.

The play of Kottabos,[3] invented in Sicily, soon propagated itself, as such inventions do, throughout the whole of Greece, and got into great vogue at Athens, where the lively temperament of the people inclined them to indulge immoderately in whatever was convivial and gay. The most usual form of the game was this,—a piece of wood like the upright of a balance having been fixed in the floor

---

[1] Plato Phædr. t. i. p. 65.

[2] Homer. Odyss. θ. 97, sqq. Eustath. p. 295, 43.

[3] Athen. xv. 2, sqq. xi. 22, 58, 75.—Suidas, v. κοταβίζειν. t. i. p. 1504, b. seq. Etym. Mag. 533. 13, sqq.

or upon a stable basis, a small cross-beam was placed on the top of it with a shallow vessel like the basin of a pair of scales, at either end.

Under each of these vessels stood a broad-mouthed vase, filled with water, with a gilt bronze statue, called Manes, fixed upright in its centre. The persons who played at the game, standing at some little distance, cast, in turn, their wine, from a drinking-cup into one of the pensile basins, which descending with the weight, struck against the head of the statue, which resounded with the blow. The victor was he who spilled least wine during the throw, and elicited most noise from the brazen head. It was, in fact, in its origin a species of divination, the object being to discover by the greater or less success obtained, the place occupied by the player in his mistress's affections. By an onomatopœa the sound created by the wine in its projection was called *latax*, and the wine itself *latagè*. Both the act of throwing and the cup used were called *ankula*, from the word which expresses the dexterous turn of the hand with which the skilful player cast his wine into the scales.[1]

Our learned Archbishop Potter, who has not unskilfully abridged the account of Athenæus, confounds the above with the *kottabos katactos*, another form of the game described both by Pollux and Athenæus.[2] In this the apparatus was suspended like a chandelier from the roof. It was formed of brass, and a brazen vessel, called the skiff, was placed beneath it. The player, standing at a little distance, with a long wand, struck one end of the kottabos, which descending came in contact with the skiff, or rather the manes within, and produced a hollow sound. Occasionally the small vessels at the extremity of the kottabos were brought down, as in the former game, by having wine cast into

---

[1] Potter, ii. 405, 406.   xv. 4.   Cf. Flor. Christian ad
[2] Pollux. vi. 109, sqq.   Athen.   Aristoph. Pac. 343.

them. Another variety required the skiff to be
filled with water, upon which floated a ball, an instrument like the tongue of a balance, a manes,
three myrtle boughs, and as many phials. In this
the great art consisted in striking some one of these
with the kottabos, and whoever could sink most of
them won the game. The prize, on these occasions,
was usually one of those cakes called *pyramos*[1] or
something similar; but instead of these it was sometimes agreed, when women were present, that the
prize should be a kiss, as in our game of forfeits.
Another kind of kottabos, chiefly practised on those
occasions which resembled our christenings, when on
the tenth day the child received its name, was a
contention of wakefulness, when the person who
longest resisted sleep, won the prize. Properly, however, kottabos was the amusement first described;
and so fashionable did it become, that persons erected circular rooms expressly for the purpose, in order
that the players might take their stand at equal
distances from the apparatus which stood in the
centre.[2]

It might, without any authority, be presumed that
when people met together for enjoyment they would
derive the greater portion of it from conversation,
which would, of course, vary and slide

" From grave to gay, from lively to severe,"

according to the character or fluctuating humour of
the company. The Spartans, like all military people,
were grievously addicted to jokes, which among them
supplied the place of that elegant badinage, alternating with profound or impassioned discourse, familiar
to the more intellectual Athenians. The latter, however, though free from the coarseness, possessed more
than the mirthfulness of the Dorians, and in the
midst of their habits of business and application to

[1] Pollux. vi. 101.   [2] Athen. xv. 7.

philosophy, knew better than any people how, amidst
wine and good-eating, to unbend and enjoy the luxury of careless trifling and an unwrinkled brow.
While some therefore retired to the kottabos-room,
which occupied the place of our billiard-room, others
still sat clustered round the table, extracting amusement from each other.   Among these of course would
be found all such as excelled in the art of small
talk, who could tell a good story or anecdote, scat-
ter around showers of witticisms, or give birth to a
pun.   Some, like the Spartans, had a Welsh passion
for genealogies, and loved to run back over the history of the "Landed Gentry" of old Hellas, to the
time of Deucalion or higher; others coined their wisdom and experience into fables, for which they exhibited an almost Oriental fondness; while the greater
number, like the princes in the Arabian Nights,
exercised their wits in propounding and resolving
difficult questions, enigmas, charades, anagrams, and
conundrums.

But the principal classes into which these contrivances were divided were two: *enigmas* and *griphoi*,[1]
the former comprehending all those terminating in
mere pleasure, the latter such questions and riddles
as involved within themselves the kernel of wisdom
or knowledge,[2] supposed to have been a dull and serious affair.   Casaubon,[3] however, vindicates it stoutly
from this charge, affirming that in the griphos the
utile was mingled with the *dulce* in due proportion;
so that it must, according to Horace's opinion, have
borne away the palm from most literary inventions.
In point of antiquity, too, the riddle may justly
boast; for, if to be old is to be noble, it has "more
of birth and better blood" even than the hungry
Dorians of the Peloponnesos, whom Mr. Mitchell

---

[1] Vid. Clem. Alexan. Protrep.
i. 1.   Diog. Laert. ii. 33.

[2] Pollux. vi. 107.

[3] Animadv. in Athen. x. 15.
Cf. Scaliger, Poet. iii. 84, where
the distinction made by Pollux is
explained.

prefers, on this account, before all nations of Ionic race. Like everything good also it comes from the East. The earliest mention of the riddle occurs in the book of Judges,[1] where Samson, during his marriage-feast at Timnath, perplexes his guests with the following riddle :

"Out of the eater came forth meat, and out of the strong came forth sweetness ; "

To which they, being instructed by his wife, replied :

"What is sweeter than honey ? and what is stronger than a lion ? "

The word griphos, in its original acceptation, signified a fishing-net, and hence by translation was employed to describe a captious or cunningly contrived question, in which the wits of people were entangled.[2] As the ancients delighted in this sort of intellectual trifling they were at the pains to be very methodical about it, dividing the riddle into several kinds, which Clearchos of Soli[3] made the subject of a separate work. This writer, a sort of Greek D'Israeli, defines the griphos to mean "a "sportive problem proposed for solution on condi- "tion, that the discovery of the sense should be "attended by a reward, and failure with punish- "ment." His description of the seven classes could scarcely be rendered intelligible, and certainly not interesting to the modern reader. It will be more to the purpose to introduce two or three specimens, prefacing them by a few remarks.

It has been above observed, that philosophical truths were often wrapped up in these sportive pro-

[1] Chap. xiv. vv. 14. 18. Chytræus, in his note on this passage, has several excellent and learned remarks on the subject. Vid. Seber. ad Poll. t. v. p. 141.

[2] Pollux. vi. 108.   Scalig. Poet. iii. 84.

[3] Schol. Aristoph. Vesp. 20. Athen. x. 69.

blems, which purposely obscured, so as to afford but dim and distant glimpses of the forms within, necessarily exercised and sharpened the wit and induced keen and persevering habits of investigation. The reward also and the penalty had the same tendency. A crown, an extra junket, and the applause of the company, cheered the successful Œdipos, while the lackwit who beat about the bush without catching the owl, had to make wry faces over a cup of brine or pickle. Theodectes, the sophist, a man distinguished for the excellence of his memory, obtained reputation as a riddle-solver, and denominated such questions the "springs of memory."[1] But whatever the interrogatories themselves may have been, the reward, to which their solution often led, was rather a source of forgetfulness, consisting of a goblet of wine which, when no interpreter could be found, passed to the propounder.[2]

The riddle was of course a mine of wealth to the comic poets, who could not be supposed to forego the use of so admirable a contrivance to raise expectation and beget surprise. But it is clear, from the examples still preserved, that they oftener missed than hit. Antiphanes's griphoi on "bringing and not bringing;" on the "porridge-pot;" on a "tart," &c., are poor things; but the following from the "Dream" of Alexis is good:

> A.   A thing exists which nor immortal is,
>   Nor mortal, but to both belongs, and lives
>   As neither god nor man does. Every day,
>   'Tis born anew and dies. No eye can see it,
>   And yet to all 'tis known.
> B.   A plague upon you!
>   You bore me with your riddles.
> A.   Still, all this
>   Is plain and easy.
> B.   What then can it be?
> A.   SLEEP—that puts all our cares and pains to flight.[3]

---

[1] Pollux. vi. 108.

[2] Etym. Mag. 341, 35, sqq.

Suidas. v. γρῖφος, t. i. p. 628, seq.

[3] Athen. x. 71.

The following from Eubulos is not amiss :

A.   What is it that, while young, is plump and heavy,
     But, being full grown, is light, and wingless mounts
     Upon the courier winds, and foils the sight ?
B.   The THISTLE'S BEARD ; for this at first sticks fast
     To the green seed, which, ripe and dry, falls off
     Upon the cradling breeze, or, upwards puffed
     By playful urchins, sails along the air.

Antiphanes, in his Sappho, introduces a very ingenious riddle, partly for the purpose of offering a
sarcastic explanation directed against the orators :

     There is a female which within her bosom
     Carries her young, that, mute, in fact, yet speak,
     And make their voice heard on the howling waves,
     Or wildest continent.   They will converse
     Even with the absent, and inform the deaf.[1]

The poet introduces the " Lesbian maid," explaining the riddle, and this passage of the Athenian
comic writer may be regarded as the original of
those fine lines in Ovid, which Pope has so elegantly translated :

     Heaven first taught LETTERS for some wretch's aid,
     Some banish'd lover, or some captive maid,
     They live, they speak, they breathe what love inspires,
     Warm from the soul, and faithful to its fires,
     The virgin's wish without her fears impart,
     Excuse the blush and pour out all the heart,
     Speed the soft intercourse from soul to soul,
     And waft a sigh from Indus to the pole.

By this time, however, the reader will probably
be of opinion, that we have lingered long enough
about the dinner-table and its attendant pastimes.
We shall therefore hasten the departure of the
guests, who after burning the tongues of the animals that had been sacrificed, to intimate that whatever had been uttered was to be kept secret, offered

                    [1] Athen. x. 73.

libations to Zeus, Hermes, and other gods, and took their leave, in ancient times before sunset; but afterwards, as luxury and extravagance increased, the morning sun often enabled them to dispense with link-boys. Examples, indeed, of similar perversions of the night occur in Homer and Virgil, but always among the reckless or effeminate in the palaces of princes, whence, in all ages, the stream of immorality has flowed downward upon society to disturb and pollute it. The company assembled at Agathon's, also, sit up all night in Plato; and Aristophanes represents drunken men reeling home through the agora by daylight.

CHAPTER VII.

THE THEATRE.

It is far from being my purpose to repeat the information which may be obtained from a hundred authors on the rise and progress of scenic representation in Greece. I shall, on the contrary, confine myself chiefly to those parts of the subject which others have either altogether neglected, or treated in a concise and unsatisfactory manner. It would, nevertheless, be beside my purpose to attempt the clearing up of all such difficulties as occur in the accounts transmitted to us of the Hellenic drama; and, in fact, notwithstanding the laborious investigations into which I have been compelled to enter, I feel that there are many points upon which I can throw no new light, and which appear likely for ever to baffle the ingenuity of architects and scholars.

Dionysos, being a deity connected with agriculture, his worship naturally took its rise, and for a long time prevailed chiefly, in the country. His festivals were celebrated with merriment; and, the power of mimicry being natural to man, the rustics, when congregated to set forth the praise of their tutelar god, easily glided into the enactment of a farcical show. And dramatic exhibitions at the outset were little superior to the feats of Punch, though, so great was their suitableness to the national character, that, in the course of time, every town of note had its own theatre, as it had of old its own dithyrambic bard;[1] and dramatic writers were

---

[1] Schol. Aristoph. Av. 1404.

multiplied incomparably beyond what they have been in any other country.

Both tragedy and comedy,[1] properly so called, took their rise in Attica, and there only, in the ancient world, flourished and grew up to perfection. The theatre, in fact, formed at length a part of the constitution, and, probably, the worst part, its tendency being to foster personal enmities, to stir the sources of malice, and, while pretending to purge off the dross of the passions by the channels of sorrow and mirth, to induce habits of idleness and political apathy, by affording in the brilliant recesses of a mock world a facile refuge from the toils and duties of the real one. Nevertheless, it may be curious to open up a view into that universe of shadows wherein the vast creations of Æschylus, of Sophocles, of Euripides, of Aristophanes, and Menander displayed themselves before the eyes of the Athenians, with a costly grandeur and magnificence never equalled save in imperial Rome.

It has been already remarked, that to the Dionysiac theatre of Athens the architectural speculations of Vitruvius on dramatic edifices apply, this building having constituted the model on which similar structures were afterwards erected.[2] By carefully studying its details, therefore, we shall be enabled to form a tolerably just conception of all the theatres once found in Greece, though each, perhaps, may have been slightly modified in plan, general arrange-

[1] See Bentley, Dissert. on Phal. i. 251.

[2] On the form and construction of ancient theatres, see Chandler, Travels, &c., who describes the ruins of the theatre of Teos. i. 110; of Ephesos, 138; of Miletos, (457 feet in length,) 168; of Myos, 191; of Stratonica, 222; of Nysa, built with a blue-veined marble, 245; of Laodicea, 262; of Ægina, ii. 16; of Athens, 113; of Eleusis, 215; on the theatre of Syracuse, see Antiq. of Athens, &c. Supplementary to Stuart, by Cockerel, Donaldson, &c. p. 38.—See a plan of the theatre in the grove of Asclepios at Epidauros, pl. 1. p. 53, and another of that of Dramysos, near Joannina, pl. 3.—(Compare on the Dionysiac Theatre, Leake, Topog. of Athens, p. 53, sqq.)

ment, and decorations, by the peculiarities of the site, and the science or taste of its architect.

The great theatre of Bacchos, partly scooped out of the rock on the face of the hill at the south-eastern angle of the Acropolis, stretched forth, on solid piers of masonry, a considerable distance into the plain, and was capable of containing upwards of thirty thousand people. The diameter, accordingly, if it did not exceed, could have fallen little short of five hundred feet.[1] For we are not to suppose that, while Sparta,[2] and Argos, and Megalopolis, cities comparatively insignificant, possessed theatres of such dimensions, Athens, incomparably the largest and most beautiful of Hellenic capitals, would have been content with one of inferior magnitude.[3]

To determine accurately the various parts of the theatre, and thus affix a distinct meaning to every term connected with it, has exercised the ingenuity of critics and architects for the last three hundred years, still leaving many difficulties to be overcome. I can scarcely hope in every case to succeed . where they have failed. But the following explanation may, perhaps, convey of its interior an idea sufficiently exact for all practical purposes.

Supposing ourselves to be standing at the foot of the Katatomè,[4] a smooth wall of rock, rising perpendicularly from the back of the theatre to the superimpending fortifications of the Acropolis, we

---

[1] Even a provincial theatre is compared by the rustic in Dion Chrysostom to a large hollow valley, i. 229 ; what then could the Abbé Dubos be thinking of when he wrote, " Il étoit impos-" sible que les altérations du " visage que le masque cache fu-" rent aperçûes distinctment des " spectateurs, dont plusieurs é-" toient éloignes de plus de douze " toises du comédien qui réci-" toit ! "—Reflex. Crit. i. 609.

[2] Scalig. Poet. i. 21.

[3] Colonel Leake, Topog. of Ath. p. 59. Cf. Wordsworth's Athens and Attica, p. 29. The conjecture of Hemsterhuis on the passage of Dicæarchos cannot be adopted. The words must apply to the theatre ; for he says the Parthenon charmed the spectators. But this could not apply to the Odeion, which was roofed.

[4] Poll. iv. 123.

behold on either hand, surmounted by porticoes, lofty piers of masonry projecting like horns down the rocky slope into the plain and united at their extremities by a wall of equal height, running in a straight line from one point of the horseshoe to the other. The space thus enclosed is divided into three principal parts, — the amphitheatre for the spectators, the orchestra,[1] filling all the space occupied by the modern pit, for the chorus, and the stage, properly so called, for the actors. Each of these parts was again subdivided. Looking down still from the Katatomè, we behold the benches of white marble, sweeping round the whole semicircle of the theatre, descend like steps to the level of the orchestra, and intersected at intervals by narrow straight passages converging towards a point below.[2] A number of the upper seats, cut off, by an open space extending round the whole semicircle, from the rest, was set apart for the women. Other divisions were appropriated to other classes of the population, as the tier of seats immediately overlooking the orchestra to the senators, or dicasts, another portion to the youth, another to foreigners and the guests of the state, while the remainder was occupied by the dense mass of citizens of all ages,[3] with crowns of flowers on their heads.

Above the level of the most elevated range of seats, and stretching round the whole sweep of the edifice,[4] arose a spacious portico,[5] designed to afford

[1] Tim. Lex. Platon. in v. ὀρχή- στρα. p. 104. Poll. iv. 123.

[2] Poll. iv. 123.—The Cunei, for greater convenience, had particular marks, numbers, or names to distinguish them: the podium of the diazoma of the theatre at Syracuse has an inscription cut on the fascia of the cornice to each cuneus. — Antiq. of Ath. &c. Supplem. to Stuart, &c., by Cockerel, Kinnaird, Donaldson, &c., p. 38.

[3] For the children, see Plat. de Rep. t. vi. p. 128. Athen. xi. 13. Cf. Aristid. t. i. p. 505. Jebb.

[4] Vitruv. v. 9. Donaldson, Theatre of the Greeks, p. 139.

[5] Among the Romans it was customary to carry along with them, as a defence against rain,

224 THE THEATRE.

shelter to the spectators during the continuance of a sudden shower. Another range of porticoes extended along the small lawn or grove within the limits of the theatre, at the back of the stage, so that there was little necessity for the Athenian people to take refuge, as some have imagined, from the weather in the public buildings, sacred or civil, in the vicinity.

It would appear from an expression in Pollux,[1] that the lower seats of the theatre, appropriated to persons of distinction, were covered with wood,[2] notwithstanding which, it was usual, in the later ages of the commonwealth, for rich persons to have cushions brought for them to the theatre by their domestics,[3] together with purple carpets for their feet. Theophrastus, accordingly, whom few striking traits of manners escaped, represents his flatterer snatching this theatrical cushion from the slave, and adjusting and obsequiously smoothing it for his patron.[4] To render their devotion to Dionysos still less irksome, it was customary to hand round cakes and wine during the representation, though, like Ho-

---

thick cloaks, rockets, or mandilions. Buleng. de Theat. i. 15. —The theatre of Regilla, built by Herodes Atticus in honour of his wife, was roofed with cedar.— Philost. Vit. Sophist. ii. 1. 5.— In later ages a velarium appears to have been extended over the great Dionysiac theatre, as was the custom at Rome.—Wordsworth, Athens and Attica, p. 90. Cf. Dion. Cass. xliii. p. 226. a. Hanov. 1606.

[1] Onomast. iv. 122.—To kick the seats with the heel was called πτερνοκοπεῖν, which they did when they wanted to drive away an actor, id. ibid. Cf. Diog. Laert. ii. 8. 4.

[2] On the old wooden theatre see Hesych. v. ἴκρια. Suid. v. ἴκρια,

t. i. p. 1234. d. Sch. Aristoph. Thesm. 395.—This theatre fell down whilst a play of Pratinas was acting.—Suid. v. Πρατίνας, t. ii. 585. d.

[3] Upon this practice Dr. Chandler has an ingenious conjecture. After attentively viewing the seats of several ancient theatres, and " considering their height, " width, and manner of arrange- " ment, I am inclined to believe " that the ancient Asiatics sate " at their plays and public spec- " tacles, like the modern, with " their legs crossed or gathered " under them, and, it is probable, " upon carpets." — Travels, &c. i. 269.

[4] Charact. c. ii. p. 10. Casaub.

mer's heroes, they were careful to fortify themselves
with a good meal before they ventured abroad. We
are informed, moreover, that when the actors were
bad there was a greater consumption of confectionary, the good people being determined to make
up in one kind of enjoyment what they lost in
another. Full cups, moreover, were habitually
drained on the entrance and exit of the chorus.[1]

The orchestra, being considerably below the level
of the stage, had in the middle of it a small square
platform, called the Thymele,[2] sometimes regarded
as a bema on which the leader of the chorus mounted
when engaged in dialogue with the actors ; sometimes
as an altar on which sacrifice was offered up to
Dionysos. That part of the orchestra which lay between the Thymele and the stage was denominated
the Dromos, while the name of Parodoi was bestowed on those two spacious side-passages,[3] the
one from the east, the other from the west, at the
extremities of the tiers of seats which afforded the
chorus ample room for marching in and out in rank
and file, in the quadrangular form it usually affected.

At the extremity of the orchestra a pier of masonry called the Hyposcenion, adorned with columns
and statues, rose to the level of the stage, where
a most intricate system of machinery and decoration represented all that was tangible to sense in
the creations of the poet. The stage was divided
into two parts ; first, the Ocribas or Logeion,[4]
floored with boards, and hollow beneath, for the
purpose of reverberating the voice ; second, the
Proscenion,[5] a broader parallelogram of solid stone-

[1] Philoch. Frag. Sieb. p. 85.
Aristot. Ethic. Nic. 5. Athen. xi.
13.

[2] Etym. Mag. 653. 7. Cf.
458. 30. 743. 30. et Suid. v.
σκηνὴ t. ii. p. 753, seq. Cf.
Thom. Magist. in v. θυμέλη, p.

458, seq. Blancard. Scalig. Poet.
i. 21. Poll. iv. 123.
[3] Sch. Aristoph. Acharn. 8. Cf.
Vesp. 270.
[4] Plat. Conviv. t. iv. 411. Tim.
Lex. v. ὀκρίβας, p. 102. Etym.
Mag. 620. 52. Poll. iv. 123.
[5] Poll. iv. 123.

work, necessary to support the vast apparatus of
machinery and decoration required by the character
of the Grecian drama. The descent from the stage[1]
into the orchestra was by two flights of steps situated at either extremity of the Logeion, at the
point where the Parodoi touched upon the Dromos.
Beyond the Proscenion arose the Scene,[2] properly
so called, the aspect of which was constantly varied,
to suit the requirements of each successive piece.
In most cases, however, it represented the front of
three different edifices, of which the central one,
communicating with the stage by a broad and lofty
portal, was generally a palace. Sometimes, as in
the Philoctetes, this portal was converted into the
mouth of a cavern,[3] opening upon the view, amid
the rocks and solitudes of Lemnos, while in other
plays it formed the entrance to the mansion of some
private person of distinction, but was always appropriated to the principal actor. The building on
the right assumed in comedy the appearance of an
inn, through the door of which the second actor
issued upon the stage, while the portal on the left
led into a ruined temple, or uninhabited house. In
tragedy the right hand entrance was appropriated
to strangers, while on the left was that of the female apartments, or of a prison.[4]

Upon the stage, in front of the doors, stood an
altar of Apollo Aguieus, and a table covered with
cakes and confectionary,[5] which appears sometimes
to have been regarded as the representative of that
ancient table, on which, in the simplicity of Pro-

---

[1] It is impossible to adopt Ge-
nelli's idea on these flights of
steps, by the injudicious position
of which in his plan, he entirely
breaks up and destroys the
beauty of the Hyposcenion, especially as the Scholiast on Aristophanes positively states, that
they led from the Parodoi to the
Logeion.—Sch.Aristoph. Eq.149.

[2] On the stage and scenery,
see Casalius.—De Trag. et Com.
c. i. ap. Gronov. Thesaur. t. viii.
p. 1603.

[3] Cf. Sch. Aristoph. Av. i.

[4] Vid. Scalig. de Art. Poet.
i. 21.

[5] Poll. iv. 123. Vid. Spanh.
ad Callim. t. ii. p. 228, seq.

thespian times, the solitary actor mounted when engaged in dialogue with the chorus.

When the stage was fitted up for the performance of comedy, there stood near the house a painted scene representing a large cattle-shed, with capacious double gates, for the admission of waggons and sumpter oxen, with herds and droves of asses, when returning from the field. In the Akestriæ of Antiphanes,[1] this rustic building was converted into a workshop. Beyond each of the side-doors on the right and left were two machines,[2] one on either hand, upon which the extremity of the periactoi abutted. The scene on the right represented rural landscapes, that on the left prospects in the environs of the city, particularly views of the harbour. On these periactoi,[3] were represented the marine deities riding on the waves, and generally all such objects as could not be introduced by machinery. By turning the periactoi on the right, the situation was changed, but when both were turned a wholly new landscape was placed before the eye. Of the parodoi, or side-passages, that on the right led from the fields, from the harbour, or from the city, as the necessities of the play required, while those arriving on foot from any other part entered by the opposite passage, and, traversing a portion of the orchestra, ascended the stage by the flights of steps before mentioned.

The machinery[4] by which the dumb economy of the play was developed consisted of numerous parts, highly complicated and curious. To avoid labour, and, perhaps, some tediousness, these might be passed over with such a remark as the above, but this would be to escape from difficulties not to diminish them. I shall descend to particulars.

First, and most remarkable, was that machine called an Eccyclema,[5] much used by the ancients when

---

[1] Scalig. reads Antipho. De Art. Poet. i. 21.

[2] Μηχαναὶ for μία. Cf. Annot. Poll. iv. 126.

[3] Poll. iv. 126, 130, seq.

[4] Vid. Buleng. De Theat. c. 21.

[5] Poll. iv. 127, seq.

scenes within-doors were to be brought to view. It consisted of a wooden structure, moved on wheels, and represented the interior of an apartment. In order to pass forth through the doors, it was formed less deep than broad, and rolled forth sideways, turning round afterwards, and concealing the front of the building from which it had issued. The channels in the floor, which were traversed by the wheels, doubtless concealed beneath the lofty basis, received the name of Eiscyclema.[1] Sometimes, as in the Agamemnon, it presented to view " the royal bathing " apartment with the silver laver, the corpse enve- " loped in the fatal garment, and Clytemnestra, be- " sprinkled with blood, and holding in her hand the " reeking weapon, still standing with haughty mien " over her murdered victim."[2] On other occasions a throne, a corpse, the interior of a tent, the summit of a building, were exhibited; and in the Clouds of Aristophanes the interior of Socrates' house was laid open to the spectators, containing a number of masks, gaunt and pale, the natural fruit of philosophy.[3] It should be remarked that the Eccyclema issued through any of the doors, as the piece required the cells of a prison, the halls of a palace, or the chambers of an inn, to be placed before the eyes of the audience.

That peculiar machine in which the gods made their appearance,[4] or such heroes as enjoyed the privilege of travelling through the air, — Bellerophon, for example, and Perseus, — stood near the left side-entrance, and, in height, exceeded the stone skreen at the back of the stage. This, in tragedy, was denominated Mechanè, and Kradè in comedy,[5] — in

[1] Poll. iv. 128.

[2] Müller, Dissert. on the Eumenid. p. 91.

[3] Sch. Aristoph. Nub. 185.

[4] Ξενοκλῆς ὁ Καρκίνου δοκεῖ μηχανὰς καὶ τερατείας εἰσάγειν ἐν τοῖς δράμασι. Πλάτων Σοφισταῖς· Ξενοκλῆς ὁ δωδεκαμήχανος ὁ Καρκίνου παῖς τοῦ Θα-λαττίου· μηχανοδίφας δὲ εἶπεν αὐτοὺς, ἐπειδὴ πολλάκις ὡς τραγῳδοὶ μηχανὰς προσέφερον, ἡνίκα Θεοὺς ἐμιμοῦντο ἀνερχομένους ἢ κατερχομένους ἐκ τοῦ οὐρανοῦ ἢ ἄλλο τι τοιοῦτον. Schol. Aristoph. Pac. 769.

[5] Poll. iv. 129. Etym. Mag. 465. 56. 534. 39.

this case resembling a fig-tree, which the Athenians called Kradè. The watch-tower, the battlements, and the turret, were constructed for the use of those watchmen, such as the old man in the Agamemnon, who looked out for signals, or indications of the coming foe. The Phructorion [1] was a pharos, or beacon-tower. Another portion of the stage was the Distegia, a building two stories high in palaces, from the top of which, in the Phœnissœ of Euripides,[2] Antigone beholds the army. It was roofed with tiles, (and thence called Keramos,) which they sometimes cast down upon the enemy. In comedy, libertines and old women, or ladies of equivocal character, were represented prying into the street for prey from such buildings.

The Keraunoskopeion [3] was a lofty triangular column, which appears to have been hollow, and furnished with narrow fissures, extending in right lines from top to bottom. Within seem to have been a number of lamps, on stationary bases, from which, as the periactos whirled round, sheets of mimic lightning flashed upon the stage from behind the scenes.

The construction of the Bronteion,[4] or thunder magazine, I imagine to have been nearly as follows: — a number of brazen plates, arranged one below another, like stairs, descended through a steep, vaulted passage behind the scene, into the bottom of a tower, terminating in a vast brazen caldron. From the edge of this, a series of metallic apertures,[5] probably spiral, pierced the tower wall, and opened without in funnels, like the mouths of trumpets.

When some deity was required to descend to earth in the midst of lightning and sudden thunder, the Keraunoskopeion was instantaneously put in motion, and showers of pebbles from the sea-shore were hurled

[1] Aristoph. Av. 1161, et Schol. Cf. Herod. ap. Const. in v. φρυκτώριον. Poll. iv. 127.

[2] Phæn. 688, cum not. et Schol. Bekk. Poll. iv. 127, 129.

[3] Poll. iv. 127. 130.

[4] Idem, Ibid.

[5] These were called ἠχεῖα. Schol. Aristoph. Nub. 292.

down the mouth of the Bronteion, and, rolling over the brazen receptacles, produced a terrific crash, which, with innumerable reverberations, was poured forth by the Echeia upon the theatre.[1]

In a lofty gallery called the Theologeion, extending over the marble skreen at the back of the stage, appeared the gods, when the drama required their presence; and hence, I imagine, the Hebrew colony which makes its appearance nightly near the roof of our own theatres have obtained the name of gods. Here Zeus, and the other deities of Olympos, were assembled in that very extraordinary drama of Æschylus, the Psychostasia, or weighing in the balance the souls of Achilles and Hector.

They employed in the theatre the machine called a Crane,[2] the point of which being lowered, snatched up whatever it was designed to bear aloft into the air. By means of this contrivance, Eos, goddess of the dawn, descended and bore away the body of Memnon, slain by Achilles before Troy. At other times strong cords, so disposed as to resemble swings, were let down from the roof, to support the gods or heroes who seemed to be borne through the air.

Though by turning the Periactoi three changes of scene could be produced, many more were sometimes required, and, when this was the case, new landscapes were dropped, like hangings, or slided in frames in front of those painted columns. These usually represented views of the sea, or mountain scenery, or the course of some river winding along through solitary vales, or other prospects of similar character, according to the spirit of the drama.

The position of the Hemicycle is more difficult to comprehend. It appears to have been a retreating semicircular scene, placed facing the orchestra, and masking the marble buildings at the back of the stage, when a view was to be opened up into some distant part of the city, or shipwrecked ma-

---

[1] Schol. Aristoph. Nub. 292, 294.   [2] Poll. iv. 130.

riners were to be exhibited buffeting with the waves. Not very dissimilar was the Stropheion,[1] which brought to view heroes translated to Olympos, or on the ocean, or in battle slain, where change of position with respect to the spectator was produced by the rotatory motion of the machine.

The position of the Charonian staircase,[2] by which spectres and apparitions ascended from the nether world, is exceedingly difficult to be determined; but that it was somewhere on the stage appears to me certain, notwithstanding the seeming testimony of Pollux to the contrary. The hypothesis which makes the ghosts issue from a door immediately beneath the seats of the spectators, and rush along the whole depth of the orchestra, among the chorus and musicians, is, at any rate, absurd. It must have been somewhere towards the back of the stage, near the altar of Loxios, the table of shewbread and those sacred and antique images which in certain dramas were there exhibited. Here, likewise, was the trap-door, through which river-gods issued from the earth, while the other trap-door, appropriated to the Furies, seems to have been situated in the boards of the Logeion, near one of the flights of steps leading down into the orchestra.

The above synopsis of the machinery and decorations employed by the Greeks in their theatrical shows may, possibly, from its imperfection, suggest the idea of a rude and clumsy apparatus. But, as the arts of poetry, sculpture, painting, and architecture reached in Greece the highest perfection, and, as this perfection was coëtaneous with the flourishing state of the drama, it is impossible to escape the conviction, that the art of scene-painting and the manufacturing of stage machinery, likewise, underwent all the improvements of which by their nature they are susceptible. For, in the first place, it is not easy to suppose, that a people, so fastidious

[1] Poll. iv. 131.   [2] Id. iv. 132.

as were the Athenians, would have tolerated in the
theatre displays of ignorance and want of skill which
everywhere else they are known to have over-
whelmed with contempt and derision ; more especially as, in the first place, the landscapes and objects
represented were usually those with which they
were most familiar, though the fancy of the poet
sometimes ventured to transport them to the most
elevated and inaccessible recesses of Mount Cauca-
sus, to the summit of the celestial Olympos, to the
palaces and harems of Persia, to the wilds of the
Tauric Chersonese,[1] or even to the dim and dreary
regions of the dead.   The names, nevertheless, of
few scene-painters, besides Agatharchos,[2] have come
down to us, though it is known, that, in their own
day, they sometimes divided with the poet the admiration of the audience, and, on other occasions,
enabled poets of inferior merit to bear away the
prize from their betters.

The character, however, of stage-scenery differed
very widely in tragedy, comedy, and satyric pieces,[3]
usually consisting, in the first, of façades of palaces,
with colonnades, architraves, cornices, niches, statues,
&c. ; in comedy, of the fronts or courts of ordinary
houses, with windows, balconies, porticoes, &c. ;
while, in the satyric drama, the fancy of the painter
and decorator was allowed to develope before the
audience scenes of rural beauty remote from cities,
as the hollows of mountains shaded with forests,
winding valleys, plains, rivers, caverns, and sacred
groves.

Of the Grecian actors,[4] whose business and profession next require to be noticed, too little by far
is known, considering the curious interest of the
subject. Their art, however, would appear to have
sprung from that of the rhapsodists, who chanted

---

[1] Cf. Æsch. Prom. 2.
[2] Vitruv. Præfat. lib. vii. Plut.
Alcib. § 16.

[3] Vitruv. v. 8.   Etym. Mag.
763. 27.
[4] Vid. Casal. c. 2.

in temples, during religious festivals, and afterwards
in the theatres, the heroic lays of Greece. To a
certain extent, indeed, the rhapsodist was himself
an actor. His art required him to enter deeply
into the spirit of the poetry he recited, to suit to
the passion brought into play the modulations and
inflexions of his voice, his tone, his looks, his gesture, so as vividly to paint to the imagination the
picture designed by the poet, and sway the whole
theatre by the powerful wand of sympathy through
all the gradations of sorrow, indignation, and joy.[1]
By some writers, accordingly, the rhapsodist is apparently confounded with the actor, that is, he is
considered an actor of epics,[2] though in reality his
imitations of character were partial and imperfect.

Actors formed at Athens part of a guild, or company, called the Dionysiac artificers,[3] among whom
were also comprehended rhapsodists, citharœdi, ci-
tharistæ, musicians, jugglers, and other individuals[4]
connected with the theatre. These persons, though
for the most part held in little estimation, were yet
somewhat more respectable than at Rome, where to
appear on the stage was infamous.[5] Like the rhapsodists, they generally led a wandering life, sometimes appearing at Athens,[6] sometimes at Corinth,

[1] Plat. Ion. t. ii. p. 183, seq.
Wolf. Proleg. p. 95. Cf. S. F.
Dresig. Comment. Lips. 1734.
Gillies, Hist. of Greece, vol. i. c. 6.

[2] Diod. Sic. xiv. 109. xv. 7.

[3] Philost. Vit. Soph. ii. 16.
Vit. Apoll. Tyan. v. 7. Vandale, Dissert. 380, seq.

[4] Casaub. ad Theoph. Char. p.
121. Athen. v. 49. Animadv.
t. viii. p. 196.

[5] Vandale. Dissert. v. p. 383.

[6] Plat. de Rep. viii. t. ii. p.
229, seq. Athen. xiii. 44. In
Roman times we find an actor
travelling from the capital to
Seville in Spain, where with

his lofty cothurni, strange dress,
and gaping mask, he frightened
the natives out of the theatre.
— Philost. Vit. Apoll. Tyan.
v. 9. Cf. Luc. de Saltat. § 27.
A taste for the amusements of
the Grecian stage was diffused
far and wide through the ancient
world, so that we find the princes
of Persia and Armenia not only
enjoying the representation of
Greek tragedies, but themselves,
likewise, in some instances, as-
piring to rival the dramatic poets
of Hellas. Thus Artavasdes, the
Armenian prince, is said to have
written tragedies, as well as his-

or Sicyon, or Epidauros, or Thebes, after the fashion
approved among the strollers of our own day. In
the course of these wanderings they now and then
fell in with rare adventures, as in the case of that
company of comedians which, on returning from
Messenia towards the Isthmus, was met by king
Cleomenes and the Spartan army near Megalopolis.[1]
To exhibit the superiority of his power and his contempt for the enemy, Cleomenes threw up, probably
with turf and boards, a temporary theatre, where
he and his army sat all day enjoying the jokes and
wild merriment of the stage, after which, he bestowed, as a prize, upon the principal performers, the
sum of forty minæ, or about one hundred and sixty
pounds sterling.

About this period, however, it was usual for the
armies of Greece, republican as well as royal, to be
followed by companies of strollers, jugglers, dancing
girls, and musicians.[2] Even in the army of Alexander, when proceeding on the Persian expedition,
the "flatterers of Dionysos"[3] were not forgotten ;
in fact, the son of Philip set a high value upon
the performances of these gentlemen, and with truly
royal munificence allowed them to enjoy their full
share of the plunder of the East. Thus, when Nico-
creon, king of Salamis, and Pasicrates, king of Soli,[4]
played the part of Choregi in Cyprus, in getting up
certain tragedies there performed for the amusement
of Alexander, and the actors, Thessalos, and Atheno-

tories and orations, some of which
still existed in the age of Plutarch. The Parthian court was
engaged in beholding the Bacchæ
of Euripides, in which Jason of
Tralles was the principal performer, when Sillaces brought in
the head of Marcus Crassus,
upon which both king and nobles
delivered themselves up to immoderate joy, and the actor, seizing upon the Roman's head, ex-

changed the part of Pentheus for
that of his mother, who appears
upon the stage bearing a bleeding
head upon her thyrsus; for this
he received a present of a talent
from the king.—Plut. Crass. §
33.   Polyæan. vii. 41. 1.

[1] Plut. Cleom. § 12.

[2] Plut. ubi supra.

[3] Διονυσοκόλακες.   Athen. vi.
56.

[4] Plut. Alex. § 29.

doros the Athenian, contended for the prize; he was piqued at the victory of the Athenian, and, though he commended the judges for bestowing the prize on him whom they regarded as the best performer, said, he would have given a part of his kingdom rather than have beheld Thessalos overcome by a rival.

Afterwards, when Athenodoros was fined by his countrymen for absenting himself from Athens during the Dionysiac festival, evidently contrary to the statutes in that case made and provided, Alexander paid the fine for his humble friend, though he refused to make application to the people for its remission.

An anecdote related of Lycon of Scarphe, also shows the high value set by the Macedonian prince upon the amusements of the stage, and the influence exercised over his mind by the Dionysiac artificers, though, according to Antiphanes, he wanted the taste to discriminate between a good play and a bad one. The Scarpheote being one day in want of money, as actors sometimes are, introduced into the piece he was performing a line of his own making, beseeching the conqueror to bestow on him ten talents; Alexander, amused by his extravagance, or captivated perhaps, by the flattery which accompanied it, at once granted his request, and thus upwards of two thousand four hundred pounds of the public money were expended for the momentary gratification of a prince.[1]

The philosophers, almost of necessity, thought and spoke of these wandering performers with extreme contempt. Plato observes, that they went about from city to city collecting together thoughtless crowds, and, by their beautiful, sonorous, and persuasive voices, converting republics into tyrannies and aristocracies. Aristotle endeavoured to account for their evil character and agency.[2] They

---

[1] Plut. Alex. § 29.

[2] Prob. xxx. 10. They were likewise corrupted by their profession, since, in female parts,

were worthless, he says, because of all men they profited least by the lessons of reason and philosophy, their whole lives being consumed by the study of their professional arts, or passed in intemperance and difficulties.

Nevertheless, even among them there were different grades, some aiming at the higher walks of tragedy and comedy ; while others were content to declaim rude, low songs, seated on waggons like mountebanks during the Lenæan festival.[1] Nor must this fashion be at all regarded as Prothespian, since it prevailed down to a very late period. And as in every thing the Greeks aimed at excellence and distinction, so even here we find that there was a contest between the poets who wrote the comic songs sung by these humble performers from their waggons.[2]

The various classes of actors known to the ancients were numerous. Among the lower grades were the Magodos, and the Lysiodos,[3] who though confounded by some, appear clearly to have been distinct ; the former personating both male and female characters ; the latter female characters only, though disguised in male costume. But the songs, and every other characteristic of their performances, were the same. The spirit of the coarse satirical farces they acted forbids my explaining their nature fully.

There were even several authors who attained a " bad eminence " in this department of literature, which especially affected the Ionic dialect, as Alexander, the Ætolian,[4] Pyretos of Miletos, a city noted for its dissolute characters, and Alexos, who obtained

they frequently indulged in immodest gestures, as is particularly related of Callipedes. Id. Poet. v. 2. Cf. Macrob. Saturnal. l. ii. c. 10.

[1] Occasionally, as among ourselves, jugglers were introduced upon the stage, swallowing swords and performing other fantastic tricks.—Plut. Lycurg. § 19.

[2] Schol. Aristoph. Eq. 545.

[3] Athen. iv. 80. v. 47. vi. 61. Cf. Eustath. ad Odyss. ψ. p. 106, sub fin.

[4] Suid. v. φλύακες, t. ii. p. 1073. b.

on this account an opprobrious sobriquet. The most remarkable, however, of this vicious brood would appear to have been Sotades [1] the Maronite, and his son Apollonios who wrote a work on his father's poems. Sotades was probably the original imitated by Pietro Aretino, who obtained in modern times a like reputation, though timely penitence may have snatched him from a similar end. The ancient libeller, enacting the part of Thersites, fastened with peculiar delight on the vices of princes, not from aversion to their manners, but because such scandal paved the way to notoriety. Thus at Alexandria, he covered Lysimachos with obloquy, which, when at the court of Lysimachos, he heaped upon Ptolemy Philadelphos. His punishment, however, exceeded the measure of his offences. Being overtaken in the island of Caunos by Patrocles, one of Ptolemy's generals, the obsequious mercenary caused him to be enclosed in a leaden box and cast into the sea. [2]

The Magodos, then, was a wandering farce actor, not unlike the tumbling mountebanks one sometimes sees in France and southern Europe. He travelled about with an apparatus of drums, cymbals, and female disguises, sometimes impersonating women, sometimes adulterers or the mean servants of vice; and the style of his dancing and performances corresponded with the low walk he selected, being wholly destitute of beauty or decorum. It seems necessary, therefore, to adopt the opinion of Aristoxenos, who considered the art of the Hilarodos as a serious imitation of tragedy; that of the Magodos as a comic parody, brought down to the level of the grossly vulgar. The latter art would appear to have derived its name from the charms, spells, or magical songs chanted by the mountebanks who likewise pretended to develope the secrets of pharmaceutics.

[1] Cf. Fabric. Bib. Græc. ii. p. 495, seq. [2] Athen. xiv. 13.

Superior in every way to the Magodos and Lysiodos was the Hilarodos,[1] who, though a wandering
singer like the Italians and Savoyards of modern
Europe, affected no little state, and was evidently
treated with some respect. His costume, in conformity with the popular taste, displayed considerable
magnificence, consisting of a golden crown, white
stole and costly sandals, though in earlier ages he
appeared in shoes. He was usually accompanied by
a youth or maiden who touched the lyre as he sung.
The style of his performances was decorous and manly. When a crown was given him in token of approbation by the audience, it was bestowed on the
Hilarodos himself, not on the musician.

A class of actors existed, also from very remote
times, among the Spartans. They were called Deikelistæ,[2] and their style of performing showed the
little value set upon the drama at Sparta. The
poetry of the piece, if poetry it could be called, was
extempore and of the rudest description, and the
characters were altogether conformable. Sometimes
the interest of the play turned upon a man robbing
an orchard, or on the broken Greek of an outlandish
physician, whom people respected for his gibberish.
This weakness, prevalent of course at Athens also,
is wittily satirised by Alexis in his Female Opium
Eater.

> " Now if a native
> Doctor prescribe, ' Give him a porringer
> Of ptisan in the morning,' we despise him.
> But in some *brogue* disguised 'tis admirable.
> Thus he who speaks of *Beet* is slighted, while
> We prick our ears if he but mention *Bate*,
> As if *Bate* knew some virtue not in *Beet*." [3]

---

[1] Cf. Athen. iv. 57. Salm.
Exercit. Plin. p. 76. Voss. In-
stitut. Poet. ii. 21. Rhinthon
was the inventor of the Hilaro-
tragœdi. i. e. Tragi-comedy.
Suid. v. 'Ρίνθων, t. ii. p. 685. b.
[2] Schol. Apoll. Rhod. i. 746.

Plut. Ages. 21. Athen. xiv. 15.
Etym. Mag. 260. 42.
[3] I have substituted this joke,
à la Smollett, " for the miserable
joke in the original." Beet, Atticé
σευτλίον, became τεύτλιον in the
Doric brogue. Athen. xiv. 15.

The Deikelistæ, however, were not confined to Laconia, but, under various names were known in most other parts of Greece. Thus, at Sicyon, they obtained the appellation of Phallophori, elsewhere they were called Autocabdali, or Improvisatori; while in Italy, (that is, among the Greek colonists,[1]) they were known by the name of Phlyakes.[2] By the common people they were called the wise men (σοφίσται), upon the same principle that actors in France are known by the name of *artistes.* The Thebans, renowned for the havoc they made in the language of Greece, denominated them the Voluntaries, alluding proleptically perhaps to the " voluntary principle." Semos, the Delian, draws an amusing picture of these Improvisatori. Those performers, he says, who are called Autocabdali made their appearance on the stage, crowned with ivy, and poured forth their verse extempore. The name of Iambi was afterwards bestowed, both on them and their poems. Another class who were called Ithyphalli,[3] wore those masks, which on the stage were appropriated to drunkards, with crowns of ivy and flowered gloves upon their hands. Their chitons were striped with white, and over these, bound by a girdle at the loins, they wore a Tarentine pelisse descending to the ankle. They entered upon the stage by the great door appropriated to royal personages, and, advancing in silence across the stage, turned towards the audience and exclaimed,—

> " Make way there, a wide space
> Yield to the god ;
> For Dionysos has a mind to walk
> Bolt upright through your midst."

---

[1] Among the mimics of this part of Italy, the most celebrated was Cleon, surnamed the Mimaulos, who dispensed with the use of a mask.—Athen. x. 78.

[2] Athen. xiv. 15. Cf. Suid. in φλύακες, t. ii. p. 1073. b.

[3] Vid. Harpocrat. in v. ἰθύφαλλοι. Mauss. p. 152.

The Phallophori made their appearance unmasked, shading their face with a drooping garland of wild thyme, intermingled with acanthus-leaves, and surmounted by an ample crown of ivy, with violets appearing between its glossy dark foliage. Their costume was the caunacè. Of these actors, some entered through the side-passages, others through the central door, advancing with measured tread, and saying,—

> " Bacchos, to thee our muse belongs,
>   Of simple chant, and varied lays ;
> Nor fit for virgin ears our songs,
>   Nor handed down from ancient days :
> Fresh flows the strain we pour to thee,
> Patron of joy and minstrelsy ! "

After which, skipping forward, they made a halt and showered their sarcasms indiscriminately on whomsoever they pleased, while the leader of the troop moved slowly about, his face bedaubed with soot.[1]

The superior classes of performers, whether actors or musicians, seem to have been held in much estimation, and to have been still more extravagantly .paid than in our own day. Thus Amœbæos, the Citharœdos, who lived near the Odeion at Athens, received, but at what period of the republic is not known, an Attic talent a day, as often as he played in public.[2] Music, however, was always in high estimation in Greece, where the greatest men, though they did not seek to rival regular professors in skill, yet learned to amuse their leisure with it. Thus the Homeric Achilles plays on the lyre, the sounds of which could not only cure diseases of the mind but of the body. A similar belief existed among the Israelites, as we learn from the example of Saul.

Though talent must have been always respected in an actor, it appears to me that anciently they

---

[1] Athen. xiv. 16.   [2] Athen. xiv. 17.

made comparatively little figure, while there were great poets to excite admiration. But, afterwards, when dramatic literature had sunk very low, the actor usurped the consideration due to the poet, as has long been the case in this country. They then contended for the prize in the tragic contests,[1] and began to entertain a high opinion of their own merits. In fact, the ignorant being better calculated to feel than to judge, the actors often obtained the first prizes in the games, and were held in higher estimation than the poets themselves.[2]

Thus persuaded of their own importance, they gradually exercised over the poor devils who composed plays for them, much the same tyranny as that in our own age complained of by the poetical servants of the theatre. That is, they despotically interfered with the framing of the plot, with the succession of the scenes, and procured episodes to be introduced, in order that they might show off their peculiar abilities. This is evident from a passage in Aristotle's Politics,[3] where he observes that the celebrated actor Theodoros would allow no inferior performer to appear before him on the stage, knowing the force of first impressions; from which it is evident that the author was compelled to yield to his caprice.

Antiquity has preserved the names of many celebrated actors, of whom several played a conspicuous though sometimes a dishonourable part in the great theatre of the world. Thus Aristodemos, who performed the first character alternately with Theodoros, became afterwards a traitor and betrayed the state to Philip. Such too was the case with Philocrates and Æschines, both actors,[4] and both rogues. Satyros, a comedian of the same period, appears to have been a man of high character and honour, who in consequence obtained the friendship of Demos-

---

[1] Aristot. Ethic. Nicom. iii. 4.   [3] Polit. vii. 17.
[2] Aristot. Rhet. iii. 1.   [4] Dem. de Fal. Leg. § 58.

thenes But the Garrick of that age seems to have
been Theocrines,[1] who by many, however, is supposed
to have afterwards degenerated into a sycophant.
Callipedes is chiefly known to us from the anecdote which describes the check his vanity received
from Agesilaos. Having acquired great reputation
as a tragic actor, he appears to have considered himself as equal at least to any king, and therefore,
meeting one day with Agesilaos, he ostentatiously
put himself forward, mingled with the courtiers and
took much pains to attract his notice. Finding all
these efforts useless, his pride was wounded, and
going up directly to the Spartan, he said,

" Dost thou not know me, king ? "

" Why," replied Agesilaos, " art thou not Callipedes, the stage-buffoon ? "[2]

The account transmitted to us of Æsopos is somewhat puzzling; he is described as one of the actors[3]
who performed in the tragedies of Æschylus, but is
said to have been at the same time a fellow of infinite merriment who turned everything into a jest,
a sort I suppose of comic Macbeth. Œagros obtained celebrity in the part of Niobe,[4] in the tragedy of Æschylus or Sophocles; and Aristophanes
enumerates among the pleasures of Dicasts the power,
should such an actor appear before them in a court
of justice, of requiring him by way of pleading his
own cause, to give them a few choice speeches of
his favourite tragic queen.

Among the most celebrated actors of antiquity was
Polos, a native of Ægina, who studied the art of
stage-declamation under Archias, known in his own
age by the infamous surname of Phugadotheras, or
the " Exile Hunter."[5] This miscreant it was, who,

[1] Dem. de Coron. § 97.
[2] Δεικηλίκτας. Plut. Ages.
§ 21. Apothegm. Lac. Ages. 57.
[3] Sch. Aristoph. Vesp. 566.
Flor. Christ. ad loc. In Plato's
time there were few or no actors
who excelled at the same time in
tragedy and comedy. Plat. de
Rep. t. vi. p. 123.
[4] Sch. Aristoph. Vesp. 579.
[5] Plut. Dem. § 28. Vit. x.
Orat. 8. Another actor obtained
the name of the Partridge. Athen.
iii. 82.

under the orders of Antipater, pursued Demosthenes
to the temple of Poseidon in Calauria, where, to escape the cruelty of the Macedonians, the orator put
a period to his own life.

Polos appears to have risen speedily to that eminence which he maintained to the last. A striking
anecdote is related of the means by which he worked
upon his own feelings, in order the more vehemently
to stir those of his audience. On one occasion,[1]
having to perform the part of Electra, he took along
with him to the theatre an urn containing the ashes
of a beloved son, whom he had recently lost, and thus,
instead of shedding, under the mask of the heroic
princess, feigned tears over the supposed remains of
Orestes, he sprinkled the urn which he bore upon
the stage with the dews of genuine and deep sorrow. He eclipsed in reputation all the actors of
his time, and was in tragedy what Theocrines, in
the preceding age, had been in comedy. His sa-
lary, accordingly, was very great, amounting at one
time to half a talent per day, out of which, to be
sure, he was required to pay the third actor.

He must have led, moreover, a life of much temperance, otherwise he would scarcely have been able
to accomplish what is related of him by Philochoros,
who says, that, at seventy years of age, a little before
his death, he performed the principal parts of eight
tragedies in four days. His devotion to his art did
not, however, carry him so far as that of the comic
poets, Philemon and Alexis, who breathed their last
upon the stage at the moment that the crown of
victory was placed upon their heads, and so were
literally dismissed for the last time from the scene
amidst the shouts and acclamations of the admiring
multitude.[2] But the passion of the Greeks for the
arts of imitation did not confine itself to the enacting of human character and human feelings. Every
species of mimicry found its patrons among them.

---

[1] Aulus Gellius, vii. 5.   [2] Plut. An. Seni. § 3.

There were, for example, persons who, by whistling, could imitate the notes of the nightingale; and Agesilaos, being once invited to witness the performances of one of these artists, replied somewhat contemptuously, " I have heard the nightingale herself."[1] Others, as Parmenion, could counterfeit to perfection the grunt of a pig,[2] though it is probable, that actors of smaller dimensions were called upon to perform in the comedy of Aristophanes, where the Megarean[3] brings on the stage his daughters in a sack, and disposes of them as porkers, having first carefully instructed them in the proper style of squeaking. Other actors obtained celebrity[4] through their power of imitating by their voice the grating or rumbling of wheels, the creaking of axletrees, the whistling of winds, the blasts of trumpets, the modulations of flutes, or pipes, or the sounds of other instruments. It was customary, too, among this class of performers, to mimic, doubtless, in pastoral scenes, the bleating of sheep, and the bark of the shepherd's dog, the neighing of horses, and the deep bellowing of bulls. They could imitate, moreover, but by what means is uncertain, the pattering of hail-storms, the dash and breaking of water in rivers or seas, with other natural phenomena. It was customary, likewise, as in modern times, to introduce boats and galleys rowed along the mimic waters of the stage, an example of which occurs on an Etruscan Chalcidone, where we behold a little vessel of extraordinary form, with a mariner at bow and stern, paddled along a bank adorned with flowers, while on a platform, occupying the

[1] Plut. Ages. § 21.

[2] Etym. Mag. 607. 25.

[3] Acharn. 834.

[4] Plut. de Aud. Poet. § 3. Plat. de Rep. t. vi. pp. 125 —127. This philosopher, it is clear, entertained a less elevated idea of art than some modern writers, who define it as follows : " Art is a representation ($\mu\acute{\iota}\mu\eta\text{-}\sigma\iota\varsigma$), i. e. an energy by means of which a subject becomes an object,"—(Müller, cited by Mr. Donaldson, Theatre of the Greeks, p. 4,) —in other words, by which a nominative becomes an accusative.

boat's waist, two naked dancers are exhibiting their saltatorial powers.[1]

Very singular figures were also introduced upon the stage, as wasps, frogs, and birds, of sufficiently large dimensions to be enacted by men; and still stranger personages occasionally made their appearance, as where, in a kind of practical parody of the story of Andromeda,[2] a whale emerges on the sea beach to snap off an old woman. In another drama the transformation of Argos was represented, after which this luckless male duenna strutted like a peacock before the audience. Io, moreover, was changed into a cow, and Euippe, in Euripides, into a mare. What there was peculiar in the appearance of Amymone it is not easy to conjecture; but she was, possibly, represented in the act of withdrawing the trident of Poseidon from the rock, from which gushed forth three fountains. The rivers, and mountains, and cities introduced[3] were, doubtless, personifications, such as we still find in many works of art. The giants were simply, in all probability, huge figures of men, made to stalk about the stage, like elephants, with an actor in each leg; and the Indians, Tritons, Gorgons, Centaurs, with other personages of terrible or fantastic aspect, owed their existence, perhaps, to masks, if we may so speak, representing the whole figures.

In what form the Seasons, the Pleiades,[4] or the nymphs of Mithakos, made their appearance on the stage, we are, I believe, nowhere told, though we possess some information respecting the costume and figure of those other strange persons of the drama, the Clouds,[5] which came floating in through the Parodoi, enveloped, some in masses of white fleecy gauze, like vapour, others in azure, or many-tinted robes,

[1] Mus. Cortonens. tab. 60.

[2] Schol. Aristoph. Nub. 548.

[3] See the figure of Alexandria in the Gemme Antiche Figurate of Agostini.

[4] Poll. iv. 142.

[5] Vid. Schol. Aristoph. Nub. 289. 343. 442.

or in drapery like piled-up flocks of wool, to represent the various aspects of the skies; while a hazy
atmosphere was probably diffused around them, as
around the other gods, by the smoke of styrax or
frankincense, burnt in profusion on the altars of the
theatre. Here and there, through these piles of
drapery, a mask with ruddy pendant nose, like the
tail of a lobster, peered forth, and a human voice
was heard chanting in richest cadence and modu-
lation the lively anapæsts of the chorus.

In the tragedy of Alcestis, the grim, spectral figure
of Death was beheld gliding to and fro through the
darkness, in front of the palace of Admetos, while
personifications still, if possible, more strange and
wild, made their appearance in other dramas,—as Justice, Madness, Frenzy, Strength, Violence, Deceit,
Drunkenness, Laziness, Envy.[1]

Plato, who entertained peculiar notions[2] respecting
the dignity of human nature, banished the theatre
from his Republic, because he thought it unbecoming
a brave man, who had political rights to watch over
and defend, to demean himself by low stage imper-
sonations; and, from his account of what he would
not have his citizens do, we learn what by others was
done. Sometimes, he observes, the actor was required to imitate a woman, (though this task often
devolved upon eunuchs,) whether young or old, revil-
ing her husband, railing at and expressing contempt
for the gods, either puffed up by the supposed stable-
ness of her felicity, or stung to desperation by the
severity of her misfortunes and sorrows. Other female
characters were to be represented, toiling, or in love,
or in the pangs of labour; which shows that there
was scarcely an act or passage in human life not
occasionally imitated on the stage.

Slaves of course performed an important part in
the mimic world of the theatre; and with these,
Plato, by some unaccountable association of ideas,

[1] Poll. iv. 141, seq.   [2] De Rep. t. vi. p. 125.

classes smiths, and madmen, and vagabonds, and low
artificers of every kind, and the rowers of galleys, and
rogues, and cowards, below which his imagination
could discover nothing in human nature.

But it was these very characters, with their low
wit, buffoonery, and appropriate actions, that constituted the most effective materials of the comic poet,
whose creed was, that

Les fous sont ici-bas pour nos menus plaisirs.

They accordingly hesitated at no degree of grotesque buffoonery and extravagance, introducing not
only low sausage-sellers with their trays of black-pud-
dings and chitterlings suspended on their paunches,[1]
and drunkards lisping, hiccuping, and reeling about
the stage,[2] but even libertines and profligates carrying on their intrigues in the view of the spectators.
An example of this kind of scene occurs on an
Etruscan bronze seal dug up near Cortona, which
represents an adulterer in conference with his mistress, together with the Leno who brought them
together.[3]

[1] Sch. Aristoph. Eq. 150.
[2] Athen. x. 33.

[3] Mus. Cortonens. tabb. 18, 19.
Cf. p. 26, seq. 1750. Rom.

CHAPTER VIII.

THEATRE *(continued)*.

INTO the various questions which have been raised respecting the origin and constitution of the chorus it is not my intention to enter. It undoubtedly appears, however, to have arisen amid the festivities of the vintage, when, after the grapes were brought home and pressed and the principal labours of the season concluded,[1] the rustics delivered themselves up to wild joy and merriment, chanting hymns and performing dances in honour of Dionysos, the protecting god of the vine. At first the number of the persons engaged in these dances could not have been fixed, since it is probable that all the vintagers, both male and female, joined in the sports, as they had previously joined in the labour. And this free and unformal character the Dithyrambic or Dionysiac chorus must have preserved, as long as it remained a mere village pastime. But when afterwards, advancing from one step to another, it assumed something of an artificial form and several chorusses arose which contended with each other for a prize, the performers must have undergone some kind of training,[2] both in singing and dancing, and then the number of the individuals constituting the chorus was possibly fixed. There appears to be some reason for thinking, that these exhibitions were more ancient than the congregation of the Athenians in one city, and that originally every tribe had its own

---

[1] Cf. Ficorini, Degli Masch. Scen. p. 15.

[2] On the importance afterwards attached to the training of the chorus, see the substance of an inscription in Chandler, ii. 72.

chorus,[1] since we find that afterwards, when all the inhabitants of Attica came to regard themselves as one people, the Choreutæ were chosen from every tribe five.

By what gradations, however, the village chorus was transformed into the Dithyrambic, the Dithyrambic into the Satyric, and the Satyric again into the Tragic, it now appears impossible to ascertain; but it seems to be quite clear,[2] that in many ancient tragedies the number of the chorus was fifty,[3] as, for example, in the "Judgment of the Arms," by Æschylus, in which silver-footed Thetis appeared upon the stage accompanied by a train of fifty Nereids.[4] Again, according to certain ancient authors,[5] in the Eumenides of Æschylus, the chorus of Furies at first amounted to fifty, which, rushing tumultuously, with frightful gestures and horrid masks,[6] into the orchestra, struck so great a terror into the people, particularly the women[7] and children, that their number was afterwards reduced by

[1] Sch. Aristoph. Av. 1404. Schneid. de Orig. Trag. Græc. c. i. p. 2. The Dithyrambic ode was said to have been invented by Arion at Corinth. Schol. Pind. Olymp. xiii. 25, seq. The first choral songs were improvisations. Max. Tyr. Dissert. xxi. p. 249.

[2] Poll. iv. 108. Sch. Aristoph. Acharn. 210.

[3] Cf. Schol. ad Æschin. Tim. Orator. Att. t. xii. p. 376. Tzetz. ad Lycoph. p. 251, sqq. See also Müller, Dissert. on the Eumenides of Æschylus, p. 54. Schol. Aristoph. Eq. 587.—" Nous savons " que sur les Théâtres Grecs les " femmes dansaient dans les " chœurs."—Winkel. Mon. Ined. iii. p. 86. I have found no proof in any ancient author that this was the practice among the Greeks.

[4] Sch. Aristoph. Acharn. 848.

[5] Vit. Æschyl. p. vi.

[6] Bœttiger, Furies, p. 2. Poll. iv. 110. Schol. Aristoph. Av. 298. Eq. 586.

[7] According to Mr. Bœttiger, however, ' chez les anciens Athe- " niens les femmes n'ont jamais " assisté aux représentations théa- " trales." — Furies, p. 3, note. But, in addition to the proofs of the contrary, accumulated in the preceding book, the reader may consult the testimony of Aristides, who severely blames his countrymen for allowing their wives and children to frequent the theatres, t. i. p. 518, cf. p. 507.—Jebb. He speaks, indeed, more particularly of the Smyrniotes; but Smyrna was an Ionian colony.—Herod. i. 149.

law. I am aware that several distinguished scholars think very differently on this subject; some maintaining, that the chorus of Furies always consisted of fifteen, while others reduce their number to three. But, though both these opinions have been supported with much learning and ingenuity, it seems difficult to admit either the one or the other. In the first place, since every thing connected with the stage was in a state of perpetual fluctuation, since the masks and costume were repeatedly altered, since the number of the actors was augmented, since almost every arrangement of the theatre, and every characteristic of the poetry, underwent numerous modifications; the chorus, also, it is probable, submitted to the same alterations or reforms till it settled in that tetragonal figure [1] and determinate number which it afterwards preserved, as long as the legitimate drama existed in Greece.

In one point of view the history of the chorus is extremely remarkable. At first, and for some time, it constituted in itself the whole of the spectacle exhibited at the Dionysiac festivals, where its songs and dances, accompanied by such rude music as the times afforded, satisfied the demands of the popular taste, and were consequently supposed to be everything that the god required. By degrees, as experience suggested improvements either in the music, in the manner of dancing, or in the materials and composition of the odes, the movements, singing, and appearance of the Chorus, assumed a more artificial form, which was necessarily carried forward many steps in the career of amelioration by the institution of rival bodies of Choreutæ, who, from the natural principle of emulation, endeavoured to excel each other. Next, a detached member of its own body, mounted on a table, enacted the part of a stranger or messenger come to announce something which it imported the servants of Dio-

[1] Cf. Schol. Aristoph. Acharn. 209.

nysos to know. This table was doubtless placed
directly in front of the altar of Bacchos, on the
steps of which the leader of the chorus was probably mounted in after ages, to hold communication with the stranger; and, as this altar ripened
through many gradations into the Thymele, so the
aforesaid table rose through innumerable changes
into the Logeion. It may be remarked, moreover,
that the slope of a hill,[1] when any such existed
near the village, would naturally be chosen on such
occasions to afford the peasants an opportunity of
standing behind each other on ascending levels, and
thus, without inconvenience, beholding the show;
and where such natural aid did not present itself,
they probably threw up embankments of turf in the
semicircular form, which experience proved to be
most convenient, and, out of this rude contrivance,
grew those vast and magnificent structures, which
afterwards constituted one of the noblest ornaments
of Greece.

The single actor, detached in the manner we have
said from the Chorus, speedily acquired greater importance, and the aid of poetry was called in to
frame and adorn his recitals; and as, during the
songs and dances of the Chorus, he necessarily remained idle, the idea soon suggested itself that a
second actor[2] would be an improvement, upon which
dialogue and the regular drama sprang into existence.

Among the principal duties of the Chorus was the
performance of certain dances, simple enough at the
outset, but, in process of time, refined and rendered
so intricate by art, that it required no little learning
and ability to execute all their varied movements
with dignity and grace. Somewhat to assist the eye
and memory, the whole pattern, as it were, of the
dance seems to have been chalked out on the floor

[1] Cf. Scalig. Poet, i. 21. Le-
roy, Ruines des plus beaux Mon-
umens de la Grèce, p. 14.

[2] Cf. Hesych. v. νέμησις ὑπο-
κριτῶν.

of the orchestra;[1] while the greatest possible pains were taken in drilling the Choreutæ to open, file off, and wheel through their labyrinthine evolutions, without confusion. The manner in which these persons usually entered the orchestra, that is to say, ranged in a square body, three in front and five deep, or five in front and three deep, has suggested to some the notion that they represented a military Lochos;[2] but besides that this is inconsistent with their Dionysiac origin, they did not always preserve this arrangement, but, on some occasions, came rushing in confusedly, while on others they traversed the Parodos in Indian file.

The musicians,[3] in the Greek theatre, took their station upon and about the steps of the Thymele, which answers as nearly as possible to the position of the orchestra in our own theatres. Here, also, stood the Rhabduchi,[4] or vergers of the theatre, whose business it was to see that order was preserved among the spectators.

With respect to the dances [5] performed by the Chorus, they were so numerous, long, and intricate, that it would be here impossible to enumerate and describe the whole. They appear to have conceived the idea of representing almost every passion and action in human life by that combination of movements and gestures which the term pantomime, borrowed from their own language, expresses much better than our word dancing.[6] A taste, in some re-

---

[1] This, however, I merely conjecture from the practice of marking with lines the station of the chorus. Hesych. v. γραμμαί.

[2] When making their exit, it is said they were preceded by a flute-player. Sch. Aristoph. Vesp. 582. These musicians wore, while playing, straps of leather called φορβείαι, bound over their mouth in order to regulate the quantity of air transmitted into the pipe.

Id. ibid. See Burney, Hist. of Music, i. 279.

[3] Cf. Torrent. in Suet. Domit. Com. p. 390. a. The best auletæ were those of Thebes. Dion Chrysost. i. 263.

[4] Suidas, v. ῥαβδοῦχοι, t. ii. p. 672. f. Scalig. Poet. i. 21.

[5] See Cahusac, Traité Historique de la Dance, ii. i. t. i. p. 61, sqq.

[6] It is said that certain ancient

spects similar, still prevails among the Orientals, whose Ghawazi and Bayadères, though relying rather upon routine and impulse than on the resources of art, perform at festivals and marriages, and before the ladies of the harem, little love-pieces and pastoral scenes, which evidently belong to the class of mimetic dances described by ancient authors.

In tragedy, such as it existed in the polished ages of Greece, the movements were slow and solemn, and, no doubt, full of dignity. The spirit of comedy required brisk and lively, and frequently tolerated, audaciously wanton dances; while the Chorus of the Satyric Drama would appear to have been rude and clownish rather than indecent, indulging in grotesque movements, ludicrous and extravagant gestures, and that rustic and farcical style of mimicry which may be supposed to have prevailed among the rough peasantry of Hellas.

In classing the various dances, it will, perhaps, be sufficient if we divide them into lively and serious,[1] joining with the latter all such as attempted to embody a symbol or an allegory.

In certain dramas of Phrynichos the Chorus represented a company of wrestlers,[2] who contrived by the quick, flexible, and varied movements of the dance, to imitate all the accidents of the palæstra. Sometimes they personated a party of scouts in the active look-out for the enemy, each with his right hand curved above the brow : this was one form of the Scops.[3] On other occasions the dancer mimicked the habits of the

poets were called orchestic, — as Thespis, Phrynichos, Pratinas, Carcinos,—not only because they adapted the subjects of their pieces to the dances of the chorusses, but, also, because they instructed in dancing the chorusses of other dramatic writers. Athen. i. 39. The above poet, Carcinos, was likewise celebrated for being the father of three sons who danced in the tragic chorusses, and, from their extremely diminutive stature, obtained the name of Quails. Schol. Aristoph. Pac. 761.

[1] Hesych. v. ἐμμέλεια. Sch. Aristoph. Nub. 532. Poll. iv. 99. Athen. xiv. 27, seq. Luc. de Saltat. § 22. 26. Plut. Symposiac. ix. 15. 1.

[2] Suid. v. Φρυνίχου πάλαισμα, t. ii. p. 1092. b. c. d.

[3] Poll. iv. 103. Athen. xiv. 27.

Scops, or mocking-owl, twirling about the head, and appearing to be absorbed in an ecstasy of imitation, until taken by the fowler. The performance of a piece like this, by a numerous Chorus, sometimes breaking off into a brisk gallopade, sometimes maintaining the same position, jigging, pirouetting, and ducking the crest, must, no doubt, have appeared infinitely comic; and yet it could have been nothing in comparison with the Morphasmos,[1] in which, not the characteristic peculiarities of a single owl, but those of the whole animal creation were "taken off." Thus we may suppose that the Hegemon of the Chorus started as a baboon, his next-door neighbour as a hog, a third as a lion, a fourth as an ass, and so on, each man accommodating his voice to the character he had, pro tempore, assumed, and gibbering, grunting, roaring, braying, as he leaped, or gamboled, or bounded, or scampered about the orchestra. Anon the frisky foresters were transformed into slaves, who would seem to have been introduced to the audience pounding something, perhaps onions and garlick, in a mortar.

The Oclasma,[2] a dance borrowed from the Persians, reminds one strongly of the performances of the negroes in the interior of Africa, the whole Chorus alternately crouching upon its heels, and springing aloft, like the frogs of Aristophanes about the fens of Acheron. Not, perhaps, un-akin to this, were those three frenzied dances, alluded to rather than described by the ancients, — that is to say, the Thermaustris,[3] which seems to have consisted of a series of violent bounds, like the performances of the Hurons and Iroquois;[4] the Mongas, which, from the name, probably represented the friskings and caracollings of a jackass; and the Kernophoros,[5] or dance of the first-fruits, wherein the Chorus appeared upon

---

[1] Poll. iv. 103. Cf. Xenoph. Conviv. vi. 4.

[2] Poll. vi. 99.

[3] Pfeiffer. Antiq. Græc. ii. 58. p. 382.

[4] Cf. Dodwell, Classical Tour in Greece, vol. i. p. 133, seq.

[5] Athen. xiv. 27. Poll. iv. 104.

the stage, some bearing censers, others fruit-baskets, evidently in a character resembling that of Bacchanals.

To this species of dance belonged, also, the Heca-terides, in which the performer interpreted his desires or passion by furious gestures of the hands. The Eclactisma was a female dance,[1] requiring the exer-tion of great force and agility, its characteristics consisting in flinging the heels backwards above the level of the shoulders. Corresponding, in some mea-sure, to the Eclactisma, was the Skistas,[2] in which the dancer bounded aloft, crossing his legs several times while in the air. There was a dance, evidently of a very extraordinary description, which they per-formed to an air called Thyrocopicon,[3] or "knocking at doors," possibly representing the frolics of such wild youths as anticipated the scape-graces of our own day. The Mothon was a loose dance, common among sailors ; the Baukismos, Bactriasmos, Apo-kinos, Aposeisis, and Sobas,[4] were laughable, but lewd dances,[5] resembling the Bolero and Fandango of the Spaniards.[6]

The Heducomos was a dance expressive of the outbreaks of joy, and the Knismos,[7] represented the pinching, struggling, and quarrels of lovers. The Deimalea was a Laconian dance performed by Sa-tyrs and Seileni, skipping and jumping about in a circle.[8] Another Spartan dance[9] was the Bryallika, of a ludicrous and licentious character, performed by women in grotesque masks, whence a courtezan at Sparta was denominated, Bryallika. The name of Hypogypones,[10] was bestowed on certain performers who imitated old men, flourishing their sticks about

[1] Poll. iv. 10. 2. Aristoph. Vesp. 1492. 1495, et Schol.

[2] Poll. iv. 105. See, in the Mus. Cortonens. tab. 60, the re-presentation of a group of dancers on a platform in a boat, on the margin of the sea.

[3] Athen. xiv. 9.

[4] Athen. xiv. 27.

[5] On the character of the old comedy, which tolerated these dances, see Plut. Lucull. § 39. Demet. § 12. Pericl. § 5.

[6] Poll. iv. 99.

[7] Id. ib.

[8] Poll. iv. 104.

[9] See Müller. ii. 354.

[10] Poll. iv. 104.

the stage, as we are informed they did in the play of Simermnos.[1] Akin in spirit to these were the Gypones,[2] who made their appearance in transparent Tarentine robes, and mounted on stilts probably in the form of goats' feet, to give them a resemblance to the Ægipanes, worshipped as gods of the woods. A peculiar dance in honour of Artemis took its rise in the village of Carya in Laconia, where its invention was attributed to Castor and Polydeukes. No description of it, so far as I know, has come down to us; but the maidens by whom it was performed probably bore, and steadied with one hand, a basket of flowers on their heads, thus forming the model of those architectural figures, still from them called Caryatides.[3] The representation of this performance was, doubtless, a favourite subject among Spartan artists or such as were employed by the Spartans, as may perhaps be fairly inferred from the circumstance, that the device on the ring, which, in return for a comb, was presented by Clearchus to Ctesias to be shown to his friends at Lacedæmon, was a dance of Caryatides.[4]

Amid the laxity of morals which prevailed in the later ages of Greece, the Pyrrhic,[5] once supposed to be peculiar to warriors, degenerated into a dance of Bacchanals, with thyrsi instead of spears, or carrying torches in one hand, while with the other they sportively cast light reeds at one another. The story told in this mimetic performance referred to remote antiquity, and was both curiously and elaborately intricate, comprehending all the adventures of Bacchos and his merry crew during the Indian expedition, and assuming towards the conclusion a tragical form, developing the sad story of Pentheus.[6]

Among the dances of a grave character are enu-

[1] Schol. Aristoph. Nub. 534.
[2] Poll. iv. 104.
[3] Vitruv. i. 1.—Poll. iv. 104.
[4] Plut. Artaxerx. § 18.
[5] Duport. ad Theoph. Char. c.

[6] p. 305, sqq. Poll. iv. 99.—Athen. xiv. 29. On the Cretan warlike dances Orsites and Epicredios, id. xiv. 26.—Luc. de Saltat. § 9. [6] Athen xiv. 29.

merated the Gingra performed like the Podismos
to slow and solemn music, the Lion and the Tetra-
comos,[1] a warlike measure performed in honour of
Heracles and supposed in its origin to have had
some connexion with the Tetracomoi of Attica, that
is, the Peiræeus, Phaleron, Oxypeteones, and Thymo-
tadæ.[2] We read, moreover, of dances in which the performers represented certain historic or mythological
personages, such as Rhodope, Phædra, or Parthenope.[3]

The Anthema,[4] or Flower-dance, appears to have
been chiefly performed in private parties by women,
who acted certain characters and chanted, as they
moved, the following verses:

> Where is my lovely parsley, say?
> My violets, roses, where are they?
> My parsley, roses, violets fair,
> Where are my flowers? Tell me where.

The Athenians, however, seem to have imagined
that there was nothing in nature which might not
be imitated in the dance, by the turns and mazes
of which they accordingly sought to represent the
movements of the stars.[5] A similar fancy, if Lucian may be credited, possessed the Indian Yoghis,
who every morning and evening before their doors
saluted the sun, at his rising and setting, with a
dance resembling his own,[6] which, as that luminary
no otherwise dances than by turning on its axis,
must have been a performance resembling that of
the whirling derwishes, whose broad symbolical petti-
coats are meant, I presume, to represent the disk of
the sun. But the dance most difficult of comprehen-
sion is that upon which they bestowed the name of

[1] Poll. iv. 99.
[2] Poll. iv. 105.
[3] Luc. de Saltat. § 2.
[4] Athen. xiv. 27.
[5] It may possibly have been in this dance that Eumelos or Arc-
tinos, an old Corinthian poet, in-
troduced Zeus himself sporting the toe:—

Μέσσοισιν δ' ὠρχεῖτο πατὴρ
ἀνδρῶν τε θεῶν τε. Athen. i. 40.
Cf. Plut. Sympos. ix. 15.
[6] Luc. de Saltat. § 17.

κόσμου εκπύρωσις,[1] or the "Conflagration of the World."
Of the figure and character of this performance antiquity, I believe, has left us no account, though it probably represented, by a train of allegorical personages
and movements, the principal events which, according
to the Stoics, are to precede the delivering up of the
Universe to fire.[2] Scaliger,[3] who does not attempt to
explain this strange exhibition, observes, however,
pertinently, that it was a dance in which Nero might
have figured, his burning of Rome deserving in some
sort to be regarded as a rehearsal of this piece.

There existed among the Spartans[4] an elegant
dance denominated Hormos, or the Necklace, performed by a chorus of youths and virgins who moved
through the requisite evolutions in a row. The line
was headed by a young man who executed his part
in the firm and vigorous steps proper to his age,
and which he would afterwards be expected to preserve in the field of battle. A maiden immediately
followed, but, instead of imitating his masculine manner, confined herself to the modest graceful paces and
gestures of her sex, and this alternation and inter-
weaving, as it were, of force and beauty, suggesting
the idea of a necklace composed of many coloured
gems, gave rise to the appellation.

The dance of the Crane,[5] among the Athenians,
in some respects resembled the above. It was, according to tradition, first invented by Theseus, who

[1] Athen. xiv. 27.
[2] Cf. Lips. Physiolog. Stoic. ii.
22. t. iv. p. 955.
[3] De Poet. i. 18.
[4] Luc. de Saltat. § 12.
[5] Poll. iv. 101. Spanh. ad
Callim. t. ii. p. 513. Plut. Thes.
§ 21. Cf. Douglas, Essay on some
points of Resemblance, &c., p. 123.

" One of the dances still per-
" formed by the Athenians has
" been supposed that which was
" called the Crane, and was said
" to have been invented by The-

" seus, after his escape from the
" labyrinth of Crete. The pea-
" sants perform it yearly in the
" street of the Frank convent at
" the conclusion of the vintage;
" joining hands and preceding
" their mules and asses, which
" are laden with grapes in pan-
" niers, in a very curved and in-
" tricate figure; the leader waving
" a handkerchief, which has been
" imagined to denote the clue
" given by Ariadne." Chandler,
ii. 151.

landing at Delos on his return from Crete, offered sacrifice to Apollo and dedicated the statue of Aphrodite which he had received from Ariadne, after which he joined the young men and women whom he had delivered, in performing a joyous dance[1] about the altar of Horns erected by Apollo, from the spoils of his sister's bow. The Choreutæ, engaged in executing the Geranos, or Crane, formed themselves into one long line with a leader in van and rear, and then, guided by the design on the floor of the orchestra, described by their movements the various mazes and involutions of the Cretan labyrinth, until, having traversed all its intricate passages, they emerged at once, like their great countryman and his companions, into light and safety. Other dances there were, which, however curious they may have been, cannot now be described from the scanty materials left us: such were the dance of Heralds, or Messengers, the dance of the Lily,[2] the Chitonea, the Pinakides, the dance of the Graces,[3] and that of the Hours, in which the performers floated about with a circle of light drapery held over the head by both hands.[4]

If from the dances we now pass to the Choreutæ,[5] by whom they were performed, we shall find that they generally made their appearance in the orchestra with golden crowns upon their heads, and habited in gorgeous raiment, frequently interwoven or embroidered with gold.[6] The Chorus, however, like the actors, must have constantly varied its costume, to suit the exigencies of the drama; sometimes to perform the part of senators, sometimes of Nereids, sometimes of female suppli-

---

[1] Like the Cyclic Chorus. Vid. Izetzes ad Lycoph. i. p. 251, sqq. Sch. Aristoph. Nub. 311.

[2] Athen. iii. 82. xiv. 27.

[3] Poll. iv. 93. Xenoph. Conviv. vii. 5. Plat. De Legg. vii. t. viii. p. 55. Cf. Herm. Comment. ad

Arist. Poet. xxvii. 3. p. 190, sqq.

[4] Scalig. Poet. i. 18.

[5] Cf. Buleng. de Theat. c. 55.

[6] Dem. cont. Mid. § 7, seq. Athen. iii. 62. Animadv. t. vii. p. 215.

ants, sometimes of urn-bearers, sometimes of clouds, or wasps, or birds. When in the tragedy of Æs-chylus they were required to personate the Furies, their exterior was the most frightful that can well be imagined,—their long but scanty robes consisting, as has been conjectured, of black lamb-skins, slit up below and exposing their tawny withered limbs to sight, while their blood-stained eyes, livid tongue hanging out, and hair like a mass of knotted serpents, easily accredited the belief of their being infernal existences. Thus habited, with fingers terminating in black claws,[1] and grasping a burning torch, they burst upon the view of the spectators, like so many hideous phantoms conjured up by an imagination diseased with terror.

The costume of the actors,[2] which some modern writers suppose to have been extremely monotonous,[3] was in reality, however, as rich, varied, and characteristic as the masks of which we shall presently have to speak. Gods, heroes, kings, chiefs, soothsayers, heralds, rustics, the hetairæ, and their mothers; gay youths, flatterers, libertines, procurers, cooks, satyrs, slaves, &c., had each and all their appropriate dresses and ornaments, modified, no doubt, from time to time by the change in public taste, and the fancy of the poets. The divinities had almost to be wholly framed by the Dionysiac artificers. Conceived to be of superhuman stature, it was necessary that the actors who represented them should, in the first place, be lifted up on Cothurni,[4] or half-boots, the soles of which were many inches high,[5] their limbs and bodies were enlarged

[1] Bœttiger, Furies, p. 28, sqq. and pl. ii. Casaub. ad Athen. xii. 2. Aristoph. Plut. 423.

[2] On the actors' wardrobe, see Poll. iv. 113, sqq.

[3] Müller, Dissert. on the Eumenides, p. 100. Mr. Donaldson, Theatre of the Greeks, p. 132, adopts this opinion.

[4] Luc. Jup. Tragœd. § 41. Cf. Xen. Cyrop. viii. 8, 17. Poll. ii. 151. vii. 62.

[5] See Winkel. Monum. Ined. t. iii. p. 84. c. ix. § 1. Les extrémités des Cothurnes étoient ronds et quelquefois un peu aigues; mais on n'en vit jamais de carrés, comme aux gravés sur

by padding, their arms lengthened by gloves, while
their countenances, which might be ignoble or even
ugly, were concealed by masks of exquisite ideal
beauty, rising above the stately forehead in a mass
of curls, which at once corresponded with the no-
bleness of their features and augmented their colossal height : add to all this robes of purple, or
scarlet, or azure, or saffron, or cloth of gold, floating about the person in graceful folds, and training
along the floor, and we have some faint idea of
the celestial personages who with gemmed sceptres
and glittering crowns made their appearance on the
Grecian stage.

The queens and heroes,[1] who were constantly beheld grouped in converse, or in action, with these
sublime dwellers of Olympos, were clad in a costume scarcely less majestic ; the former, for example,
in times of prosperity, issued forth from their palaces in white garments, with loose sleeves reaching
to the elbow, and closed on the upper part of the
arm by a succession of jewelled agraffes,[2] their
tresses confined in front by a golden sphendone, or
fillet, crusted with gems, while their robes terminated below in long sweeping trains of purple.[3] But
when their houses were visited by misfortune, the

---

l'estampe, de Vasali. p. 85. Cf.
Luc. de Saltat. § 27. Their
height depended first upon the
stature of the actor, second, upon
that of the character represented.
Sometimes they were satisfied
with attributing four cubits even
to the heroes.—Aristoph. Ran.
1046. Cf. Athen. v. 27. But
the ghost of Achilles when it appeared to Apollonios of Tyana,
rose five cubits in height, and, no
doubt, the spectre was careful to
accommodate itself to public opinion.—Philost. Vit. Apoll. Tyan.
iv. 16. Aul. Gell. iii. 10. See,
also, Scalig. Poet. i. 13. Scaliger

relates à propos of the Cothurnus
a facetious remark of his father :
" Italas mulieres altissimis soccis
" usas vidimus ; quamvis diminu-
" tiva dicant voce Socculos. Pa-
" tris mei perfacetum dictum
" memini. Ejusmodi uxorum
" dimidio tantùm in lectis frui
" maritos, alter dimidio cum
" soccis deposito," p. 53.

[1] Poll. iv. 119.

[2] Cf. Mus. Chiaramont. tavv.
3. 7. 16.

[3] Poll. vii. 60. Bœttiger, Furies, p. 32. Luc. Jup. Tragoed.
§ 41.

milk-white pelisse was exchanged for one quince-coloured or blue, while the purple train was converted into black. The costume of the kings,[1] likewise varied by circumstances, consisted usually of an ample robe of purple, or scarlet, or dark green, descending to the feet, a rich cloak of cloth of gold, or of some delicate colour, adorned with gold embroidery, and a lofty mitre on the head.[2] When any of these characters, as Tydeus or Meleager, was engaged in hunting or war, he wore the scarlet or purple mantle called Ephaptis,[3] which in action was wrapped about the left arm. Athenæus, in describing the horsemen of Antiochos, observes, that these Ephaptides [4] were embroidered with gold and adorned with the figures of animals. Bacchanals and soothsayers, like Teiresias, generally appeared upon the stage in an extraordinary garment, denominated Agrenon,[5] formed of a reticular fabric of wool of various colours. Dionysos himself,[6] in whose honour the theatre with all its shows was created, descended from Olympos in a saffron-coloured robe compressed below the bosom by a broad flowered belt, and bearing a thyrsus in his hand.[7] This girdle, in the case of other gods, or heroes, was sometimes

---

[1] On voit parmi les plus belles peintures d'Herculaneum un de ces premiers acteurs, ou protagonistes, avec une large ceinture de couleur d'or, une sceptre dans une main, et l'épée au côté.— Winkelmann. Monum. Ined. t. iii. p. 84. Pitt. Ercol. i. 4. i. 41.—Plutarch observes, that, together with their royal garments, actors assumed the very strut of kings.—Vit. Demet. § 18.— Demetrius moreover, is said to have resembled a tragic actor, because he went clad in cloth of purple and gold, and wore sandals of purple and gold tissue. § 41.

[2] Aristoph. Av. 512, et Schol.

Nub. 70. Poll. iv. 115. Suid. v. *Ξυστὶς*. t. ii. p. 264. e.—The actor who personated Heracles made his appearance with club and lion's skin.—Luc. de Saltat. § 27.

[3] Poll. iv. 116, 117. Aristoph. Nub. 71, et Schol. Lysist. 1189.

[4] Deipnosoph. v. 22.

[5] Poll. iv. 117. Hesych. v. *ἀγρηνὸν*.

[6] Poll. iv. 118.

[7] It behoved the actors, however, to take care of their gold and jewels, since it would appear that thieves found their way even to the stage. — Aristoph. Acharn. 258.

replaced by one of gold.[1] Persons overtaken by
calamity, especially exiles, wore garments dirty-
white, or sad-coloured, or black, or quince-coloured,
or bluish. The costume of Philoctetes, Telephos,
Œneus, Phœnix, Bellerophontes, was ragged. The
Seileni appeared in a shaggy Chiton, and the other
personages of the Satyric drama in the skins of
fawns, or goats, or sheep, or pards, and, sometimes,
in the Theraion or Dionysiac garment, and a flowered
cloak and a scarlet Himation. Old men were distinguished by the Exomis,[2] a white Chiton of mean
appearance, having no seam or arm-hole on the
left side—young men by the Campulè,[3] a scarlet or
deep purple Himation, — the parasites by bearing
the Stlengis and flask (as country people by the
Lagobalon) and by black or sad-coloured robes, except in the play of the Sicyonians, where a person
of this class, being about to be married, sported a
white garment,—the cook by an Himation double
and unfulled, — priestesses by white robes, — comic
old women by such as were quince-coloured or dusky,
like a cloudy morning sky in autumn,—the mothers
of the hetairæ wore a purple fillet about the head,
—the dresses of young women were white and delicate,—of heiresses the same with fringes. Pornoboski
wore garments of various colours, with flowered
cloaks, and carried a straight wand, called ἀρέσκος.[4]
There were, likewise, female characters which wore
the Parapechu and the Symmetria, a chiton reaching
to the feet, with a border of marine purple.

We now come to the masks,[5] a subject upon which

---

[1] Poll. iv. 118.

[2] Dion. Chrysost. i. 231. Scalig. Poet. i. 13.

[3] Poll. iv. 119, sqq.

[4] Scalig. Poet. i. 13.

[5] When actors displeased the
audience they were sometimes
compelled to take off their masks
and face those who hissed them,

which was regarded as a serious
punishment. Duport. ad Theoph.
Char. p. 308. We ought, perhaps,
to understand Lucian *cum grano*,
when he informs us that actors
who performed their parts ill
were scourged. Piscator, § 33.
On the derivation of the word
persona, Aul. Gell. v. 7.   Cf.

much has been written, though very little has been
explained. The primary difficulty connected with
them is, to determine whether they were so constructed as to resemble a speaking-trumpet,[1] which,
by narrowing the stream, and compressing, as it were,
the particles of the voice, cast it forth condensed
and corroborated upon the theatre,[2] which it was thus
enabled to penetrate and fill, even to its utmost
extremities. My own opinion, after bestowing much
attention upon the subject, is, that the mask was in
reality so constructed as to communicate additional
force and intensity to the voice; but whether by
roofing or encircling the artificial mouth by metallic plates, or thin laminæ of the stone called Chalco-
phonos,[3] it is now scarcely possible to determine.
Be this, however, as it may, there existed in some
theatres other contrivances for conveying and augmenting the volume of the actor's voice; these were
the Echeia,[4] vases generally of metal, finely toned,
and arranged according to the musical scale, in a
succession of domed cells,[5] running in diverging lines
up the hollow face of the theatre. They rested with
one edge upon a smooth and polished pavement, the
mouth outward, and the external edge reposing on the
summit of a small, blunt obelisk,[6] while a low opening in each cell enabled the resonances, or echoes,
thus created, to issue forth, and fill the air with

Aristoph. Poet. c. 5. Scalig. Poet.
i. 13, on the derivation of πρόσ-
ωπον. Etym. Mag. 691. 1.
[1] Vid. Cassiod. iv. 51. Plin.
xlvii. 10. Solin. cxxxvii. Lucian. de Saltat. § 27. De Gym-
nast. § 23. A tragic poet,
Hieronymos, exposed himself to
ridicule by introducing into one
of his pieces a mask of frightful
aspect. Aristoph. Acharn. 390.
[2] Cf. Suid. v. φλοιός. t. ii. p.
1073. Diog. Laert. iv. p. 27.
[3] Plin. xxxvii. 56.
[4] See Burney's Hist. of Music,

i. 153. sqq. Scalig. Poet. i. 21.
Antiq. of Athens, &c., Supple-
mentary to Stuart, by Cockerell,
Kinnaird, Donaldson, &c. p. 39.

[5] Vitruv. v. 6. Antiq. of Ath.
by Cockerell, Donaldson, &c. p.
39. Tectum porticus quod est
in summa gradatione, respondet
Sienæ altitudinem, ut vox cre-
scens æqualiter ad summas gra-
dationes et tectum perveniat.
Buleng. de Theat. c. 17.

[6] Marinus's edition of Vitruv.
t. iv. tab. 81.

sound,[1] which, however the fact may be accounted
for, produced no isolated reverberations, no confusion.

The materials wherewith the masks were constructed varied, no doubt, considerably in different ages;[2]
but that they were ever manufactured of bronze or
copper is scarcely credible, if we reflect upon the
weight of so voluminous an apparatus, covering the
entire head and neck, composed of either of those
metals. Such metallic specimens as have come down
to us are to be regarded simply as model-masks,
or as works of art, designed by the statuary as ornaments. The intention, at first, of this disguise being
to give additional boldness and self-confidence to the
actor, by concealing from his neighbours the shame-
facedness which a raw performer would sometimes
naturally feel while strutting about in imperial robes,
and pouring forth the *sesquipedalia verba* of Pelias
and Telephos, they were contented to cover the face
with a piece of linen, having openings for the eyes
and a breathing-place.[3] To this appears to have
succeeeded a mask manufactured from the flexible
bark of certain trees,[4] shaped, of course, and coloured
to resemble the human countenance. The next step
was to employ wood, some kinds of which, while
possessing the advantage of extreme lightness, might
be wrought with all the delicacy and fineness of a
statue, while, better than any other material, it would
receive that smooth and polished enamel by which
were represented the texture[5] and complexion of
the skin. Specimens of masks of this kind have been
found among nations in a very rude state ; among the

---

[1] Empty pots were built into
the walls of certain public edifices to augment the sound of the
voice. Aristot. Prob. xi. 8. i. 1. v.
5. The orchestra was sometimes
strewed with chaff, which was
found to deaden the voice. 25.
Plin. ii. 51.

[2] Scalig. Poet. i. 14. Poll. iv.
143.

[3] Suid. in θέσπις, p. 1315. d.
Poll. x. 167.

[4] Virg. Georg. ii. 387.

[5] Vid. Horat. de Art. Poet.
278. Athen. xiv. 77. Suid. v.
χοιρίλλος, t. ii. p. 1160. f. Etym.
Mag. 376. 47. Poll. iv. 133,
sqq. Schol. Soph. Œdip. Tyr.
80.

inhabitants, for example, of Nootka Sound, whose dress, we are told,[1] " is accompanied by a mask represent- " ing the head of some animal: it is made of wood, " with the eyes, teeth, &c., and is a work of consi- " derable ingenuity. Of these masks they have a " great variety, which are applicable to certain cir- " cumstances and occasions. Those, for example, " which represent the head of the otter or any other " marine animals, are used only when they go to " hunt them. In their war expeditions, but at no " other time, they cover the whole of their dress " with large bear-skins."

But while the above improvements were going on in the national theatre,[2] the rustic drama con- tinued to preserve its original simplicity, the actors to prevent their being recognised, shading their brows with thick projecting crowns of leaves, and daubing their faces[3] with lees of wine. Thus disguised they chanted their songs upon the public roads, sitting in a waggon,[4] whence the proverb, "he speaks as from the waggon," i. e. he is shamelessly abusive, which was in fact the case with the comic poets.

The masks were divided into three kinds, the Tragic, the Comic, and the Satyric. Those be- longing to Tragedy were again subdivided into nu- merous classes, representing every marked variety of character, and every stage of human life from childhood to extreme old age. In the highly varied range of countenances thus brought into play, the mask-maker enjoyed abundant opportunities of ex- hibiting his skill. The hair, of course, was real and adjusted on the mask like a wig,[5] differently fa-

[1] Meare's Voyage, p. 254.

[2] On the Roman Stage the actors appeared in hats up to the age of Livius Andronicus. Ros- cius Gallus was the first who put on a mask, which he did on ac- count of his squinting. Ficorini, Masch. Scen. p. 15. On the ori- gin of the Mask see Paccichelli De Larvis, Capillamentis, et Chi- rothecis. Neap. 1693.

[3] Schol. Aristoph. Nub. 29. Scalig. Poet. i. 13.

[4] Schol. Aristoph. Eq. 545. Nub. 29.—Demosth. De Coron. § 37. Ulp. in. § 5.

[5] Scalig. Poet. i. 13.—Poll. iv. 133, sqq.

shioned and coloured according to the age, habits, and complexion of the wearer. In some cases it was gathered together and piled up on the forehead,[1] in a triangular figure,[2] adding many inches to the actor's stature; at other times it was combed smoothly downwards, from the crown, twisted round a fillet and disposed like a wreath about the head as we sometimes find it in the figures of Asclepios and the philosopher Archytas. Some characters were represented wholly bald, with a garland of vine-leaves or ivy wreathed about the brow,[3] others were simply bald in front, while a third class exhibited a bushy fell of hair, something like a lion's mane. Young ladies displayed a profusion of pendant curls, kept in order by the fillet or sphendone, or gathered up in nets, or twisted about the head in braided tresses. In representing certain characters the eye-sockets were left open, so that the actor's eyes could be seen moving and flashing within;[4] but on other occasions, when the part of a squinter was to be acted by a performer who did not squint or vice versa, as in the case of Roscius Gallus, the mask-maker must have represented the eyes by glass or some other transparent substance, through which the actor could see his way. This was ne-

---

[1] Cf. Thucyd. i. 6, et Schol. Ælian.Var. Hist. iv. 22.

[2] See a beautiful head of Aphrodite with a pole of curls. (ὄγκος) Mus. Chiaramont. tav. 27. Cf. a tragic female mask, with the hair bound by a fillet, in the Cabinet d' Orleans. pl. 52.

[3] It may be remarked that persons ridiculed upon the stage were introduced with masks exactly resembling their countenances. They seized, however, upon the ludicrous features, which any one happened to possess, as the eyebrows of Chærephon, and the baldness of Socrates. Sch.

Aristoph. Nub. 147, 224. This applies to living characters. The dead were protected from ridicule by the laws. Sch. Pac. 631. The Comic mask was said to have been invented by Mason. Athen. xiv. 77. The Comte de Caylus, however, attributes the invention of masks to the Etruscans. Recueil d' Antiq. i. 147, seq.

[4] Cic. de Orat. ii. 46. See in Agostini Gemme Antiche, pl. 17, a representation of one of these masks. For examples of hideous masks see Mus. Florent. t. i. pp. 45—51.

cessarily the case in the part of the poet Thamyris,[1] who, like our own Chatterton, had eyes of different colours, one blue, the other black, which, as Aristotle informs us, was common among the horses of Greece.

The time of acting, as is well-known, was during the Dionysiac and Lenæan festivals, in the spring and autumn.[2] The theatres being national establishments, in the proper sense of the word, were therefore open, free of expense, to all the citizens, who were not called together as with us by playbills,[3] but for the most part knew nothing of what they were going to see till they were seated in the theatre, and the herald[4] commanded the chorus of such and such a poet to advance. Previously to the commencement of the performance the theatre was purified by the sacrifice of a young hog, the blood of which was sprinkled on the earth.[5]

[1] Poll. iv. 141. Dubos, Reflex. Crit. sur la Poes. et sur la Peint. i. 603.

[2] Schol. Aristoph. Eq. 545. Acharn. 336. Cf. Dem. cont. Mid. § 4, et annot. Plut. Vit. x. Rhet. Lycurg.

[3] Winkelmann, however, supposes they had a kind of play-bill, Monum. Ined. iii. p. 86, founding his opinion upon a misinterpretation of Pollux, iv. 131.

[4] Aristoph. Acharn. 10, sqq.

[5] Sch. Æschin. Tim. p. 17. Orator. Att. t. xiii. p. 377. Vales. ad Harpoc. 99, 296. Suid. v. καθάρσιον, t. i. p. 1346. a. Poll. viii. 104.

BOOK V.

RURAL LIFE.

CHAPTER I.

THE VILLA AND THE FARMYARD.

IF we now, for a moment, quit the city and its amusements, and observe the tone and character of Hellenic rural life, we shall find, perhaps, that there existed in antiquity a still greater contrast between town and country than in modern times. From the poetry of Athens, rife with sylvan imagery, we, no less than from its history, discover how deeply they loved the sunshine and calm and quiet of their fields. The rustic population confined to the city during the Peleponnesian war almost perished of nostalgia within sight of their village homes. Half the metaphors in their language are of country growth. The bee murmurs, the partridge whirrs, the lark, the nightingale, the thrush, pour their music through the channels of verse and prose. The odours of ripe fruit, of new wine "pur-" ple and gushing," the fresh invigorating morning breeze from harvest fields, from clover meadows dotted with kine, the scent of milk-pails, of honey, and the honey-comb, still breathe sweetly over the Attic page, and prove how smitten with home delights the Athenian people were,

> " With plesaunce of the breathing fields yfed."

This their manly and healthful taste, however,

constantly, in time of war, exposed them to the malice of their enemies. For the valleys and grassy uplands of Attica, being thickly covered with villas and farmhouses,[1] the first act of an invading army was to lay all those beautiful homesteads in ashes. Thus the Persians, in their two invasions, destroyed the whole with fire and sword. But the gentlemen, immediately on their return, rebuilt their dwellings[2] with greater taste and magnificence, so that, before the breaking out of the Peloponnesian war, it is probable that, as a scene of unambitious affluence, taste, high cultivation, and rustic contentment, nothing was ever beheld to compare with Attica. Here and there, throughout the land, perched on rocks, or shaded by trees, were small rustic chapels dedicated to the nymphs, or rural gods.[3] On the mountains, and in solitary glens, and wherever springs gushed from the cliffs, caverns were scooped out by the hands of the leisurely shepherds,[4] and consecrated by association with mythology. Fountains, also, and water-courses, altars, statues,[5] and sacred groves,[6] protected at once by religion and the laws,[7] imprinted on the landscape features of poetry and elegance.

Another cause which, in the eyes of the Athenians, imparted sanctity to their lands, was the practice of burying in them their dead. The spot selected for this sacred purpose seems usually to have been the orchard, where, amid fig-trees and trailing vines,[8] often near the boundaries of the estate, might be seen the ancient and venerable monuments of the dead. All Attica, therefore, in their eyes, ap-

---

[1] Demosth. in Ev. et Mnes. § 15.
[2] Thucyd. ii. 65.
[3] In the neighbourhood of the Isthmus the shepherds of the present day often pass the winter months in mountain caverns.— Chandler, ii. p. 261.
[4] Theocrit. i. 143, seq.
[5] Cf. Iliad. ϛ. 305, seq.

[6] On the wild olive and other trees, of which these groves were composed, the eye of the passenger usually beheld suspended a number of votive offerings.—Sch. Aristoph. Ran. 943.
[7] Cf Plat. Phæd. t. i. p. 9.
[8] Eurip. Bacch. 10, seq. Cf. Kirch. de Funer. Rom. iii. 17.

peared holy as a sepulchre ; and, as every one guarded
his own ancestral ashes, to sell a farm cost a man's
feelings more than in countries where people inter
those they love in public cemeteries; and this circumstance with many would operate like a law of
entail.[1]

But it is easy thus to present to the imagination
a general picture of the country. What we want
is to thrust aside the impediments, to dissipate the
obscurity of two thousand years, and lift the latch
of a Greek farmhouse, such as it existed in the days
of Pericles.

In the first place it was common in Attica to
erect country-houses in the midst of a grove of silver firs,[2] which in winter protect from cold, and in
summer attract the breezes that imitate in their
branches the sound of trickling runnels, or the distant murmur of the sea. Towards the centre of the
grove, with a spacious court in front and a garden
behind, stood the house,[3] sometimes with flat, sometimes with pointed roof, ornamented with a picturesque porch, and surrounded with verandahs or
colonnades. Occasionally opulent persons had on the
south front of their houses large citron trees,[4] growing in pots, on either side the door, where they
were well watered and carefully covered during winter.[5] In the plainer class of dwellings, numerous
outhouses, as stables, sheds for cattle,[6] henroosts,
pigstyes, &c., extended round the court, while the

---

[1] Demosth. in Callicl. § 4.

[2] Schol. Aristoph. Eq. 406.
On the music of the pine-groves,
the Schol. on Theocritus, i. 1, has
an amusing passage : ἡ πίτυς ἐκεί-
νη, ἡδύ τι μελουργεῖ, κατὰ τὸ
ψιθύρισμα. κ. τ. λ.

[3] Called in Latin pagus from
πηγὴ, a fountain. Serv. ad Virg.
Georg. 182. See also the note of
Gibbon, t. iii. p. 410.

[4] Geop. x. 7. 11. These pots,

like those in which the palm-tree
was cultivated, were pierced at
the bottom like our own. Theoph.
Hist. Plant. iv. 4. 3.

[5] As the orange-tree is still in
Lemnos. Walp. Mem. i. 280.

[6] The stalls for cattle were built
as often as convenient, near the
kitchen and facing the east, because when exposed to light and
heat they became smooth-coated.
Vitruv. vi. 9. Cf. Varro. i. 13.

back-front, generally in the East the principal, opened
upon the garden or orchard.

Much pains was usually taken in selecting the site
of a farmhouse,[1] though opinions of course varied
according to the peculiar range of experience on
which they were based.   In general such positions
were considered most favourable as neighboured the
sea, or occupied the summits or the slopes of mountains,[2] more especially if looking towards the north.[3]
The vicinity of swamps and marshes, and as much
as possible of rivers, was avoided, together with
coombs, or hollow valleys, and declivities facing the
south or the setting sun.   If necessitated by the
nature of the ground to build near the banks of a
stream, the front of the dwelling was carefully turned
away from it, inasmuch as its waters communicated
an additional rigour to the winds in winter, and in
summer filled the atmosphere with unwholesome
vapours.   The favourite exposure was towards the
east whence the most salubrious breezes were supposed to blow, while the cheerful beams of the sun,
as soon as they streamed above the horizon, dissipated the dank fogs and murkiness of the air.   Notwithstanding the warmth of the climate, moreover,
they loved such situations as were all day long illu-
minated by the sun, whilst every care was taken
to fence out the sirocco, a moist and pestilential
wind, blowing across the Mediterranean from the
deserts of Africa.   In Italy, nevertheless, the farmer often selected for the site of his mansion the
southern roots of mountains, further defended from
Alpine blasts by a sweep of lofty woods.

According to the fashion prevailing in antiquity,

---

[1] Geop. ii. 3.   Cf. Vitruv. i. 4.

[2] Petatur igitur aer calore et
frigore temperatus, quem fere me-
dius obtinet collis, quod neque
depressus hieme pruinis torpet,
aut torret æstute vaporibus, neque
elatus in summa montium per-
exiguis ventorum motibus, aut

pluviis omni tempore anni sævit.
Columell. De Re Rust. i. 4.

[3] The same opinion is held by
Hippocrates, De Morbo Sacro. cap.
7. p. 308, ed. Foes. Ὁ Βορέης
ὑγιεινότατός ἐστι τῶν ἀνέμων.
Cf. Plin. ii. 48.   Varro. i. 12.

farmhouses were built high, large, and roomy, though
Cato[1] shrewdly advises, that their magnitude should
bear some relation to that of the domain, lest the
villa should have to seek for the farm, or the farm
for the villa.

Much, however, would depend upon the taste of
the individual; but in a plain farmhouse more attention appears to have been paid to substantial comfort, and something like rough John-Bullism, than to
that cold finical elegance which certain persons are
fond of associating with whatever is classical. An
Attic farmer of the true old republican school was
anything but a fine gentleman. He scorned none
of the occupations or productions by which he lived.
On entering his dwelling you found no small difficulty in steering between bags of corn,[2] piles of
cheeses, hurdles of dried figs[3] or raisins, while the
racks groaned with hams[4] and bacon flitches. If
they resembled their descendants,[5] too, even their
bedchambers were invaded by some species of provisions, for there in the present day you often behold long strings of melons suspended like festoons
from the rafters. In one corner of the ground-floor
stood a corbel filled with olive-dregs, recently pressed,
in another a wool-sack or a pile of dressed skins.[6]
Yonder in the room looking into the garden, with
the honey-suckle twining about the open lattice,
were madam's loom and spinning-wheel, and carding
apparatus, and work-baskets; and there with the
lark[7] might you see her, serene and happy, suckling
her young democrat, and rocking the cradle of a

---

[1] De Re Rust. 3. "Ita ædi-
"fices, ne villa fundum quærat,
"neve fundus villam. Cf. Colum. De Re Rust. i. 4. It
may here by the way be observed that, during the flourishing periods of Roman agriculture,
farms were generally rather small
than large. Plin. Hist. Nat. viii.
21. Schulz. Antiq. Rustic. § vii.

[2] Schol. Aristoph. Nub. 45.

[3] Philost. Icon. ii. 26. p. 851.

[4] Cf. Athen. iv. 38.

[5] Walp. Mem. i. 281.

[6] Aristoph. Nub. 45, seq. et
Schol.—Schol. Eq. 803.

[7] Plat. De Legg. vii. t. viii. p.
40. Aristoph. Lysist. 18, sqq.

second with her foot, thriftily giving directions the while to Thratta, Xanthia or "the neat-handed" Phillis.[1]

The kitchen must sometimes have been in fine disorder; geese and ducks waddling across the floor, picking up the spilled grain, or snatching away the piece of bread and honey which my young master had just put down on the stool to play at a game of romps with Thratta. Up in the dusky corner there, behind a huge armchair or settle, you may discern a very suspicious looking enclosure, from which, at intervals, issues a suppressed grunt; it is the pigsty.[2] But be not offended; the practice is classical; and pigs, in my apprehension, are as pleasant company as geese and many other animals. Now, that geese were fed even about palaces, we have the testimony of Homer, whose Penelope, the the *beau idéal* of a good housewife, says—

> "Full twenty geese have we at home, that feed
> On wheat in water steeped."[3]

But the whole economy of geese-feeding[4] has been transmitted to us; in the first place, the birds usually preferred were those most remarkable for their size and whiteness.[5] The ancients esteemed the variegated, or spotted, as of inferior value. The same rule applied to fowls. The chenoboscion,[6] or enclosure in which the geese were kept, was commonly situated near ponds or freshes,[7] abounding with rich grass and aquatic plants. Geese, it was observed, are not nice in the article of food, but devour eagerly nearly all kinds of plants, though the chick-pea, and the couch-grass, the laurel and

[1] Aristoph. Acharn. 272. Vesp. 824. Pac. 1138. Thesm. 286, seq. Suid. v. Θρᾶττα. t. p. 1330. a.

[2] Ἐπὶ τῆς ἑστίας τρέφουσι χοίρους. — Schol. Aristoph. Vesp. 844. Lysist. 1073, Poll. ix. 16.

[3] Odyss. τ. 536.

[4] Cf. Vict. Var. Lect. p. 891.

[5] Geop. xiv. 22. Varro. iii. 10. Colum. viii. 14.

[6] Poll. ix. 16. Heresbach. De Re Rust. lib. iv. p. 285. a.

[7] Cf. Pallad. i. 30. Plin. x. 79. Plaut. Trucul. ii. 1. 41.

the laurel-rose,[1] were by the ancients supposed to be hurtful to them. Of their eggs some were hatched by hens, but such as were designed to be sitten on by the goose herself, (who, during the period of incubation [2] was fed on barley steeped in water,) were marked by writing or otherwise, to distinguish them from the eggs of their neighbours, which it was thought she would not be at the pains to hatch. For the first ten days after they had broken the shell the young goslings were kept within-doors, where they were fed on wheat steeped in water, *polenta* a preparation of barley-meal dried at the fire, and chopped cresses. This period over, they were driven out to feed and afterwards to water; they who tended them taking great care that they should not be stung by nettles, or pricked by thorns, or swallow the hair [3] of pigs or kids, which they imagined to be fatal to them.

When full-grown geese were intended to be fattened, the custom was, to confine them in dark and extremely warm cells.[4] Their food was scientifically varied and regulated, proceeding from less to more nutritious, until they were judged fit for the table.

---

[1] Ælian. De Nat. Anim. v. 29. This ingenious writer, anxious to remove from geese the reputation of folly, relates that, when traversing Mount Taurus, conscious of their disposition to cackling, they carry stones in their bills, and thus frequently escape the eagles which inhabit that lofty ridge of mountains. This the poet Phile undertakes to confirm in verse :—

Λίθον δὲ τῷ στόματι μὴ κλάγξῃ
στέγων
Ὄνπερ καλοῦσι Ταῦρον, ἀμείβει
πάγον
Τοὺς ἀετοὺς γὰρ φασὶ τοὺς χηνο-
σκόπους,
Εκεῖσε δεινῶς ἐλλοχᾷν πρὸ τοῦ
ψύχους.

Iamb. De Animal. Proprietat. c. 15. p. 62.

[2] Which according to Aristotle was thirty days. — Hist. Anim. vii. 6.

[3] Pallad. i. 30. Cavendum est etiam, ne pulli eorum setas glutiant.

[4] The Quintilian Brothers, ap. Geop. xiv. 22. For the fate of these illustrious authors, Maximus and Condianus, see Gibbon, i. 142. " Sint calido et tene- " broso loco : quæres ad creandas " adipes multum conferunt." Colum. viii. 14.

At first their diet consisted of a preparation composed of two parts *polenta*, and four parts bran boiled in water. Of this they were permitted to eat as much as they pleased three times a day, and once again at midnight, while water was furnished them in abundance. When they had continued on this regimen for some time, they were indulged with a more luxurious table, — nothing less than the most exquisite dried figs, which, being chopped small, and dissolved in water, were served up as a sort of jelly for twenty days, after which the pampered animal itself was ready for the spit.

Occasionally that delicate and humane device, for the practice of which Germany has, in modern times, obtained so enviable a celebrity, of enlarging preternaturally the dimensions of the liver, was resorted to by the ancients,[1] whose mode of proceeding was as follows : during five-and-twenty days, being cooped up as before in a place of high temperature, the geese were fed with wheat and barley steeped in water, the former of which fattened, while the latter rendered their flesh delicately white. For the next five days certain cakes or balls, denominated collyria,[2] the composition of which is not exactly known, were given them at the rate of seven per day, after which the number was gradually augmented to fifteen, which constituted their whole allowance for other twenty days. To this succeeded the most extraordinary dish of all, consisting of bolusses of leavened dough, steeped in a warm decoction of mallows, by which they were puffed up for four days. Their drink, meanwhile, was still more delicious than their food, being nothing less than hydromel,[3] or water mingled with honey. During the last six days dried figs, chopped fine, were added to their leaven, and the process being thus brought to a conclusion, the gourmands for whom they were intended, feasted on

[1] Eupolis, ap. Athen. ix. 32.   Mag. 526. 26.   Schol. Aristoph.
[2] Cf. Suid. v. κολλύρα. t. i. p.   Pac. 122.
1489. a. Poll. i. 248. Etym.   [3] Cf. Dioscor. v. 30.

the tenderest geese and the largest livers in the
world. It should be added, however, that before
being cooked the liver was thrown into a basin of
warm water, which the *artistes* several times changed.
Geese, adds the ingenious gastronomer to whom we
are indebted for these details, are, both for flesh and
liver, much inferior to ganders. The Greeks did
not, however, like the Romans and the moderns,
select young geese for this species of culinary apo-
theosis, but birds of a mature age and of the largest
size, from two to four years old, which only proves
the superior strength and keenness of their teeth.

Ducks were kept in ponds, carefully enclosed, and,
perhaps, covered over that they might not fly away.
In the centre were certain green islets,[1] planted with
couch-grass, which the ancients considered as beneficial to ducks as it was hurtful to geese. Their usual
food, which was cast in the water encircling the
islets, consisted of wheat, millet, barley, sometimes
mixed with grape-stones and grape-skins. Occasionally they were indulged with locusts, prawns, shrimps,[2]
and whatever else aquatic birds habitually feed
on. Persons desirous of possessing tame ducks were
accustomed to beat about the lakes and marshes[3]
for the nest of the wild bird. Giving the eggs
to a hen to sit on, they obtained a brood of duck-
lings perfectly domesticated.[4] Wild ducks were
sometimes caught by pouring red wine, or the lees
of wine, into the springs whither they came to
drink.

With respect to barn-door fowl, originally introduced from India and Media into Greece, the
greatest care appears to have been taken to vary
and improve the breeds. For this purpose cocks

---

[1] Geop. xiv. 23. Varro, iii. 11.
Ælian. De Nat. Anim. v. 33.
Aristot. De Hist. Anim. viii.
3. Athen. ix. 52. Phile, De
Anim. Proprietat. c. 14. p. 59.

[2] Athen. iii. 64. Κουρίδες·

καρίδες, ἢ τὰς μικρὰς ἐγχλώρας,
τὰς δὲ ἐρυθρὰς καμμάρους. Hesych.

[3] Cf. Philost. Icon. i. 9. p. 776.

[4] Colum. viii. 15. Heresbach.
De Re Rust. lib. iv. p. 288. a.

and hens were imported[1] from the shores of the
Adriatic, from Italy, Sicily, Numidia, and Egypt,
while those of Attica were occasionally exported
to other countries. There appears to have been
a prejudice against keeping more than fifty fowls[2]
about one farmyard, some traces of which may
also be discovered in the practice of the Arabs.[3]
The fowl-house furnished with roosts,[4] as with us,
was so contrived and situated as to receive from
the kitchen a tolerable supply of smoke, which was
supposed to be agreeable to these Median strangers.
The food of fowls[5] being much the same all the
world over, it is unnecessary to observe more than
that the green leaves of the Cytisus were supposed
to render them prolific. To preserve them from
vermin, the juice of rue, by way I suppose of
charm, was sprinkled over their feathers.[6] The
proportion of male birds was one to six. Hens
were usually put to sit about the vernal equinox,
during the first quarter of the moon, in nests carefully constructed of boards, and strewed with fresh
clean straw, into which, as a sort of talisman against
thunder, they threw an iron nail, heads of garlic, and
sprigs of laurel.[7] During the period of incubation,
the eggs which had previously been kept in bran
were turned every day.

The other inhabitants of the farmyard were peacocks,[8] commonly confined in beautiful artificial islands

[1] Athen. vii. 23. Of these
birds the black were esteemed
less than the white. ix. 15. On
the fighting cocks. Plin. x. 24.
Æsch. Eum. 864, 869. Schol.
ad Æsch. Tim. Orat. Attic. t.
xii. p. 379. Schol. Aristoph. Eq.
492.   [2] Geop. xiv. 7, 9.
[3] Arabian Nights, Story of the
Ass, the Ox, and the Labourer,
vol. 1. p. 23.
[4] Ταῤῥοί. Sch. Aristoph. Nub.
227.
[5] Beans, however, were eschewed as they were supposed to
prevent them from laying.—Geo-
ponic. ii. 35. But cocks were suffered to feed on them, at least when
they belonged to poor men.—Luc.
Mycill. § 4.   [6] Dioscor. iii. 52.
[7] Geop. xiv. 7. 11. Colum.
viii. 5.
[8] Schol. Aristoph. Acharn. 63.
Petit. Leg. Att. p. 277. Geop.
xiv. 18. 1. Athen. xiv. 70. See
the poetical description of this
bird by Phile: De Animal. Proprietat. c. 8. p. 32, sqq.

provided with elegant sheds; pheasants[1] from the shores of the Black Sea;[2] guinea-fowls from Numidia,[3] though according to other authors they were originally found in Ætolia;[4] partridges, quails, and the attagas. Thrushes were bred in warm rooms with slight perches projecting from the walls, and laurel boughs or other evergreens fixed in the corners.[5] Over the clean floor was strewed their food, dried figs, which had been steeped in water, and mixed with flour or barley meal, together with the berries of the myrtle; the lentiscus, the ivy, the laurel, and the olive. They were fattened with millet, panic, and pure water.[6] Other still smaller birds were reared, and fattened in like manner. Every farmhouse had, moreover, its columbary and dovecotes,[7] sometimes so large as to contain five thousand birds. They usually consisted of spacious buildings,[8] roofed over and furnished with windows closed by lattice work, made so close that neither a lizard nor a mouse could creep through them. In the floor were channels and basins of water, in which these delicate birds[9] might wash and plume them-

---

[1] Geop. xiv. 19. Colum. viii. 12. Pallad. i. 28. Athen. ix. 37, seq. Suid. v. φασιανοὶ. t. i. p. 1033. a. b. Aristoph. Nub. 109.

[2] According to Diogenes Laertius, (i. iv. 51) both pheasants and peacocks were familiar to the Greeks in the days of Solon.

[3] Athen. xiv. 71. Ælian. De Nat. Anim. v. 27. Aristot. Hist. Anim. vi. 2. A number of these birds were kept on the Acropolis of Athens.—Suid. v. μελεαγρίδες. t. ii. p. 122. a.

[4] Within the enclosure for these birds pellitory of the wall was probably planted, as they loved to roll in and pluck it up.— Theoph. Hist. Plant. i. 6. 11.

[5] Cf. Pollux. ii. 24.

[6] Geop. xiv. 24. 5, seq.

[7] The king of Tuban, in Java, had formerly his bed surrounded by cages of turtle-doves, which roosted on perches of various coloured glass. — Voyage de La Compagnie des Indes, i. 533.

[8] Varro. iii. 7. Columell. viii. 8. Pallad. i. 24.

[9] For the food with which they were supplied, see Geopon. xiv. 1. 5. Occasionally when the birds were permitted to fly abroad, their owners sprinkled them with unguents, or gave them cumin seed to eat, in order that they might attract and bring back with them flights of doves or wild pigeons to their cells.—Id. xiv. 3. 1. So also Palladius: Inducunt alias, si

selves, and adjoining was a chamber into which such
as were required for sale, or the table, were en-
ticed. Even jackdaws were kept about farmyards,
and like common fowls had perches set up for
them.[1]

Much pains was taken by the ancients to improve the breed of animals.[2] Polycrates, tyrant of
Samos, introduced into that island the Molossian
and Spartan dogs, goats from Scyros and Naxos,
and sheep from Attica and Miletos.[3] The fineness
and beauty of Merinos were also known to the ancients, who purchased from Spain rams for breeding at a talent each, that is, about two hundred
and forty-one pounds sterling.[4]

Horses were at all times few, and, consequently,
dear in Greece; they were, therefore, seldom employed in agriculture, but bred and kept chiefly for
the army, for religious pomps and processions, and
for the chariot races at Olympia. Originally, no
doubt, the horse was introduced from Asia, and, up
to a very late period, chargers of great beauty and
spirit, continued to be imported from the shores of
the Black Sea.[5] Princes, in the Homeric age, appear to have obtained celebrity for the beauty of
their steeds, as Laomedon, Tros, and Rhesos; and
it was customary for them to possess studs of brood
mares in the rich pasture lands on the sea-shore.
That of Priam, for example, lay at Abydos, on the
Hellespont.[6]

The high estimation in which horses[7] were held
in remote antiquity, may be gathered from the nu-

cumino pascantur assidue, vel
hirci alarum balsami liquore tan-
gantur, i. 24. Cf. Plin. x. 52.

[1] Schol. Aristoph. Vesp. 129.

[2] Cf. Arist. Hist. Anim. vii.
6. 5.

[3] Athen. xii. 57.

[4] Strab. iii. 2. t. i. p. 231.

[5] Aristoph. Nub. 109. Suid.
v. φασιανοί. t. ii. p. 1033.
b. Thom. Magist. v. φασιανοί.

p. 885. Blancard. Of the commentators on Aristophanes, however, some by the word φασιανοί
understand horses, and some
pheasants. The probability is,
that they imported both, and
that the poet means to play upon
the word.

[6] Iliad. δ. 500.

[7] See also Iliad. ε. 358. Wolf.
Proleg. 80, seq.

merous fables invented respecting them,—as that of
the centaurs in Thessaly, of the winged courser of
Bellerophontes, and the Muses, and of the marvellous steeds presented by Poseidon to Peleus on his
marriage with Thetis. They were reckoned, likewise, among the most precious victims offered in
sacrifice to the gods. Thus we find the Trojans
plunging live horses into the whirlpool of the Sca-
mander[1] to deprecate the anger of that divinity.
The Romans, likewise, in later times, sacrificed horses
to the ocean;[2] and, in many parts of Asia, it appears to have been customary in nearly all ages, to
offer up, as anciently in Laconia,[3] this magnificent
animal on the altars of the sun.[4] Thus, among the
Armenians, whose breed, though smaller than that
of the Persians, was far more spirited, this practice
prevailed as it still does in Northern India, and
Xenophon,[5] a religious man, observes in the Ana-
basis, that he gave his steed, worn down with the
fatigues of the march, to be fed and offered up by
the Komarch, with whom he had been for some
days a guest. From Homer's account of Pandarus
we may infer, that the possessors of fine horses
often submitted to great personal inconvenience
rather than hazard the well-being of their favourites.
For this wealthy prince,[6] who possessed eleven car-

---

[1] Iliad φ. 132.

[2] Fest. v. October, t. ii. p. 521,
seq. v. Panibus, p. 555. Lomeier,
de Lustrat. cap. 23. p. 292, seq.
Propert. iv. i. 20, with the note
of Frid. Jacob, in whose edition
it is, v. i. 20.

[3] Pausan. iii. 20. 4. Fest.
v. October, t. ii. p. 520, tells us
that this horse was sacrificed to
the winds.

[4] Herod. i. 216. Brisson. de
Regn. Pers. ii. 5. The reason why
the horse was selected as a victim
to the sun, was that its swiftness
appeared to resemble that of the

god:— ὡς ταχύτατον τῷ ταχύτατῳ.
Bochart. Hierozoic. pt. i. l. ii.
c. 10. Olear. in Philost. Vit.
Apoll. Tyan. i. 31. p. 29. Justin. i. 10. Suid. v. μίθρου. t. ii.
p. 162, f. This practice is likewise mentioned by Ovid, (Fast.
i. 385, seq.)

Placat equo Persis radiis Hyperi-
    ona cinctum,
Ne detur celeri victima tarda deo.

Cf. Vigenere, Images des Philostrates, p. 773. Par. 1627.

[5] Anab. iv. 5. 35.

[6] Iliad. ε. 192, seq.

riages and twenty-two steeds, came on foot to the assistance of Priam, lest they should not find a plentiful supply of provender at Troy.

Several countries were famous [1] for their breed of horses, as Cyrene, Egypt, Syria, Phrygia, and the Phasis.[2] Thessaly, too, particularly the neighbourhood of Triccæ, abounded in barbs, as did likewise Bœotia. But one of the most remarkable races was that produced in Nisæon,[3] a district of Media, which seems to have been white, or of a bright cream colour,[4] and of extraordinary size and swiftness. On one of these Masistios[5] was mounted during the expedition into Greece. Apollo, in an oracle is said to have spoken of the beauty of mares, alluding, perhaps, to those of Elis, which were remarkable for their lightness and elegance of form; and Aristotle celebrates a particular mare of Pharsatis, called Dicæa, which was famous for bringing colts resembling their sires.[6] Among the Homeric chiefs, Achilles and Eumelos boasted the noblest coursers, as we learn from a picturesque and striking passage in the Catalogue :[7] "And now, O Muse, "declare, which of the leaders and their horses were "most illustrious. Excepting those of Achilles, the "finest steeds before Troy were those of Eume-"los from Pheræ, swift as birds, alike in mane, in "age, and so equal in size, that a rule would stand "level on their backs. They were both bred by "Apollo in Pieria, both mares, and they bore with "them the dread of battle. Noblest of all, how-

[1] Sch. Pind. Pyth. iv. 1.

[2] Sch. Aristoph. Nub. 110.

[3] Strab. xi. 13. p. 453. Τοὺς δὲ Νησαίους ἵππους, οἷς ἐχρῶντο οἱ βασιλεῖς ἀρίστοις οὖσι καὶ μεγίστοις. Cf. Herod. i. 189, on the sacred horses of Persia.

[4] Suid. v. ἵππος Νισαῖος. t. i. p. 1271. d. who relates that, according to some, the breed was found near the Erythrean Sea.

[5] Herod. ix. 20. Cf. Il. ε. 583. δ. 142, seq. In Philostratus we find mention made of a black Nisæan mare with white feet, large patch of white on the breast, and white nostrils.—Icon. ii. 5. p. 816.

[6] Hist. Anim. vii. 6.

[7] Il. ε. 760, sqq.

" ever, were the coursers of Achilles. But he, in
" his lunar-prowed, sea-passing ships remains in-
" censed against Atreides, the shepherd of his
" people; his myrmidons amuse themselves on the
" sea-shore with pitching the quoit, launching the
" javelin, and drawing the bow; their horses, stand-
" ing beside the chariots, feed upon lotus, trefoil and
" marsh parsley; and the chariots themselves, well
" covered with hangings, are drawn up in the tents
" of the chiefs, while the soldiers, sighing for the
" leading of their impetuous general, stroll carelessly
" through the camp without joining in the war."

The food of the Homeric horses,[1] was little inferior to that of their masters, since, besides the
natural delicacies of the meadows, they were indulged with sifted barley and the finest wheat.[2]
The halter with which, while feeding, they were tied
to the manger seems usually to have been of leather.
Aristotle,[3] remarks, that horses are fattened less by
their food than by what they drink, and that, like
the camel,[4] they delight in muddy water, on which
account they usually trouble the stream before
they taste it.

The Greek conception of equine beauty[5] differed

---

[1] Iliad. θ. 560. Cf. ι. 123, seq.
265, 407. κ 565, seq.

[2] Il. ε 196. On an ancient
crystal engraved in Buonaroti a
man with cap and short breeches
is represented feeding an ass with
corn. Osserv. Istorich. sop. alc.
Medagl. Antich. p. 345.

[3] Hist. Anim. viii. 10.

[4] Phile applies the same observation to the elephant :
"Ὕδωρ δὲ πίνει πλῆθος ἄφθονον
πάνυ·
Πλὴν οὐ καθαρὸν, καὶ διειδὲς οὐ
θέλει,
'Αλλ' οὖν ῥυπαρὸν καὶ κατεσπι-
λωμένον.
Iamb. de Animal. Pro-
prietat. c. 39. p. 56, 165, seq.

[5] Geop. xvi. 2. Philost. Icon.
i. 28. p. 804. Notwithstanding
the admiration of the Greeks for
horses we do not find that they
made any attempt to naturalize
among them those Shetlands of
the ancient world which, according to a very grave naturalist,
were no larger than rams. These
diminutive steeds were found in
India :—Παρά γε τοῖς ψύλλοις
καλουμένοις τῶν 'Ινδῶν, εἰσὶ γὰρ
καὶ Λιβύων ἕτεροι, ἵπποι γίνονται τῶν κριῶν οὐ μείζους.
Ælian. de Animal. xvi. 37.
Modern writers relate the same
thing of a certain breed of oxen
in India : " Naturalists speak of
" a diminutive breed of oxen in

but little from our own, since they chiefly loved
horses of those colours which are still the objects of
admiration : as snow-white, with black eyes like those
of Rhesos, which Plato thought the most beautiful;
cream-coloured, light bay, chestnut, and smoky grey.
They judged of the breeding of a horse by the short-
ness of its coat and the dusky prominence of its
veins. As a fine large mane greatly augments the
magnificent appearance of this animal, they were
careful after washing to comb and oil it[1] while they
gathered up the forelock in a band of gilded leather.[2]
The floors of their stables were commonly pitched
with round pebbles bound tight together by curbs
of iron.[3]

Horses were usually broken[4] by professed grooms,
who entered into a written agreement with the
owners implicitly to follow their directions.[5] The
process was sufficiently simple. They began with
the year-and-a-half colts,[6] on which they put a halter
when feeding, while a bridle was hung up close to
the manger, that they might be accustomed to the
touch of it, and not take fright at the jingling of
the bit.[7] The next step was to lead them into the
midst of noisy and tumultuous crowds in order to
discover whether or not they were bold enough to
be employed in war.[8] The operation was not completely finished till they were three years old. When,
on the course or elsewhere, horses had been well
sweated,[9] they were led into a place set apart for

"Ceylon, and the neighbourhood
"of Surat, no larger than a New-
"foundland dog, which, though
"fierce of aspect, are trained to
"draw children in their little
"carts." Hindoos, i. 23.

[1] Iliad, χ 281, seq.

[2] Il. ε 358.

[3] Xenoph. de Re Equest. iv. 4.

[4] Plat. de Rep. t. vi. p. 158.

[5] Xenoph. de Re Equest. ii. 2.
Cf. Œconom. iii. 11. xiii. 7.

[6] Geop. xvi. i. 11.

[7] Xen. de Re Equest. 10. 6.
Poll. viii. 184.

[8] The swimming powers of the
war-horse were probably augmented by exercise, since we find
them passing by swimming from
Rhegium to Sicily. Plut. Ti-
mol. § 19. This feat, however,
was nothing to that of the stags
which swam from Syria to Cyprus!
Ælian. De Nat. Anim. v. 56.

[9] Sch. Aristoph. Nub. 32. Cf.
25, 28.

the purpose, and, in order to dry themselves, made to roll in the sand. It was customary for owners to mark their horses with the Koppa,[1] or other letter of the alphabet, whence they were sometimes called Koppatias, Samphoras, &c.

The mule and the ass were much employed in rural labours, the former both at the cart and the plough, the latter in drawing small tumbrils, and in bearing wood[2] or other produce of the farm to the city.[3] The wild ass[4] was sometimes resorted to for improving the breed of mules, which, in the Homeric age, were found in a state of nature among the mountains of Paphlagonia.[5]

But their cares extended even to swine, which, if King Ptolemy may be credited, were sometimes distinguished in Greece for their great size and beauty. He, in fact, observes in his Memoirs, that in the city of Assos he saw a milk-white hog two cubits and a half in length, and of equal height; and adds, that King Eumenes had given four thousand drachmæ, or nearly two hundred pounds sterling, for a boar of this enormous size, to improve the breed of pigs in his country.[6] So that we perceive those great generals, whom posterity usually contemplates only in the cabinet or in the battle-field, were, at the same time, in their domestic policy, the rivals of the Earls Spencer and Leicester. Superstition, among the Cretans, prevented the improvement of bacon; for as a sow was said to have suckled the

[1] Aristoph. Eq. 601. Nub. 25. Spanh. in loc. Athen. xi. 30.

[2] In carting wood from Mount Ida in the Troad oxen are at present substituted for asses, and the bodies of the vehicles they draw, in form resembling ancient cars, are constructed of wickerwork. Chandler. i. 47.

[3] Lucian. Luc. siv. Asin. §

43. Cf. Artemid. Oneirocrit. ii. 12. p. 97.

[4] Geop. xvi. 21. Varro ii. 6. 3. To account for this care it may be observed, that rich men sometimes rode, as they still do in the East, on asses superbly caparisoned and adorned with bells. Lucian. Luc. sive Asin. § 48.   [5] Il. ε. 852.

[6] Athen. ix. 17. Cf. Steph. De Urb. 184. e.

infant Jupiter, and defended his helpless infancy, they, in gratitude,[1] abstained from hog's flesh.

In all farms the care of cattle necessarily formed a principal employment. The oxen[2] were used in ploughing, treading out the corn, drawing manure to the fields, and bringing home the produce of the harvest. To prevent their being overcome by fatigue while engaged in their labours, the husbandmen of Greece had recourse to certain expedients, one of which was, to smear their hoofs with a composition of oil and terebinth, or wax, or warm pitch:[3] while, to protect them from flies, their coats were anointed with their own saliva, or with a decoction of bruised laurel berries and oil.[4] Their milch cows, in the selection of which much judgment was displayed,[5] were commonly fed on cytisus and clover; and, still further to increase their milk, bunches of the herb dittany were sometimes tied about their flanks. The usual milking-times[6] were, in the morning immediately after the breaking-up of the dawn, and in the evening about the close of twilight; though, occasionally, both cows, sheep, and goats were milked several times during the day. In weaning calves they made use of a species of muzzle,[7] as the Arabs do in the case of young camels. Their pails, like our own, were of wood,[8] but somewhat differently shaped, being narrow above, and spreading towards the bottom. When conveyed into the dairy the milk

[1] Athen. ix. 18.

[2] Scheffer, De Re Vehic. p. 80; et vid. Dickenson, Delph. Phæ-nicizant. c. 10. p. 116, seq. Heresbach. De Re Rust. p. 236, sqq.

[3] Geop. xvii. 9, with the note of Niclas. Aristoph. Hist. Anim. viii. 7. 23. Cato. De Re Rust. 72. Plin. xxviii. 81.

[4] African. ap. Geop. xvii. 11.

[5] Geop. xvii. 2. 8.

[6] Buttm. Lexil. p. 86.

[7] Hesych. v. πύσσαχος.

[8] Eustath. ad Odyss. ε. p. 219. Their milk-cups were sometimes of ivy. Eurip. Fragm. Androm. 27. Athen. xi. 53. Macrob. Sat. v. 21. Cf. on the milk-pans and cheese-vats, Poll. x. 130; Theocrit. Eidyll. v. 87. Milk-pails were sometimes called πέλλαι, ἀμολγοὶ, γαλακτοδόκα, and out of these they sometimes drank. Schol. i. 25.

was poured into pans,[1] on the form of which I have
hitherto found no information.[2] That they skimmed
their milk is evident (whatever they may have done
with the cream), from the mention of that thin
pellicle which is found on it only when skimmed,
whether scalded or not. " Here, drink this!" said
Glycera to Menander, when he had returned one
day in exceeding ill-humour from the theatre. " I
" don't like the wrinkled skin," replied the poet to
the lady, whose beauty, it must be remembered,
was at this time on the wane. " Blow it off," replied
she, immediately comprehending his meaning, " and
take what is beneath."[3] Milk, in those warm latitudes, grows sour more rapidly than with us; but
the ancients observed that it would keep three days
when it had been scalded, and stirred until cold with
a reed or ferula.[4]

The Greeks of classical times appear to have made
no use of butter,[5] though so early as the age of Hippocrates they were well enough acquainted with its
existence and properties.[6] Even in the present day
butter is much less used in Greece than in most
European countries, its place being supplied by fine
olive oil. For cheese, however, they seem to have
entertained a partiality, though it is probable that
the best they could manufacture would have lost
very considerably in comparison with good Stilton
or Cheshire, not to mention Parmasan. It was a
favourite food, however, among soldiers in Attica,
who during war used to supply themselves both with

[1] Cf. Il. π. 642, et Schol. Venet. Etym. Mag. 659. 41. Athen.
xi. 91.
[2] Even Philostratus, while
mentioning these vessels, filled to
the brim with milk, on which
the cream lies rich and shining,
omits to furnish any hint of their
form : — ψυκτῆρες γάλακτος, οὐ
λευκοῦ μόνον, ἀλλὰ καὶ στιλπ-
νοῦ· καὶ γὰρ στίβειν ἔοικεν, ὑπὸ

τῆς ἐπιπολαζούσης αὐτῷ πιμελῆς.
Icon. i. 31. p. 809.
[3] Athen. xiii. 49.
[4] Geop. xviii. 19. 4.
[5] See Beckman. Hist. of Inv. i.
372, seq. Butter is made at
present in Greece by filling a skin
with cream and treading on it.
Chandler, ii. 245.
[6] Foes, Œconom. Hippoc. v.
πικέριον, p. 306.

cheese and meal.[1] Their cheese-lope or rennet in most cases resembled our own, consisting of the liquid substance found in the ruen of new-born animals, as calves, kids, or hares, which was considered superior to lamb's rennet.[2] Occasionally they employed for the same purpose burnt salt or vinegar, fowl's crop or pepper, the flowers of bastard saffron, or the threads which grow on the head of the artichoke. For these again, was sometimes substituted the juice of the fig-tree;[3] or a branch freshly cut[4] was used in stirring the milk while warming on the fire. This cheese would seem, for the most part, to have been eaten while fresh and soft,[5] like that of Neufchatel, though they were acquainted with various means of preserving it for a considerable space of time. Acidulated curds were kept soft by being wrapped in the leaves of the terebinth tree, or plunged in oil, or sprinkled with salt. When desirous of preserving their cheese for any length of time, they washed it in pure water, and, after drying it in the sun, laid it upon earthen jars with thyme and summer savory. Some other kinds were kept in a sort of pickle, composed of sweet vinegar or oxymel or sea-water, which was poured into the jars until it entirely penetrated and covered the whole mass. When they wished to communicate a peculiar whiteness to the cheese, they laid it up in brine. Dry cheese was rendered more solid and sharp-tasted by being placed within reach of the smoke. If from age it were hard or bitter,

---

[1] Sch. Aristoph. Pac. 394.

[2] Varro. De Re Rust. ii. 11. 4. Colum. vii. 8. Eustath ad Il. ε. p. 472. Hesych. v. ὀπὸς.— Mœris: ὀπός ’Αττικοί, πυτία Ἕλληνες, p. 205. Cf. Aristot. Hist. Anim. iv. 21.

[3] The cheese made in this manner was called ὀπίας. Eurip. Cyclop. 136. Athen. xiv. 76. Schol. Aristoph. Vesp. 353.

Dioscor. i. 183. Plin. xxiii. 63. Plut. Sympos. vi. 10.

[4] Geop. xviii. 12. These cheeses were sometimes made in box-wood moulds. Colum. vii. 8.

[5] Philostratus describes one of these delicate little cheeses freshly made and quivering like a slice of blanc-manger:—καὶ τρυφαλὶς ἐφ’ ἑτέρου φύλλου νεοπαγὴς, καὶ σαλεύουσα. Icon. i. 31. p. 809.

it was thrown into a preparation of barley-meal, then soaked in water, and what rose to the top was skimmed off.[1]

That the milk-women in Greece understood all the arts of their profession may be gathered from the instructions which have been left us on the best methods of detecting the presence of water in milk. If you dip a sharp rush into milk, says Berytios, and it run off easily, there is water in it. And again, if you pour a few drops upon your thumb-nail, the pure milk will maintain its position, while the adulterated will immediately glide away![2]

Their mode of fattening cattle[3] was as follows: first they fed them on cabbage chopped small and steeped in vinegar, to which succeeded chaff and gurgions during five days. This diet was then exchanged for barley, of which for nearly a week they were allowed four cotylæ a-day, the quantity being then gradually augmented for six other days. As of necessity the hinds were stirring early, the cattle began even in winter to be fed at cock-crowing; a second quantity of food was given them about dawn, when they were watered, and their remaining allowance towards evening. In summer their first meal commenced at day-break, the second at mid-day, and the third about sunset. They were at this time of the year suffered to drink at noon and night of water rendered somewhat tepid; in winter it was considerably warmer.

About Mossynos, in Thrace, cattle were sometimes fed upon fish, which was likewise given to horses, and even to sheep. Herodotus, who mentions a similar fact, calls food of this description χόρτος, "fodder,"[4] though hay or dried straw was, doubtless, its original meaning. The provender of cattle in the district about Ænia appears to have been

[1] Geop. xviii. 19.
[2] Geop. xviii. 20.
[3] Geop. xvii. 12. Heresbach. p. 233. a.

[4] Herod. v. 16. Athen. vii. 72. Ælian. de Nat. Anim. v. 25. Cf. Sch. Aristoph. Pac. 891.

so wholesome, that the herds which fed upon it
were never afflicted by the mange.[1]

Among the animals domesticated and rendered
useful by the Greeks we must, doubtless, reckon
bees,[2] which, in the heroic ages, had not yet been
confined in hives. For, whenever Homer describes
them, it is either where they are streaming forth
from a rock,[3] or settling in bands and clusters on
the spring flowers. So, likewise, in Virgil, they

> Hunt the golden dew ;
> In summer time on tops of lilies feed,
> And creep within their bells to suck the balmy seed.

In that Bœotian old savage, Hesiod,[4] however, we
undoubtedly find mention of the hive where he is
uncourteously comparing women to drones—

> As when within their well-roofed hives the bees
> Maintain the mischief-working drones at ease,
> Their task pursuing till the golden sun
> Down to the western wave his course hath run,
> Filling their shining combs, while snug within
> Their fragrant cells, the drones, with idle din,
> As princes revel o'er their unpaid bowls,
> On others' labours cheer their worthless souls.

As the honey of Attica constantly, in antiquity,
enjoyed the reputation of being the finest in the
world,[5] the management of bees naturally formed in

---

[1] Theoph. Hist. Plant. iv. 14. 3.

[2] Athen. iii. 59. Sch. Aristoph. Vesp. 107.

[3] Il. ϛ. 87. μ. 67. Odyss. ν. 106.

[4] Theogon. 594, seq.—Pro σίμ-
ϐλοισι, quod præbet R. S., cæteri
Mss. σμήνεσσι. Schæferus tamen
malebat σίμϐλοισιν ἐπηρεφέεσι.
Gœttling. But Goguet, who has
considered this passage, does not
think that " hives " are meant ;
because, if their use had been
known in the times of Hesiod,

he would not have failed to leave
us some directions on the subject.
Origine des Loix, t. iii. p. 399.
Wolff, following in the footsteps
of Heyne, gets easily over the
difficulty by pronouncing the
whole passage, v. 590 — 612,
spurious. Gœttling, p. 55. Cf.
Schol. Aristoph. Nub. 937.
Phile, de Animal. Proprietat. c.
28. p. 87, seq.

[5] The pasturage of Hymettos,
however, was, by Pausanias, regarded as second to that of the

that country an important branch of rural economy. The natural history, moreover, of the bee was studied with singlar enthusiam by the Greeks in general. Aristomachos of Soli, devoted to it fifty-eight years, and Philiscos, the Thasian, who passed his life among bees in a desert, obtained on that account the name of the Wild Man. Both wrote on the subject.[1]

This branch of rural economy was carried to very great perfection in Attica. The vocabulary[2] connected with it was extensive, as every separate operation had its technical term, by the study of which, chiefly, an insight into their practice is obtained. Thus, from certain expressions employed by Aristotle[3] and Pollux, it seems clear that bee-managers, whom we may occasionally call melitturgi, constituted a separate division among the industrious classes; and these, instructed by constant experience, probably anticipated most of the improvements imagined in modern times. For example, instead of destroying the valuable and industrious little insects for the purpose of obtaining possession of their spoils, they in some cases compelled them by smoke to retire temporarily from the hive, whence their treasures were to be taken; and in the mining districts about Laureion they understood the art, concerning which, however, no particulars are known, of procuring the virgin honey pure and unsmoked.[4]

The grounds of a melitturgos or bee-keeper were

Alazones on the river Halys, where the bees were tame, and worked in common in the fields. i. 32. 1.

[1] Plin. Hist. Nat. xi. 9.

[2] Poll. i. 254. Artemid. Oneirocrit. ii. 22. p. 109.

[3] Hist. Anim. v. 22. ix. 40. Etym. Mag. 458. 44.

[4] Τοῦ δὲ μέλιτος, ἀρίστου ὄντος τῶν πάντων τοῦ Ἀττικοῦ, πολὺ βέλτιστον φάσι τὸ ἐν τοῖς ἀργυ-ρέοις, ὁ καὶ ἀκαπνίστον καλοῦσιν ἀπὸ τοῦ τρόπου τῆς σκευασίας. Strab. ix. 2. t. ii. p. 246. — Wheler describes the modern method observed by the Athenians in taking honey without destroying the bee, but in a style so lengthy and uncouth, that I must content myself with a reference to his travels. Book vi. p. 412, seq.

chosen and laid out with peculiar care.[1] In a sheltered spot, generally on the thymy slope of a hill,
the hives were arranged in the midst of flowers and
odoriferous shrubs. And if the necessary kinds had
not by nature been scattered there, they were planted
by the gardener. Experience soon taught them what
blossoms and flowers yielded the best honey,[2] and
were most agreeable to the bees. These, in Attica,
were supposed to be the wild pear-tree, the bean,
clover, a pale-coloured vetch, the syria, myrtle, wild
poppy, wild thyme, and the almond-tree.[3] To which
may be added the rose, balm gentle, the galingale
or odoriferous rush, basil royal, and above all the
cytisus,[4] which begins to flower about the vernal
equinox, and continues in bloom to the end of September.[5] Of all the plants, however, affected by the
bee, none is so grateful to it as the thyme, which
so extensively abounds in Attica and Messenia[6] as
to perfume the whole atmosphere. In Sicily too,
all the slopes and crests of its beautiful hills, from
Palermo to Syracuse, are invested with a mantle of
thyme,[7] and other odoriferous shrubs, which, according to Varro, gives the superior flavour to the Sicilian honey. Box-wood abounded on mount Cytoros,

[1] On the management of bees
in Circassia and other countries
on the Black Sea, see Pallas,
Travels in Southern Russia, ii.
p. 204.

[2] On the coast of the Black Sea
bees sucked honey from the grape.
Geop. v. 2.

[3] Arist. Hist. Anim. ix. 26, 27.

[4] Geop. xv. 2. 6.

[5] Varro, De Re Rust. iii. 16.

[6] Sibthorpe in Walpole's Memoirs, t. ii. p. 62.   Geop. xv. 2.
5. Speaking of Hymettos, Chandler observes, that it produces a
succession of aromatic plants,
herbs, and flowers, calculated to
supply the bee with nourishment
both in winter and summer, ii. p.

143. " Les montagnes (des îles)
" sont couvertes de thym et de
" lavande. Les abeilles, qui y
" volent par nuées, en tirent un
" miel qui est aussi transparent
" que notre gelée."   Della Rocca,
Traité sur les Abeilles, t. i. 6.

[7] This plant in Greece flowers
about midsummer, and those who
kept bees conjectured whether
honey would be plentiful or not,
according as it was more or less
luxuriant. Theoph. Hist. Plant.
vi. 2, 3.   The wild thyme of
Greece was a creeping plant which
was sometimes trained on poles or
hedges, or even in pits, the sides
of which it speedily covered.   Id.
vi. 7. 5.

in Galatia, and in the island of Corsica, on which account the honey of the latter country was bitter.[1]

In selecting a spot for hives, the ancients observed a rule which I do not recollect to have been mentioned by modern bee-keepers, and that was to avoid the neighbourhood of an echo,[2] which by repeating their own buzzing and murmuring suggested the idea perhaps of invisible rivals. Place them not, says Virgil,[3]

> Near hollow rocks that render back the sound,
> And doubled images of voice rebound.

Care was taken to conduct near the hives small runnels of the purest water, not exceeding two or three inches in depth with shells or pebbles rising dry above the surface, whereon the bees might alight to drink.[4] When of necessity the apiary was situated

[1] Theoph. Hist. Plant. iii. 15. 5. The honey of modern Crete is esteemed of a good quality. Pashley, Travels, vol. i. p. 56.

[2] Echo, in the mythology, is said to have been beloved of Pan, by which she seems tacitly to be connected with the generation of Panic Terrors Polyæn. Stratagem. i. 2. 1. Offensive smells are often reckoned among the aversions of bees, but I fear without good reason. At least they have sometimes been found to select strange places wherein to deposit their treasures of sweets. In the book of Judges, chap. xiv. ver. 8, seq., it is related that, when Samson, on his way to Timnath, turned aside to view the carcass of a young lion which he had a short time previously slain, " be-" hold, there was a swarm of bees " and honey in the carcass of the " lion, and he took thereof in his " hands and went on eating, and " came to his father and mother,

" and he gave them and they " did eat, but he told not them " that he had taken the honey " out of the carcass of the lion." Upon this passage the following may serve as a note : — " Among this pretty collection " of natural curiosities, (in the " cemetery of Algesiras,) one in " particular attracted our atten-" tion ; this was the contents of a " small uncovered coffin in which " lay a child, the cavity of the " chest exposed and tenanted by " an industrious colony of bees. " The comb was rapidly progress-" ing, and I suppose, according to " the adage of the poet, they were " adding sweets to the sweet, if " not perfume to the violet." Napier, Excursions on the Shores of the Mediterranean, v. i. 127.

[3] Georg. iv. 50, with the commentaries of Servius and Philargyrius ; and Varro, De Re Rust. iii. 16.

[4] Cf. Geop. xv. 2, 3, 4.

on the margin of lakes or larger streams other contrivances were had recourse to for the convenience
of the airy labourers.

> Then o'er the running stream or standing lake
> A passage for thy weary people make,
> With osier floats the standing water strow,
> Of massy stones make bridges if it flow,
> That basking in the sun thy bees may lie
> And resting there their flaggy pinions dry,
> When late returning home the laden host
> By raging winds is wrecked upon the coast.

Their hives were of various kinds and shapes.
Some, like the modern Circassians, they made with
fine wicker-work, of a round form and carefully plastered on the inside with clay.[1]   Other hives were
constructed of bark, especially that of the cork-tree,
others of fig, oxya, beech, and pine-wood,[2] others, as
now in Spain, of the trunk of a hollow tree, others
of earthenware, as is the practice in .Russia; and
others again of plaited cane of a square shape, three
feet in length and about one in breadth, but so contrived that, should the honey materials prove scanty,
they might be contracted, lest the bees should lose
courage if surrounded by a large empty space.   The
wicker-hives were occasionally plastered both inside
and outside with cow-dung to fill up the cavities
and smooth the surface.[3]   A more beautiful species
of hive was sometimes made with the lapis specularis,[4] which, being almost as transparent as glass,
enabled the curious owner to contemplate the movements and works of the bees.[5]   When finished, they
were placed on projecting slabs, so as not to touch
or be easily shaken.   There were generally three

---

[1] Vir. Georg. iv. 34, seq. Var-
ro, iii. 16.   Colum. ix. 2—7.
Sch. Aristoph. Nub. 295. Vesp.
241.   Callim. Hymn. i. 50.   Cf.
Wheler, Travels into Greece.
Book vi. p. 411.

[2] Geop. xv. 2. 7. Cf. Theoph.
Hist. Plant. iii. 10. 1.

[3] Geop. xv. 2. 8. Varro, iii. 16.
Colum. ix. 14.   Pallad. vii. 8.
Cato. 81.

[4] Plin. xxi. 47.

[5] At present the hives, we are
told, are set on the ground in
rows enclosed within a low wall.
Chandler, ii. 143.

rows of hives rising above each other like Egyptian
tombs on the face of the wall, and there was a prejudice against adding a fourth.

The fences of apiaries were made high and strong
to protect the inmates from the inroads of the bears,[1]
which would otherwise have overthrown the hives
and devoured all the combs.[2] Another enemy of the
bee was the Merops,[3] which makes its appearance
about Hymettos towards the end of summer.[4]

There were, in ancient times, two entrances,
one on either hand, and on the top a lid, which
the Melitturgos could remove when he desired to
take the honey, or inspect the condition of the bees.
The best of these lids were made of bark, the worst
of earthenware, which were cold in winter, and in
summer exceedingly hot.[5] It was considered necessary during spring and the succeeding season
for the bee-keeper to inspect the hives thrice a
month, to fumigate them slightly, and remove
all filth and vermin. He was careful, likewise, to
destroy the usurpers if there were more than one
queen,[6] since, in Varro's[7] opinion, they gave rise to

[1] Phile gives a long list of the bees' foes, which begins as follows:

Ὄφις, δὲ καὶ σφὴξ, καὶ χελιδὼν,
καὶ φρύνος,
Μύρμηξ τε, καὶ σὴς, αἰγιθαλὴς,
καὶ φάλαγξ,
Καὶ σαῦρος ὠχρὸς, καὶ φαγεῖν
δεινὸς μέροψ,
Σμήνει μελισσῶν δυσμενεῖς ὁδοσ-
τάται.

Iamb. De Animal. Proprietat.
c. 30, p. 104, seq.

[2] Arist. Hist. Anim. viii. 5.
Plin. Nat. Hist. viii. 54.

[3] Besides this enemy the bees of America have another still more audacious, that is to say, the monkey, which either carries off their combs or crushes them for the purpose of dipping his tail in

the honey, which he afterwards sucks at his leisure. Schneider, Observ. sur Ulloa, t. ii. p. 199.— See a very amusing chapter on the enemies of the bee in Della Rocca, iii. 219, sqq.

[4] Sibthorpe in Walp. Mem. i. 75. The practice, moreover, of stealing hives was not unknown to the ancients. Plat. De Legg. t. viii. p. 104.

[5] Colum. ix. 6. Della Rocca, however, considers this kind as equal to any other, except that it is more fragile. t. ii. p. 17.

[6] Geop. xv. 2. 15.

[7] De Re Rust. iii. 16, 18. Colum. ix. 9. 6. Hist. Anim. v. 19, 22. Xenoph. Œconom. vii. 32.

sedition ; but Aristotle thinks there ought to be
several, lest one should die, and the hive along
with it. Of the queen bees there are three kinds,
the black, the ruddy, and the variegated; though
Menecrates, who is good authority, speaks only of
the black and variegated.[1]   Aristotle, however, describes the reddish queen bee as the best. Even
among the working insects there are two kinds, the
smaller, in form round, and variegated in colour,
the larger, which is the tame bee, less active and
beautiful. The former, or wild bee,[2] frequents the
mountains, forests, and other solitary places, labours
indefatigably, and collects honey in great quantities;
the latter, which feeds among gardens, and in man's
neighbourhood, fills its hive more slowly.[3]   With
respect to the drones, or males, which the working
bees generally expel at a certain time of the year,
the Attic melitturgi got rid of them in a very ingenious manner. It was observed, that these gentlemen though no way inclined to work, would yet
occasionally, on very fine days, go abroad for exercise, rushing forth in squadrons, mounting aloft into
the air, and there wheeling, and sporting, and ma-
nœuvring in the sun.[4]   Taking advantage of their
absence, they spread a fine net over the hive-en-
trance, the meshes of which, large enough to
admit the bee, would exclude the drone. On returning, therefore, they found themselves, according
to the old saying, " on the smooth side of the door,"
and were compelled to seek fresh lodgings.[5]

In late springs, or when there is a drought or
blight, the bees breed very little, but make a great
deal of honey, whereas in wet seasons they keep
more at home, and attend to breeding. Swarms in
Greece[6] appeared about the ripening of the olive.

[1] Cf. Geop. xv. 2, 6.
[2] On the humble bee, see Sch.
Aristoph. Acharn. 831.
[3] Varro, De Re Rust. iii. 16.
[4] Arist. Hist. Anim. ix. 27.

[5] Arist. Hist. Anim. v. 21.
Cf. Xenoph. Œcon. xvii. 14, seq.
[6] Cf. Sch. Aristoph. Vesp. 425.
In the island of Cuba, where the
tame bee was originally intro-

Aristotle is of opinion, that honey is not manufactured by the bee, but falls perfectly formed from the atmosphere, more especially at the heliacal rising or setting of certain stars, and when the rainbow appears. He observes, too, that no honey is found before the rising of the Pleiades,[1] which happens about the thirteenth of May.[2] This opinion is in exact conformity with the fact, that at certain seasons of the year what is called the honey dew descends, covering thick the leaves of the oak, and several other trees, which at such times literally drop with honey. On these occasions the bees find little to do beyond the labour of conveying it to their cells, and, accordingly, have been known to fill the hive in one or two days. It has been observed, moreover, that autumn flowers, which yield very little fragrance, yield, also, little or no honey. In the kingdom of Pontos there was a race of white bees which made honey twice a month ; and at Themiscyra there were those which built their combs both in hives and in the earth, producing very little wax, but a great deal of honey.[3]

duced by the English, it has been found to swarm and multiply with incredible rapidity, each hive sometimes sending forth two swarms per month, so that the mountains are absolutely filled with them. This rapid increase seems to have taken place chiefly in the neighbourhood of the sugar plantations, which they were long since supposed to deteriorate by extracting too much honey from the cane. Don Ulloa, Memoires Philosophiques, &c., t. i. p. 185. In North America where bees are known among the natives by the name of the " English Flies," they betray an invariable tendency for migrating southward. Kalm. t. ii. 427. Schneider, Observ. sur Ulloa, ii. 198.

[1] Hist. Anim. v. 22. Orion rises on the 9th of July, Gœttling ad Hesiod. Opp. et Dies, 598. Arcturus, 18th September. Id. 610.

[2] A similar opinion has been sometimes maintained also by the moderns :—" I have heard," observes Lord Bacon, " from one " that was industrious in hus- " bandry, that the labour of the " bee is about the wax, and that " he hath known in the beginning " of May, honey combs empty " of honey, and within a fort- " night when the sweet dews " fall filled like a cellar."—Sylva Sylvarum, 612.

[3] Arist. Hist. Anim. v. 22. In the Crimea wild bees are found in great abundance in the clefts

When the time of year arrived for robbing the
bee, some hives were found to produce five, others
ten, others fifteen quarts of honey, still leaving sufficient for winter consumption.[1] And in determining
what quantity would suffice great judgment was required; for if too much remained the labourers grew
indolent, if too little they lost their spirits. However, in this latter case the bee-keepers, having ascertained that they were in need of food, introduced
a number of sweet figs, and other similar fruit into
the hive, as now we do moist sugar in a split cane.
Elsewhere the practice was to boil a number of
rich figs in water[2] till they were reduced to a jelly,
which was then formed into cakes and set near the
hive. Together with this, some bee-keepers placed
honey-water, wherein they threw locks of purple
wool, on which the bees might stand to drink.[3]
Certain melitturgi, desirous of distinguishing their
own bees[4] when spread over the meadows, sprinkled
them with fine flour. Mention is made of a person

and caverns of the mountains.—
Pallas, Travels in Southern Russia, iii. 324. Among the numerous species of wild bees found in
America there is one which pre-
eminently deserves to be introduced into Europe and brought
under the dominion of man. This
bee does not, like the ordinary
kind, deposit its honey in combs
but in separate waxen cells about
the size and shape of a pigeon's
egg. As the honey of this bee is
of an excellent quality, many
persons in South America have
been at the pains to tame its
maker, whose labours have proved
extremely profitable.—Schneider,
Observ. sur Ulloa, ii. 200.

[1] Arist. Hist. Anim. ix. 27.
24. In Attica, the honey was
taken about the summer solstice;

at Rome about the festival of
Vulcan, in the month of August.
—Winkelmann. Hist. de l' Art,
i. 65. But commentators are
not at all agreed respecting the
meaning of Pliny, whom this
writer relies upon. xi. 15. Cf.
Sch. Aristoph. Eq. 797.

[2] Arist. Hist. Anim. ix. 27.
19. Sch. Aristoph. Eq. 752. Cf.
Meurs. Græc. Ludib. p. 13.

[3] Varro, de Re Rust. iii. 16.

[4] A gentleman in Surrey desirous of knowing his own bees,
when he should chance to meet
them in the fields, touched their
wings with vermilion as they
were issuing from the hive. Being one fine day in summer on
a visit at Hampstead, he found
them thickly scattered among the
wild flowers on the heath.

who obtained five thousand pounds' weight of honey annually; and Varro[1] speaks of two soldiers who, with a small country house, and an acre of ground left them by their father, realised an independent fortune.

Theophrastus, in a fragment[2] of one of his lost works, speaks of three different kinds of honey, one collected from flowers, another which, according to his philosophy, descended pure from heaven, and a third produced from canes. This last, which was sometimes denominated Indian honey, is the sugar of modern times. There appear, likewise, to have been other kinds of sugar manufactured from different substances, as Tamarisk and Wheat.[3] The honey-dew, on the production of which the ancients[4] held many extraordinary opinions, was supposed to be superior to the nectar of the bee.

Amyntas, in his Stations of Asia, cited by Athenæus, gives a curious account of this sort of honey which was collected in various parts of the East, particularly in Syria. In some cases they gathered the leaves of the tree, chiefly the linden and the oak, on which the dew was most abundantly[5] found, and pressed them together like those masses of Syrian figs, which were called *palathè*. Others allowed it to drop from the leaves and harden into globules, which, when desirous of using, they broke, and, having poured water thereon in wooden bowls called *tabaitas*, drank the mixture. In the districts of Mount Lebanon[6] the honey-dew fell plentifully

[1] De Re Rust, iii. 16.

[2] Preserved by Photius. Biblioth. cod. 278. p. 529. b.

[3] Herod. vii. 31. Cf. iv. 194.

[4] On the origin of the honey-dew, see the Quarterly Journal of Agriculture, No. XLIV. p. 499, sqq.

[5] Theoph. Hist. Plant. iii. 7. 6. Cf. Hes. Opp. et Dies, 232. seq. Cf. Lord Bacon, Sylva Sylvarum. 496.

[6] Schneid. Comm. ad Theoph. Frag. t. iv. p. 822.

several times during the year, and was collected
by spreading skins under the trees, and shaking
into them the liquid honey from the leaves; they
then filled therewith numerous vessels, in which it
was preserved for use. On these occasions, the
peasants used to exclaim, " Zeus has been raining
honey!"

CHAPTER II.

GARDEN AND ORCHARD.

LORD BACON, who loved to be surrounded by plants and trees and flowers, delivers it as his opinion, that the scientific culture of gardens affords a surer mark of the advance of civilisation than any improvement in the science of architecture, since men, he observes, enjoyed the luxury of magnificent palaces before that of picturesque and well-ordered garden-grounds. This, likewise, was the conviction of the ancient Greeks,[1] in whose literature we everywhere discover vestiges of a passion for that voluptuous solitude which men taste in artificial and secluded plantations, amid flower-beds and arbours and hanging vines and fountains and smooth shady walks. No full description, however, of an Hellenic garden has survived ; even the poets have contented themselves with affording us glimpses of their " studious walks and shades." We must, therefore, endeavour, by the aid of scattered hints, chance expressions, fragments, and a careful study of the natural and invariable productions of the country, to work out for ourselves a picture of what the gardens of Peisistratos, or Cimon, or Pericles, or Epicurus, whom Pliny[2] denominates the *magister hortorum*, or

---

[1] But see Dr. Nolan on the Grecian Rose, Trans. Roy. Soc. ii. p. 330, and Poll. i. 229.

[2] Hist. Nat. xix. 4. Dr. Nolan, p. 330. Nic. Caussin. De Eloquent. xi. p. 727, seq. Cic. De Senect. § 17. Ælian. De Nat. Anim. xiii. 18, has a brief but interesting description of the gar-den of the Indian kings, with its evergreen groves, fish-ponds, and flights of peacocks, pheasants, and parrots, reckoned sacred by the Brahmins. Cf. Xenoph. Œconom. iv. 13, where he celebrates the fondness of the Persian kings for gardens.

any other Grecian gentleman, must in the best ages
have been.

That portion of the ground [1] which was devoted
to the culture of sweet-smelling shrubs and flowers,
usually approached and projected inwards between
the back wings of the house, so that from the windows the eye might alight upon the rich and variegated tints of the parterres [2] intermingled with verdure, while the evening and morning breeze wafted
clouds of fragrance into the apartments. [3] The lawns,
shrubberies, bosquets, thickets, arcades, and avenues,
were, in most cases, laid out in a picturesque though
artificial manner, the principal object appearing to
have been to combine use with magnificence, and
to enjoy all the blended hues and odours which the
plants and trees acclimated in Hellas could afford.
Protection, in summer, from the sun's rays, is, in those
southern latitudes, an almost necessary ingredient
of pleasure, and, therefore, numerous trees, as the
cedar, [4] the cypress, the black and white poplar, [5] the
ash, the linden, the elm, and the platane, rose here
and there in the grounds, in some places singly, elsewhere in clumps, uniting their branches above, and
affording a cool and dense shade. Beneath these
umbrageous arches the air was further refrigerated
by splashing fountains, [6] whose waters, through nu-

---

[1] Here sometimes were grown
both vegetables, as lettuces, radishes, parsley, &c., and flowering
shrubs, as the wild or rose-laurel,
which was supposed to be a deadly poison to horses and asses.
Lucian. Luc. siv. Asin. § 17.

[2] Luc. Piscat. § 6.

[3] Geop. x. 1. 1. xii. 2.

[4] The cedar still grows wild
on the promontory of Sunium.
Chandler, ii. 8.

[5] Sibth. Flor. Græc. t. i. pl. 4.

[6] Plato describes, though not
in a garden, a fountain and a
plane-tree, in language so pic-

turesque and harmonious, that it
has captivated the imagination of
all succeeding writers, many of
whom have sought to express
their admiration by imitating it
in their own style: —Ἥ τε γὰρ
πλάτανος αὕτη μάλ' ἀμφιλαφής
τε καὶ ὑψηλή, τοῦ τε ἄγνου τὸ
ὕψος καὶ τὸ σύσκιον πάγκαλον,
καὶ ὡς ἀγμὴν ἔχει τῆς ἄνθης, ὡς
ἂν εὐωδέστατον παρέχοι τὸν τό-
πον· ἥ τε αὖ πηγὴ χαριεστάτη
ὑπο τῆς πλατάνου ῥεῖ μάλα ψυχροῦ ὕδατος, ὥς τε γε τῷ ποδὶ
τεκμήρασθαι· νυμφῶν τέ τινων καὶ
Ἀχελώου ἱερὸν ἀπὸ τῶν κορῶν τε

merous fair channels, straight or winding, as the use
demanded of them required,[1] spread themselves over
the whole garden, refreshing the eye and keeping
up a perpetual verdure. Copses of myrtles, of roses,
of agnus-castus,[2] and other odoriferous shrubs intermingled, clustering round a pomegranate-tree, were
usually placed on elevated spots,[3] that, being thus
exposed to the winds, they might the more freely
diffuse their sweetness. The spaces between trees
were sometimes planted with roses,[4] and lilies, and
violets, and golden crocuses;[5] and sometimes presented a breadth of smooth, close, green sward,
sprinkled with wild-flowers, as the violet and the blue
veronica,[6] the pink, and the pale primrose, the golden
motherwort, the cowslip, the daisy, the pimpernel,
and the periwinkle. In many gardens the custom

καὶ ἀγαλμάτων ἔοικεν εἶναι· εἰ
δ᾽ αὖ βούλει, τὸ εὔπνουν τοῦ
τόπου ὡς ἀγαπητὸν καὶ σφόδρα
ἡδύ· θερινόν τε καὶ λιγυρὸν ὑπηχεῖ τῷ τῶν τεττίγων χορῷ, πάντων δὲ κομψότατον τὸ τῆς πόας ὅτι
ἐν ἠρέμα προσάντει ἱκανὴ πέφυκε
κατακλινέντι τὴν κεφαλὴν παγ-
κάλως ἔχειν. Phæd. t. i. p. 8,
seq. The prevailing image in
this passage is thus expressed by
Cicero : " Cur non imitamur So-
" cratem illum, qui est in Phæ-
" dro Platonis ; nam me hæc tua
" platanus admonuit, quæ non
" minus ad opacandum hunc lo-
" cum patulis est diffusa ramis,
" quam illa cujus umbram secu-
" tus est Socrates quæ mihi vi-
" detur non tam ipsa aquula,
" quæ describitur, quam Platonis
" oratione crevisse." De Orat. i.
7. The picture is slightly varied by Aristinætos, who introduces it into a garden : — Ἡ δὲ
πηγὴ χαριεστάτη ὑπὸ τῇ πλα-
τάνῳ ῥεῖ ὕδατος εὖ μάλα ψυχροῦ,
ὥς γε τῷ ποδὶ τεκμήρασθαι, καὶ
διαφανοῦς τοσοῦτον, ὥστε συν-

επινηχομένων καὶ διὰ διαυγὲς ὑδά-
τιον διαπλεκομένων ἐπαφροδίτως
ἀλλήλοις, ἅπαν ἡμῶν φανερῶς
ἀποκαταφαίνεσθαι μέλος. Epist.
Lib. i. Epist. 3. p. 14. On the epithet ἀμφιλαφὴς, which Ruhnken
(ad Tim. Lex. p. 24) observes
was almost exclusively appropriated by the ancients to the
Plane tree, see Apollon. Rhod. ii.
733. Wellauer. et schol.

[1] Where running water was not
to be obtained, they constructed
two gardens, the one for winter,
which depended on the showers,
the other on a northern exposure,
where a fresh, cool air was preserved throughout the summer.
Geop. xii. 5.

[2] Used by rustics in crowns.
Athen. xv. 12. Prometheus was
crowned with agnus-castus. 13.

[3] Geop. xi. 7. Plin. xv. 18.

[4] Geop. x. 1. 3.

[5] Which delighted particularly
in the edges of paths and trodden
places. Theoph. Hist. Plant. vi. 6.1.

[6] Sibth. Flor. Græc. t. i. pl. 5,
sqq.

was, to plant each kind of tree in separate groups, and each species of flower-bed also had, as now in Holland,[1] a distinct space assigned to it; so that there were beds of white violets,[2] of irises, of the golden cynosure,[3] of hyacinths, of ranunculuses, of the blue campanula, or Canterbury bells, of white gilliflowers, carnations, and the branchy asphodel.

One of the principal causes which induced the Greeks to attend to the culture of ornamental shrubs and flowers, was the perpetual use made of them in crowns and garlands.[4] Nearly all their ceremonies, whether civil or religious, were performed by individuals wearing certain wreaths about their brow.

[1] Laing, Notes of a Traveller, p. 6.

[2] Geop. xi. 21, 23, sqq.

[3] Sibth. Flor. Græc. t. i. pl. 79. pl. 203. pl. 334, &c.

[4] Πρῶτον μὲν γὰρ ἀφ᾽ ὧν ζῶσιν οἱ ἄνθρωποι, ταῦτα ἡ γῆ φέρει ἐργαζομένοις· καὶ ἀφ᾽ ὧν τοίνυν ἡδυπαθοῦσι προσεπιφέρει. —Ἔπειτα δὲ ὅσα κοσμοῦσι βωμοὺς καὶ ἀγάλματα, καὶ οἷς αὐτοὶ κοσμοῦνται, καὶ ταῦτα μετὰ ἡδίστων ὀσμῶν καὶ θεαμάτων παρέχει. κ. τ. λ. Xenoph. Œconom. v. 2, seq.

Pliny has a curious passage on the use of crowns among the Romans, which Holland has thus translated: "Now when these "garlands of flowers were taken "up and received commonly in all "places for a certain time, there "came soon after into request "those chaplets which are named "Egyptian; and after them, "winter coronets, to wit, when "the earth affordeth no flowers "to make them, and these con- "sisted of horn shavings dyed "into sundry colours. And so "in process of time, by little and "little crept into Rome, also the "name of corolla, or as one would "say, petty garlands; for that "these winter chaplets at first "were so pretty and small: and "not long after them, the costly "coronets and others, corolla- "ries, namely, when they are "made of thin leaves and plates "and latten, either gilded or sil- "vered over, or else set out with "golden and silvered spangles, "and so presented." xxi. 2. Pollux affords a list of the principal flowers used in crowns by the Greeks: τὰ δὲ ἐν τοῖς στεφάνοις ἄνθη, ῥόδα, ἴα, κρίνα, σισύμβρια, ἀνεμῶναι, ἔρπυλος, κρόκος, ὑάκινθος, ἐλίχρυσος, ἡμεροκαλές, ἐλένειον, θρυαλὶς, ἀνθρίσκος, νάρκισσος, μελίλωτον, ἀνθεμὶς, παρθενὶς, καὶ τἄλλα ὅσα τοῖς ὀφθαλμοῖς τέρψιν, ἤρισὶν ἡδεῖαν ὄσφρησιν ἔχει. Cratinus enumerates among garland flowers, those of the smilax and the cosmosandalon. Onomast. vi. 106. Athen. xv. 32. Cf. Theoph. Hist. Plant. vi. 1. 2 —6. 4. Persons returning from a voyage were sometimes crowned with flowers. Plut. Thes. § 22. Soldiers also going to battle. Ages. § 19. Cf. Philost. Icon. i. 24. p. 799. Plut. Sympos. iii. 1.

Thus the Spartans, during the Promachian festival,[1] shaded their foreheads with plaited tufts of reeds— priests and priestesses, soothsayers,[2] prophets, and enchanters, appeared in their several capacities before the gods in temples or sacred groves with symbolical crowns encircling their heads, as the priests of Hera, at Samos, with laurel,[3] and those of Aphrodite with myrtle,[4] while the statues of the divinities themselves were often crowned with circlets of these "earthly stars." In the festival of Europa, at Corinth, a crown of myrtle, thirty feet in circumference, was borne in procession through the city.[5] The actors, dancers, and spectators of the theatre usually appeared crowned with flowers,[6] as did every guest at an entertainment, while lovers suspended a profusion of garlands on the doors of their mistresses, as did the devout on the temples and altars of the gods.[7]

Most of the flowers cultivated, moreover, suggested poetical or mythological associations; for the religion of Greece combined itself with nearly every object in nature, more particularly with the beautiful, so that the Greek, as he strolled through his garden, had perpetually before his fancy a succession of fables connected with nymphs and goddesses and the old hereditary traditions of his country. Thus the laurel recalled the tale and transformation of Daphnè,[8] the object of Apollo's love—the cypresses or graces of the vegetable kingdom,[9] were the everlasting representatives of Eteocles' daughters, visited by death because they dared to rival the goddesses in dancing—the myrtle[10] was a most beautiful maiden of Attica, fairer than all her countrywomen, swifter and more patient of toil than the youth, who there-

[1] Athen. xv. 15.
[2] Id. xv. 16.
[3] Id. xv. 13.
[4] Id. xv. 18.
[5] Id. xv. 22.
[6] Id. xv. 26.

[7] Athen. xv. 9.
[8] Geop. xi. 2.   Ovid. Metam. 550.
[9] Geop. xi. 4.
[10] Geop. xi. 6.

fore slew her through envy—the pine[1] was the tall
and graceful mistress of Pan and Boreas—the mint
that of Pluto—while the rose-campion sprung from
the bath of Aphrodite, and the humble çabbage from
the tears of Lycurgus, the enemy of Dionysos.[2]

It has sometimes been supposed,[3] that the flower
which constitutes the greatest ornament of gardens
was wholly unknown in the earlier ages of Greece.
But this theory, imagined for the purpose of destroying the claims of the Anacreontic fragments to
be considered genuine,[4] is entirely overthrown by
the testimony of several ancient writers, more particularly Herodotus,[5] who speaks of the rose of sixty
leaves, as found in the gardens of Midas in Thrace,
at the foot of the snowy Bermios. Elswhere, too,
he compares the flower of the red Niliac lotus[6] to
the rose; and Stesichoros,[7] an older poet than Anacreon, distinctly mentions chaplets composed of this
flower.

> Many a yellow quince was there
> Piled upon the regal chair,

---

[1] Geop. xi. 10. Cf. Plut. Sympos. vol. iii. 1, where he assigns
the reason why the pine was sacred to Poseidon and Dionysos.
The foliage of the pine-forests
was so dense in Bœotia as to per-
mit neither snow nor rain to penetrate through. Theoph. Hist.
Plant. iii. 9. 6. The shade of
such trees, therefore, would be
more especially coveted.

[2] Sch. Aristoph. Eq. 537. Geop.
xii. 17. 16.

[3] By Dr. Nolan. See his paper
on the Grecian Rose. Trans. Roy.
Soc. of Lit. ii. 327, sqq.

[4] Cf. Athen. xv. 11.

[5] Οἱ δὲ, ἀπικόμενοι ἐς ἄλλην
γῆν τῆς Μακεδόνιης, οἴκησαν πέ-
λας τῶν κήπων τῶν λεγομένων
εἶναι Μίδεω τοῦ Γορδίεω. ἐν τοῖσι
φύεται αὐτόματα ῥόδα, ἓν ἕκαστον

ἔχον ἑξήκοντα φύλλα ὀδμῇ δὲ
ὑπερφέροντα τῶν ἄλλων· ἐν τού-
τοισι καὶ ὁ Σιληνὸς τοῖσι κήποισι
ἥλω, ὡς λέγεται ὑπὸ Μακεδόνων.
ὑπὲρ δὲ τῶν κήπων οὖρος κέεται,
Βέρμιον οὔνομα, ἄβατον ὑπὸ χειμῶνος. viii. 138. On the arts
and manners of this Midas, who,
together with Orpheus and Eumol-
pos was the founder of the Hellenic religion, see J. G. Voss. de
Idololat. i. 24, and Bouhier, Dissert. sur Herod. ch. 80.

[6] Cf. Theop. Hist. Plant. iv. 87.

[7] Athen. iii. 21. Stesichoros
lived before Christ about 632.
Clint. Fast. Hellen. ii. 5. Crowns
of roses are mentioned by Cratinus who was born 519 B.C. which
shows that roses must have been
largely cultivated in his time.
Athen. xv. 27.

Many a verdant myrtle-bough,
Many a rose-crown featly wreathed,
With twisted violets that grow
Where the breath of spring has breathed.

Homer,[1] too, it is evident, was familiar with the
rose, to whose fragrant petals he compares the
fingers of the morning, and not, as has been imagined, to the blood-red flower of the wild pomegranate tree.[2]

According, moreover, to a tradition preserved to
later times, the seasons of the year, which in remote
antiquity were but three, they symbolically represented by a rose, an ear of corn, and an apple.[3]
This division is thought to have been borrowed
from the Egyptians, in whose country, however, the
apple was never sufficiently naturalised to be taken
as an emblem of one of the seasons of the year.

But, at whatever period the rose began to be
cultivated, it evidently, as soon as known, shared
with the violet the admiration of the Athenian people, whose extensive plantations of this most fragrant
shrub recall to mind the rose gardens of the Fayoum, or Serinaghur. The secret, moreover, was early
discovered of hastening or retarding their maturity,
so as to obtain an abundant supply through every
month in the year.[4] Occasionally, too, numbers of

---

[1] Il. α. 477. ι. 703. Cf. Hesiod. Opp. et Dies, 610. To
place the matter beyond dispute,
Homer speaks of oils rendered
fragrant by the perfume of the
rose :—ῥοδόεντι δὲ χρῖεν ἐλαίῳ.
Il. ψ. 186.

[2] Dioscor. i. 154.

[3] " Les Egyptiens, selon le dé-
" partement de leur Roy Horus,
" n'en mettaient que trois (sai-
" sons): le printemps, l'esté, et
" l'automne : leur attribuans
" quatre mois à chacune, et les
" figurans par une rose, une
" espy, et une pomme, ou rai-

" sin." Les Images de Platte
Peinture des deux Philostrates,
par Vigenère, Paris, fol. 1627,
p. 555.

[4] Geop. xi. 18. A species of
perpetual rose is said to have
been recently discovered in France,
where " A Parisian florist, we are
" told, has succeeded in producing
" a new hybrid rose from the
" Bourbon rose and Gloire de
" Rosomène, the flowers of which
" he had fertilised with the pol-
" len of some Damask and hy-
" brid China roses. The plant
" is extremely beautiful, the co-

rosebuds were laid among green barleystalks, plucked up by the roots, in unglazed amphoræ, to be brought forth and made to blow when wanted. Others deposited them between layers of the same material on the ground, or dipped them in the liquid dregs of olives. Another mode of preserving the rose was exceedingly curious,—cutting off the top of a large standing reed, and splitting it down a little way, they inserted a number of rosebuds in the hollow, and then bound it softly round and atop with papyrus in order to prevent their fragrance from exhaling.[1] How many varieties of this flower[2] were possessed by the ancients it is now, perhaps, impossible to determine; but they were acquainted with the common, the white, and the moss rose, the last, in Aristotle's[3] opinion, the sweetest, together with the rose of a hundred leaves,[4] celebrated by the Persian poets. Even the wild rose was not wholly inodorous in Greece.[5] Roses were artificially blanched by being exposed while unfolding to powerful and repeated fumigations with sulphur.[6] The roses which grew on a dry soil were supposed to be the sweetest, while their fragrance was augmented by planting garlic near the root.[7] To cause them to bloom in January, or in early spring (for even in the most southern parts of

" lour bright crimson shaded with " Maroon purple, and is further " enriched with a powerful fra-" grance." TIMES, March 24th, 1841.

[1] Geop. xi. 18. 12.

[2] Plinius varia genera commemorat, Milesia ardentissimo colore, Alabandica albicantibus foliis, Spermonia vilissima, Damascenæ albæ distillandis aquis usurpantur. Differunt foliorum multitudine, asperitate, lævore, colore, odore.—Heresbachius, de Re Rustica, lib. ii. p. 121. a.

[3] Problem. xii. 8. Theoph. Hist. Plant. vi. 6. 5.

[4] Athen. xv. 29. Plin. xxi. 10. Cf. Theoph. Hist. Plant. vi. 6. 4.

[5] As Dr. Nolan seems to suppose. On the Grecian Rose. Transact. Roy. Soc. ii. 328. Though Theophrastus states the contrary very distinctly. Hist. Plant. vi. 2. 1—6. 4—7. 5. The white rose appears at present to be commonly cultivated in Attica.—Chandler, ii. 181.

[6] Geop. xi. 18. 13.

[7] Geop. xi. 18. 1.

Greece the rose season only commences in April)[1] various means were resorted to; sometimes, the bushes were watered twice a-day during the whole summer; on other occasions, a shallow trench was dug at a distance of about eighteen inches round the bush, into which warm water was poured morning and evening;[2] while a third, and, perhaps, the surest, method was to plant them in pots, or baskets, which, during the winter months, were placed in sheltered sunny spots by day,[3] and carried into the house at night; afterwards, when the season was sufficiently advanced, these portable gardens were buried in the earth.

Another favorite denizen of Hellenic gardens was the lily, which, probably, introduced from Suza or from Egypt, beheld the virginal snow of its bells compelled, by art, to put on various hues, as deep red and purple,[4]—the former, by infusing, before planting, cinnabar into the bulb,—the latter, by steeping it in the lees of purple wine. This flower naturally begins to bloom[5] just as the roses are fading; but, to produce a succession of lilies at different seasons, some were set near the surface, which grew up and blossomed immediately, while others were buried at different depths, according to the times at which they were required to flower.

Along with these, about the dank borders of streams or fountains, grew the favourite flower of the Athenian people, purple, double, white, and gold,[6]

> " The violet dim,
> But sweeter than the lids of Juno's eyes,
> Or Cytherea's breath ; "[7]

---

[1] Pashley, Trav. i. 8, who observes, that the rose is common in February at Malta.

[2] Geop. xi. 18. 5. Plin. xxi. 4. Pallad. iii. 21. 2.

[3] Geop. xi. 18. 4. Cf. xii. 19. 3.

[4] Geop. xi. 20. Heresbach. de Re Rust. p. 122. b. Theoph. Hist. Plant. vi. 6. 4, 8.

[5] Plin. xxi. 13.

[6] Colum. De Cultu Hortorum, x. 102.

[7] Winter's Tale, iv. 5.

the pansy,[1] "freaked with jet;" the purple cyperus, the iris, the water-mint,[2] and hyacinth,[3] and the narcissus,[4] and the willow-herb, and the blue speed-well, and the marsh-marigold, or, brave bassinet, and the jacinth, and early daffodil,

> " That come before the swallow dares, and take
> The winds of March with beauty."

A netting of wild thyme[5] tufted with sweet mint, and marjoram,[6] which, when crushed by the foot, yielded the most delicious fragrance, embraced the sunny hillocks, while here and there singly, or in beds, grew a profusion of other herbs and flowers, some prized for their medicinal virtues, others for their beauty, others for their delicate odour, as the geranium, the spike-lavender, the rosemary,[7] with its purple and white flowers, the basil,[8] the flower-gentle, the hyssop, the white privet, the cytisus, the

---

[1] Sibth. Flor. Græc. t. i. tab. 222, tab. 318. Schol. Aristoph. Eq. 1320. Theoph. Hist. Plant. vi. 6. 4. The finest violets, crocusses, &c., in the ancient world, were supposed to be found in Cyrene. Id. vi. 6. 5.

[2] Dioscor. ii. 155.

[3] On the birth of the Hyacinth, see Eudocia in the Anecdota Græca, i. 408.

[4] Theoph. Hist. Plant. vi. 6. 9. 8. 2. This flower flourishes after the setting of Arcturus, about the autumnal equinox.— " We were ferried over a narrow " stream fringed with Agnus- " Castus, into a garden belonging " to the convent. A number of " vernal flowers now blossomed " on its banks; the garden ane- " mone was crimsoned with an " extraordinary glow of colour- " ing. The soil which was a

" sandy loam, was further enli- " vened with the Ixia, the grass- " leaved Iris, and the enamel- " blue of a species of speedwell, " not noticed by the Swedish " Naturalist." Sibth. Walp. Mem. i. 282, seq.

[5] This plant was brought from Mount Hymettos, to be culti- vated in the gardens of Athens. The Sicyonians, likewise, trans- planted it to their gardens from the mountains of Peloponnesos.— Theoph. Hist. Plant. vi. 7. 2.

[6] Theoph. Hist. Plant. vi. 7. 4.

[7] Dioscor. iii. 89. Sibth. Flor. Græc. t. i. tab. 14, tab. 192, seq. tab. 310, tab. 518, tab. 549. Colum. x. De Cult. Hort. 96, sqq.

[8] The basil-gentle was water-ed at noon, other plants morning and evening. — Theoph. Hist. Plant. vii. 5. 2.

sweet marjoram, the rose-campion, or columbine,[1]
the yellow amaryllis, and the celandine.   Here, too,

> " Their gem-like eyes
> The Phrygian melilots disclose," [2]

with the balm-gentle, the red, the purple, and the
coronal anemone,[3] the convolvulus, yellow, white, pale
pink, and blue, together with our Lady's-gloves, the
flower of the Trinity, southernwood,[4] and summer-
savory,[5] œnanthe,[6] gith, the silver sage,[7] Saint Mary's
thistle, and the amaranth, while high above all rose
the dark pyramidal masses of the rhododendron,[8] with
its gigantic clusters of purple flowers.

How many of the lovely evergreens[9] that abound
in Greece were usually cultivated in a single garden,
we possess no means of ascertaining, though all appear occasionally to have been called in to diversify
the picture.   The myrtle,[10] whose deep blue berries
were esteemed a delicacy,[11] in some places rose into
a tree, while elsewhere it was planted thick, and bent

---

[1] Dioscor. iii. 114.

[2] Colum. x. 399, seq. Engl.
Trans.

[3] The anemone among other
flowers beautifies the fields of
Attica, so early as the month of
February. — Chandler, ii. 211.
" Les campagnes et les collines
" sont rouges d'anémones." —
Della Rocca, Traité sur les A-
beilles, t. i. p. 5.

[4] Cultivated usually in pots,
resembling the gardens of Adonis.
Theoph. Hist. Plant. vi. 7. 3.
Thickets of this shrub constitute
one of the greatest beauties of
the islands of the Archipelago.
" Les lauriers roses, que l'on con-
" serve en France avec tant de
" soin, viennent à l'aventure dans
" les prairies, et le long des ruis-
" seaux qui en sont bordés.
" Rien n'est plus agréable que
" de voir ces beaux arbres, de

" la hauteur de douze à quinze
" pieds, variés de fleurs rouges et
" blanches, se croiser par les
" branches d'en haut, sur un
" ruisseau ou sur le lit d'une
" fontaine, et faire un berceau
" qui dure quelquefois un grand
" quart de lieue."   Della Rocca,
Traité Complet sur les Abeilles,
t. i. p. 6.

[5] Schol. Aristoph. Acharn. 253.

[6] Theoph. Hist. Plant. vi. 8. 2.

[7] Sibth. Flor. Græc. t. i. tab.
27.

[8] Known also by the names of
νηρίον and ῥοδοδάφνη.—Dioscor.
iv. 82.   Geop. ii. 42. 1.

[9] Theoph. Hist. Plant. i. 9. 3.

[10] Cf. Clus. Hist. Rar. Plant.
i. 43. p. 65.

[11] Plat. De Rep. t. vi. p. 85.
The berry, both of the myrtle
and the laurel, assumed, we are
told, a black colour in the garden

and fashioned into bowers,[1] which, when sprinkled
with its snowy blossoms, combined, perhaps, with
those of the jasmine, the eglantine, and the yellow
tufts of the broad-leaved philyrea,[2] constituted some
of the most beautiful objects in a Greek paradise.
Thickets of the tamarisk,[3] the strawberry-tree,[4] the
juniper, the box, the bay, the styrax, the andrachne,
and the white-flowered laurel, in whose dark leaves
the morning dew collects and glistens in the sun like
so many tiny mirrors of burnished silver, varied the
surface of the lawn, connecting the bowers, and the
copses, and the flower beds, and the grassy slopes
with those loftier piles of verdure, consisting of the
pine tree, the smilax, the cedar, the carob, the
maple,[5] the ash, the elm tree, the platane,[6] and
the evergreen oak which here and there towered
in the grounds. In many places the vine shot up
among the ranges of elms or platanes, and stretched its long twisted arm from trunk to trunk, like
so many festoons of intermingled leaves and tendrils, and massive clusters of golden or purple
grapes.[7] Alternating, perhaps, with the lovely fa-

---

of Antandros.—Theophrast. Hist.
Plant. ii. 2. 6.

[1] Hemsterhuis,   Annot.   ad
Poll. ix. 49. p. 943. Cf. Dion.
Chrysost. i. 273.

[2] Sibthorp. Flor. Græc. t. i.
tab. 2, tab. 367, tab. 374, seq.

[3] Theoph. Hist. Plant. i. 9. 3.

[4] The strawberry-tree is found
flourishing in great beauty and
perfection on Mount Helicon, and
its fruit is said to be exceedingly
sweet.—Chandler, ii. 290.

[5] Sibth. Flor. Græc. tab. 361.

[6] Ἔνθα πλάτανος μὲν ἀμφιλαφής τε καὶ σύσκιος, πνεῦμα δὲ
μέτριον, καὶ πόα μαλθακὴ, ὥρα
θέρους ἐπανθεῖν εἰωθυῖα. Aristænet. Epist. lib. i. Epist. 3. p.
13. There was, according to
Varro, an evergreen platane tree

in Crete, i. 7. The same platane
is mentioned by Theophrastus,
who informs us, that it grew beside a fountain in the Gortynian
territory where Zeus first reclined
on landing from the sea with
Europa, i. 9. 5. Near the city
of Sybaris, there is said to have
grown a common oak which enjoyed the privilege of being unde-
ciduous. Ibid.

[7] Ἄμπελοι δὲ παμμήκεις σφόδρα τε ὑψηλαὶ περιελίττονται
κυπαρίττους ὡς ἀνακλᾶν ἡμᾶς
ἐπὶ πολὺ τὸν αὐχένα πρὸς θέαν
τῶν κύκλῳ συναιωρουμένων βο-
τρών, ὧν οἱ μὲν ὀργῶσιν, οἱ δὲ
περκάζουσιν οἱ δὲ ὄμφακες, οἱ δὲ
οἰνάνθαι δοκοῦσιν. — Aristænet.
Epist. lib. i. Ep. 3. p. 13, seq.

vourite of Dionysos, the blue and yellow clematis [1] suspended their living garlands around the stems, or along the boughs of the trees, in union or contrast with the dodder, or the honeysuckle, or the delicate and slender briony.   And, if perchance a silver fir, with its bright yellow flowers,[2] formed part of the group, large pendant clusters of mistletoe, the food sometimes of the labouring ox,[3] might frequently be seen swinging thick among its branches. In some grounds was probably cultivated the quercus suber,[4] or cork tree, with bark four or five inches thick, triennially stripped off,[5] after which it grows again with renewed vigour.   Occasionally, where streams and rivulets [6] found their way through the grounds, the black and white poplar, the willow, and the lentiscus, with a variety of tufted reeds, crowded about the margin, here and there shading and concealing the waters.

Proceeding now into the orchard we find, that, instead of walls, it was, sometimes at least, if it touched on the confines of another man's grounds, surrounded by hedges [7] of black and white thorn, brambles, and barberry bushes, as at present [8] by impenetrable fences of the Indian cactus.[9]   On the

[1] Sibth. Flor. Græc. tab. 516.

[2] Theophrast. Hist. Plant. i. 13. 1.

[3] Dodwell, ii. 455. Sibth. in Walp. Mem. i. 283. There was a species of mistletoe called the Cretan, which found equally congenial the climates of Achaia and Media. Theoph. Hist. Plant. ix. 1, 3.

[4] That is to say at a late period, for in the time of Theophrastus it would seem not to have been common in Greece, if it had been at all introduced. Hist. Plant. iii. 17. 1.

[5] Dodwell, ii. 455.

[6] Even the platane, also, delights in humid places. Theoph.

Hist. Plant. i. 4. 2. The black poplar was said to bear fruit in several parts of Crete. iii. 3. 5.

[7] Geop. v. 44. Cf. Artemid. Oneirocrit. ii. 24. p. 112.

[8] Walp. Mem. i. 60.

[9] The cactus, as most travellers will have remarked, flourishes luxuriantly in Sicily even among the beds of lava where little else will grow ; it appears, however, to delight in a volcanic soil. Spallanzani, Travels in the Two Sicilies, " i. 209. In the Æolian Islands it " thrives so well that it usually " grows to the height of ten, " twelve, and sometimes fifteen " feet, with a stem a foot or more " in diameter. The fruits, which

banks of these hedges, both inside and out, were
found, peculiar tribes of plants and wild flowers, in
some places enamelling the smooth close turf, elsewhere flourishing thickly in dank masses of verdure,
or climbing upwards and interlacing themselves with
the lofty and projecting thorns, such as the enchan-
ter's nightshade, the euphorbia, the iris tuberosa, the
red-flowered valerian, the ground-ivy,[1] the physalis
somnifera, with its coral red seeds in their inflated
calyces,[2] the globularia, the creeping heliotrope, the
penny-cress,[3] the bright yellow scorpion-flower, and
the broad-leaved cyclamen or our Lady's-seal, with
pink flower, light green leaf, veined with white and
yellow beneath. The ancient Parthians surrounded
their gardens with hedges of a fragrant, creeping
shrub denominated philadelphos or love-brother, [4]
whose long suckers they interwove into a kind of
network forming a sufficient protection against man
and beast. In mountainous districts, where rain-
floods were to be guarded against, the enclosures
frequently consisted of walls of loose stones,[5] as is
still the case in Savoy on the edge of mountain
torrents.

It was moreover the custom, both in Greece and
Italy, to plant, on the boundary line of estates, rows
of olives or other trees,[6] which not only served to

" are nearly as large as turkeys'
" eggs, are sweet and extremely
" agreeable to the palate. It is
" well-known that the fruits grow
" at the edges of the leaves, the
" number on each leaf is not con-
" stant, but they are frequently
" numerous, as I have counted
" two and twenty on a single
" leaf." iv. 97.

[1] Sibth. Flor. Græc. t. i. tab. 29.
tab. 157. tab. 185.

[2] Sibth. in Walp. Trav. p. 73,
seq. On the seasons of these
wild flowers see Theoph. Hist.
Plant. vii. 9. 2.

[3] Dioscor. ii. 186.

[4] Athen. xv. 29.

[5] Demosth. in Callicl. § 1. 3,
seq.

[6] Cf. Varro. i. 15. Magii Mis-
cellan. lib. iv. p. 187. b. As the
cotton-tree in modern times has
been supposed not to thrive at a
much greater distance than twenty miles from the sea ; so, among
the ancients, the olive was supposed not to flourish at a greater
distance than three hundred stadia.
Theoph. Hist. Plant. vi. 2. 4. Both
opinions are probably erroneous,
as the olive-tree is found in perfection in the Fayoum, and the
cotton-plant in Upper Egypt.

mark the limits of a man's territory, but shed an air of beauty over the whole country. A proof of this practice prevailing in Attica, has with much ingenuity[1] been brought forward from the "Frogs," where Bacchos, addressing the poet Æschylus in the shades, observes "It will be all right provided your anger does not transport you beyond the olives." It may likewise be remarked that in olive-grounds,[2] the trees, excepting the sacred ones called *moriæ*, were always planted in straight lines, from twenty-five to thirty feet[3] apart, because, in order to ripen the fruit,[4] it is necessary that the wind should be able freely to play upon it from all sides. And further because they delight in a warm dry air like that of Libya, Cilicia,[5] and Attica, the best olive-grounds were generally supposed to be those which occupied the rapid slopes of hills where the soil is naturally stony and light. The oil of the plains was commonly coarse and thick.

Among these olive grounds in summer, the song of the tettix[6] is commonly heard; for this musical insect loves the olive, which, like the sant of the Arabian desert, yields but a thin and warm shade.[7]

[1] Vict. Var. Lect. p. 874. But the Scholiast (Aristoph. Ran. 1026) gives a different though less probable interpretation to the passage.
[2] Cf. Sibth. Flor. Græc. t. i. tab. 3.
[3] Cato. De Re Rusticâ 6. They were sometimes also grafted, we are told, on lentiscus stocks. Plut. Sympos. ii. 6. 1.
[4] In Syria and some other warm countries the olive was said to produce fruit in clusters. Theophrast. Hist. Plant. i. 11. 4. And when this fruit was found chiefly on the upper branches, they augured a productive year. id. i. 14. 2. Geop. ix. 2. 4. The ancients entertained extraordinary ideas concerning the purity of the olive,

which they imagined bore more freely when cultivated by persons of chaste minds. Thus the olive-grounds of Anazarbos, in Cilicia, were thought to owe their extraordinary fertility to the reserved and modest manners of the youths who cultivated them. Id. ix. 2. 6.
[5] Geop. ix. 3. 1. Virg. Georg. ii. 179. The heads of olive-stocks when freshly planted were covered with clay, which was protected from the wet by a shell. Xenoph. Œconom. xix. 14. The pits for the planting of the olive and other fruit-trees were of considerable depth and dug long beforehand. Theoph. Hist. Plant. i. 6. 1.
[6] Cf. Hesiod. Opp. et Dies, 582, seq.
[7] Οὐ γίνονται δὲ τέττιγες ὅπου

The tettix, in fact, though never found in an un-
wooded country, as in the plains about Cyrene,
equally avoids the dense shade of the woods.[1] Here
likewise[2] are found the blackbird, the roller, and
three distinct species of butcher-bird—the small grey,
the ash-coloured, and the redheaded.

In an Attic orchard were most of the trees reared
in England, together with many which will not stand
the rigour of our climate.—The apple,[3] cultivated
with peculiar care in the environs of Delphi and
Corinth ; the pear,[4] the cherry from Cerasos on the
southern shore of the Black Sea,[5] which sometimes
grew to the height of nearly forty feet,[6] the damascene,[7] and the common plum. Along with these
were likewise to be found the quince,[8] the apricot,
the peach, the nectarine, the walnut, the chestnut,
the filbert, introduced from Pontos,[9] the hazel nut,
the medlar, and the mulberry, which, according to
Menander, is the earliest fruit of the year.[10] With
these were intermingled the fig, white, purple, and
red, the pomegranate,[11] from the northern shores of
Africa, the orange,[12] still planted under artificial shel-

μὴ δένδρα ἐστίν· διὸ καὶ ἐν Κυρήνῃ
οὐ γίνονται ἐν τῷ πεδίῳ, περὶ δὲ
τὴν πόλιν πολλοί, μόλιστα δ᾽ οὐ
ἐλαῖαι· οὐ γὰρ γίνονται παλίν
σκίοι. Aristot. Hist. Anim. v. 30.
Cf. Phile, de Animal. Proprietat.
c. 25. p. 81.

[1] In Spain, however, these insects exhibit a somewhat different
taste, being there found amid the
foliage of the most leafy trees.
" Every oak in the cork-wood
near Gibraltar was the abode if
not of harmony, at least of noise,
and the concert kept up amidst
the foliage by the numerous
grass or rather tree-hoppers was
quite deafening." Napier, Excursions on the shores of the
Mediterranean, ii. p. 2.

[2] Sibth. in Walp. Mem. i. 75.

[3] On the cultivation of the apple see Theophrast. Hist. Plant. i.
3. 3. Geop. xviii. 18.

[4] Athen. xiv. 63. Etym. Mag.
122. 20.

[5] Geop. x. 41. Plin. xv. 25.
Athen. ii. 35.

[6] Theoph. Hist. Plant. iii. 13. 1.

[7] Etym. Mag. 211. 4, sqq.

[8] Geop. x. 3. 73.

[9] Geop. xiii. 19. Athen. ii. 38.

[10] Athen. ii. 12. Vid. Cœl.
Rhodigin. vii. 15. Bochart, Geog.
Sac. col. 629.

[11] Theophrast. Hist. Plant. i. 3.
3. The fruit of the pomegranate-
tree lost much of its acidity in
Egypt. Id. Hist. Plant. ii. 2. 7.

[12] In Greece the orange-tree
and the lemon blossom in June,
Chandler, ii. 238.

ter at Lemnos, the citron, the lemon,[1] the date-palm,[2] the pistachio, the almond, the service, and the cornel-tree.

.As these gardens were arranged with a view no less to pleasure than to profit, the trees were plant-ed in lines, which, when sufficiently close, formed a series of umbrageous avenues, opening here into the lawn and there into the vineyard, which gene-rally formed part of a Greek gentleman's grounds. And such an orchard decked in its summer pride with foliage of emerald and fruit, ruddy, purple, and gold, the notes of the thrush, the nightingale,[3] the tettix, with the "amorous thrill of the green-finch,"[4] floating through its boughs, and the perfume of the agnus-castus, the myrtle, the rose, and the violet, wafting richly on all sides, was a very paradise.

Not unfrequently, common foot-paths traversed these orchards and vineyards, in which case the passers-by were customarily, if not by law, permit-ted to pick and eat the fruit,[5] which seems also from the account of our Saviour to have been the practice in Judæa. The contrary is the case in modern Europe. In Burgundy and Switzerland, where pathways traverse vineyards, it is not un-common to see the grapes smeared with something resembling white lime which children are assured

---

[1] Cf. Chandler, ii. 250.

[2] In Babylonia the palm-tree was by some thought to be propa-gated by off-shoots. Theophrast. Hist. Plant. ii. 2. 2. In Greece, the fruit seldom ripened complete-ly. iii. 3. 5.

[3] Ἔτι δὲ τὸ ἔμπνουν τῆς αὔρας λιγυρὸν ὑπηχεῖ τῷ μουσικῷ τῶν τεττίγων χορῷ δι' ἣν καὶ τὸ πνί-γος τῆς μεσημβρίας ἠπιώτερον ἐγεγόνει ἡδὺ καὶ ἀηδόνει, περὶ πετόμεναι τὰ νάματα, μελῳδοῦ-σιν. ἀλλὰ καὶ τῶν ἄλλων ἡδὺ φώ-νων κατηκούομεν ὀρνίθων, ὥσπερ

ἐμμελῶς ὁμιλούντων ανθρώποις. Aristænet. Epist. lib. i. Ep. 3. p. 17.

[4] "The amorous thrill of the "green-finch was now heard dis-"tinctly. The little owl hooted "frequently round the walls of "the convent. In the river be-"low, otters were frequently "taken. On the sides of the "banks were the holes of the "river-crabs; and the green-back-"ed lizard was sporting among "the grass." Sibth. in Walp. Trav. p. 76.

[5] Plat. De Legg. t. viii. p. 107.

is a deadly poison.   This, while in the country, I
regarded as a mere stratagem, intended to protect
the vineyards from depredation, though there seems
after all to be too much reason to believe the nefarious practice to exist in several localities.   At
least two children were recently killed at Foix by
eating poisoned grapes on the way-side.

The Greeks placed much of their happiness in
spots like those we have been describing, as may
be inferred from such of their fabulous traditions,[1] as relate to the garden of the Hesperides,[2]
the gardens of Midas, with their magnificent roses,
and those of Alcinoös,[3] which still shed their fragrance over the pages of the Odyssey.   From the
East, no doubt, they obtained, along with their noblest fruit-trees, the art of cultivating them, and,
perhaps, that sacred tradition of the Garden of
Eden, preserved in the Scriptures, formed the basis
of many a Hellenic legend.[4]   The Syrians acquired
much celebrity among the ancients for their knowledge of gardening, in which, according to modern
travellers, they still excel.   Of the manner of cultivating fruit-trees in the earlier ages very little is
known.   No doubt they soon discovered that some
will thrive better in certain soils and situations than
in others, and profited by the discovery; but the
art of properly training and grafting trees is comparatively modern.[5]

No mention of it occurs in the Pentateuch, though
Moses there gives directions how to manage an orchard.   For the first three years the blossoms were
not to be suffered to ripen into fruit, and even in
the fourth all that came was sacred to the Lord.

[1] Eudoc. Ionia. 434.

[2] Plin. xix. 19.   Athen. xi. 39.

[3] Bœttig. Fragm. sur les Jar. des
Anciens, in Magaz. Encycloped.
Ann. vii. t. i. p. 337.   Cardinal
Quirini, Primordia Corcyræ, c.
vii. p. 60, sqq.

[4] See in Xenophon a brief description of the gardens of Cyrus.
Œconom. iv. 21.   Upon this passage our countryman, Sir Thomas
Browne, has written an elaborate
treatise.

[5] On the various methods of
propagating trees see Theophrast.
Hist. Plant. ii. 1. 2.

From the fifth year, onward, they might do with it what they pleased. Of these regulations the intention was to prevent the early exhaustion of the trees. Homer, also, is silent on the practice of grafting, nor does any mention of it occur in the extant works of Hesiod, though Manilius [1] refers to his poems in proof of the antiquity of the practice. By degrees, however, it got into use; [2] and, in the age of Aristotle,[3] was already common, as at present almost everywhere, save in Greece,[4] since no fruit was esteemed excellent unless the tree had been grafted. Some few of the rules they observed in this process may be briefly noticed. [5] Trees with a thick rind were grafted in the ordinary way, and sometimes by inserting the graft between the bark and the wood, which was called infoliation.[6] Inoculation, also, or introducing the bud of one tree into the rind of another, was common among Greek gardeners.[7] They were extremely particular in their choice of stocks.[8] Thus the fig was grafted only on the platane [9] and the mulberry; the mulberry on

[1] Astronomicon, ii. p. 30. l. 4. Scalig. et not. p. 67.

[2] Cf. Athen. xiv. 68.

[3] De Plantis, ii. 6.

[4] Hobhouse, Travels, i. 227. Thiersch, Etat Actuel de la Grèce, t. i. p. 297.

[5] Geop. iii. 3. 9. Clem. Alexand. Stromat. l. vi. Opera, t. ii. p. 800. Venet. 1657.

[6] Geop. xii. 75. x. 75. 19.

[7] Geop. x. 77. Colum. v. 11. 1. Pallad. vii. 5. 2. Plin. xvii. 26. Cato. 42. Virg. Georg. ii. 73, sqq.

[8] Geop. x. 76.

[9] Introduced by Dionysios the elder into Rhegium, where it attained, however, no great size. Theoph. Hist. Plant. iv. 5. 6. The same naturalist speaks of two plane trees, the one at Delphi, the other at Caphyæ in Arcadia, said to have been planted by the hand of Agamemnon, which were still flourishing in his own days, iv. 13. 2. This tree attains a prodigious size in Peloponnesos. Chandler, Travels, ii. 308. Our traveller was prevented from measuring the stem by the fear of certain Albanian soldiers who lay asleep under it; but Theophrastus gives us the dimensions of a large platane, at Antandros, whose trunk, he says, could scarcely be embraced by four men, while its height before the springing forth of the boughs was fifteen feet. Having described the dimensions of the tree, he relates a very extraordinary fact in natural history, namely, that this platane,

the chestnut,[1] the beech, the apple, the terebinth, the wild pear, the elm, and the white poplar, (whence white mulberries;) the pear on the pomegranate, the quince, the mulberry, (whence red pears,) the almond, and the terebinth; apples[2] on all sorts of wild pears and quinces, (whence the finest apples called by the Athenians Melimela,)[3] on damascenes, also, and *vice versâ*, and on the platane, (whence red apples.)[4] Another method of communicating a blush to this fruit was to plant rose-bushes round the root of the tree.[5] The walnut was grafted on the strawberry-tree only;[6] the pomegranate on the myrtle[7] and the willow; the laurel on the cherry[8] and the ash; the white peach on the damascene and the almond; the damascene on the wild pear, the quince, and the apple; chestnuts on the walnut, the beech, and the oak;[9] the cherry

---

having been blown down by the winds and lightened of its branches by the axe, rose again spontaneously during the night, put forth fresh boughs, and flourished as before. The same thing is related of a white poplar in the museum at Stagira, and of a large willow at Philippi. In this last city a soothsayer counselled the inhabitants to offer sacrifice, and set a guard about the tree, as a thing of auspicious omen. Theoph. Hist. Plant. iv. 16. 2, seq. Cf. Plin. xvi. 57. In corroboration of the narrative of Theophrastus, Palmerius relates, that, during the winter of 1624-25, while Breda was besieged by Ambrosio Spinola, he himself saw in Brabant an oak twenty-five feet high, and three feet in circumference, overthrown by the wind, and recovering itself exactly in the manner described by the great naturalist. The vulgar, who regarded it as a mi-

racle, preserved portions of its bark or branches as amulets.— Excercitationes, p. 598.

[1] Plut. Sympos. ii. 6. 7.

[2] " It is reported," observes Lord Bacon, " that, in the low " countries, they will graft an ap- " ple scion upon the stock of a " colewort, and it will bear a " great flaggy apple, the kernel " of which, if it be set, will be a " colewort and not an apple." Sylva Sylvarum, 453.

[3] Geop. x. 20. 1. Varro. i. 59. Mustea (mala) a celeritate mitescendi : quæ nunc melimela dicuntur, a sapore melleo.—Plin. xv. 15. Dioscor. i. 161.

[4] Plut. Sympos. ii. 6. 1.

[5] Geop. x. 19. 15, cum not. Niclas.

[6] Inseritur vero ex fœtu uncis arbutus horrida. Virg. Georg. ii. 69, with the note of Servius.

[7] Plut. Sympos. ii. 6. 1.

[8] Plin. xvii. 14.

[9] Castanea inseritur in se, et

on the terebinth, and the peach ; the quince on the oxyacanthus ; the myrtle on the willow ; and the apricot on the damascene, and the Thasian almond-tree. The vine, also, was grafted on a cherry and a myrtle-stock, which produced, in the first case, grapes in spring,[1] in the second, a mixed fruit, between the myrtle-berry and the grape.[2] When the gardener desired to obtain black citrons, he inserted a citron-graft into an apple-stock, and, if red, into a mulberry-stock.

Citrons were likewise occasionally grafted on the pomegranate-tree. In the present day, the almond, the chestnut, the fig, the orange, and the citron, with many other species of fruit-trees, are no longer thought to require grafting.[3]

In illustration of the prolific virtue of the Hellenic soil it may be mentioned, that young branchless pear-trees, transplanted from Malta to the neighbourhood of Athens, in the autumn of 1830, were the next year covered thick with fruit, which hung even upon the trunk like hanks of onions.[4]

Notwithstanding the early season of the year at which Gaia distributes her gifts in Greece, numerous arts were resorted to for anticipating the productions of summer,[5] though of most of them the nature is unknown. It is certain, however, that they

---

in salice, sed ex salice tardius maturat, et fit asperior in sapore. Pallad. xii. 7. 22. Cf. Virg. Georg. ii. 71. Plutarch speaks of certain gardens on the banks of the Cephissos, in Bœotia, in which he beheld pears growing on an oak-stock : ἦσαν δὲ καὶ δρύες ἀπίους ἀγαθὰς ἐκφέρουσαι. Sympos. ii. 6. 1.

[1] Geop. x. 41. 3. iv. 12. 5.

[2] Geop. iv. 4.

[3] Thiersch, Etat Actuel de la Grèce, t. i. p. 298.

[4] Idem. t. i. p. 288. Speaking of

the fertility of the islands, Della Rocca remarks : " Le terroir y " est si bon, et les arbres y vien- " nent si vîte, que j'ai vu à " Naxie des pépins d'orange de " Portugal pousser en moins de " huit ans de grands orangers, " dont les fruits étoient les plus " délicieux du monde, et la tige " de l'arbre si haute, qu'il falloit " une longue échelle pour y mon- " ter. " — Traité Complet des Abeilles, t. i. p. 6.

[5] On the artificial ripening of dates, Theoph. ii. 8. 4.

possessed the means of ripening fruits throughout the winter, either by hothouses or other contrivances equally efficacious.[1] During the festival celebrated in honour of the lover of Aphrodite, the seeds of flowers were sown in those silver pots, or baskets, called the gardens of Adonis,[2] and with artificial heat and constant irrigation compelled to bloom in eight days. Among the modern Hindùs corn is still forced to spring up in a few days, by a similar process, during the festival of Gouri.[3] To produce rathe figs,[4] a manure, composed of dove's dung and pepper and oil, was laid about the roots of the tree. Another method was that which is still employed under the name of caprification, alluded to by Sophocles.[5] For this purpose care was taken to rear, close at hand, several wild fig-trees, from which might be obtained the flies made use of in this process,[6] performed by cutting off bunches of wild figs and suspending them amid the branches of the culti-vated species,[7] when a fly issuing from the former

---

[1] Athen. iii. 19. Plut. Phoc. § 3. Xenoph. Vectigal. i. 3.

[2] Ὁ νοῦν ἔχων γεωργός, ὧν σπερμάτων κήδοιτο καὶ ἔγκαρπα βούλοιτο γενέσθαι, πότερα σπον-δῇ ἂν θέρους εἰς Ἀδώνιδος κή-πους ἀρῶν χαίροι θεωρῶν καλοὺς ἐν ἡμέραισιν ὀκτὼ γιγνομένους. —Plat. Phœd. t. i. p. 99. Suid. v. Ἀδώνιδ. κῆπ. t. i. p. 84. b. Theoph. Hist. Plant. v. 7. 3. Caus. Plant. i. 12. 2. Eustath. ad Odyss. λ. p. 459. 4.

[3] Tod, Annals of Rajast'han, vol. i. p. 570.

[4] Cf. Athen. iii. 12. Theo-phrast. Hist. Plant. i. 3. 3. The fruit of the Egyptian sycamore, or Pharaoh's fig-tree, was eaten in antiquity as now. Athenæus, who was a native of the Delta, says they used to rip open the skin of the fruit with an iron claw, and leave it thus upon the tree for three days. On the fourth it was eatable, and ex-haled a very agreeable odour. Deipnosoph. ii. 36. Theophras-tus adds, that a little oil was likewise poured on the fruit when opened by the iron. De Caus. Plant. i. 17. 9. ii. 8. 4. In Malta figs are still sometimes ripened by introducing a little olive oil into the eye of the fruit, or by puncturing it with a straw or feather dipped in oil. Napier, Excursions along the Shores of the Mediterranean, vol. ii. p. 144. Cf. Lord Bacon, Sylva Sylvarum, 446.

[5] Ap. Athen. iii. 10. Cf. Theoph. Hist. Plant. i. 8. 1.

[6] Aristot. de Gen. Anim. t. i.

[7] Suid. v. ἐρινεός. t. i. p. 1038. d.

pricked the slowly ripening fruit and accelerated its maturity.[1] In growing the various kinds of fig they were careful to plant the Chelidonian, the Erinean, or wild fig, the Leukerinean, and the Phibaleian[2] on plains. The autumn-royals would grow anywhere. Each sort has its peculiar excellence. The following were the best: the colouroi, or truncated, the formi- nion, the diforoi, the Megaric, and the Laconian, which would bear abundantly if well-watered.[3] Rhodes was famous for its excellent figs, which were even thought worthy to be compared with those of Attica.[4] Athenæus, however, pretends that the best figs in the world were found at Rome. There were figs with a ruddy bloom in the island of Paros, the same in kind as the Lydian fig.[5] The Leukerinean produced the white fig.[6]

The fancy of Hellenic gardeners amused itself with effecting numerous fantastic changes in the appearance and nature of . fruit. Thus citrons, le- mons, &c., were made, by the application of a clay mould, to assume the form of the human face, of birds and other animals.[7] Occasionally, too, they were introduced, when small, into the neck of a bottle provided with breathing holes, the figure of which they assumed as they projected their growth into all its dimensions. We are assured, moreover, that, by a very simple process, they could produce

---

[1] Cf. Tournefort, t. ii. p. 23.

[2] Schol. Aristoph. Acharn. 76 7

[3] Athen. iii. 7. The Laconian fig-tree was not commonly planted in Attica. Frag. Aristoph. Georg. 4. Brunck. This kind of fig re- quires much watering, which was found to deteriorate the flavour of other kinds. Theoph. Hist. Plant. i. 7. 1.

[4] Athen. iii. 8.

[5] Athen. iii. 9. In the fig- tree orchards of Asia Minor the spaces between the trees are sown, as in vineyards, with corn, and the bushes are often filled with nightingales. — Chandler, i. 244.

[6] Athen. iii. 10. There was, also, a species which received its name from resembling the crow in colour. Sch. Aristoph. Pac. 611. Philost. Icon. i. 31. p. 809, where figs are enumerated in his elegant description of the Xenia. Cf. Pausan. i. 37. Vi- truv.

[7] Geop. x. 9. Clus. Rar. Plant. Hist. i. 4.

peaches, almonds,[1] &c., covered, as though by magic, with written characters. The mode of operation was this,—steeping the stone of the fruit in water for several days, they then carefully divided it, and taking out the kernel inscribed upon it with a brazen pen whatever words or letters they thought proper. This done, they again closed the stone over the kernel, bound it round with papyrus, and planted it; and the peaches or almonds which afterwards grew on that tree bore every one of them, *mirabile dictu !* the legend inscribed upon the kernel. By similar arts[2] they created stoneless peaches, walnuts without husks, figs white one side, and black the other, and converted bitter almonds into sweet.[3]

The rules observed in the planting of fruit-trees were numerous.[4] Some, they were of opinion, were best propagated by seed, others by suckers wrenched from the root of the parent stock,[5] others, again, by branches selected from among the new wood on the topmost boughs. A rude practice, too, common enough in our own rural districts, appears to have been in much favour among them,—bending some long pendant bough to the ground, they covered a part of it with heavy clods, allowing, however, the extremity to appear above the earth. When it had taken root it was severed from the tree and transplanted to some proper situation. At other times, the points of boughs were drawn down and fixed in the ground, which even thus took root, and sent the juices backwards, after which the bough was

---

[1] Geop. x. 14. 60. Pallad. ii. 15. 13.

[2] Geop. x. 16. 53. 76.

[3] Geop. x. 59. Theoph. Hist. Plant. ii. 8. 1. Caus. Plant. i. 9. 1. Plin. xvii. 43. Pallad. ii. 15. 11.

[4] Geop. x. 3. Cf. Xenoph. Œconom. xix. 3.

[5] Plin. xvii. 13. When a tree was barren, or had lost its strength in blooming, they split it at the root, and put a stone into the fissure to keep it open, after which it was said to bear well. Theoph. Hist. Plant. ii. 7. 6. It was customary, moreover, to wound the trunks of almond, pear, and other trees, as the service-tree in Arcadia, in order to render them fertile. Id. ii. 7. 7. The berries of the cornel and service-trees were sweeter and ripened earlier wild than when cultivated. iii. 2. 1.

cut off and a new stock produced. Trees generated by this method, as well as those planted during the waning moon,[1] were supposed to spread and grow branchy, while those set during the waxing moon attained, though weaker, to a much greater height. It ought, perhaps, to be further added, that all seeds and plants were put into the ground while the moon was below the horizon.[2] Those trees which it was customary to renew by seed were the pistachio, the filbert, the almond, the chestnut, the white peach, the damascene, the pine-tree, and the edible pine, the palm, the cypress, the laurel, the ash, the maple, and the fig. The apple,[3] the cherry, the rhamnus jujuba, the common nut, the dwarf laurel, the myrtle, and the medlar, were propagated by suckers; while the quicker and surer mode of raising trees from boughs was frequently adopted in the case of the almond, the pear, the mulberry, the citron,[4] the apple, the olive, the quince,[5] the black and white poplar, the ivy, the jujube-tree, the myrtle, the chestnut, the vine, the willow, the box, and the cytisus.

But the thrifty people of Hellas seldom devoted the orchard-ground entirely to fruit-trees. The custom seems to have been to lay out the whole in beds and borders for the cultivation of vegetables, and to plant trees, at intervals, along the edges and at the corners. These beds, moreover, were often, as with us, edged with parsley and rue; whence the proverb, — "You have not proceeded beyond the rue," for "You know nothing of the matter."[6]

---

[1] The ancients believed that the moon ripens fruit, promotes digestion, and causes putrefaction in wood, and animal substances. Athen. vii. 3. Cf. Plut. Sympos. iii. 10.

[2] Geop. x. 2. 13.

[3] Cf. Vigenère, Images des Philostrates, p. 48.

[4] " Les orangers et les citron-" niers perfument l'air par la " quantité prodigieuse des fleurs " dont ils sont chargés, et qui " s'épanouissent aux premières " chaleurs."—Della Rocca, Traité sur les Abeilles, t. i. p. 5.

[5] Originally of Crete. Pashley, i. 27. κοδύμαλον in the ancient dialect of the country. Athen. iii. 2.

[6] Schol. Aristoph. Vesp. 480. Geop. xii. 1. 2.

The rustics of antiquity, who put generally great
faith in spells and talismans, possessed an extraordinary charm for ensuring unfailing fertility to their
gardens; they buried an ass's head deep in the middle of them, and sprinkled the ground with the juice
of fenugreek and lotus.[1] Somewhat greater efficacy,
however, may be attributed to their laborious methods
of manuring and irrigation.[2]

The aspect of such a garden differed very little,
except perhaps in luxuriance, from a similar plot of
ground in Kent or Middlesex. Here you perceived
beds of turnips, or cabbages, or onions; there, lettuces, or endive, or succory,[3] in the process of blanching, or the delicate heads of asparagus, or broad-
beans, or lentils, or peas, or kidney-beans, or arti-
chokes. In the most sunny spots were ranges of
boxes or baskets for forcing cucumbers.[4] Near the
brooks, where such existed, were patches of water-
melons,[5] the finest in the world; and here and there,
clasping round the trunks of trees,[6] and, suspending
its huge leaves and spheres from among the branches,
you might behold the gourd,[7] as I have often seen
it in the palm-groves of Nubia. It may be added,
that the pumpkin, or common gourd, was eaten by
the Greeks,[8] as it is still in France and Asia Minor.[9]

Lettuces [10] were blanched by being tied a-top, or

1 Geop. xii. 6. Pallad. i. 35. 16.
2 Lucian. Luc. siv. Asin. § 43.
3 Geop. ii. 37. 40.
4 These were covered with
plates of the lapis specularis, and
furnished with wheels, that they
might the more easily be moved
in and out from under cover.
Colum. De Re Rust. xi. 3. p.
461 : see also Castell, Villas of
the Ancients, p. 4.
5 These are found growing at
present even in the cemeteries.
" Des melons d'eau qui végètent
" çà et là sur ces tombes aban-
" données, resemblent, par leur

" forme et leur pâleur, à des
" crânes humains qu'on ne s'est
" pas donné la peine d'ensève-
" lir." Chateaub. Itin. i. 27.
These fruit are considered so in-
nocent in the Levant as to be
given to the sick in fevers. Chandler, i. p. 77.
6 Colum. De Cult. Hortor. 234.
7 Sch. Aristoph. Acharn. 494.
8 Athen. iii. 1.
9 Chandler, i. 317.
10 See Strattis's Invocation to
the Caterpillar. Athen. ii. 79.
Theoph. Hist. Plant. vii. 2. 4.
5. 4.

being buried up to a certain point in sand.[1] They were, moreover, supposed to be rendered more rich and delicate by being watered with a mixture of wine and honey, as was the practice of the gourmand Aristoxenos, who having done so over-night, used next morning to cut them, and say they were so many green cakes sent him by mother Earth.[2]

The Greek gardeners appear to have delighted exceedingly in the production of monstrous vegetables. Thus, in the case of the cucumber, their principal object appears to have been to produce it without seed, or of some extraordinary shape.[3] In the first case they diligently watched the appearance of the plant above ground, and then covering it over with fresh earth, and repeating the same operation three times, the cucumbers it bore were found to be seed-less. The same effect was produced by steeping the seeds in sesamum-oil for three days before they were sown. They were made to grow to a great length by having vessels of water [4] placed daily within a few inches of their points, which, exciting by attraction a sort of nisus in the fruit, drew them forward as far as the gardener thought necessary.[5] They were made, likewise, to assume all sorts of forms by the use of light, fictile moulds,[6] as in the case of the citron. Another method was, to take a large reed,[7] split it, and clear out the pith; then introducing the young cucumber into the hollow, the

[1] Geop. xii. 13. 3. Pallad. ii. 14. 2.

[2] Athen. i. 12.

[3] Geop. xii. 19. 1, sqq. Pallad. iv. 9. 8.

[4] Plin. xix. 23. Pallad. iv. 9. 8.

At qui sub trichila manantem
    repit ad undam,
Labentemque sequens nimio te-
    nuatur amore,
Candidus, effœtæ tremebundior
    ubere porcæ.
Colum. x. De Cult. Hortor. 394.

[5] Lord Bacon, having noticed this fact, adds the following sage remark : " If you set a stake or prop " at a certain distance from it (the " vine), it will grow that way, " which is far stranger than the " other : for that water may work " by a sympathy of attraction; but " this of the stake seemeth to be " a reasonable discourse." Sylva Sylvarum, 462.

[6] Theoph. Hist. Plant. vii. 3. 5. Plin. Hist. Nat. xix. 24.

[7] Plin. xix. 23.

sections of the reed were bound together, and the
fruit projected itself through the tube until it acquired an enormous length. It is observed by Theophrastus, that if you steep the seeds of cucumbers
in milk, or an infusion of honey, it will improve
their flavour.[1] They were, moreover, believed to expand in size at the full of the moon, like the sea-
hedgehog.[2] A fragrant smell was supposed to be
communicated to melons[3] by constantly keeping the
seed in dry rose-leaves. To preserve the seed for
any length of time, it was sprinkled with the juice
of house-leek.

The Megaréans, in whose country melons, gourds,[4]
and cucumbers were plentiful, were accustomed to
heap dust about their roots during the prevalence of
the Etesian winds, and found this answer instead of
of irrigation.[5] It appears from the following proverb,
— " The end of cucumbers and the beginning of pom-
pions," — that the former went out of season as the
latter came in.[6]

To procure a plentiful crop of asparagus, they used
to bury the shavings of a wild ram's horn, and well
water them.[7] By banking up the stalks, moreover,
immediately after cutting the heads, they caused new
shoots to spring forth, and thus enjoyed a fresh supply throughout the year. This plant was probably
obtained from Libya,[8] where it was said to attain,
in its wild state, the height of twelve, and sometimes
even of thirty cubits;[9] and on the slopes of Lebanon,

---

[1] Cf. Athen. iii. 5.

[2] Athen. iii. 2.

[3] The best melons at present
known in Greece are those of
Cephalonia, which lose their flavour if transplanted. Hobhouse,
Trav. &c., i. 227. Cf. Chandler, i.
p. 14.

[4] Schol. Aristoph. Acharn. 494.

[5] Theoph. Hist. Plant. ii. 7.
5.

[6] Schol. Aristoph. Pac. 966.

[7] Geop. xii. 18. 2. Plin. xix.
42. Dioscor. ii. 152. The physician, however, modestly professes
his unbelief: ἔνιοι δὲ ἱστόρησαν,
ὅτι ἐάν τις κριοῦ κέρατα συγκόψας
κατορύξῃ, φύεται ἀσπάραγος· ἐμοὶ
δὲ ἀπίθανον.

[8] The asparagus, however, has
been found, in modern times,
growing wild among the ruins of
Epidauros. Chandler, ii. 249.

[9] Athen. ii. 62.

in Syria, it has in our own day been seen from twelve
to fifteen feet high.

That kind of cabbage which we call savoys was
supposed to flourish best in saline spots, on which
account the gardeners used to sift pounded nitre[1]
over the beds where it was sown, as was the practice also in Egypt. In and about Alexandria,[2] however, there was said to be some peculiar quality in
the earth which communicated a bitter taste to the
cabbage. To prevent this they imported cabbage-
seed from the island of Rhodes, which produced good
plants the first year, but experienced in the second
the acrid influence of the soil.[3] Kumè was celebrated for its fine cabbages, which, when full-grown,
were of a yellowish green colour, like the new leather
sole of a sandal. Broccoli and sea-kale and cauli-
flowers would appear to have been commonly cultivated in the gardens of the ancients. There was,
likewise, among them a sort of cabbage supposed to
have some connexion with the gift of prophecy;[4]
and by this, probably, it was, that certain comic
personages used to swear, as Socrates by the dog,
and Zeno by the caper-bush.

Radishes[5] were rendered sweet by steeping the
seeds in wine and honey, or the fresh juice of grapes:
Nicander speaks of preserved turnips.[6] Parsley-seed
was put into the earth in an old rag, or a wisp of
straw,[7] surrounded with manure, and well-watered,
which made the plant grow large. Rue they sowed in
warm and sunny spots, without manure.[8] It was defended from the cold of winter by being surrounded
with heaps of ashes,[9] and was sometimes planted in

[1] Geop. ii. 41.
[2] Athen. ix. 9. Suid. v. κράμβη. t. i. p. 1518. b. Cf. Foës. Œconom. Hippoc. v. κραμβίων. p. 214.
Dioscorid. ii. 146.
[3] Cf. Steph. Byzant. de Urb.
p. 488. b.
[4] Cf. Casaub. Animadv. in
Athen. ix. 9. t. x. p. 24.

[5] Theoph. Hist. Plant. vii. 1. 3.
[6] Athen. iv. 11.
[7] Theoph. Hist. Plant. vii. 4.
2. 6. 4. Aristoph. Concion. 355,
et schol.
[8] Geop. xii. 1.
[9] Geop. xii. 25. 1.

pots, probably to be kept in apartments for the sake of its bright yellow flowers,[1] and because, when smelt, it was said to cure the head-ache. The juice of wild rue, mixed with woman's milk, sharpened the sight, in the opinion of the ancients.[2] The juice of sweet mint, which was a garden herb, squeezed into milk,[3] was supposed to prevent coagulation, even should rennet be afterwards thrown into it.

Both the root and bean of the nymphæa nelumbo or red lotus,[4] were eaten in Egypt,[5] where its crimson flowers were woven into crowns which diffused an agreeable odour, and were considered exceedingly refreshing in the heat of summer.[6] This plant was by the Greeks of Naucratis denominated the melilotus, to distinguish it from the lotus with white flowers. Theophrastus[7] observes, that it grows in the marshes to the height of four cubits, and has a striped root and stem. This lotus was also anciently found in Syria and Cilicia, but did not there ripen. In the environs of Toronè in Chalcidice,[8] however, it was found in perfection in a small marsh.

The lupin,[9] and the caper-bush, probably cultivated for the beauty of its delicate white flowers,[10] deteriorated in gardens,[11] as did likewise the mallows,[12]

---

[1] Cf. Sibth. Flor. Græc. tab. 368.

[2] Dioscor. iii. 53. Geop. xii. 25. 4.

[3] Geop. xii. 24.

[4] The rose-coloured lotus was said by the poet Pancrates to have been produced from the blood of the lion slain by the Emperor Adrian. Athen. xv. 21.

[5] Athen. iii. 1.

[6] Nicander in Georgicis ap. Athen. iii. 1.

Σπείρειας κύαμον Αἰγύπτιον, ὄφρα
    θερείης
῎Ανθεα μὲν στεφάνους ἀνύῃς· τὰ
    δὲ πεπτηῶτα
᾽Ακμαίου καρποῖο κιβώρια δαινυ-
    μένοισιν

'Ες χέρας ἠΐθεοισι, πάλαι ποθέου-
    σιν, ὀρέξῃς
'Ρίζας δ' ἐν θοίνῃσιν ἀφεψήσας
    προτίθημι.

See the note of Schweighæuser, t. vii. 10.

[7] Histor. Plant. iv. 10.

[8] It was also found in Thesprotia. Athen. iii. 3.

[9] Geop. ii. 39. Apuleius relates that the lupin-flower turned round with the sun, even in cloudy weather, so that it served as a sort of rural clock. Cf. Plin. xviii. 67.

[10] The caper-bush blossoms in June. Chandler, ii. 275.

[11] Theoph. Hist. Plant. i. 3. 6. Cf. Sibth. Flor. Græc. tab. 488.

[12] Athen. ii. 52.

which, together with the beet, were said to acquire in gardens the height of a small tree.[1] The stem of the mallows was sometimes used as a walking stick. Its large pale red flower which

Follows with its bending head the sun,[2]

constituted one of the ornaments of the garden.

Besides these the ancients usually cultivated in their grounds two species of cistus, one with pale red flowers now called the long rose, the other which about midsummer has on its leaves a sort of fatty dew, of which laudanum is made;[3] together with the blue eringo,[4] rocket, cresses, (which were planted in ridges,) bastard parsley, penny-royal, anis,[5] water-mint, sea-onions, monk's rhubarb, purslain, a leaf of which placed under the tongue quenched thirst, garden coriander, hellebore, yellow, red, and white, bush origany,[6] with its pink cones, flame-coloured fox-glove, brank-ursine, or bear's foot, admired for its vast pyramid of white flowers, chervil, skirwort,

[1] Theoph. Hist. Plant. i. 9. 2. Cf. vii. 3, 3. Hesiod reckons the mallow and the asphodel among edible plants. Opp. et Dies, 41. Gœttling, therefore, (in loc.) wonders Pythagoras should have prohibited the mallow. Cf. Aristoph. Plut. 543. Suid. v. θύμος. t. 1. p. 1336. e. Horat. Od. i. 32. 16.

[2] Colum. de Cult. Hortor. 253. Cardan in his treatise De Subtilitate having undertaken to assign the cause why certain flowers bend towards the sun, his antagonist, J. C. Scaliger, remarks upon his philosophy as follows:—" De floribus, qui ad Solem convertuntur non pessime ais: tenue humidum ad Solis calorem, se habere, ut corii ad ignem. Cæterum adhuc integra restat quæstio. Rosis enim tenuissimum esse humidum testantur omnia. Non convertuntur tamen. Platonici flores quosdam etiam Lunæ dicunt esse familiares: qui sane huic Sideri, sicut illi suo canant hymnos, sed mortalibus ignotos auribus." Exercit. 170, § 2. " The cause (of the bowing of the " heliotrope) is somewhat obscure; " but I take it to be no other, but " that the part against which the " sun heateth, waxeth more faint " and flaccid in the stalk, and " thereby less able to support the flower." Bacon, Sylva Sylvarum § 493.

[3] Sibth. Flor. Græc. t. 1. tab. 258, seq.

[4] Colum. x. de Cult. Hortor. 230, sqq. Sch. Aristoph. Nub. 235.

[5] Theoph. Hist. Plant. i. 72. 2.

[6] Schol. Aristoph. Acharn. 826, 837.

the mournful elecampane, giant fennel, dill, mustard
and wake-robin, which was sown,

> Soon as the punic tree, whose numerous grains,
> When thoroughly ripe, a bright red covering hides,
> Itself did with its bloody blossoms clothe.[1]

Other garden herbs were the cumin, the seed
of which was sown with abuse and curses,[2] the sperage-
berry, the dittander, or pepperwort, turnips,[3] and
parsnips, (found wild in Dalmatia,)[4] with onions, garlic, and leeks.[5] For these last Megara was famous,
as Attica was for honey, which suggested to the
Athenians an occasion of compliment to themselves,[6]
it having been a saying among them, that they were
as superior to the Megareans as honey is to garlic
and leeks.

The cultivation of that species of leek called ge-
thyllis was carried to great perfection at Delphi,[7]
where it was an established custom, evidently with
a view to the improvement of gardening, that the
person who, on the day of the Theoxenia,[8] presented
the largest vegetable of this kind to Leto should
receive a portion from the holy table.[9] Polemo, who
relates this circumstance says, that he had seen on
these occasions leeks nearly as large as turnips. The
cause of this ceremony was said to be, that Leto
when great with Apollo longed for a leek.

Mushrooms[10] were sedulously cultivated by the ancients, among whose methods of producing them
were the following. They felled a poplar-tree[11] and

[1] Colum. x. De Cult. Hortor.
374. English Translation. Theoph.
Hist. Plant. vii. 12. 1.

[2] Theoph. Hist. Plant. vii. 3. 3.
Cf. Dioscor. iii. 68, seq.

[3] Athen. iv. 11.

[4] Athen. ix. 8.

[5] Theoph. Hist. Plant. vii. 4.
7, 10, 11. Aristoph. Plut. 283,
et schol. Eq. 675. 494. Vesp.
680. Acharn. 166, 500. Plut.
283.

[6] Schol. Aristoph. Pac. 246.
252.

[7] Cf. Schol. Aristoph. Eq. 675.

[8] This passage has escaped the
diligence of Meursius, Græc. Feriat. p. 150.

[9] Athen. ix. 13.

[10] Dioscor. ii. 200, seq. Plin.
xix. 11.

[11] Athen. ii. 57. Schol. Aristoph.
Nub. 189, 191. Eccles. 1092.
Geop. xii. 36.

laying its trunk in the earth to rot, watered it assi-
duously, after which mushrooms, at the proper time
sprung up. Another method was to irrigate the
trunk of the fig-tree after having covered it all round
with dung, though the best kind in the opinion of
others were such as grew at the foot of elm and pine-
trees.[1] Those springing from the upper roots were
reckoned of no value.

On other occasions[2] they chose a light sandy soil
accustomed to produce reeds, then burning brush-
wood, &c., when the air was in a state indicating
rain, this ambiguous species of vegetable started
forth from the earth with the first shower. The
same effect was produced by watering the ground
thus prepared, though this species was supposed to
be inferior. In France, the most delicate sort of
mushrooms are said to proceed from the decayed
root of the Eryngium.

This vegetable appears to have been a favourite
dish among the ancients, together with the truffle,[3]
eaten both cooked and raw;[4] and the morrille.[5]
That particular kind, called geranion, is the modern
crane's bill. The Misu, another sort of truffle,[6]
grew chiefly in the sandy plains about Cyrene, and,
as well as the Iton,[7] found in the lofty downs of
Thrace, was said to exhale an agreeable odour resembling that of animal food. These fanciful luxuries, which were produced among the rains and
thunders[8] of autumn, continued to flourish in the
earth during a whole year, but were thought to be

[1] A similar observation is made
in France respecting the truffles,
the best of which are supposed to
grow about the roots and under
the shadow of the oak. Trollope's
Summer in Western France, ii.
352.

[2] Geop. xii. 41. 2.

[3] Sch. Aristoph. Nub. 189.

[4] This was more particularly
the case on the Tauric Chersonese.—Theoph. Hist. Plant. vii.
13. 8.

[5] Theophrast. Hist. Plant. i.
10. 7.

[6] Theoph. Hist. Plant. i. 6.
13.

[7] Athen. ii. 62.

[8] Plut. Sympos. iv. 2. 1. who
relates that the ὕδνα attained to
a very large size in Elis.

in season in spring. Truffle-seed was usually imported from Megara, Lycia, and Getulia; but in Mytelene the inhabitants were spared this expense, their sandy shores being annually sown from the neighbouring coast by the winds and showers. It has been remarked, that neither truffles nor wild onions were found near the Hellespont.[1]

What methods the ancients employed for discovering the truffle, which grows without stem or leaf in a small cell beneath the surface of the earth, I have nowhere seen explained. At present[2] their existence is said to be detected in Greece, not by the truffle hound, but by the divining rod. On the dry sandy downs of the Limousin, Gascogne, Angoumois, and Perigord, as well as in several parts of Italy,[3] they are collected by the swineherds; for the hogs being extremely fond of them utter grunts of joy, and begin to turn up the earth as soon as they scent their odour, upon which the herdsmen beat the animals away, and carefully preserve the delicacy for the tables of the rich. At other times they are discovered in the following manner: the herdsmen stooping down, and looking horizontally along the surface of the Landes, observe here and there, on spots bare of grass and full of fissures, clouds of very diminutive flies hatched in the truffle, and still regaling themselves with its perfume. In some parts of Savoy they have been found two pounds in weight.

[1] Vid. Theoph. Hist. Plant. i. 6. 13.
[2] Walp. Mem. i. 284.
[3] Valmont de Bomare, Dict. D'Hist. Nat. t. ii. p. 21, seq.

CHAPTER III.

VINEYARD, VINTAGE, ETC.

ONE of the principal branches of husbandry [1] in Greece was the culture of the vine, probably introduced from Phœnicia.[2] Long before the historical age, however, it had spread itself through the whole country, together with several parts of Asia Minor, as may be inferred from the language of Homer,[3] who frequently enumerates vineyards among the possessions of his heroes. Like most things the origin of which was unknown, the vine furnished the poets and common people with the subjects of numerous fables, some of which were reckoned of sufficient importance to be treasured up and transmitted to posterity. Thus, among the Ozolian Locrians, it was said [4] to have sprung from a small piece of wood, brought forth in lieu of whelps by a bitch. Others supposed a spot near Olympia [5] to have given birth to the vine, in proof of which the

---

[1] The importance of this branch of cultivation in some countries may be perceived from the fact, that in France it is said to afford employment to 2,200,000 families, comprising a population of 6,000,000, or nearly one-fifth of the population of the entire kingdom. Times, Aug. 3, 1838. The quantity of land devoted to the culture of the vine was estimated in 1823, at 4,270,000 acres, the produce of which amounted to 920,721,088 gallons, 22,516,220*l.* 15*s.* sterling. Redding, Hist. of Modern Wines,

chap. iv. p. 56. In the Greek Budget of 1836, the tax on cattle produced 2,100,000 drachmas, on bees 35,000, olive-grounds 64,776, and on vineyards and currant-grounds 58,269.—Parish, Diplomatic History of the Monarchy of Greece, p. 175.

[2] Or according to Athenæus, from the shores of the Red Sea. Deipnosoph. xv. 17.

[3] Iliad. β. 561. γ. 184. ι. 152, 294. Cf. Pind. Isth. viii. 108.

[4] Paus. x. 38. 1.

[5] Athen. i. 61.

inhabitants affirmed a miracle was wrought annually among them during the Dionysiac festival. They took three empty brazen vessels, and having closely covered and sealed them in the presence of witnesses, again opened them after some interval of time, not stated, when they were found full of wine. According to other authorities, the environs of Plinthinè, in Egypt, had the honour of being the cradle of Dionysos, on which account the ancient Egyptians were by some accused of inebriety, though in the age of Herodotus[1] there would appear to have been no vineyards in the whole valley of the Nile. In reality,[2] the vine appears to be a native of all temperate climates, both in the old world and the new, and will even flourish[3] and produce fine grapes in various situations within the tropics, where clusters in different stages of ripeness may be observed upon its branches at all seasons of the year.

The opinions of Grecian writers respecting the soil best suited to the cultivation of the vine, having been founded on experience, generally agree with those which prevail in modern times.[4] They preferred for their vineyards the gentle acclivities of hills,[5] where the soil was good, though light and porous, and abounding in springs at no great depth from the surface.[6] A considerable degree of moisture was always supposed to be indispensable, on which account, in arid situations, large hollow sea-shells, and fragments of sandstone[7] were buried in the soil, these being regarded as so many reservoirs of humidity.

[1] ii. 77.

[2] Cf. Redding History of Modern Wines, chap. i. p. 2. An interesting and able work.

[3] Nienhoff in Churchill's Collection, ii. 264. Barbot, iii. 13. Ulloa, Memoires Philoso-phiques, t. ii. p. 15. Voyages, t. i. p. 487, 491.

[4] Virg. Georg. ii. 276.

[5] " Quòd colles Bacchus ama-" ret." Manil. Astronom. ii. p. 31. 6. Scalig.

[6] Geop. v. 1.

[7] Geop. v. 9. 8. Virg. Georg. ii. 348.

By some the vine was even thought to delight in the rich alluvial soil of plains, such as is found in Egypt,[1] where, in later times, the banks of the Nile, from Elephantinè to the sea, seem to have presented one vast succession of vineyards.[2] But superior vines were produced on a few spots only, as at Koptos, and in the neighbourhood of Lake Mareotis, where showers of sand, pouring in from the desert or the sea-shore, diminished the fatness of the ground. With respect to Koptos, we possess, however, no precise information,[3] but are expressly told, that the Mareotic vineyards covered a series of sandy swells, stretching eastward from the lake towards Rosetta.[4] On the southern confines of Egypt, in the rocky and picturesque island of Elephantinè, the vine was said [5] never to shed its leaves; but as none grow there at present, the traveller has no opportunity of deciding this question. In Greece the vineyards of the plains were generally appropriated to the production of the green grape, the purple being supposed to prefer the sides of hills, or even of mountains, provided it were not exposed to the furious winds upon their summits. Several sorts of

[1] Καλλίστη δὲ γῆ καὶ ἡ ὑπὸ τῶν ῥεόντων ποταμῶν χωσθεῖσα, ὅθεν καὶ τὴν Αἴγυπτον ἐπαινοῦμεν.—Florent. ap. Geop. v. 1. 4.

[2] Jemaleddin. Maured Allatafet, p. 7. All these vines it will be remembered were cut down by order of the Caliph Beamrillah, even in the province of the Fayoum. Some vestiges, however, of vineyards were here discovered by Pococke. "I observ-" ed," says he, "about this lake "(Mœris) several roots in the "ground, that seemed to me to "be the remains of vines, for "which the country about the "lake was formerly famous. "Where there is little moisture "in the air, and it rains so sel-

"dom, wood may remain sound "a great while, though it is not "known how long these vine-"yards have been destroyed." Vol. i. p. 65.

[3] Though with regard to the nature of the wine itself we are told, that it was so light as to be given to persons in fevers,—ὁ δὲ κατὰ τὴν Θηβαΐδα, καὶ μάλιστα ὁ κατὰ τὴν Κόπτον πόλιν, οὕτως ἐστὶ λεπτὸς, καὶ εὐανάδοτος, καὶ ταχέως πεπτικὸς, ὡς τοῖς πυρεταίνουσι διδόμενος μὴ βλάπτειν. Athen. i. 60.

[4] Athen. i. 60. Horat. Od. i. 37. 14. Strab. xvii. 1. t. iii. p. 425.

[5] Theoph. Hist. Plant. i. 3. 5. Varro, i. 7.

white grape, also, as the Psillian, Corcyrean, and the Chlorian, delighted in elevated vineyards,[1] though it was often judged necessary to reverse these rules, and compel the hill-nurslings to descend to the plains, while those of the plains were in their turn exposed to the climate of the mountains.

Much judgment was thought to be required in selecting the site of a vineyard, though almost everything depended on the climate and general configuration of the district in which it was situated. Thus in warm countries, as in the Pentapolis of Cyrene, the vineyards sloped towards the north; in Laconia, they occupied the eastern face of Mount Taygetos, while in Attica and the islands, the hills often appear to have been encircled with vines. Upon the whole, however, those were most esteemed which looked towards the rising sun and enjoyed, without obstruction, the first rays of the morning.[2] And this also is the case in the Côte d'Or, where the best wines, as the Chambertin, the Vin de Beaune, and that of the Clos Vougeot, are grown on eastern declivities. In some parts of Greece, the vine was strongly affected by the prevalence of certain winds, as those of the east and the west in Thessaly, which in the forty cold days of winter were attended by frost that killed its upper extremities, and sometimes the whole trunk. At Chalcis, in Eubœa likewise, the Olympias, a western wind, parched and shrivelled, or, as the Greeks express it, burnt up the leaves, sometimes completely destroying the shrub itself.[3] In such situations it was accordingly found necessary to protect it by a covering[4] during the prevalence of cold winds. At Methana, in Argolis, when

---

[1] Geop. v. 1. 15. Cf. Geop. iii. 2. "The shifting of ground "is a means to better the tree "and fruit, but with this caution, "that all things do prosper best "when they are advanced to the "better." Bacon, "Sylva Syl-"varum," 439.

[2] Geop. v. 4. 1.

[3] Theoph. Caus. Plant. v. 12. 5. Cf. Hist. Plant. iv. 14. 11. And yet the neighbourhood of the sea was considered propitious to the vine. Geop. v. 5.

[4] Theoph. Caus. Plant. v. 12. 5.

the south-east in spring blew up the Saronic gulf,[1] the inhabitants, to defend them from it, spread over their vines the invisible teguments of a spell; which was effected in the following manner: taking a milk-white cock, and cutting it in halves, two men seized each a part, and then, standing back to back, started off in opposite directions, made the tour of the vine-yard, and, returning whence they had set out, buried the cock's remains in the earth. After this the Libs might blow as it listed, since it possessed no power to injure any man's property within the consecrated circle.[2] The prevalence of the north wind during autumn was considered auspicious, as they supposed it to hasten the ripening of the fruit.

When the husbandman had resolved on the for-mation of a new vineyard, he first, of course, en-circled the spot with a hedge[3] which was made both thick and strong for the purpose of repelling the flocks and herds, which, as well as goats, foxes, and soldiers, loved to prey upon the vine.[4] His next care was to root up the hazel bush and the ole-aster, the roots of the former being supposed to be inimical to the Dionysiac tree, while the oily bark of the latter rendered it peculiarly susceptible of taking fire, by which means vineyards would often appear to have been reduced to ashes. So at least says Virgil.[5]

> Root up wild olives from thy laboured lands,
> For sparkling fire from hinds' unwary hands
> Is often scattered o'er their unctuous rinds,
> And often spread abroad by raging winds;
> For first the smouldering flame the trunk receives,
> Ascending thence it crackles in the leaves;

---

[1] On the prevalence of these winds in winter and spring, toge-ther with the causes of the pheno-menon, see Aristot. Problem. xxvi. 16.

[2] Paus. ii. 34. 2.   Chandler, Travels, ii. 248.

[3] Virg. Georg. ii. 371, sqq.

[4] Aristoph. Eq. 1073, seq. Küst.

[5] Georg. ii. 299, sqq. Dryden's Translation.

At length victorious to the top aspires,
Involving all the wood in smoky fires.
But most when driven by winds the flaming storm
Of the long files destroys the beauteous form;
In ashes then the unhappy vineyard lies,
Nor will the blasted plants from ruin rise,
Nor will the withered stock be green again,
But the wild olive shoots, and shades th' ungrateful plain.

The next operation[1] was to trench the ground and throw it into lofty ridges, which, by the operation of the summer sun, and the rain and winds and frosts of winter, were rendered mellow and genial. Occasionally a species of manure, composed[2] of pounded acorns, lentils, and other vegetable substances, was dug in for the purpose of giving to the soil the warmth and fertility required by the vine.

The ground having remained in this state during a whole year, its surface was levelled, and a series of shallow furrows traced for the slips by line, rather close, on rich alluvial plains, but diverging more and more[3] in proportion to the elevation of the site. Generally the vine was propagated by slips of moderate length, planted sometimes upright or à l'aiguille,[4] as the phrase is in Languedoc, sometimes obliquely,[5] which was generally supposed to be the better fashion. Along with the slip a handfull of grape-stones was usually cast into the furrow,[6] those of the green grape with the purple vine, and those of the purple with the green, in order to cause it the sooner to take root. With some

---

[1] Geop. iii. 4. Cf. Virg. Georg. ii. 259, seq. et Serv. ad loc.

[2] Geop. v. 24.

[3] Virg. Georg. ii. 274, seq.

[4] Skippon in Churchill, Collection of Voyages, vi. 730.

[5] Πότερα δὲ ὅλον τὸ κλῆμα ὀρθὸν τιθεὶς πρὸς τὸν οὐρανὸν βλέπον ἡγῇ μᾶλλον ἂν ῥιζοῦσθαι αὐτὸ, ἢ καὶ πλάγιόν τι ὑπὸ τῇ ὑποβεβλημένῃ γῇ θείης ἂν, ὥστε κεῖσθαι ὥσπερ γάμμα ὕπτιον;

οὕτω νὴ Δία· πλείονες γὰρ ἂν οἱ ὀφθαλμοὶ κατὰ γῆς εἶεν· ἐκ δὲ τῶν ὀφθαλμῶν καὶ ἄνω ὁρῶ βλαστάνοντα τὰ φυτά. Xenoph. Œconom. xix. 9, seq.

[6] Geop. v. 9. This practice is noticed by Lord Bacon who advises gardeners to extend the experiment by laying " good store " of other kernels about the roots of trees of the same kind. Sylva Sylvarum, i. 35.

the practice was always to set two slips together, so that if one missed the other might take, and when both grew, the weaker was cut off or removed. Several stones, [1] about the size of the fist, were placed round the slip above whatever manure was used, the belief being, that they would aid in preventing the root from being scorched by the sun in the heats of summer. [2] Some touched the lower point of the slip with cedar oil which prevented it from decaying, and likewise by its odour repelled vermin.

To produce grapes without stones the lower end of the slip was split, and the pith carefully extracted with an ear-pick. [3] It was then bound round with a papyrus leaf, thrust into a sea-onion and thus planted. Vines producing medicinal grapes were created by withdrawing the pith from the lower part of the slip, but without splitting, and introducing certain drugs into the hollow, [4] closing up the extremity with papyrus and thus setting it in the earth. The wine, the grape, the leaves, and even the ashes of such a vine were thought to be a remedy against the bite of serpents and dogs, though no security against hydrophobia. Another mode of producing stoneless grapes was to cut short all the branches of a vine already growing, extract the pith from the ends of them, and fill up the

---

[1] Virg. Georg. ii. 348.

[2] A similar remark is made by Lord Bacon : " It is an as-
" sured experience, " he says,
" that an heap of flint or stone
" laid about the bottom of a wild
" tree, as an oak, elm, ash, &c.,
" upon the first planting, doth
" make it prosper double as much
" as without it. The cause is
" for that it retaineth the mois-
" ture which falleth at any time
" upon the tree and suffereth it
" not to be exhaled by the sun."
Sylva Sylvarum, 422.

[3] Geop. iv. 7. Mention of the stoneless grapes of Persia occurs in many travellers, and, by Mr. Fowler, one of the most recent, are enumerated under the name of *kismis,* among the choicest fruits of that country. Three Years in Persia, vol. i. p. 323. It may here be remarked, that certain sorts of vines, among others the Capneion, produced sometimes white clusters, sometimes purple. Theophrast. Hist. Plant. ii. 3. 2. Cf. de Caus. Plant. v. 3. 1. κ. τ. λ.

[4] Geop. iv. 8.

cavity once a-week with the juice of sylphion,[1] binding them carefully to props that the liquor might
not escape. A method was also in use of producing
green and purple grapes on the same cluster.[2] This
was to take two slips as nearly as possible of the
same size, the one of the white, the other of the
black grape, and, having split them down the middle, carefully to fit the halves to their opposites,
so that the buds, when divided, should exactly
meet. They were then bound tight together with
papyrus thread, and placed in the earth in a sea-
onion,[3] whose glutinous juice aided the growing together of the severed parts. Sometimes instead of
slips, offshoots removed from the trunk of a large
vine, with roots attached to them, were used. On
other occasions the vine was grafted, like any other
fruit-tree, on a variety of stocks,[4] each modifying
the quality and flavour of the grape. Thus a vine
grafted on a myrtle-stock,[5] produced fruit partaking
of the character of the myrtle-berry. Grafted on a
cherry-tree, its grapes underwent a different change,
and ripened, like cherries, in the spring. As the
clay encircling the junctures of these grafts grew dry,
and somewhat cracked in hot summers, it was customary for gardeners to moisten them every evening
with a sponge dipped in water.[6]

The husbandmen of antiquity were often somewhat
fanciful in their practices. In order, when forming
a nursery,[7] to coax the young plants to grow, the
beds to which they were transferred, were formed
of a stratum of earth brought from the vineyard

[1] Geop. iv. 7.

[2] Geop. iv. 14.

[3] It has been remarked also by
ancient naturalists that a fig-tree
planted in a sea-onion, grows
quicker and is more free from
vermin. Theoph. Hist. Plant. i.
5. 5.

[4] Colum. v. 11.
—Adultâ vitium propagine
    Altas maritat populos,
    Inutilesque falce ramos ampu-
        tans
    Feliciores inserit.
        Horat. Epod. ii. 9, seq.
[5] Geop. iv. 4, seq.
[6] Geop. iv. 12.
[7] Virg. Georg. ii. 265, seq.

whence they also were taken. Another nicety was to take care, that they occupied precisely the same position with respect to the quarters of the heavens [1] as when growing on the parent stock.[2]

> " Besides to plant it as it was they mark
> The heaven's four quarters on the tender bark,
> And to the north or south restore the side
> Which at their birth did heat or cold abide,
> So strong is custom ; such effects can use
> In tender souls of pliant plants produce."

When desirous of extending the plantation in an old vineyard, instead of the methods above described, they had recourse to another, which was to bend down [3] the vine branch, and bury it up to the point in the earth, where it would take root, and send forth a new vine, and in this way a long series of leafy arcades [4] may sometimes have been formed. At the foot of their vines some cultivators were in the habit of burying three goats' horns [5] with their points downwards, and the other end appearing above the soil. These they regarded as so many receptacles for receiving and gradually conveying water to the roots, and, consequently, an active cause of the vines' fertility.

[1] Lord Bacon gives this experiment a place in his philosophy, observing, that " in all trees " when they be removed (especially fruit-trees) care ought to " be taken that the sides of the " trees be coasted (north and " south) and as they stood be-" fore." Sylva Sylvarum, 471.

[2] Virg. Georg. ii. 270, seq.

[3] An analogous practice is observed in the pepper gardens of Sumatra :—" When the vines " originally planted to any of the " chinkareens (or props) are ob-" served to fail or miss ; instead " of replacing them with new " plants, they frequently conduct " one of the shoots, or suckers, " from a neighbouring vine, to " the spot, through a trench " made in the ground, and there " suffer it to rise up anew, often " at the distance of twelve or " fourteen feet from the parent " stock." Marsden, History of Sumatra, p. 111.

[4] Virg. Georg. ii. 26. Serv. ad loc.

[5] Geop. iv. 2. The nymphs are said to have been the nurses of Bacchos, because water supplied moisture to the vine. The explanation of Athenæus is forced and cold. ii. 2.

Respecting the seasons of planting,[1] opinions were divided, some preferring the close of autumn, immediately after the fall of the leaf, when the sap had forsaken the branches, and descended to the roots; others chose, for the time of this operation, the early spring, just before the sap mounted; while a third class delayed it until the buds began to swell, and the tokens of spring were evident. To these varieties of practice Virgil makes allusion,—

> When winter frosts constrain the field with cold,
> The fainty root can take no steady hold;
> But when the golden spring reveals the year,
> And the white bird returns whom serpents fear,
> That season deem the best to plant thy vines;
> Next that, is when autumnal warmth declines,
> Ere heat is quite decayed, or cold begun,
> Or Capricorn admits the winter sun.

But the above were not the only rules observed; for, besides the general march of the seasons, they took note of the phases of the moon,[2] whose influence over vegetation all antiquity believed to be very powerful. Some planted during the four days immediately succeeding the birth of the new moon, while others extended their labours through the first two quarters. The act of pruning[3] was performed when that planet was in its wane.

There were in Greece[4] three remarkable varieties of the vine, created by difference in the mode of cultivation.[5] The first consisted of plants always kept short, and supported on props, as in France;

[1] Geop. v. 7, seq. Virg. Georg. ii. 323, sqq.

[2] Geop. v. 10.

[3] Geop. iii. 1.

[4] Cf. Theoph. Caus. Plant. iv. 3. 6.

[5] The low vines of Asia Minor are now pruned in a very particular manner. " As we approach- " ed Vourla the little valleys " were all green with corn, or " filled with naked vine-stocks in " orderly arrangement, about a " foot and a half high. The peo- " ple were working, many in a " row, turning the earth, or " encircling the trunks with tar, " to secure the buds from grubs " and worms. The shoots which " bear the fruit are cut down " again in winter." Chandler, i. 98.

the second of tree-climbers, thence called Anadendrades; the third sort enjoyed neither of these advantages,[1] but being grown chiefly in steep and stony
places, spread their branches over the earth, as is still
the fashion in Syra[2] and other islands of the Archipelago.

Vine-props[3] appear to have commonly consisted of
short reeds, which, accordingly, were extensively cultivated both in Hellas and its colonies of Northern
Africa, where the musical cicada, whose excessive
multiplication betokened a sickly year, bored through
the rind, and laid its eggs in the hollow within.[4]
From an inconvenience attending the use of this kind
of support came the rustic proverb, " The prop has
defrauded the vine;"[5] for these reeds sometimes took
root, outgrew their clients, and monopolized the moisture of the soil.

In rich and level lands,[6] particularly where the
Aminian vine[7] was cultivated, the props often rose
to the height of five or six feet; but in hill-vine-
yards, where the soil was lighter and less nutritive,
they were not suffered to exceed that of three feet.

---

[1] On the cultivation of the Corinth grape, see Chandler, ii. 339.

[2] Abbé Della Rocca, Traité
Complet des Abeilles, i. 203.
Lord Bacon, who had heard of
this manner of cultivating the
vine, observes, that in this state
it was supposed to produce grapes
of superior magnitude, and advises to extend the practice to
hops, ivy, woodbine, &c. Sylva
Sylvarum, 623.

[3] Geop. v. 22. 27. Reeds delight in sunny spots, and are
nourished by the rain. They
were cultivated for props, and,
if thoroughly smoked, the insects
called Ἶπες were killed, which
would otherwise breed in them,
to the great injury of the vine.
v. 53. Plin. xviii. 78. Cf.

Schol. Aristoph. Acharn. 1140.
983. Varro, i. 8. In the island
of Pandataria the vineyard was
filled with traps, to protect the
grapes from the mice. Id. ib.

[4] Aristoph. Hist. Anim. v. 24.
3.

[5] Sch. Aristoph. Vesp. 1282.
Cf. Thom. Magist. v. χάραξ. p.
911, seq. Blancard. cum not.
Stieber. et Oudendorp. Ammon.
v. χάραξ. p. 145, with the note
of Valckenaer. Liban. Epist. 218.
p. 104 seq. Wolf.

[6] Geop. v. 27.

[7] Cf. Geop. iv. 1. Dioscor. v.
6. Virg. Georg. ii. 97. Servius,
on the authority of Aristotle, relates that the Aminian vines were
transplanted from Thessaly into
Italy. Cf. Pier. ad loc.

Where reeds were not procurable, ash-props[1] were substituted, but they were always carefully barked, to prevent cantharides, and other insects hurtful to the vine, from making nests in them. Their price would appear to have been considerable, since we find a husbandman speaking of having laid out a hundred drachma in vine-props.[2] To prevent their speedily decaying they were smeared a-top with pitch, and carefully, after the vintage, collected and laid up within doors.[3]

A vineyard, consisting wholly of Anadendrades,[4] most common in Attica, presented, in spring and summer, a very picturesque appearance, especially when situated on the sharp declivity of a hill.[5] The trees designed for the support of the vines,[6] planted in straight lines, and rising behind each other, terrace above terrace, at intervals of three or four and twenty feet, were beautiful in form and varied in feature, consisting generally of the black poplar, the ash, the maple, the elm,[7] and probably, also, the platane, which is still employed for this purpose in Crete.[8] Though kept low in some situations, where the soil was scanty, they were, in others, allowed to run to thirty or forty, and sometimes, as in Bithynia, even to sixty feet in height.

The face of the tree along which the vine climbed was cut down sheer like a wall, against which the purple or golden clusters hung thickly suspended,

---

[1] Sch. Aristoph. Vesp. 1116. Acharn. 1177. In the Æolian islands the vines are supported on a frame-work of poles and trees, over which they spread themselves with extraordinary luxuriance. Spallanzani, iv. 99.

[2] Sch. Aristoph. Pac. 1262.

[3] Virg. Georg. 408, seq.

[4] Which were pruned in January (Geop. iii. 1), and esteemed the most useful, iv. 1. The solidest and hardest vines were thought to bear the least fruit. Theoph.

Hist. Plant. v. 4. 1.   Cf. Chandler, i. 98.

[5] Dem. in Nicostrat. § 5.

[6] " Vitem viduas ducit ad arbores."
        Hor. Carm. iv. 5. 30.

[7] Virg. Georg. ii. 361, seq. An amictâ vitibus ulmo. Hor. Epist. i. 16. 3.

[8] Pashley, Travels, ii. 22. The oak is now used for the same purpose in Asia Minor. Chandler, i. 114.

while the young branches crept along the boughs, or over bridges of reeds,[1] uniting tree with tree, and, when touched with the rich tints of autumn, delighting the eye by an extraordinary variety of foliage. As the lower boughs of these noble trees were carefully lopped away, a series of lofty arches was created, beneath which the breezes could freely play, abundant currents of pure air being regarded as no less essential to the perfect maturing of the grape [2] than constant sunshine. Sometimes the vine, in its ascent, was suffered to wind round the trunk of its supporter, which, however, by the most judicious husbandmen, was considered prejudicial, since the profusion of ligatures which it threw out in its passage upwards was thought to exhaust too much of its strength, to prevent which wooden wedges[3] were here and there inserted between the vine stem and the tree. In trailing the branches, moreover, along the boughs, care was taken to keep them as much as possible on the upper side, that they might enjoy a greater amount of sunshine, and be the more exposed to be agitated by the winds.

These Anadendrades,[4] which were supposed to produce the best and most lasting wines, probably, as at present, ripened their produce much later than the other sorts of vines on account of the trees by which

---

[1] Gœttling ad Hesiod. Scut. Heracl. 298.

[2] Another means of augmenting the fertility of the vine is noticed by Lord Bacon, whose diligent study of antiquity was at least as remarkable as his superior intellect. " It is strange, " which is observed by some of " the ancients, that dust helpeth " the fruitfulness of trees and of " vines by name ; insomuch as " they cast dust upon them of " purpose. It should seem that " powdring when a shower cometh " maketh a kind of soiling to the " tree, being earth and water " finely laid on. And they note " that countries where the fields " and waies are dusty bear the " best vines." Sylva Sylvarum, 666.

[3] Geop. iv. 1. 16.

[4] These vines were likewise called ἀμαμάξυες. Aristoph. Vesp. 325, et Schol. The rustics engaged in pruning them, feeling themselves secure in their lofty station, used to pour their rough raillery and invectives on the passers-by. Horace, Satir. i. 7. 29, seq.

they were shaded. In modern Crete,[1] where, however, they are never pruned, their grapes seldom
ripen before November, and sometimes they furnish
the bazaar of Khania with fresh supplies till Christ-
mas. The same is the case also in Egypt.

Occasionally, too, more especially in Cypros, the
Anadendrades grew to an enormous size. At Po-
pulonium, in Etruria, there was a statue of Jupiter
carved from a single vine; the pillars of the temple
of Hera, at Metapontum, consisted of so many vines;
and the whole staircase leading to the roof of the
fane of Artemis, at Ephesos, was constructed with
the timber of a single vine from Cypros. To render these things credible, we are informed, that, at
Arambys, in Africa,[2] there was a vine twelve feet
in circumference, and modern travellers have found
them of equal dimensions in other parts of the
world.[3] In France, for example, the celebrated
Anne, Duc de Montmorenci, had a table made
with a single slab of vinewood, which, two hundred
years afterwards, Brotier[4] saw preserved at the town
of Ecouen.

To return, however : the wide spaces between the
trees were not in this class of vineyards allowed to
remain entirely idle, having been sometimes sown[5]
with corn, or planted with beans, and gourds, and
cucumbers, and lentils.[6] The cabbage[7] was carefully
excluded,[8] as an enemy to Dionysos. In other cases
these intervals were given up to the cultivation of
fruit-trees, such as the pomegranate, the apple, the
quince, and the olive. The fig-tree was regarded as

---

[1] On the vines of this island
cf. Meurs. Cret. c. 9. p. 103.

[2] Bochart. Geog. Sac. Pars
Alt. l. i. c. 37. p. 712. Cf. Plin.
Hist. Nat. v. i.

[3] Tozzeli, Viaggi. t. iv. p. 208.

[4] Not. ad Plin. xiv. i. 1.

[5] Geop. iv. 1. v. 7, seq.

[6] Barley and other grain are
still in modern times sown be-

tween the vines in Asia Minor.
Chandler, i. 114. The same
practice has been partially introduced into the Æolian islands.
Spallanzani, iv. 100.

[7] Suid. v. κράμβη, t. i. p. 1518.
b. — παρὰ ἀμπέλῳ οὐ φύεται.
Etym. Mag. 534. 47.

[8] So was the laurel. Theoph.
Caus. Plant. ii. 18. 4.

pernicious, though often planted in rows on the outside of the vineyard.

Respecting those vines which were cultivated without the aid of props,[1] or trees, we possess little information, except that there were such. But, as they
are still found in the country, it is probable, that
the mode of dressing them now prevailing nearly
resembles that of antiquity. They are generally, in
Syria, planted along the steep sides of mountains,
where they spread and rest upon the stones, and
have their fruit early ripened by the heat reflected
from the earth. Frequently, also, they are planted
on more level ground, in which case, as soon as
the grapes acquire any size, the husbandman passes
through the vineyard with an armful of forked
wooden props which he skilfully introduces beneath
the branches and fixes firmly so as to keep the
clusters from touching the mould. The reason for
adopting this method is the furious winds which
at certain seasons of the year prevail in many of
the Grecian islands, preventing the growth of woods
and prostrating the fig and every other fruit-tree to
the earth. The spaces between the lines are turned
up annually by a peculiar sort of plough [2] drawn by
oxen, in front of which a man advances, lifting up
the vines and holding them aside while they pass.
This destroys the weeds, and, at the same time, all
the upper roots of the vine, which compels it to
descend deeper into the earth, where it finds a
cooler and more abundant nourishment. In this
respect the practice of the Syrotes closely resembles
that of their ancestors. Some husbandmen were
careful, likewise, while weeding,[3] to remove the
larger stones, though they are often supposed, by
preserving moisture, to do more good than harm.

---

[1] This creeping vine, cultivated
sine ridicis, was common in Spain.
Varro, i. 8.

[2] Della Rocca, Traité Complet

sur les Abeilles, t. i. p. 203, sqq.
Cf. Thiersch, Etat Actuel de ·la
Grèce, t. i. p. 288. 296. Damm.
Nov. Lex. Græc. Etym. 1122.

[3] Geop. v. 19.

It is a peculiar feature in the character of the
ancients that they loved to attribute to the inferior
animals the first hints of various useful practices.
Thus they maintained it was the ass that, by browsing on the extremities of the vine, which only made
it bear the more luxuriantly, taught them the art
of pruning as well perhaps as that of feeding on
the tendrils and tender branches,[1] which among them
were esteemed a delicacy. To manifest their gratitude for this piece of instruction they erected at
Nauplia,[2] a marble statue in honour of this ill-used
quadruped, who has seldom, I fear, from that day
to this, been so well treated. The rules observed
in pruning[3] resembling those still in use, it is unnecessary to repeat them, though it may be worth
mentioning, that the husbandman, who coveted an
abundant vintage, was careful to lop his vines[4] with
his brows shaded by an ivy crown. They esteemed
it a sign of a fruitful year when the fig-tree and
the white vine put forth luxuriantly in spring,[5] after
which they had only to petition the gods against
too much rain, or too much drought,[6] and those
terrible hailstorms which sometimes devastate whole
districts. Against this calamity, however, they had
a preservative, which was to bind an amulet in the
shape of a thong of seal-hide or eagle's wing, about
one of the stocks,[7] after which the whole vineyard
was supposed to be secure from injury. The same

[1] Theoph. Caus. Plant. vi. 12.
9. After the vintage the goat
and the camel, among the modern
Asiatics, are sometimes let into
the vineyard to browse upon the
vine. Chandler, i. 163.

[2] Paus. ii. 38. 3. See, however,
another interpretation of the passage in the Tale of a Tub, where
the author gravely insists, that,
by Ass, we are to understand a
critic. Sect. iii. p. 96.

[3] Cf. Plat. De Rep. t. vi. p. 53.

Schol. Aristoph. Eq. 166. See
an exact representation of the
pruninghook in the hand of Ver-
tumnus. Mus. Cortonens. pl.
36. This instrument was usually
put into requisition about the
vespertinal rising of Arcturus.
Hesiod. Opp. et Dies, 566, sqq.

[4] Geop. v. 24.

[5] Theoph. Caus. Plant. i. 20. 5.

[6] Sch. Aristoph. Nub. 1117.
Küst.

[7] Geop. i. 14. Cf. Sch. Aris-

effect was produced by striking a chalezite stone with a piece of iron on the approach of a storm, and by hanging up in the vineyard a picture of a bunch of grapes at the setting of the constellation of the Lyre.[1] To repel the ascent of vermin along the trunk it was smeared with a thick coat of bitumen,[2] imported from Cilicia, while to preserve the branches from wasps a little olive-oil was blown over them.[3]

While the grapes were growing, the ancients, following in the track of nature, supposed them to need shade, since the leaves at that time put forth most abundantly, to screen the young fruit from the scorching sun; but when they began to don their gold or purple hues, observing the foliage shrivel and shrink from about them, in order to admit the warm rays to penetrate and pervade the fruit they then stripped the branches and hastened the vintage,[4] plucking moreover the clusters as they ripened, lest they should drop off and be lost. But this partial gathering of the grapes could only take place in their gardens, or where the vine was trained about the house; for in the regular vineyards the season of the vintage was regulated by law,[5] as in Burgundy and the south of France, in order to protect the public against the pernicious frauds which would otherwise be practised. This, in Attica, usually coincided with, the heliacal rising of the constellation Arcturus.[6]

When the magistrate had declared that the season of the vintage[7] was come, the servants of Bac-

toph. Nub. 1109. Husbandmen were accustomed to nail the heads and feet of animals to the trunks of trees to prevent their being withered by the operation of the evil eye. Sch. Ran. 943.

[1] Geop. ii. 14.

[2] Theoph. De Lapid. § 49. Schneid. Cf. Sir John Hill, notes,

p. 200. It was likewise obtained from Seleucia Pieria in Syria. Strab. vii. 5. t. ii. p. 106.

[3] Geop. iv. 10.

[4] Xenoph. Œcon. xix. 9.

[5] Plat. De Legg. t. viii. 106. Geop. v. 45.

[6] Cf. Geop. i. 9. 9.

[7] Cf. Plut. Thes. § 22.

chos hurried forth to the vine-clad hills, converting
their labours into a pretext for superabundant mirth
and revelry.   The troops of vintagers, composed of
youths and maidens, with crowns of ivy on their
heads, and accompanied by rural performers on the
flute or phorminx, moved forward with shout, and
dance, and song, to the sacred enclosures of Dionysos, surrounded with plaited hedgerows, and blue
streamlets.[1]   Here, where

> "——————— the showering grapes
> In Bacchanal profusion reel to earth
> Purple and gushing,"

they at once commenced their joyous task.   With
sharp pruning-hooks[2] they separated the luxuriant
clusters, gold or purple, from the vine, and piling
them in plaited baskets of osier or reed, bore them
on their shoulders to the wine-press.   In this operation, as I have said, both men and women joined;
but the press was trodden by men only,[3] who, half
intoxicated by pleasure,[4] and the fumes of the young
wine, chanted loudly their ancient national lays in
praise of Bacchos.

The wine-press, which stood under cover, sometimes consisted of two upright, and many cross
beams,[5] which descending with great weight upon
the grapes squeezed forth all their juices, and these
falling through a species of strainer,[6] upon an in-

---

[1] Il. σ. 561, sqq.

[2] Scut. Heracl. 291, seq. On
the modern modes of gathering
the grapes, see Redding Hist.
of Modern Wines, chap. ii. 26,
et seq.

[3] The practice is still the same
in the Levant :—" The vintage
" was now begun, the black
" grapes being spread on the
" ground in beds exposed to the
" sun to dry for raisins ; while
" in another part, the juice was
" expressed for wine, a man with
" feet and legs bare, treading the

" fruit in a kind of cistern, with
" a hole or vent near the bottom,
" and a vessel beneath it to re-
" ceive the liquor." Chandler, ii.
p. 2.

[4] Anacreon, Od. 52.   See a
representation of the whole process in the Mus. Cortonens, pl. 9,
where the vintagers are clad in
skins ; and Cf. Zoëga, Bassi Rilievi, tav. 26.

[5] Antich. di Ercol. t. i. tav. 35,
p. 187.

[6] Schol. Aristoph. Pac. 527.

clined slab, were poured through a small channel formed for the purpose, into a broad open vessel communicating with the vat. Into the process of wine-making [1] it is unnecessary to enter. It will be sufficient, perhaps, to say that, when made, it was laid up in skins or large earthen jars until required for use. The wines of modern Attica and the Morea [2] are preserved from becoming acid by a large infusion of resin. [3]

The sports, [4] which took place during the vintage, were loud and frolicsome, and distinguished sometimes for their excessive licence. They brought forth a number of wine skins, filled tight, to the village green, and there smearing them liberally with oil the staggering rustics sought, each in his turn, to leap and stand upon one of them with his naked foot. [5] The missing, slipping, and falling, the awkward figure they sometimes made upon the ground, the jokes, and shouts, and laughter of the bystanders, mingled with the twanging of rustic instruments, and the roar of Bacchanalian songs, constituted the charm of the rural Dionysia, out of which, through many changes and gradations, arose, as we have seen, the Greek drama. In order without shame to give the freer licence to their tongues, they sometimes covered their faces with masks, formed with the bark of trees, which, there can be no doubt, led to those afterwards employed in the theatre. Sometimes a sort of farce [6] was acted,

---

[1] For the making of the sweet wine (βίβλινος οἶνος) which resembled, perhaps, our Constantia or Malaga, and enjoyed extraordinary favour among the ancients Hesiod gives particular directions. Opp. et Dies, 611, sqq. Colum. xii. 39. Plin. Hist. Nat. xiv. 8. Pallad. xi. 19.

[2] Sibth. in Walp. Mem. ii. 235. Chandler, ii. 251.

[3] A few drops of the oil which ran from olives without pressing were supposed by the ancients to render the wine stronger and more lasting.—Geop. vii. 12. 20. On the boiled wine, σίραιον. Cf. Sch. Aristoph. Vesp. 878.

[4] Virg. Georg. ii. 580, sqq. Hes. Scut. Heracl. 291, sqq. Cf. Schol. Theocrit. i. 48.

[5] See Book ii. chapter 3.

[6] Serv. ad Virg. Georg. ii. 389

representing the search of the Athenians for the
bodies of Icarios and Erygone. The former, according to tradition, was the person who taught the inhabitants of Attica the use of wine, with which on
a certain occasion he regaled a number of shepherds.
These demi-savages, observing their strength and
their reason fail, imagined themselves to have been
poisoned, and falling, in revenge, upon the donor,
put him to death. His dog Mœra escaped, and
leading Erygone to the spot where her father had
been murdered, she immediately hung herself on
the discovery of the corpse. Upon this they were
all transported to the skies, and changed into so
many constellations, namely Boötes, [1] the Dog, and
the Virgin, by whose brilliancy we are still re-
joiced nightly. Soon afterwards the maidens of Attica were seized with madness and hung themselves
in great numbers, upon which the oracle being consulted, commanded the Athenians to make search
for the bodies of Icarios and Erygone. Being able
to discover them nowhere on earth, they suspended
ropes from the branches of lofty trees, by swinging
to and fro on which they appeared to be conducting their search in the air; but many of these adventurous explorers receiving severe falls, they were
afterwards contented with suspending to the ropes
little images after their own likeness, which they
sent hither and thither in the air as their substi-
tutes.

But all the produce of the vineyards was not appropriated to the making of wine, great quantities
of grapes [2] being preserved for the table, or converted into raisins. [3] The latter were sometimes
made by being carefully gathered after the full
moon, and put out to dry in the sun, about ten
o'clock in the morning, when all the dew was eva-

[1] Æl. de Anim. vi. 25.

[2] Geop. iv. 15. Cato, 7. Colum. xii. 39. Pallad. 11. 22.

[3] In the warm climate of Asia
Minor grapes were sometimes
turned into raisins, on the stalk,
by the sun.—Chandler, i. 77.

porated. For this purpose, there was in every
vineyard, garden, and orchard, a place called Thei-
lopedon,[1] which would seem to have been a smooth
raised terrace, where not grapes only, but myrtle-
berries, and every other kind of fruit, were exposed to the sun on fine hurdles. Here, likewise,
the berries of the Palma Christi [2] were prepared
for the making of castor oil. Another method was
to twist the stem of the cluster [3] and allow the

---

[1] Eustath. ad Odyss. η. p. 276.
Schol. Aristoph. Nub. 51. κρε-
μάθρα, fruit-baskets, 219.

[2] Dioscor. i. 38.

[3] Geop. v. 52. This we find
is still the practice in the islands
of the Archipelago, for the purpose of making sweet wine. M. l'
Abbé della Rocca, who mentions
it, enumerates at the same time
the most delicious sorts of grapes
now cultivated in Greece—" On
" peut juger si les vins y sont
" exquis, et si les anciens eurent
" raison d'appeler Naxie l'île de
" Bacchus. Les raisins y sont
" monstrueux, et il arrive sou-
" vent que dans un repas, on n'en
" sert qu'un seul pour le fruit ;
" mais aussi couvre-t-il toute la
" profondeur d'un grand bassin :
" les grains en sont gros comme
" nos damas noirs. Il y a dans
" les îles des raisins de plus de
" vingt sortes: les muscats de
" Ténédos et de Samos l'empor-
" tent sur tous les autres ; ceux
" de Ténédos sont plus ambrés ;
" ceux de Samos, plus délicats.
" Les Sentorinois, pour donner
" une saveur plus exquise à leurs
" raisins, leur tordent la queue
" lorsqu'ils commencent à mûrir ;
" après quelques jours d'un soleil
" ardent, les raisins deviennent
" à demi flétris, ce qui fait un
" vin dont ceux de la Cieutat et

" de Saint-Laurent n'approchent
" pas. Les autres sortes de rai-
" sins sont l'aïdhoni, petit raisin
" blanc qu'on mange vers la mi-
" juillet ; le samia gros raisin
" blanc qu'on fait sécher ; le
" siriqui, ainsi nommé parce qu'il
" a le goût de la cerise ; l'œtony-
" chi, qui a la figure de l'ongle
" d'un aigle, et qui est très sa-
" voureux ; le malvoisie, le mus-
" cat violet, le corinthe, et plu-
" sieurs autres dont les noms
" me sont échappés." Traité
sur les Abeilles, t. i. p. 6, seq.
Speaking of the prodigious pro-
ductiveness of vines, Columella
mentions one which bore upwards
of two thousand clusters, De Re
Rust. iii. 3. A vine producing
a fifth of this quantity has been
thought extraordinary in modern
Egypt : " Il n'est pas croyable
" combien rapporte un seul pied
" de vigne. Il y en a un dans
" la maison Consulaire de France,
" qui a porté 436 grosses grappes
" de raisin, et qui en donne or-
" dinairement 300."—De Mail-
" let, Description de l'Egypte, p.
17.* In the Grecian Archipelago, however, the vine has
been known to yield still more
abundantly than in Egypt : " On
" a compté pendant trois ans
" consécutifs, cent trente-quatre
" grappes de raisin sur une

grapes to dry on the vine. They were then laid up in vessels among vine leaves, dried also in the sun, covered close with a stopper, and deposited in a cold room free from smoke.

To preserve the grapes fresh some cut off with a sharp pruninghook the clusters separately, others the branches on which they grew, after which, dipping the stem into pitch and removing the damaged grapes with a pair of scissors, they spread them in cool and shady rooms, on layers of pulse-halm, or hay, or straw.[1] The halm of lentils was usually preferred, because it is hard and dry, and repels mice. On other occasions, the branches were kept suspended, having sometimes been previously dipped in sweet wine. Grapes were likewise preserved in pitched coffers, immersed in dry saw-dust of the pitch tree, or the silver fir, or the black poplar, or even in millet flour. Others plunged the bunches in boiling sea-water, or if this were not at hand, into a preparation of wine, salt, and water, and then laid them up in barley straw. Others boiled the ashes of the fig-tree, or the vine, with which they sprinkled the bunches. Others preserved grapes by suspending them in granaries, where the grain beneath was occasionally moved, for the dust rising from the corn settled on the outside of the clusters, and protected them from the air. Another method was to boil rain-water to a third, and then, after cooling it in the open air, and pouring it into a pitched vessel, to fill it with clusters perfectly cleansed. The vessel was then covered, luted with gypsum, and laid by in a cold place. The grapes in this way remained quite fresh, and the water

"souche; et sur un autre cep "de vigne planté dans un terrain "très-gras, on a compté jusqu'à "quatre cent quatre - vingts "grappes; et l'intendant de "l'évêché de notre île m'a plus

"d'une fois assuré qu'on avoit "fait soixante-quinze bouteilles "de vin, avec le raisin d'un seul "cep." Della Rocca, t. i. p. 65.

[1] Geop. iv. 15 . 4.

itself acquiring a vinous taste was administered to sick persons in lieu of wine. Occasionally, also, grapes as well as apples were kept in honey.

The most extraordinary, and perhaps the most effectual contrivance,[1] however, was to dig near the vine a pit three feet deep, the bottom of which was covered with a layer of sand. A few short stakes were then fixed upright in it, and to these a number of vine branches laden with clusters were bent down and made fast. The whole was then closely roofed over so as completely to keep out the rain, and in this way the grapes would remain fresh till spring.

The labours of the vintage being concluded, the husbandman next turned his attention to olive gathering and the making of oil. This, in Greece, was a matter of great importance. The olives, therefore,[2] for all the better sorts of oil, were picked by hand, and not, as in Italy, suffered to fall. When as many were gathered as could conveniently be pressed during the following night and day, they were spread loosely on fine hurdles, and not heaped up lest they should heat and lose the delicacy of their flavour. They were, likewise, cleansed carefully from leaves and every particle of wood, these substances, it was supposed, impairing the quality and durability of the oil. Towards evening a little salt was sprinkled over the olives, which were then put into a clean mill,[3] and so arranged that they could be bruised without crushing the stones, from the juice of which the oil contracted a bad taste. Having been sufficiently bruised, they were conveyed in small vessels to the press, where they were covered with hurdles of green willows, upon which, at first, was placed a moderate weight, — for that which flows from slight pressure is the

---

[1] Geop. iv. 11. Pallad. xii. 12.

[2] Geop. ix. 19. 2.

[3] The fruit of the terebinth was ground, like the olive, in a mill, for the making of oil. The kernels were used in feeding pigs, or for fuel. Geop. ix. 18.

sweetest and purest oil, on which account it was drawn off in clean leaden vessels,[1] and preserved apart. Greater weight was then added, and the mass having been well writhen, the second runnings were laid up in separate vessels. The next step was to cause the precipitation of the lees, which was effected by mingling with the crude oil a little salt and nitre. It was then stirred with a piece of olive-wood, and left to settle, when the amurca or watery part sank to the bottom. The pure oil was then skimmed off with a shell, and laid up in glass vases, this substance having been preferred on account of its cold nature. In default of these, pickle-jars, glazed with gypsum, were used, which were deposited in cool cellars facing the north.[2]

The Greeks had a variety of other oils besides that procured from the olive,[3] as walnut-oil, oil of terebinth, oil of sesamum, oil of violets, oil of almonds, oil of Palma Christi, or castor-oil, oil of saffron, oil of Cnidian laurel, oil of datura, oil of lentisk, oil of mastic, oil of myrtle, and oil of mustard. They had, likewise,[4] the green and wild-olive oil, and the double-refined oil of Sicyon, together with imitations of the Spanish and Italian oils.

As fruit of all kinds was in great request among the Greeks, they had recourse to numerous contrivances[5] for ensuring an unfailing supply throughout the year. At many of these our gardeners may, perhaps, smile, but they were, nevertheless, most of them ingenious, and, probably, effectual, though the fruit thus preserved may have been dear when brought to market. Into the details of all their methods it will be unnecessary to enter: the following were the

---

[1] Cf. Cato, De Re Rust. 66. This clear pure oil, sometimes rendered odoriferous by perfumes, (Il. ψ. 186,) was chiefly employed in lubricating the body. Thus we find the virgin in Hesiod anointing her limbs with olive-oil to defend herself from the winter's cold. Opp. et Dies, 519, sqq.

[2] Vitruv. vi. 9.

[3] Geop. ix. 18.

[4] Geop. ix. 19, seq. iii. 13. Dioscor. i. 140.

[5] Geop. x. 10—70. Cf. Mazois, Pal. de Scaurus, p. 182, seq.

principal and most curious. Walnuts, chestnuts,
filberts, &c., were gathered and kept in the ordinary
way. They understood the art of blanching almonds,
which were afterwards dried in the sun. Medlars,
service-berries, winter-apples, and the like, having
been gathered carefully, were simply laid up in straw,
whether on the loft-floor or in baskets. This, likewise, was sometimes the case with quinces, which,
together with apples and pears, were, on other occasions, deposited in dry fig-leaves. For these, in the case
of pears and apples, walnut-leaves were often substituted, sometimes piled under and over them in
heaps, at other times wrapped and tied about the
fruit, the hues and odours of which they were supposed greatly to improve.

Citrons,[1] pomegranates,[2] apples, quinces, and pears,
were preserved in heaps of sand, grapestones, oak,
poplar, deal, or cedar sawdust, sometimes sprinkled
with vinegar, chopped straw, wheat, or barley, or
the seeds of plants, all of which sufficed equally to
exclude the external air. Another method with
apples[3] was to lay them up surrounded with sea-
weed in unbaked jars, which were then deposited
in an upper room free from smoke and all bad
smells. When sea-weed was not procurable they
put each apple into a small separate jar closely
covered up and luted. These apple-jars were
often lined with a coating of wax. Figs were, in
like manner, preserved green [4] by being enclosed
in so many small gourds. Citrons and pomegranates
were often suffered to remain throughout the winter

[1] Palladius, iv. 10.

[2] We find mention in modern
times of a species of pomegranate,
the kernels of which are without
stones, peculiar apparently to the
island of Scio. " It is usual to
" bring them to table, in a plate,
" sprinkled with rose-water."
Chandler, i. 58.

[3] Cf. Philost. Icon. t. 31. p.
809. ii. 2. p. 812.

[4] Ficus virides servari possunt
vel in melle ordinatæ, ne se in-
vicem tangant, vel singulæ intra
viridem cucurbitam clausæ, locis
unicuique cavatis, et item tessera,
quæ secatur, inclusis, suspensa ea
cucurbita, ubi non sit ignis vel
fumus. Pallad. iv. 10.

on the tree, defended from wet and wind by being capped with little fictile vases bound tightly to the branches to keep them steady. Others enclosed these fruits, as well as apples, in a thick coating of gypsum, preventing their falling off by binding the stem to the branches with packthread. Nor was it unusual, even when gathered, to envelope apples, quinces, and citrons, in a covering of the same material, or potter's clay, or argillaceous earth, mixed with hair, sometimes interposing between the fruit and this crust a layer of fig-leaves, after which they were dried in the sun. When at the end, perhaps, of a whole year the above crust was broken and removed the fruit came forth perfect as when plucked from the bough. It is possible, therefore, that, in a similar manner, mangoes, mangusteens, and other frail and delicate fruit of the tropics, might be brought fresh to Europe, and that, too, in such abundance as to make them accessible to most persons. To render pears and pomegranates durable, their stems were dipped in pitch, after which they were hung up. In the case of the latter the fruit itself was sometimes thus dipped ; and, at other times, immersed in hot sea-water, after which it was dried in the sun. One mode of preserving figs was to plunge them in honey so as neither to touch each other, nor the vessel in which they were contained ; another, to cover a pile of them with an inverted vase of glass, or other pellucid substance, closely luted to the slab on which it stood. Cherries were gathered before sunrise, and put, with summer savory above and below, into a jar, or the hollow of a reed, which was then filled with sweet vinegar, and closely covered. Mulberries were preserved in their own juice, apples and quinces in pitched coffers, wrapped in clean locks of wool, pears by being placed in salt [1] for five days, and afterwards dried in the sun, as were also figs, which were strung by the stalks to

---

[1] Cato, 7. Varro. i. 59. Colum. xii. 14.

a piece of cord or willow twig, like so many hanks of onions [1] as they are sold in modern times. Elsewhere they were preserved, as dates in Egypt, by being pressed together in square masses, like bricks.[2] Damascenes were kept in must or sweet wine, as were also pears, adding sometimes a little salt and jujubes, with leaves, above and below. The same course was pursued with apples and quinces, which communicated to the liquor additional durability and the most exquisite fragrance. Quinces, whose sharp effluvia prevented their being placed with other fruit, were often put into closely-covered jars, and kept floating in wine to which they imparted a delicious perfume. The same custom was observed with respect to figs, which were cut off on the bearing branch a little before they were ripe, and hung, so as not to touch each other, in a square earthen jar. Upon the same principle apples were preserved in jars hermetically sealed, which, for the sake of coolness, were plunged in cisterns or deep wells.[3]

It may, perhaps, be worth while to mention, in passing, that, like ourselves, the ancients possessed the art of extracting perry and cider [4] from their pears and apples; and from pomegranates a species of wine which is said to have been of an extremely delicate flavour. The Egyptians, also, made wine from the fruit of the lotos.[5]

[1] Schol. Aristoph. Eq. 755. Sibth. in Walp. Mem. ii. 61.
[2] Phot. ap. Brunckh. ad Aristoph. Pac. 574.
[3] Pallad. iii. 25.
[4] Pallad. iii. 25. Colum. xii. 45.
[5] Theoph. Hist. Plant. iv. 3. i.

CHAPTER IV.

STUDIES OF THE FARMER.

In other branches of rural economy the country gentlemen of Attica exhibited no less enthusiasm or skill. Indeed, throughout Greece, there prevailed a similar taste. Every one was eager to instruct and be instructed ; and so great in consequence was the demand for treatises on husbandry, theoretical and practical, that numerous writers, the names of fifty of whom are preserved by Varro,[1] made it the object of their study. Others without committing the result of their experience to writing, devoted themselves wholly to its practical improvement. They purchased waste or ill-cultivated lands, and, by investigating the nature of the soil, skilfully adapting their crops to it, manuring, irrigating, and draining, converted a comparative desert into a productive estate.[2] We can possibly, as Dr. Johnson insists, improve very little our knowledge of agriculture by erudite researches into the methods of the ancients ; though Milton was of opinion, that even here some useful hints might be obtained. In describing, however, what the Greeks did, I am not pretending to enlighten the present age, but to enable it to enjoy its superiority by instituting a comparison with the ruder practices of antiquity.

Already in those times the men of experience and routine,[3] had begun to vent their sneers against philosophers for their profound researches into the nature of soils,[4] in which, however, they by no means

[1] De Re Rusticâ, i. 1. Cf. Colum. i. 1.

[2] Xenoph. Œconom. xx. 22, sqq.

[3] Cf. Plat. De Legg. t. vii. p. 111. t. viii. p. 103.

[4] Xenoph. Œconom. xvi. 1, sqq.

designed to engage the husbandman, but only to present him, in brief and intelligible maxims, with the fruit of their labours. Nevertheless the practical husbandman went to work a shorter way. He observed his neighbour's grounds,[1] saw what throve in this soil, what in the other, what was bettered by irrigation, what in this respect might safely be left to the care of Heaven; and thus, in a brief space, acquired a rough theory wherewith to commence operations. An agriculturist, the Athenians thought, required no recondite erudition, though to his complete success the exercise of much good sense and careful observation was necessary. Every man would, doubtless, know in what seasons of the year he must plough and sow and reap, that lands exhausted by cultivation must be suffered to lie fallow, that change of crops is beneficial to the soil, and so on. But the great art consists in nicely adapting each operation to the varying march of the seasons, in converting accidents to use, in rendering the winds, the showers, the sunshine, subservient to your purposes, in mastering the signs of the weather, and guarding as far as possible against the injuries sustained from storms of rain or hail.

There was in circulation among the Greeks a small body of precepts, addressed more especially to husbandmen, designed to promote the real object of civilisation. Quaint, no doubt, and ineffably commonplace, they will now appear, but they served, nevertheless, in early and rude times, to soften the manners and regulate the conduct of the rustic Hellenes. Who first began to collect and preserve them is, of course, unknown; they are thickly sprinkled through the works of Hesiod,[2] and impart to them

[1] The sight of a rich and thriving neighbour operated likewise as a spur to his industry :—

Εἰς ἕτερον γάρ τίς τε ἰδὼν ἔργοιο χατίζων
Πλούσιον ὅς σπεύδει μὲν ἀρόμμεναι ἠδὲ φυτεύειν,

Οἶκόν τ' εὖ θέσθαι· ζηλοῖ δέ τε γείτονα γείτων
Εἰς ἄφενον σπεύδοντ' ἀγαθὴ δ' Ἔρις ἥδε βροτοῖσι.

Hesiod. Opp. et Dies, 21, sqq.

[2] Opp. et Dies, 298, sqq.

an air of moral dignity which relieves the monotony that would otherwise result from a mere string of agricultural maxims. The chief aim of the poet seems to be, to promote peace and good neighbourhood, to multiply among the inhabitants of the fields occasions of joining the " rough right hand,"[1] to apply the sharp spur to industry, and thus to augment the stores, and, along with them, the contentment, of his native land. Be industrious, exclaims the poet, for famine is the companion of the idle. Labour confers fertility on flocks and herds, and is the parent of opulence. He who toils is beloved by gods[2] and men, while the idle hand is the object of their aversion. The slothful man envies the prosperity of his neighbour; but glory is the reward of virtue. Prudence heaps up that which profligacy dissipates. Be hospitable to the stranger, for he who repels the suppliant from his door is no less guilty than the adulterer, than the despoiler of the orphan, or the wretch who blasphemes his aged parent on the brink of the grave: of such men the end is miserable, when Zeus rains down vengeance upon them in recompense for their evil actions. Be mindful that thou offer up victims to the gods with pure hands and holy thoughts, — to pour libations in their temples, adorn their altars, and render them propitious to thee in all things. When about to ascend thy couch to enjoy sweet sleep, and when the sacred light of the day-spring first appears, omit not to demand of heaven a pure heart and a cheerful mind, with the means of extending thy possessions, and protection from loss. When thou makest a feast, invite thy friends and thy neighbours, and in times of trouble they will run to thy assistance half-clad, while thy relations will tarry to buckle on their girdles. Borrow of thy neighbour, but, in repaying him, exceed rather than fall short of what

---

[1] Sch. Aristoph. Pac. 190.

[2] Καί τ’ ἐργαζόμενος πολὺ φίλτερος ἀθανάτοισιν.

῞Εσσεαι ἠδὲ βροτοῖς· μάλα γὰρ στυγέουσιν ἀεργούς.
Opp. et Dies. 309, seq.

is his due. Rise betimes. Every little makes a mickle. Store is no sore. Housed corn breaks no sleep. Drink largely the top and the bottom of the jar; be sparing of the middle :[1] it is niggardly to stint your friends when the wine runs low. Do unto others as they do unto you.—These seeds of morality are simple, as I have said, and far from recondite; but they produced the warriors of Marathon and Platæa, and preserved for ages the freedom and the independence of Greece.

The other branches of an Hellenic farmer's studies comprehended something like the elements of natural philosophy,—the influence of the sun and moon, the rising and setting of the stars, the motion of the winds, the generation and effects of dews, clouds, meteors, showers and tempests, the origin of springs and fountains, and the migrations and habits of birds and other animals. In addition to these things, it was necessary that he should be acquainted with certain practices, prevalent from time immemorial in his country, and, probably, deriving their origin from ages beyond the utmost reach of tradition. The source of these we usually denominate superstition, though it would, perhaps, be more proper to regard them as the offspring of that lively and plastic fancy which gave birth to poetry and art, and inclined its possessors to create a sort of minor religion, based on a praiseworthy principle, but developing itself chiefly in observances almost always minute and trifling, and sometimes ridiculous. To describe all these at length would be beside my present purpose, which only requires that I mention by the way the more remarkable of those connected especially with agriculture.

The knowledge of soil was called into play both in purchasing estates and in appropriating their several parts to different kinds of culture. According to their notions, which appear to have been founded on long experience, and in most points, I believe,

---

[1] Cf. Plut. Sympos. vii. 3.

agree with those which still prevail, a rich black mould, deep, friable, and porous,[1] which would resist equally the effects of rain and drought, was, for all purposes, the best. Next to this they esteemed a yellow alluvial soil, and that sweet warm ground which best suited vines, corn, and trees. The red earth, also, they highly valued, except for timber.

Their rules for detecting the character and qualities of the soil appear to have been judicious. Good land, they thought, might be known even from its appearance, since in drought it cracks not too much, and during heavy and continued showers becomes not miry, but suffers all the rain to sink into its bosom. That earth they considered inferior which in cold weather becomes baked, and is covered on the surface by a shell-like incrustation. They judged, likewise, of the virtue of the soil by the luxuriant or stunted character of its natural productions :[2] thus they augured favourably of those tracts of country which were covered by vast and lofty timber-trees, while such as produced only a dwarfed vegetation, consisting of meagre bushes, scattered thickets, and hungry grass, they reckoned almost worthless.

Not content with the testimony of the eye, some husbandmen were accustomed to consult both the smell and the taste; for, digging a pit of some depth, they took thence a small quantity of earth, from the odour of which they drew an opinion favourable or otherwise. But to render surety doubly sure, they then threw it into a vase, and poured on it a quantity of potable water, which they afterwards tasted, inferring from the flavour the fertility or barrenness of the soil. This was the experiment most relied

[1] Geop. ii. 9. In these rich loams, particularly on the banks of the Stymphalian and Copaic lakes, wheat has been known to yield a return of fifty-fold. Thiersch, Etat Act. de la Grèce. t. ii. p 17. Other spots, again, return thirty-fold. Sibth. in Walp. Mem. i. 60.

[2] The pitch-pine indicated a light and hungry soil; the cypress, a clayey soil. Philost. Icon. ii. 9. p. 775.

on; though many considered that soil sweet which produced the basket-rush, the reed, the lotos, and the bramble. On some occasions they employed another method, which was, to make a small excavation, and then, throwing back the earth into the opening whence it had been drawn, to observe whether or not it filled the whole cavity:[1] if it did so, or left a surplus, the soil was judged to be excellent; if not, they regarded it as of little value. Soils possessing saline qualities were shunned by the ancients, who carefully avoided mingling salt with their manure, though lands of this description were rightly thought to be well adapted to the cultivation of palm-trees,[2] which they produce in the greatest perfection,[3] as in Phœnicia, Egypt, and the country round Babylon.[4]

Another art in which the condition of the husbandman required him to be well versed was that of discovering the signs of latent springs,[5] the existence of which it was necessary to ascertain before laying the foundation of a new farm. The investigation was complicated, and carried on in a variety of ways. First, and most obvious, was the inference drawn from plants and the nature of the soil itself; for those grounds, they thought, were intersected below by veins of water which bore upon their surface certain tribes of grasses and herbs and bushes, as the couch-grass, the broad-leaved plantain, the heliotrope, the red-grass, the agnus-castus, the bramble, the horse-tail, or shave-grass, ivy, bush-calamint, soft and slender reeds,[6] maiden-hair, the melilot, ditch-dock, cinque-

[1] Geop. ii. 11.
[2] The Grecian husbandman, therefore, when planting palm-trees in any other than a sandy soil, sprinkled salt on the earth immediately around. Theoph. Hist. Plant. i. 6. 2.
[3] Geop. ii. 10.
[4] Xenoph. Anab. ii. 3. 16. The

doom-palm, generally, I believe, supposed to be peculiar to Upper Egypt and the countries beyond the cataract, was anciently cultivated also in Crete. Theoph. Hist. Plant. i. 6. 3.

[5] Geop. ii. 4, sqq.

[6] Philost. Icon. ii. 9. p. 775.

foil, or five leaf-grass, broad-leaved bloodwort, the
rush, nightshade, mil-foil, colt's-foot or foal's-foot, trefoil or pond-weed, and the black thistle. Spring-heads
were always supposed to lurk beneath fat and black
loam, as, likewise, in a stony soil, especially where
the rocks are dark and of a ferruginous colour. But
in argillaceous districts, particularly where potter's-
clay abounds, or where there are many pebbles and
pumice-stones,[1] they are of rare occurrence.

To the above indications they were in most cases
careful to add others. Ascending ere sunrise to a
higher level than the spot under examination, they

[1] Spallanzani, in his scientific
Travels in the Two Sicilies, describes and explains the cause of
the rarity of springs in volcanic
countries. In some districts
among the roots of Ætna the female peasants are compelled to
travel ten miles, at certain seasons of the year, in search of
water, a jar of which costs, consequently, almost a day's journey. vol.
i. p. 299, sqq. In another part of
the same work he investigates the
origin of springs in the Æolian
isles, which he illustrates by the
example of Stromboli. iv. 128.
In this island there are two fountains, one of slightly tepid water,
at the foot of the mountain, the
other on its slope. " Je recon-
" trai," observes Monsieur Do-
lomieu, " à moitié hauteur une
" source d'eau froide, douce, légère
" et très bonne à boire, qui ne
" tarit jamais et qui est l'u-
" nique ressourse des habitans
" lorsque leurs cîternes sont épui-
" sées et lorsque les chaleurs ont
" desséché une seconde source qui
" est au pied de la montagne
" ce qui arrive tous les étés."
He then adds with reason : "Cette
" petite fontaine dans ce lieu très
" élevé au milieu des cendres

" volcaniques, est très remarqua-
" ble, elle ne peut avoir son ré-
" servoir que dans une pointe
" de montagne isolée, toute de
" sable et de pierres poreuses, ma-
" tières qui ne peuvent point
" retenir l'eau, puisqu'elles sont
" perméables à la fumée." Voyage aux Iles de Lipari, t. i. p.
120. He then endeavours to account for its existence by evapo-
ration. In the island of Saline,
among the same Æolian group,
there is another never-failing
spring, which, as some years no
rain falls in these islands during
the space of nine months, has
greatly perplexed the theories of
naturalists. Spallanzani conceives,
however, that the phenomenon
may be explained in the usual
way : " It appears to me," he
says, " extremely probable, that
" in the internal parts of an
" island which, like this, is the
" work of fire, there may be im-
" mense caverns that may be fill-
" ed with water by the rains ;
" and that in some of these which
" are placed above the spring,
" the water may always continue
" at nearly the same height."
Travels in the Two Sicilies, vol.
iv. p. 136.

observed by the first rays and before the light thickened, whether they could detect the presence of any
exhalations, which were held unerringly to indicate
the presence of springs below. Sometimes inquisi-
tion was made during the bright and clear noon,
when the subterraneous retreats of the Naiads were
supposed in summer to be betrayed by cloudlets of
thin silvery vapour, and in the winter season by
curling threads of steam. In this way the natives
of southern Africa discover the existence of hidden
fountains in the desert.[1] Swarms of gnats flitting
hither and thither, or whirling round and ascending
in a column, were regarded as another sign.

When not entirely satisfied by any of the above
means, they had recourse to the following experiment:[2] sinking a pit to the depth of about four feet
and a half, they took a hemispherical pan or lead
basin, and having anointed it with oil, and fastened
with wax a long flake of wool to the bottom, placed
it inverted in the pit. It was then covered with
earth about a foot deep, and left undisturbed during a whole night. On its being taken forth in
the morning, if the inside of the vessel were covered
thickly with globules, and the wool were dripping

[1] Le Vaillant, t. viii. p. 162.
Even in the southern provinces of
France, the discovery of hidden
springs is an art of no mean importance; and the persons who
possess it are regarded as public
benefactors. Thus, as I learn
from my friend M. Louis Fro-
ment, of the department of the
Lot, M. Paramelle, a curé having a living in that part of the
country, is held in high estimation on account of the power
he possesses of discovering the
lurking retreats of spring-heads.
He is able, from a certain distance, and without the least hesi-
tation, to point out the source of

living water, determine the depth
at which it is to be found, say,
without ever falling into error,
what is the quantity and what
the quality of the water. Without seeking to penetrate the plan,
of which he keeps the secret, his
countrymen avail themselves of
the advantages offered to them;
and the inhabitants of one village,
situated on a calcareous table-
land, have discovered, by the
assistance of M. Paramelle, a
source in their market-place,
whilst before they were compelled
to seek water at a distance of five
miles.

[2] Geop. ii. 4.

wet, it was concluded there were springs beneath, the depth of which they calculated from the scantiness or profusion of the moisture. A similar trial was made with a sponge covered with reeds.

Since most streams and rivers take their rise in lofty table-lands or mountains, which by the ancients were supposed to be richer in springs in proportion to the number of their peaks, it would seem to follow, that scarcely any country in Europe should be better supplied with water than Greece. Experience, however, shows, that this in modern times is not the fact, several rivers supposed to have been of great volume in antiquity, having now dwindled into mere brooks, and innumerable streamlets and fountains become altogether dry; on which account the credit of Greek writers is often impugned, it being supposed that the natural characteristics of the country must necessarily be invariable. But this is an error. For the existence of springs and rivulets depends less perhaps on the presence of mountains than on the prevalence of forests, as Democritos[1] long ago observed. Now, from a variety of causes, still in active operation, the ridges and hills and lower eminences of modern Greece have been almost completely denuded of trees, along with which have necessarily disappeared the well-springs, and runnels, and cascades, and rills, and mountain tarns, which anciently shed beauty and fertility over the face of Hellas, whose highlands were once so densely clad with woods[2] that the peasants requiring a short cut from

---

[1] Geop. ii. 6.

[2] Cf. Hesiod. Opp. et Dies, 233, where he speaks of swarms of wild bees on the slopes of the mountains.

In another passage this poet describes the ravages and devastation of a hurricane amid the fountain forests:

Μῆνα δὲ Ληναιῶνα, κάκ᾽ ἤματα,
βουδόρα πάντα,
τοῦτον ἀλεύασθαι, καὶ πηγάδας,
αἵτ᾽ ἐπὶ γαῖαν
πνεύσαντος Βορέαο δυσηλεγέες
τελέθουσιν,
ὅστε διὰ Θρήκης ἱπποτρόφου εὑρέϊ
πόντῳ
ἐμπνεύσας ὤρινε· μέμυκε δὲ γαῖα
καὶ ὕλη.

one valley to another, were compelled to clear themselves a pathway with the axe.[1] To restore to
Greece, therefore, its waters, and the beauty and
riches depending on them, the mountains must be
again forested, and severe restraint put on the wantonness of those vagrant shepherds who constantly
expose vast woods to the risk of entire destruction
for the sake of procuring more delicate grass for
their flocks.[2]

In Attica,[3] both fields and gardens were chiefly
irrigated by means of wells which, sometimes, in
extremely long and dry summers, failed entirely,
thus causing a scarcity of vegetables.[4] The water,

πολλὰς δὲ δρῦς ὑψικόμους ἐλάτας
  τε παχείας
οὔρεος ἐν βήσσῃς πιλνᾷ χθονὶ
  πουλυβοτείρῃ
ἐμπίπτων, καὶ πᾶσα βοᾷ τότε
  νήριτος ὕλη.
      Opp. et Dies, 504, sqq.

The pine and pitch trees, it is
related by Theophrastus, were
often uprooted by the winds in
Arcadia. Hist. Plant. iii. 6. 4.

[1] Theoph. Hist. Plant. iii. 3.
7. In all countries, small and
great, the progress of civilisation
has been inimical to forests. Thus
in the little island of Stromboli,
containing about a thousand inhabitants, attempts were made
towards the end of the eighteenth
century to enlarge the cultivable
ground by clearing away the
woods. Spallanzani, Travels in
the Two Sicilies. vol. iv. p. 126,
seq. The difficulty of extirpating
trees is illustrated by Theophrastus who relates that, in a spot
near Pheneon in Arcadia, a well-
wooded tract was overflowed by
the water and the trees destroyed.
Next year, when the flood had
subsided and the mud dried, each
kind of tree appeared in the situa-

tion which it had formerly occupied. The willow, the elm, the
pine, and the fir, growing in its
own place, doubtless from the
roots of the former trees. Hist.
Plant. iii. 1. 2. Again: the
Nessos, in the territory of the
Abderites, constantly changed its
bed, and in the old channels trees
sprung up so rapidly that, in three
years, they were so many strips
of forest. Id. iii. 1. 5.

[2] Thiersch, Etat Actuel de la
Grèce. t. i. p. 276. It is remarked
by Theophrastus, however, that
pine forests, being destroyed by
fire, shot up again, as happened
in Lesbos, on a mountain near
Pyrrha. Hist. Plant. iii. 9. 4.

[3] Cf. Chandler, i. p. 261.
The apparatus now used in irrigation by the Sciots exactly
resembles that of the Egyptian
Arabs. Id. i. 315.

[4] Demosth. Adv. Polycl. §
16. On the supply of water to
Athens we possess little positive
information, though we cannot
doubt that all possible advantage
was taken of those pure sources
which are still found in its neighbourhood. " In no country ne-

we find, was drawn up by precisely the same machinery as is still employed for the purpose. The invention of these conveniences of primary necessity having preceded the birth of tradition, has, by some writers, been attributed to Danaos, who is supposed to have emigrated from Egypt into Greece. Arriving, we are told, at Argos, he, upon the failure of spontaneous fountains, taught the inhabitants to dig wells, in consequence of which he was elected chief. But where was Danaos himself to have learned this art? He is said to have been an Egyptian, and Egypt is a country so entirely without springs, that two only exist within its limits, and of these but one was known to the ancients. Of wells they had none. Danaos could, therefore, if he was an Egyptian, have known nothing of springs or wells; and, if he had such knowledge, he must have come from some other land.[1]

Where there existed neither wells nor fountains, people were compelled to depend on rain-water, collected and preserved in cisterns.[2] For this purpose troughs were in some farm-houses run along the eaves both of the stables, barns, and sheep-cotes, as well as of the dwelling of the family, while others used only that which ran from the last, the roof of which was kept scrupulously clean. The water was conveyed through wooden pipes[3] to the cisterns, which appear to have been frequently situated in

"cessity was more likely to have "created the hydragogic art "than in Attica; and we have "evidence of the attention be-"stowed by the Athenians upon "their canals and fountains in "the time of Themistocles, as "well as in that of Alexander "the Great." Col. Leake, on some disputed points in the Topography of Athens. Trans. Lit. Soc. iii. 189. Cf. Aristoph. Av. Schol. 998. Plut. Themist. § 31. Arist. Polit. vi. 8. vii. 12. We find, from Theophrastus, that there was in his time, an aqueduct in the Lyceum with a number of plane trees growing near it. Theoph. Hist. Plant. i. 7. 1.

[1] Mitford, i. 33, seq. In Bœotia, Babylonia, Egypt, and Cyrenaica, the dew served instead of rain. Theoph. Hist. Plant. viii. 4. 6.

[2] Λακκοὶ. Machon. ap. Athen. xiii. 43.

[3] Geop. ii. 7.

the front court.[1] Bad water they purified in several ways : by casting into it a little coral powder,[2] small linen bags of bruised barley, or a quantity of laurel leaves, or by pouring it into broad tubs and exposing it for a considerable time to the action of the sun and air. When there happened to be about the farms ponds of any magnitude, they introduced into them a number of eels or river crabs, which opened the veins of the earth and destroyed leeches.

A scarcely less important branch of the farmer's studies was that which related to the weather and the general march of the seasons.[3] Above all things, it behoved him to observe diligently the rising and setting of the sun and moon. He was, likewise, carefully to note the state of the atmosphere at the disappearance of the Pleiades, since it was expected to continue the same until the winter solstice, after which a change sometimes immediately supervened,

---

[1] Sir W. Hamilton, Acc. of Discov. at Pompeii, p. 13.

[2] Water was cooled by being suspended in vessels over the mouths of wells; and sometimes boiled previously to render the process more complete. For, according to the Peripatetics, πᾶν ὕδωρ προθερμανθὲν ψύχεται μᾶλλον, ὥσπερ τὸ τοῖς βασιλεῦσι παρασκευαζόμενον, ὅταν ἐψηθῇ μέχρι ζέσεως, περισωρεύουσι τῷ ἀγγείῳ χιόνα πολλὴν, καὶ γίνεται ψυχρότερον. Plut. Sympos. vi. 4. 1.

[3] Geop. i. 2—4. 11. Theophrast. De Signis Pluviarum et de Ventis, *passim*. Our own agriculturists, also, were formerly much addicted to these studies. Thus, " The oke apples, if broken in " sunder about the time of their " withering, do foreshewe the se- " quel of the yeare, as the ex- " pert Kentish husbandmen have

" observed, by the living things " found in them : as, if they " find an ant, they foretell plen- " tie of graine to insue ; if a " whole worm, like a gentill or " maggot, then they prognosticate " murren of beasts and cattle ; " if a spider, then (saie they) " we shall have a pestilence or " some such like sickness to fol- " lowe amongst men. These " things the learned, also, have " observed and noted : for Ma- " thiolus, writing upon Diosco- " rides saith, that before they " have an hole through them, " they conteine in them either " a flie, a spider, or a worme ; " if a flie, then warre insueth ; if " a creeping worme, then scarcitie " of victuals ; if a running spi- " der, then followeth great sick- " ness and mortalitie." Gerrard, Herball, Third Book, c. 29. p. 1158. Cf. Lord Bacon, Sylva Sylvarum, 561.

otherwise there was usually no alteration till the vernal equinox.[1] Another variation then took place in the character of the weather, which afterwards remained fixed till the rising of the Pleiades, undergoing successively fresh mutations at the summer solstice and the autumnal equinox. According to their observations, moreover, a rainy winter[2] was followed by a dry and raw spring, and the contrary; and a snowy winter by a year of abundance. But as nature by no means steadily follows this course, exhibiting many sudden and abrupt fluctuations, it was found necessary to subject her restless phenomena to a more rigid scrutiny, in order that rules might be obtained for foretelling the approach of rain, or tempests, or droughts, or a continuance of fair weather. Of these some, possibly, were founded on imperfect observation or casual coincidences, or a fanciful linking of causes and effects; while others, we cannot doubt, sprang from a practical familiarity with the subtler and more shifting elements of natural philosophy.

As nothing more obviously interests the husbandman than the seasonable arrival and departure of rains, everything connected with them, however remotely, was observed and treasured up with scrupulous accuracy. Of all the circumstances pre-signifying their approach the most certain was supposed to be the aspect of the morning; for if, before sunrise, beds of purpurescent clouds[3] stretched along the verge of the horizon, rain was expected that day, or the day after the morrow. The same augury they drew, though with less confidence, from the appearance of the setting sun,[4] especially if in winter

[1] Cf. Hesiod, Opp. et Dies, 486, seq.
[2] Cf. Lord Bacon, Sylva Sylvarum, 675. 812.
[3] Cf. Arato. Prognost. 102, sqq. But, on the other hand, " purus " oriens, atque non fervens, se-

" renum diem nuntiat." Plin. Hist. Nat. xviii. 78. Aristot. Problem. xxvi. 8.
[4] The sun-sets of the Mediterranean exhibit, as most travellers will have observed, a variety of gorgeous phenomena, which, as

or spring it went down through an accumulation of clouds or with masses of dusky rack on the left. Again, if, on rising, the sun looked pale, dull red, or spotted;[1] or, if, previously, its rays were seen streaming upwards;[2] or, if, immediately afterwards, a long band of clouds extended beneath it, intersecting its descending beams; or if the orient wore a sombre hue; or if piles of sable vapour towered into the welkin; or if the clouds were scattered loosely over the sky like fleeces of wool;[3] or came waving

betokening certain states of the atmosphere serve as so many admonitions to the husbandman. The sun before going down " as-" sumed," observes Dr. Chandler, " a variety of fantastic shapes. " It was surrounded, first, with " a golden glory of great extent, " and flamed upon the surface of " the sea in a long column of " fire. The lower half of the " orb soon after emerged in the " horizon, the other portion re-" maining very large and red, " with half of a smaller orb be-" neath it, and separate, but in " the same direction, the circular " rim approaching the line of its " diameter. These two, by de-" grees, united, and then changed " rapidly into different figures, " until the resemblance was that " of a capacious punch-bowl in-" verted. The rim of the bot-" tom extending upward, and " the body lengthening below " it, became a mushroom on a " stalk with a round head. It " was next metamorphosed into " a flaming caldron, of which " the lid, rising up, swelled " nearly into an orb and va-" nished. The other portion put " on several uncircular forms, " and, after many twinklings and " faint glimmerings, slowly dis-

" appeared, quite red, leaving the " clouds hanging over the dark " rocks on the Barbary shore fine-" ly tinged with a vivid bloody " hue." Travels, i. p. 4. Appearances similar, though of inferior brilliance and variety, are sometimes witnessed in the Western Hemisphere. Describing the beauties of an evening on the Canadian shore, Sir R. H. Bonnycastle observes: " First, there " was a double sun by reflec-" tion, each disk equally dis-" tinct; afterwards, when the " orb reached the mark x, a solid " body of light, equal in breadth " with the sun itself, but of great " length from the shore, shot " down on the sea, and remained " like a broad fiery golden co-" lumn, or bar, until the black " high land hid the luminary " itself." The Canadas in 1841. v. i. p. 34.

[1] Ille ubi nascentem maculis variaverit ortum
Conditus in nubem, medioque refugerit orbe;
Suspecti tibi sint imbres.
      Virg. Georg. i. 441, sqq.
[2] Plin. Hist. Nat. xviii. 78. Aratus, Prognost. 137, sqq.
[3] Cf. Plin. xviii. 82. " Si " nubes ut vellera lanæ spargen-" tur multæ ab oriente, aquam

up from the south in long sinuous streaks — the
"mares' tails" of our nautical vocabulary — the husbandman reckoned with certainty upon rain, floods,
and tempestuous winds. Among the signs of showers
peculiar to the site of Athens may be reckoned these
following: if a rampart of white ground-fogs begirt
at night the basis of Hymettos; or, if its summits
were capped with vapour;[1] or, if troops of mists
settled in the hollow of the smaller mount, called
the Springless; or, if a single cloud rested on the
fane of Zeus at Ægina.[2] The violent roaring of the
sea upon the beach was the forerunner of a gale,
and they were enabled to conjecture from what
quarter it was to blow, by the movements of the
waters, which retreated from the shore before a north
wind; while, at the approach of the sirocco, they
were piled up higher than usual against the cliffs.
Elsewhere, in Attica, they supposed wet weather
to be foretold by the summits of Eubœa rising clear,
sharp, and unusually elevated through a dense floor
of exhalations, which, when they mounted and gathered in blowing weather about the peaks of Caphareus,[3] on the eastern shores of the island, presaged an impending storm of five days' continuance.
But here these signs concerned rather the mariner
than the husbandman, since the cliffs that stretched
along this coast are rugged and precipitous, and
the approaches so dangerous that few vessels which
are driven on it escape. Scarcely are the crews
able to save themselves, unless their bark happen
to be extremely light. Another portent of foul weather was the apparition of a circle about the moon,

"in triduum præsagient;" and Virg. Georg. i. 397:
Tenuia nec lanæ per cœlum vel-
lera ferri.
[1] If the Mounts Parnes and Brylessus appeared enveloped in clouds, the circumstance was thought to foretel a tempest.

Theoph. de Sign. Pluv. iii. 6. Cf. Strabo. ix. 11. t. ii. p. 253.

[2] Pausan. ii. 30. 3. Pind. Nem. v. 10. Dissen. — Müll. Æginetica, § 5. p. 19.

[3] Dion. Chrysost. i. 222. Cf. Aristot. Prob. xxvi. 1.

while, by the double reflection of its orb north and
south, that luminary appeared to be multiplied into
three. At night, also, if the nubecula,[1] called the
Manger, in the constellation of the Crab, shone
less luminously, it betokened a similar state of the
atmosphere. A like inference [2] was drawn when
the moon at three days old rose dusky; or, with
blunt horns; or, with its rim, or whole disk, red;
or blotted with black spots; or encircled by two
halos.[3]

The phenomena of thunder and lightning, likewise, instructed the husbandman who was studious
in the language of the heavens: thus, when thunder was heard in winter or in the morning, it betokened wind; in the evening or at noon, in summer, rain; when it lightened from every part of
the heavens, both. Falling stars[4] likewise denoted
wind or rain, originating in that part of the heavens where they appeared.

Among our own rustics the whole philosophy of
rainbows has been compressed into a couple of dis-
tichs :

> A rainbow at night
> Is the shepherd's delight.
> A rainbow in the morning
> Is the shepherd's warning.

And upon this subject,[5] the peasants of Hellas
had little more to say; their opinion having been

---

[1] This is explained by Lord
Bacon. " The upper regions of
" the air," he observes, " perceive
" the collection of the matter of
" tempest and wind before the air
" here below. And, therefore, the
" observing of the smaller stars is
" a sign of tempests following."
Sylva Sylvarum, 812.

[2] Similar observations have
been made in most countries, as
we find from the signs of the
weather collected by Erra Pater,
and translated by Lilly, Part iv.
§ 3—5.

[3] Cf. Seneca. Quæst. Nat. i.
c. 2.

[4] Aristot. Problem. xxvi. 24.
Alexand. Aphrodis. Problem. i.
72. Plin. xviii. 80. Virg. Georg.
i. 365, sqq.

> Sæpe etiam stellas, vento im-
> pendente, videbis
> Præcipites cœlo labi, noctisque
> per umbram
> Flammarum longos à tergo al-
> bescere tractus.

[5] On the effects of the rainbow the ancients held a curious
opinion, which Lord Bacon thus

that, in proportion to the number of rainbows, would be the fury and continuance of the showers with which they were threatened.

Other signs of mutation in the atmosphere they discovered in almost every part of nature; for example, when bubbles rose on the surface of a river they looked for a fall of rain; as also when small land-birds were seen drenching their plumage; when the crow was beheld washing his head upon the rocky beach,[1] or the raven flapping his wings, while with his voice he imitated amidst his croaking the pattering of drops of rain; when the peasant was awakened in the morning by the cry of the passing crane,[2] or the shrill note of the chaffinch within

expounds : — " It hath been ob-
" served by the ancients, that
" where a rainbow seemeth to
" hang over or to touch, there
" breathed forth a sweet smell.
" The cause is, for that this hap-
" peneth but in certain matters
" which have in themselves some
" sweetness, which the gentle dew
" of the rainbow doth draw forth,
" and the like to soft showers, for
" they also make the ground
" sweet, but none are so delicate as
" the dew of the rainbow where
" it falleth." Sylva Sylvarum.
" 832. His Lordship here, as in many other places, adopts the explanation of the Peripatetics while he seems to be himself assigning the cause of the phenomenon. Aristotle (Problem. 12. 3) enters fully into the subject, which appears to have been brought under the notice of philosophers by the shepherds who had observed that when certain thickets had been laid in ashes the passing of a rainbow over the spot caused a sweet odour to exhale from it. The same fact is noticed by Theo-

phrastus, De Caus. Plant. 6. 17. 7. Cf. Plin. Hist. Nat. 12. 52 21. 18. 2. 60. To many among the older philosophers that comparatively rare phenomenon, the lunar rainbow, was unknown. (Arist. Meteor. iii. 2 : νύκτωρ δ' ἀπὸ σελήνης ὡς μὲν οἱ ἀρχαῖοι ᾤοντο οὐκ ἐγίγνετο·) but in the time of Aristotle it had been observed, and the cause of its pearly whiteness investigated. Cf. Meteorol. iii. 4. 5. Senec. Quæst. Nat. i. 2, sqq.

[1] Cf. Ælian. De Nat. Anim. vii. 7.

[2] Φράζεσθαι δ', εὖτ' ἂν γεράνου
φωνὴν ἐπακούσῃς
ὑψόθεν ἐκ νεφέων ἐνιαύσια κεκ-
ληγυίης·
ἥτ' ἀρότοιο τε σῆμα φέρει, καὶ
χείματος ὥρην
δεικνύει ὀμβρηροῦ· κραδίην δ'
ἔδακ' ἀνδρὸς ἀβούτεω.

Hesiod. Opp. et Dies, 448, sqq. To the same purpose, Homer : — Il. γ 3, sqq.

Ἠΰτε περ κλαγγὴ γεράνων πέ-
λει οὐρανόθι πρὸ,
αἵτ' ἐπεὶ οὖν χειμῶνα φύγον
καὶ ἀθέσφατον ὄμβρον,

his dwelling. Flights of island birds flocking to the continent,[1] preceded drought; as a number of jackdaws and ravens flying up and down, and imitating the scream of the hawk, did rain. The incessant shrieks of the screech-owl and the vehement cawing of the crow, heard during a serene night, foretold the approach of storms. The barn-door fowl and the house-dog also played the part of soothsayers, teaching their master to dread impending storms by rolling themselves in the dust. Of similar import was the flocking of geese with noise to their food, or the skimming of swallows along the surface of the water.[2] Again, when troops of dolphins were seen rolling near the shore, or oxen licking their fore-hoofs, or looking southwards, or, with a suspicious air, snuffing the elements,[3] or going bellowing to their stalls; when wolves approached the homesteads; when flies bit sharp,[4] or frogs croaked vociferously, or the ruddock, or landtoad, crept into the water; when the salamander lizard appeared, and the note of the green-frog was

κλαγγῇ ταίγε πέτονται ἐπ' Ὠ-
κεανοῖο ῥοάων.

And Aristophanes: — (Av. 710, sqq.)

Πρῶτα μὲν ὥρας φαίνομεν ἡ-
μεῖς ἦρος, χειμῶνος, ὀπώρας·
Σπείρειν μὲν, ὅταν γέρανος
κρώζουσ' ἐς τὴν Λιβύην μετα-
χωρῇ,
καὶ πηδάλιον τότε ναυκλήρῳ
φράζει κρεμάσαντι καθεύ-
δειν.

[1] All birds which frequent the sea, more particularly those which fly high, are observed to seek terra firma at the approach of foul weather : — Ἀριστοτέλους ἀκούω λέγοντος, ὅτι ἄρα γέρανοι ἐκ τοὺς πελάγους εἰς τὴν γῆν πετόμενοι, χειμῶνος ἀπειλὴν ἰσχουραὶ ὑποσημαίνουσι τῷ συνιέντι. Ælian. De Nat. Anim. vii. 7.

Before the great earthquake of 1783, which shook the whole of Calabria and destroyed the city of Messina, the mews and other aquatic birds were observed to forsake the sea and take refuge in the mountains. Spallanzani, Travels in the Two Sicilies. vol. iv. p. 158.

[2] Aut arguta lacus circumvolitat hirundo. Virg. Georg. i. 377. "Hirundo tam juxta aquam volitans, ut penna sæpe percutiat" Plin. xviii. 87.

[3] Plin. xviii. 88. Virg. Georg. i. 375.— Ælian, De Nat. Anim. vii. 8, describes the ox before rain snuffing the earth, and adds : πρόβατα δὲ ἐρυττοντα ταῖς ὁπλαῖς τὴν γῆν, ἔοικε σημαίνειν χειμῶνα.

[4] Cf. Ælian De Nat. Anim. viii. 8.

heard in the trees, the rustic donned his capote, and prepared, like Anaxagoras at Olympia,[1] for a shower. The flight of the storm-birds, kepphoi,[2] was supposed to indicate a tempest from the point of the heavens towards which they flew. When in bright and windless weather clouds of cobwebs,[3] floated through the air, the husbandman anticipated a drenching for his fields, as also when earthen pots and brass pans emitted sparks; when lamps spat; when the wick made mushrooms;[4] when a halo encircled its flame,[5] or when the flame itself was dusky. The housewife was forewarned of coming hail-storms, generally from the north, by a profusion of bright sparks appearing on the surface of her charcoal fire; when her feet swelled she knew that the wind would blow from the south.[6] Heaps of clouds like burnished copper rising after rain in the west portended fine weather; as did likewise the tops of lofty mountains, as Athos, Ossa, and Olympos, appearing sharply defined against the sky; while an apparent augmentation in the height of promontories and the number of islands foreshowed wind.

[1] Diog. Laert. i 3. 5. Ælian (De Nat. Anim. vii. 8) relates a curious anecdote of Hipparchos who, from some change in the goatskin cloak he wore, likewise foretold a rain storm to the great admiration of Nero.

[2] Probably the storm-finch observed frequently on the wing flying along the Ægean sea, particularly when it is troubled. Sibth. in Walp. Mem. i. 76.

[3] Cf. Aristot. Problem. xxvii. 63, where he investigates the causes of the phenomenon; and Plin. Nat. Hist. xi. 28.

[4] Vid. Aristoph. Vesp. 262. The Scholiast entertains a somewhat different notion: — φασὶν ὅτι ὑετοῦ μέλλοντος γενέσθαι οἱ περὶ τὴν θρυαλλίδα τοῦ λύχνου σπινθῆρες ἀποπηδῶσιν, οὓς μύκητας νῦν λέγει, ὡς τοῦ λύχνου ἐναντιουμένου τῷ νοτερῷ ἀέρι· καὶ Ἄρατος " ἢ λύχνοιο μύκητες ἐγείρονται περὶ μύξαν, νύκτα κατὰ νοτίην."

[5] Aristot. Meteorol. iii. 4. Seneca, Quæst. Nat. i. 2.

[6] Cf. Aristot. Problem. xxvi. 17.

CHAPTER V.

THE VARIOUS PROCESSES OF AGRICULTURE.

IF we now pass to the actual labours of the farm, and the implements by which they were usually carried on, we shall find that the Grecian husbandman was no way deficient in invention, or in that ingenuity by which men have in all countries sought to diminish their toils. For the purpose of procuring at a cheap rate whatever was wanted for the use of the establishment,[1] smiths, carpenters, and potters, were kept upon the land or in its immediate neighbourhood; by which means also the necessity was avoided of often sending the farm-servants to the neighbouring town, where it was observed they contracted bad habits, and were rendered more vicious and slothful.[2] Waggons, therefore, and carts, and ploughs, and harrows, were constructed on the spot, though it was sometimes necessary perhaps to obtain from a distance the timber used for these implements, which was generally cut in winter-time. They exhibited much nicety in their choice of wood. Thus they would have the poplar or mulberry-tree for the felloes of their wheels; the ash, the ilex, and the oxya, for the axle-tree, and fine close-grained maple for the yokes of their oxen,[3] sometimes carved in the form of serpents which seemed to wind round the necks of the animals, and project their heads

[1] Geop. ii. 49. Illustrating the wretched condition of a tyrant dwelling in the midst of a nation that abhors him, Plato draws the picture of a man being in a remote part of the country with his wife and children, surrounded by a gang of fifty or sixty slaves, with scarcely a free neighbour at hand to whom, in case of necessity, he might fly. In what terror, he says, must this man live, lest his slaves should set upon and murder him, with all his family! De Repub. t. vi. p. 439.

[2] Carts were sometimes roofed with skins. Scheffer, De Re Vehic. p. 246, seq. Justin, ii. 2.

[3] Theoph. Hist. Plant. v. 7. 6.

on either side.[1] Their harrows, it is probable, were
formed like our own. The construction of the
plough,[2] always continued to be extremely simple.
In the age of Hesiod[3] it consisted of four parts,
the handle, the socket, the coulter, and the beam;
and very little alteration seems afterwards to have
been made in its form or structure, till the introduction of the wheel-plough, which did not, it is
believed, occur until after the age of Virgil. The
more primitive instrument, however, would seem to
have consisted originally of two parts only, one
serving the purpose of handle, socket, and share, the
other being the beam by which it was fastened to
the yoke. In the antique implement[4] the beam was
sometimes made of laurel or elm, the socket of oak,
and the handle of ilex.

Before mills were invented, the instrument by
which they reduced corn into flour was a large
mortar, scooped out of the trunk of a tree, furnished with a pestle upwards of four feet in length,
exactly resembling that still in use among the Egyptian Arabs. To give the pestle greater effect it was
fixed above in a cross-bar, seven feet long, and
worked by two individuals.[5] By this rude contrivance, it is possible to produce flour as fine as that
proceeding from the most perfect boulting machine.
In addition to these they possessed winnowing fans,
scythes, sickles, pruning-hooks, fern or braken-scythes,
saws and hand-saws, used in pruning and grafting,
spades, shovels, rakes, pick-axes, hoes, mattocks,—one,
two, and three pronged,—dibbles, fork-dibbles, and
grubbing-axes.[6] When rustics were clearing away

---

[1] Scheffer, De Re Vehic. p.114.
[2] Pollux. x. 128. Goguet,
Orig. des Lois, i. 189, seq. Pallad. i. 43. Colum. ii. 2.
[3] Opp. et Dies, 467, seq. Vid.
Gœttl. ad v. 431. Etym. Mag.
173, 16. Poll. i. 252. The
Syrians used a small plough, with
which they turned up extremely

shallow furrows. Theoph. Hist.
Plant. viii. 6. 3.
[4] Hesiod, Opp. et Dies, 435, seq.
[5] Idem, 423, seq.
[6] Poll. x. 129. Pallad. i. 51.
Brunckh. not. ad Aristoph. Pac.
567. Cf. Eurip. Bacch. 344.
Sch. Aristoph. Pac. 558, seq. 620.
Plat. de Repub. t. vi. p. 81. Ar-

underwood or cutting down brakes, they went clad in hooded skin-cloaks, leather gaiters, and long gloves.[1]

On the subject of manure[2] the Greeks appear to have entertained very just notions, and have left behind them numerous rules for using and preparing it. In lean lands which required most the help of art, they were still careful to avoid excess in the employment of manure, spreading it frequently rather than copiously; for as, left to themselves, they would have been too cold, so, when over enriched by art, their prolific virtue was thought to be consumed by heat. In applying it to plants, they were careful to interpose a layer of earth lest their roots should be scorched. Of all kinds of manure they considered that of birds the best,[3] except the aquatic species, which, when mixed, however, was not rejected. Most husbandmen set a peculiar value on the sweepings of dovecotes,[4] which, in small quantities, were frequently scattered over the fields with the seed.

On the preparation of manure-pits they bestowed much attention.[5] Having sunk them sufficiently deep in places abundantly supplied with water, they cast therein large quantities of weeds, with all descriptions of manure, among which they reckoned even earth itself, when completely impregnated with humidity. When they had lain long enough to be

---

temid. Oneirocrit. ii. 24. p. 111. Lutet.

[1] Pallad. i. 43. Colum. i. 8.

[2] Geop. ii. 21, seq. Theoph. Hist. Plant. vii. 5. 1. i. 7. 4. To exemplify the importance of manure, it is remarked by this writer, that manured corn ripens twenty days earlier than that which wants this advantage, viii. 7. 7.

[3] Geop. ii. 21. 4. From a speech of the Earl of Radnor, in the House of Lords, May 25, 1841, we learn that our own farmers have begun to make experiments with this kind of manure on the lands of Great Britain, and that ship-loads of bird's dung have been imported for the purpose from the Pacific. The rocks and smaller islands along the American coast are sometimes white with this substance. Keppel, Life of Lord Keppel, i. 48.

[4] Geop. xii. 4. 3. v. 26. 3.

[5] Xenoph. Œconom. xx. 10. Cf. Artemid. Oneirocrit. ii. 26. p. 114.

entirely decayed, they were fit for use.   To the above
were sometimes added wood-ashes, the refuse of
leather-dressers, the cleansing of stables, and cow-
houses, with stubble, brambles, and thorns reduced
to ashes.   In maritime situations sea-weed,[1] also,
having been well washed in fresh water, was mingled in large proportion with other materials, and,
where possible, a channel was made conducting
the muck and puddle [2] of the neighbouring road
into the pit, which at once accelerated the putres-
cence of the manure and augmented it.   The Attic
husbandmen had a mode of enriching their lands [3]
somewhat expensive, and, as far as I know, peculiar
to themselves; having sown a field, they allowed
the corn to spring up and the blade to reach a
considerable height, upon which they again ploughed
it in as a kind of sacrifice to the earth.   A practice,
not altogether unlike, still prevails in the kingdom
of Naples, where the husbandmen sometimes bury
their beans and lupins, just before flowering, for manure.[4]

In ploughing there was great variety of practice,
and in small farms, where the soil was light, they
had recourse to what may be denominated spade
husbandry.   Most lands were ploughed thrice; first,
immediately after the removal of the preceding crop;
secondly, at a convenient interval of time; and, thirdly,[5] in the sowing season, when the ploughman scattered the grain in the furrows as they were laid
open while a lad followed at his heels with a hoe
breaking the clods and covering the seed that it might

---

[1] Geopon. ii. 22.

[2] The practice of mingling water with the manure was in great
use among the ancients, particularly in the island of Rhodes, in
the cultivation of the palm-trees.
Theoph. Hist. Plant. i. 6. 3.

[3] Xenoph. Œconom. xvii. 10.
Cf. Earl of Aberdeen, Walp. Mem.
i. 250.   In such lands the farmers
suffered their cattle to eat down
the young corn to prevent its too
great luxuriance.   Theoph. Hist.
Plant. viii. 7. 3.

[4] Swinburne, Letters from the
Courts of Europe, i. 144.

[5] Cf. Xenoph. Œconom. xvi.
10, seq.   Theoph. Hist. Plant.
vi. 5. 1.

not be devoured by the birds.[1] Occasionally, in very
hot weather, and in certain situations, the farmer
ploughed all night;[2] first, out of consideration to the
oxen, whose health would have suffered. from the
sun; secondly, to preserve the moisture and richness of the soil; and, thirdly, by the aid of the dew,
to render it more pliable. On these occasions, it
was customary to employ two pair of oxen and a
heavier share in order to produce the deeper furrows, and turn up the hidden fat of the earth. In
choosing a ploughman they took care that he should
be tall and powerful,[3] that he might be able to
thrust the share deeper into the ground and wield
it generally with facility : and yet they would not,
if posssible, that he should be under forty years of
age, lest, instead of attending to his duties, his eye
should be glancing hither and thither, and his mind
be roving after his companions.[4] When in particular haste to complete his task, the ploughman often
carried a long loaf under his arm, which, like the
French peasants, he ate as he went along.[5] In this
department of rural labour it may be observed, mules
were sometimes employed as well as oxen.[6] Both
were directed and kept in order by a sharp goad.[7]

As the Greeks well understood the practice of fal-
lowing, their lands were then, as now, suffered to

---

[1] Hesiod. Opp. et Dies, 469,
seq.

[2] Geop. ii. 28.

[3] Geop. ii. 2.

[4] Hesiod. Opp. et Dies, 443,
sqq.

[5] Hesiod. Opp. et Dies, 442.
" Vide Athenæum, quem Lanzius
laudavit, iii. p. 114. e. hæc ex
Philemone referentem : βλωμι-
λίους ἄρτους ὀνομάζεσθαι λέγει
τοὺς ἔχοντας ἐντομάς, οὓς Ῥω-
μαῖοι, καδράτους λέγουσι. ὀκτά-
βλωμον Spohnius intelligit de
servo celeriter edente. Minime
verò. Panes rustici incisuras

suas habent, ut servis omnibus
æquas partes frangendo possis di-
rimere. v. Philostrat. Imagg. p.
95. 16. Jacobs." Gœttling in loc.
p. 173.

[6] Hesiod. Opp. et Dies, 46.
Dickinson. Delphi Phœnicizantes,
c. 10. p. 101, sqq.

[7] Scheffer. de Re Vehic. 186,
seq. Schol. Aristoph. Nub. 449.
The necks of these animals, when
galled by the yoke, were cured
by the leaves of black briony
steeped in wine. Dioscor. iv.
185.

regain their strength by lying for a time idle ;[1] and
it seems to have been as much their custom as it
is still of their descendants,[2] for the poor, at least,
to roam over these fallow grounds, collecting nettles,[3]
mallows, the sow-thistle or jagged lettuce,[4] dande-
lions, sea-purslain, stoches, hartwort, briony sprouts,
gentle-rocket, usually found in the environs of towns,
and about the courts of houses, gardens, and ruins,
with other wild herbs for salads, or to be eaten as
vegetables.

The rules observed in sowing were numerous, and,
in many instances, not a little curious. As a matter
of course, they were careful to adapt the grain to
the soil :[5] thus rich plains were appropriated to wheat,
and in the intervals cropped with vegetables; mid-
dling grounds to barley;[6] while poor and hungry
spots were given up to lentils, vetches, lupins, and
such other pulse as were cultivated on a large scale.
Beans and peas, however, were supposed to thrive
best in fat and level lands. The principal sowing-
time[7] was in autumn ; for, as soon as the equi-

---

[1] Xenoph. Œconom. xvi. 13,
seq. Cf. Schulz. Antiquitat.
Rustic. § 7.

[2] Sibthorpe, in Walp. Mem. v.
i. p. 144.

[3] Sch. Aristoph. Eq. 420. Hesiod alludes to this diet where he
celebrates the inferiority of the
half to the whole :—

Νήπιοι, οὐδὲ ἴσασιν ὅσῳ πλέον
ἥμισυ παντός,
Οὐδ' ὅσον ἐν μαλάχῃ τε καὶ ἀσ-
φοδέλῳ μέγ' ὄνειαρ.
Opp. et Dies, 40, seq.

Cf. on the proverb in the first
verse, Diog. Laert. i. 4. 2. Aristot. Ethic. Nicom. i. 7. Ovid.
Fast. v. 718.

[4] Theoph. Hist. Plant. vi. 4.
8.

[5] Geop. ii. 12.

[6] A fine kind of barley was
cultivated on the plain of Marathon, which obtained the name
of Achillean, on account, as Dr.
Chandler conjectures, of its tall-
ness. ii. 184. Attica, in fact,
produced the best barley known
to the ancients. Theoph. Hist.
Plant. viii. 8. 2.

[7] Geop. ii. 14. — Ἐπειδὰν ὁ
μετοπωρινὸς χρόνος ἔλθῃ, πάντες
που οἱ ἄνθρωποι πρὸς τὸν θεὸν
ἀποβλέπουσιν, ὁπότε βρέξας τὴν
γῆν ἀφήσει αὐτοὺς σπείρειν. Xenoph. Œconom. xvii. 2. There
was a second sowing-time in the
spring, and a third in summer
for millet and sesame. Theoph
Hist. Plant. viii. 1. 2, sqq. In
Phocis, and other cold parts of
Greece, they sowed early, that
the corn might be strong before

noctial rains had moistened the earth, the sower immediately went forth to sow, committing to the ground the hopes of the future year. The best time for scattering wheat they' placed somewhere in November, about the setting of the constellation called the Crown. They were careful in this operation to avoid the time when the south wind [1] blew, and, generally, all cold and raw weather, as it rendered the earth ungenial, and little apt to fructify that which was entrusted to it. Great skill was supposed to be required in scattering the seed: in the first place, that it should be equally distributed; and, secondly, that none should fall between the horns of the oxen, superstition having taught them the belief that such grain, which they denominated Kerasbolos,[2] if it sprang up at all, would produce corn which could neither be baked nor eaten. A favourite sowing sieve was made of wolf's-hide, pierced with thirty holes as large as the tips of the fingers. In later ages much virtue was supposed to reside in the barbarous term Phriel,[3] which they accordingly wrote on the plough. The choice of grains for sowing necessarily afforded much exercise[4] to their ingenuity: seed wheat, they thought, should be of a rich gold colour, full, smooth, and solid; barley, white and heavy; both not exceeding one year old, for they quickly deteriorated, and, after the third year, would not they supposed grow. This, however, was an error, since barley has been known to preserve its vitality upwards of two thousand years.

It was customary often to renew seed by sowing the produce of mountains on plains; of dry places in moist, and the contrary.[5] To try the compara-

the winter came on. § 7. In ancient Italy corn was chiefly committed to the ground in September and October; though in mild seasons the work of sowing went on throughout the winter. Schulze, Antiquitates Rusticæ, § 4. p. 6.

[1] Cf. Aristot. Problem, xxvi. 3.
[2] Plat. de Legg. t. viii. p. 119. Tim. Lex. Plat. p. 85. Ruhnk. Plut. Sympos. vii. 2.
[3] Geop. ii. 19.
[4] Geop. ii. 16.
[5] Geop. ii. 17.

tive value of different qualities of grain [1] they took
a sample of each, and sowed the whole in separate
patches of the same bed, a little before the rising
of the Dog-star.   If the produce of any of these
samples withered, through the influence they supposed of Syrius, the wheat which it represented was
rejected.   As corn when committed to the earth is
exposed to numerous enemies, they had recourse to
a variety of contrivances for its preservation : to
protect it from birds, mice, and ants, [2] they steeped
it in the juice of houseleeks, or mixed it with hellebore and cypress leaves, and scattered it out of a
circle, or sprinkled it with water into which river
crabs had been thrown for eight days, or with powdered hartshorn or ivory.   Not satisfied with these
precautions, they had likewise recourse to scare-
crows, [3] fixing up long reeds here and there in the
fields, with dead birds suspended to them by the
feet.   This long list of contrivances they closed by
a spell: taking a live toad, they carried it round
the field by night, after which they shut it up carefully in a jar, which they buried in the middle of
the grounds.

When the corn began to spring up it was diligently weeded [4] a first and a second time.   They
would not trust entirely, however, to the industry of
their hands, but called in to their aid certain characteristic enchantments, some two or three of which
may be worth describing.   First, to subdue the
growth of choke-weed they planted sprigs of rose-
laurel, at the corner and in the middle of their
fields, or set up a number of potsherds, upon which
had been drawn with chalk the figure of Heracles

---

[1] Geop. ii. 15.

[2] Geop. ii. 18. " The bunting,
" the yellow-hammer, and a spe-
" cies of Emberiza, nearly related
" to it, frequent the low bushes
" in the neighbourhood of corn-
" fields." Sibth. in Walp. Mem.
i. 77.

[3] Among the husbandmen of
Asia Minor people are employed to drive away the birds as the
corn ripens.   Chandler, i. 100.

[4] Geop. ii. 24. Cf. Xen. Œconom. xv. 1. 13, seq.

strangling the lion. But the most effectual of
all spells, was for a young woman, naked and with
dishevelled hair, to take a live cock in her hands
and bear him round the fields, upon which, not only
would the choke-weed and the restharrow vanish,[1]
but all the produce of the land would turn out of
a superior quality.[2]

As the ancients well understood the value of hay,
they took much pains in the formation and management of meadows. In the first place, all stones,
stumps, bushes, and brambles,[3] were diligently removed, together with whatever else might interrupt
the free play of the scythe in mowing. They avoided, moreover, letting into them their droves of hogs,
which were found to turn up the soil and destroy
the roots of the young grass. In moist lands, too,
even the larger cattle were excluded, as the holes
made by their hoofs[4] in sinking broke up the fine
level of the turf. Old hayfields, in districts where
much rain fell, grew in time to be clothed with a
coating of moss,[5] which some farmers sought to remove by manuring the ground with ashes ; but the
more scientific agriculturists ploughed them up, and
took precisely the same steps as in the formation of
a new meadow, that is, they sowed the ground with
beans, turnips, or rape-seed, which, in the second year,
were succeeded by wheat; on the third it was thoroughly cleared out, and sown with hay-seed, mingled with vetches, after which the whole field was
finely levelled by the harrow.

The rules observed by them in the regulation of
their hay harvest[6] were, first, to mow before the
grass or clover was withered, when it became less
rich and nutritive ; second, to beware in making the

---

[1] Cf. Schulz. Antiquit. Rustic.
§ vii.

[2] Geop. ii. 42.   Theoph. Hist.
Plant. vi. 5. 3.

[3] Colum. ii. 18.   Varro, i. 49.

[4] Cf. Hesiod. Opp. et Dies, 489.

[5] Lord Bacon, Sylva Sylvarum,
539.

[6] Much hay was laid up in
Euboea for consumption during
the winter months.—Dion Chrysost. i. 225.

ricks, that it was neither too dry nor too damp, since in the former case it was little better than straw, and in the latter was liable to spontaneous combustion.[1] It may be observed further, that clover [2] was usually sown in March or April, and though commonly mown six, or at least five, times in the twelve months, did not require to be re- newed in less than ten years.[3]

Harvest usually commenced in Greece about the rising of the Pleiades,[4] when the corn had already acquired a deep gold colour, though not yet so ripe as to fall from the ear, which in barley happens earlier than in wheat, the grain having no hose.[5] Among the Romans operations were preceded by the sacrifice [6] of a young sow to Ceres, with liba- tions of wine, the burning of frankincense, and the offering of a cake to Jove, Juno, and Janus. They, at the same time, addressed their prayers to the last-mentioned gods, nearly in the following words :— " O father Janus or Jupiter, in making an obla- "tion of this cake I offer up my prayers that thou " wouldst be propitious to me and my children, my " house, and my family ! " [7]

At Athens, as soon as the season for reaping[8] had

---

[1] Colum. ii. 19.

[2] Καὶ τὴν βοτάνην δὲ, τὴν μάλιστα τρέφουσαν τοὺς ἵππους ἀπὸ τοῦ πλεονάζειν ἐνταῦθα ἰδίως Μηδικὴν καλοῦμεν. Strab. xi. 13. t. ii. p. 453.

[3] Pallad. v. 1. Schol. Aris- toph. Eq. 604.

[4] Geop. ii. 25. Hesiod. Opp. et Dies, 383. xiv. cal. June. Cf. Plin. Hist. Nat. xviii. 69.

[5] Pallad. vii. 2.

[6] The custom with which the modern Greeks hail the approach of summer is picturesque and beautiful : " On the first of May " at Athens, there is not a door " that is not crowned with a gar- " land, and the youths of both " sexes, with the elasticity of " spirits so characteristic of a " Greek, forget or brave their " Turkish masters, while with " guitars in their hands, and " crowns upon their heads,

' They lead the dance in hon- our of the May.' " Douglas, p. 64.

[7] Cato, 134.

[8] The harvest began earlier in Salamis than in the neighbour- hood of Athens. Theoph. Hist. Plant. viii. 2. 11. Chandler, vol. ii. p. 230. In Egypt barley was reaped on the sixth month after sowing, and wheat on the seventh. Theoph. Hist. Plant. viii. 2. 7.

come round, those hardy citizens who lived by letting out their strength for hire,[1] ranged themselves
in bands in the agora, whither the farmers of the
neighbourhood resorted in search of harvesters. They
then, in consequence of the hot weather, proceeded
half-naked[2] to the fields, where, taking the sickle in
hand, and separating into two divisions, they stationed
themselves at either end of the piece of corn to be
reaped, and began their work with vigour and emulation, each party striving to reach the centre of
the field before their rivals.[3] On other occasions
they took advantage of the wind,[4] moving along with
it, whereby they were supposed to benefit considerably, avoiding the beard or chaff which it might
have blown into their eyes, and having by its action
the tall straw bent to their hand.

In Greece, barley required seven or eight months to ripen ; wheat still more. This latter grain came to maturity more speedily in Sicily, and returned thirty-fold. § 8. In a district in the island of Rhodes they reaped barley twice in the year. § 9. Harvest was thirty days earlier in Attica than in the Hellespont. 8. 10. There was a kind of wheat in Euboea which ripened very early ; and there was introduced from Sicily into Achaia another kind which was fit for the sickle in two months. Id. viii. 4. 4. Wheat returned in Babylonia, even to negligent husbandmen, fifty-fold, and to such as properly cultivated their lands, a hundred-fold. Id. viii. 7. 4.

[1] Dem. De Cor. § 16.

[2] Or perhaps wholly so when they happened to be inhabitants of the warm lowlands on the sea-shore and valleys. At least this is the opinion of Hesiod who counsels the husbandman, γυμνὸν

σπείρειν, γυμνὸν δὲ βοωτεῖν, γυμνὸν δ᾽ ἀμάαν, εἴ χ᾽ ὥρια πάντ᾽
ἐθέλησθα ἔργα κομίζεσθαι Δημή-
τερος. Opp. et Dies, 391, sqq.

Aristophanes alludes to the same custom. Lysist. 1175.

Ἤδη γεωργεῖν γυμνὸς ἀποδὺς βούλομαι. And Virgil. " Nudus ara, sere nudus," Georg. i. 299, upon which Servius remarks : " Non dicit nudum esse debere, " quasi aliter non oporteat aut " possit ; sed sub tanta serenitate " dicit hæc agenda, ut et amictus " possit contemni." Be this, how-ever, as it may, the precept of Hesiod and Virgil is literally ob-served in Egypt, where the rustics often perform their labour stark naked.

[3] Il. λ. 67, seq.

[4] Πότερα οὖν τέμνεις, ἔφη, στὰς ἔνθα πνεῖ ἄνεμος, ἢ ἀντίος ; οὐκ ἀντίος, ἔφην, ἔγωγε· χαλεπὸν γὰρ, οἶμαι, καὶ τοῖς ὄμμασι καὶ ταῖς χερσὶ γίγνεται, ἀντίον ἀχύρων καὶ ἀθέρων θερίζειν. Xenoph. Œconom. xviii. 1.

In many parts of Greece, though the practice was not general, the women joined in these labours. The reapers, as they advanced, laid the corn behind them in long lines upon the stubble, and were followed by two other classes of harvesters, one of whom bound it into sheaves which the others bore back and piled up into mows. Of the whole of these operations, together with the plenteous feast which interrupted or terminated their toils, Homer has left us a graphic picture in the Iliad : [1]

> There in a field 'mid lofty corn, the lusty reapers stand,
> Plying their task right joyously, with sickle each in hand.
> Some strew in lines, as on they press, the handfuls thick behind,
> While at their heels the heavy sheaves their merry comrades bind.
> These to the mows a troop of boys next bear in haste away,
> Piling upon the golden glebe the triumphs of the day.
> Among them wrapped in silent joy, their sceptered king appears,
> Beholding, in the swelling heaps, the stores of future years.
> A mighty ox beneath an oak the busy heralds slay,
> With grateful sacrifice to close the labours of the day.
> While near, the husbandman's repast the rustic maids prepare,
> Sprinkling with flour the broiling cates whose savour fills the air.

In these remote and unsettled times it behoved the rustic to keep a sharp look-out on the sheaves left behind him on the field, as there were usually prowlers,[2] lurking amid the neighbouring woods and thickets, ready to pounce upon and carry off whatever they saw unguarded.

The implement used in cutting wheat seems always to have been the sickle, while in the case of barley and other inferior grains, the scythe was commonly employed. In some parts of ancient Gaul, where no value was set upon the straw, corn was reaped by a sort of cart,[3] armed in front with scythes, having the edges inclined upwards, which, as it was driven along by an ox, harnessed behind, cut off the ears of corn, which were received into the tum-

---

[1] σ. 550, seq.

[2] Ἡμερόκοιτοὶ ἀνδρες, an elegant euphonism for " thieves."

Hesiod. Opp. et Dies, 605. Cf. the note of Gœttling on verse 375.

[3] Pallad. vii. 2.

bril. In this manner the produce of a whole field might be got in easily in a day. Reaping among the ancient inhabitants of Italy[1] was performed in three ways : first they reaped close, as in Umbria, and laid the handfuls carefully on the ground, after which the ears were separated from the straw, and borne in baskets to the threshing-floor. Elsewhere, as in Picenum, they made use of a ripple or serrated hook, having a long handle with which the ears only were cut off, leaving the straw standing to be afterwards collected and raked up into mows.

In the neighbourhood of Rome they reaped with the common sickle, holding the upper part of the straw in their left hand, and cutting it off in the middle. This tall stubble was afterwards mown and carried off to be used as fodder or bedding for cattle. In Upper Egypt and Nubia, the dhoura stalks are left about two feet in height to support the crop of kidney-beans which succeeds next in order. Among the Athenians[2] when the corn grew tall the stubble was suffered to remain to be burned for manure ; but, when short, the value of the straw led them to reap close.

In separating the grain from the straw the ancients made use of horses, oxen, and mules, which, passing round and round over the threshing-floor, trod out the corn. All the labourer had to do was to guide the movements of the cattle, and take care that no part of the sheaf remained untrodden.[3] From

---

[1] Varro. i. 50.

[2] Καὶ ἀκροτομοίης δ'ἂν, ἔφη, ἢ παρὰ γῆν τέμνοις; ἢν μὲν βραχὺς ᾖ ὁ κάλαμος τοῦ σίτου, ἔγωγ', ἔφην, κάτωθεν ἂν τέμνοιμι, ἵνα ἱκανὰ τὰ ἄχυρα μᾶλλον γίγνηται. Ἐὰν δὲ ὑψηλὸς ᾖ, νομίζω ὀρθῶς ἂν ποιεῖν μεσοτομῶν, ἵνα μήτε οἱ ἀλοῶντες μοχθῶσι περιττὸν πόνον, μήτε οἱ λικμῶντες, ὧν οὐδὲν προσδέονται. Τὸ δὲ ἐν τῇ γῇ λειφθὲν

ἡγοῦμαι καὶ κατακαυθὲν συνωφελεῖν ἂν τὴν γῆν καὶ εἰς κόπρον ἐμβληθὲν τὴν κόπρον συμπληθύνειν. Xenoph. Œconom. xviii. 2.

[3] Xenoph. Œconom. xviii. 4. The same custom still prevails in Southern Europe and in the East. " Corn is trodden out in Granada " in circular-formed threshing- " floors, in the open fields ; the " animals employed are mules

a very humane law in the Old Testament we
learn, that among some nations it was customary
to tie up the mouths of such animals as they employed in this labour, which was forbidden the Israelites : " Thou shalt not," says the Scripture, " muzzle the ox that treadeth out the corn." Nor was
it practised among the Greeks in the age of Homer,[1]
whom we find describing the oxen bellowing as
they made their unwearied round. The threshing-
floor, which was of a circular form,[2] stood on a
breezy eminence, in the open field, where, as at
present, in modern Greece, and in the Crimea,[3] a
high pole was set up in the centre, to which the
cattle were tied by a cord determining the extent
of the circle they had to describe.[4] The end being
nailed, every turn made by the cattle coiled the
rope about the pole and diminished their range, until, at length, they were brought quite close to the
centre, after which, their heads were turned about,
and by moving in an opposite direction the cord
was unwound. Great pains were taken in the construction of this threshing-floor, which was somewhat elevated about the centre, in order, as Varro
observes, that what rain fell might speedily run off.
It was sometimes paved with stone, or pitched with
flints, but more commonly coated with stucco, made
level by a roller, and well soaked with the lees of
oil which at once prevented the growth of weeds

" or oxen." Napier, Excursions,
&c., i. 156. Again, in the Troad,
" The oxen or horses being har-
" nessed to a sort of sledge, the
" bottom part of which is arm-
" ed with sharp flints, are dri-
" ven over the corn, the person
" who guides the cattle balancing
" him or herself with great dex-
" terity whilst rapidly drawn
" round in revolving circles." Id.
ii. 171. Cf. Fowler, Three Years
in Persia, i. 173, and Chandler,
i. 320. ii. 234.

[1] Iliad, v. 495, seq. Hesiod.
Opp. et Dies, 599.

[2] Suid. v. ἀλωά t. i. p. 186. c.
Philoch. Frag. Siebel. p. 86. E-
tym. Mag. 73. 56, seq. Colum.
ii. 20. Geop. ii. 26. Senec.
Quæst. Nat. i. 2,

[3] Earl of Aberdeen in Walp.
Mem. i. 150. Pallas, Trav. in
South. Russia. vol. iv. p. 148,
seq.

[4] Schneid. ad Xenoph. Œcon.
xviii. 8.

and grass, preserved it from cracking, and repelled the approach of mice, ants, and moles, to which oil-lees are destructive.[1] Though some authorities advise that it should be situated under the master's, or at least the steward's, eye, it was generally thought advisable to keep it at a distance from the house and gardens, since the finer particles of chaff, borne thickly through the air, caused ophthalmia, and often blindness,[2] and proved exceedingly injurious to all plants and pulpy fruits, more particularly grapes. In some parts of the ancient world, exposed to the chances of summer rains, the threshing-floor was covered; and, even in Italy, an umbracula,[3] or shed, was always constructed close at hand, into which the corn could be removed in case of bad weather. But this in the sunnier climate of Greece was judged unnecessary. In obedience to a notion prevalent among Hellenic farmers, the sheaves were piled up with the straw towards the south, by which means they believed the grain was enlarged and loosened from the hose. When the farmer happened to be scant of cattle he made use of a threshing-machine,[4] which consisted of a kind of heavy sledge, toothed below with sharp stones or iron. Occasionally, too, the flail[5] was used, especially in the case of such corn as was laid up in the barn and threshed during winter.

In winnowing,[6] when the breeze served, they simply threw the grain up into the air with a scoop, until the wind had completely cleared away the chaff. In serene days they had recourse to a winnowing machine, which, though turned by the hand, was of great power, as we may judge from its being employed in cleansing vetches, and even beans.[7] To receive the chaff, which was too valuable to be lost, pits

---

[1] Varro. de Re Rust. i. 51.

[2] Geop. ii. 26.

[3] Varro. i. 51.   Pallad. i. 36.

[4] Mathem. Vett. p. 85.   Theoph. Hist. Plant. iii. 8.

[5] Colum. ii. 21.

[6] Plat. Tim. t. vii. p. 65. Xenoph. Œconom. xviii. 8.

[7] Il. *v.* 588.

appear to have been sunk all round the threshing-
floor, which, for the passage of the men and cattle,
would appear to have been covered, save in the
direction of the wind.[1] When the corn was designed
for immediate use, one winnowing was deemed sufficient ; but that which was intended to be laid up
in the granary [2] underwent the operation a second
time.

On the building and preparation of granaries [3] the
ancients bestowed great pains. Every means which
could communicate to grain firmness and durability
appears to have been tried by them ; and their success was answerable to their diligence, for, in their
granaries, wheat was preserved in perfection fifty,
and millet a hundred years.[4] Their methods, however, were various ; some laid up their grain in hollow rocks and caves, as in Thrace and Cappadocia ;
others sank deep pits in the earth [5] where they found
it to be perfectly free from humidity, as in Farther
Spain, while others, as in Hither Spain, Apulia, and
Greece,[6] erected their granaries on lofty basements
fronting the East, and with openings towards the
north and west winds.[7] There was usually a range of
numerous diminutive windows near the roof, to supply

---

[1] Il. ε. 562.

[2] See on the vessels in which
the produce of the harvest was
received, Pollux. x. 129.

[3] Cf. Pallad. l. 19. Colum.
i. 6. A granary, commonly σιτο-
φυλακεῖον, was, by Menander, in
his Eunuch, denominated σιτο-
ξόλιον ; among the Siciliotes and
Greek colonists of Italy ῥογος ;
as in the Busiris of Epicharmos.
Poll. ix. 45.

[4] Varro. i. 57.

[5] The same practice is still
found in several of the Grecian
islands. " Ils font dans les champs
" un trou proportionné à la quan-
" tité de bled qu'ils y veulent
" serrer ; il est ordinairement de

" cinq pieds de diamètre, sur
" deux ou trois de profondeur.
" On en tapisse l'intérieur
" d'environ un demi-pied de paille
" brisée sous les pieds des bœufs ;
" on y serre ensuite le grain, de
" manière qu'il s'élève par des-
" sus la terre, à une hauteur
" à-peu-près égale à la profondeur
" du trou ; on le couvre avec
" un demi-pied de paille, sur la-
" quelle on met trois ou quatre
" pouces de terre." Della Rocca,
Traité Complet sur les Abeilles,
t. i. p. 198, seq.

[6] Geop. ii. 27.

[7] Cf. Lord Bacon. Hist. Life
and Death, p. 5.

free vent for the heated air, while the floor, in many cases, contained small apertures for the admission of the cool breezes beneath. The walls were built with suitable solidity, and having, together with the floor, been plastered with rough mortar,[1] made commonly with hair, for which chaff was sometimes substituted, received a coat of fine stucco, on the preparation of which much care was bestowed. It was generally composed of lime, sand, and powdered marble, moistened with the lees of oil, the peculiar flavour and odour of which were supposed effectually to repel the approaches of mice,[2] weevils, and ants. Instead of this a common stucco, formed of clay, was often used. Occasionally the grain was packed up in baskets or large jars,[3] such, it may be presumed, as those still employed for the purpose in Africa, where they are commonly kept in a corner outside the door. Beans and other pulse were preserved in oil-jars rubbed with ashes.[4]

Before the produce of the new year was carried in, the granaries, having been carefully swept, were

[1] But, according to Theophrastus, corn kept best in granaries unplastered with lime. Hist. Plant. viii. 10. 1. In a certain part of Cappadocia called Petra, corn would keep fit for sowing forty years, and for food sixty or seventy, although in that district cloths and other articles decay rapidly. Id. viii. 10. 5.

[2] Among tame animals designed to protect the farmstead from vermin, the weasel was sometimes used. Hom. Batrachom. 52. Ovid. Met. ix. 323. Luc. Timon. § 21. Perizon. ad Ælian. Var. Hist. xiv. 4. Muncker, ad Anton. Liber. 29. Plin. Hist. Nat. xix. 16. Welcker. ad Simon. Amorg. p. 43.

[3] From which they carefully cleansed the spider's webs: ἐκ δ' ἀγγέων ἐλάσειας ἀράχνια. Hesiod.

Opp. et Dies, 475. Cf. 600. A similar method still prevails in the islands of the Archipelago when the grain is intended for the market: " Ceux qui veulent porter " leurs grains à la ville, les met- " tent dans des vases de terre " cuite, qu'ils remplissent à deux " ou trois pouces près ; ensuite " ils étendent par dessus quelques " feuilles de figuier sauvage, ap- " pelé orni, et en Latin caprifi- " cus ; enfin ils achèvent de rem- " plir les vases avec de la cen- " dre, et les couvrent d'une espèce " d'ardoise, mais plus forte et plus " épaisse que celle dont on se " sert en France pour couvrir les " maisons." Della Rocca, Traité Complet sur les Abeilles, t. i. p. 200.

[4] Varro. i. 57.

smeared all over with oil-lees. Various other precautions were, likewise, taken to protect the sacred
gifts of Demeter from depredation, such as drawing
on the floor broad lines of chalk,[1] or strewing handfuls of wild origany round the heaps, or sprinkling
them with the ashes of oaken twigs or dry cow's
dung, or sprigs of wormwood and southernwood, or,
in greater quantity, the leaves of the everlasting.
Instead of these, in some cases, they made use of
powdered clay [2] or dry pomegranate leaves, rubbed
small, and passed through a sieve, a chœnix of which
was sprinkled over a bushel of corn. The favourite
plan, however, seems to have been, to spread a layer
of half-withered fleabane over the floor, on which
were poured about ten bushels of wheat, then a layer
of fleabane, and so on, until the granary was full.[3]

[1] Geop. ii. 29.

[2] This substance was brought
from Olynthos and Cerinthos, in
Eubœa. It is said to have improved
the appearance of the wheat,
though it deteriorated its quality
as an article of food. Theoph.
viii. 10. 7.

[3] The granaries of the island
of Syra, with the contrivance by
which corn is there preserved at
the present day, are thus described
by Della Rocca : — " Les granges,
" appelées en Grec θεμονέα, ont
" communément une vingtaine
" de pieds de long, sur huit à dix
" de hauteur et de largeur. On
" les remplit jusqu'à la moitié
" de leur hauteur, de paille bien
" foulée : on pratique un espace
" de trois ou quatre pieds, que
" l'on remplit de grain. A côté
" on en forme un autre, que l'on
" remplit de même, et ainsi de
" suite, selon l'étendue de la
" grange, et la quantité de grain
" que l'on a ; cela fait, par des
" ouvertures pratiquées dans la
" couverture, on recouvre de paille

" tout le bled, jusqu'à ce que la
" grange soit exactement remplie.
" Quand on veut en faire usage,
" on commence par le tas le plus
" voisin de la porte ; on enlève
" d'abord la paille avec beau-
" coup de précaution : plus on
" approche, plus cette précaution
" augmente ; enfin, pour ôter les
" derniers brins de paille, on se
" sert d'un balai de milleper-
" tuis ou d'autres plantes que
" l'on fait sécher ; et si malgré
" tous ces soins, la surface du
" monceau de grain n'est pas bien
" nette, on achève d'en enlever
" toutes les menues pailles en
" la vannant avec un chapeau
" car les paysans de nos îles por-
" tent comme ici, dans les champs,
" des chapeaux ronds de feutre ;
" ils en portent aussi de paille,
" que l'on travaille avec beau-
" coup de délicatesse à Sifanto."
Traité Complet sur les Abeilles.
t. i. p. 199, seq. Among the tribes
of Northern Africa a more complete system of preserving grain
prevails. " The Arabs, in lieu

Wheat thus layed up was supposed not only to last many years, but also to preserve its weight in bread-making. To render barley durable, they strewed over it laurel leaves, or the ashes of laurel wood, as, like-wise, everlasting, calaminth, and gypsum, or placed a tightly-corked bottle of vinegar,[1] in the middle of the heap. To communicate greater plumpness to all kinds of grain, they sprinkled over the piles a mixture composed of nitre,[2] spume of nitre, and fine earth, which, likewise, acted as a preservative. To render flour more durable, they thrust into it small maple branches, stripped of their leaves, or little cakes of salt and cumin.[3]

The fruits of the earth having been thus safely lodged within doors, the grateful husbandmen cele-brated in honour of their rural gods, Demeter and Dionysos, a festival which may, perhaps, be denomi-nated that of the Harvest Home. In Attica it took place in the great temple at Eleusis, and continued

" of granaries, preserve all their " grain in pits : forty or fifty of " these are made, each to con-" tain about a thousand bushels : " the spot selected is a dry, " sandy soil, the hole being form-" ed in the shape of a large earth-" en jug, the sides are plastered " with mortar about a foot in " thickness, and the wheat or " grain filled up to the mouth, " which is left just large enough " for a man to get in at, and " is about three feet below the " surface of the ground ; this " is now plastered over also, and " filled with the soil around " to the same level as the sur-" rounding country. The earth " taken out in forming the pits " is removed to a distance, and " being scattered abroad, in a " month or two the grass grows " over the surface, and no one, " unless those who have buried " this treasure, would imagine " that there was anything be-" neath their feet. The grain " thus buried preserves for many " years. I have eaten bread at " the Esmailla made from wheat " as old as the Sultan, having " been buried the year of his " birth, and it was as good as " that made of flour from this " year's crop." Colonel Scott, Journal of a Residence in the Esmailla of Abd-el-Kader. p. 155, seq. Mandelslo (lib. ii. c. iii.) found corn-vaults of similar construction in the Azores ; and most travel-lers who have visited the island of Malta will have observed in the fortifications of Valetta that series of curious and beautiful granaries excavated in the form of a bottle in the solid rock.

[1] Geop. ii. 30, seq.
[2] Geop. ii. 28.
[3] Geop. ii. 30.

during several days. No bloody sacrifices were on this occasion offered up; but, in lieu of them, oblations of cakes and fruit with other rustic offerings, designed at once to express their gratitude for past blessings, and to render the gods propitious to them in future. The first loaf made from the new corn was probably eaten or offered up on this day, since it received the name of Thargelos, or Thalusios, from Thalusia, the denomination of the festival.[1]

Before we quit the farm, it may be observed, that the ancients kept a number of slaves, constituting a kind of rural police, whose occupation wholly consisted in guarding the boundaries of estates.[2] These, among the Romans, were denominated rangers, or foresters. There were others to whom the care of the fruit was entrusted; and both these classes of persons were probably elderly men, remarkable for their diligence and fidelity, who were rewarded, by appointment to this more easy duty, for their honest discharge in youth of such as were more painful and laborious. Boys were sometimes set to keep watch over vineyards,[3] as we may see in the first Eidyll of Theocritus, where he gives us a lively sketch of such a guardian plotted against by two foxes.

---

[1] Vid. Theoc. Eidyll. vii. 3. Etym. Mag. 444. 13. Athen. xiii. 65. iii. 80. Meurs. Græc. Fer. p. 15. p. 142. Dem. adv. Neær. § 27, with the authorities collected by Taylor.

[2] Such of these as had charge of the timber may be denominated wood-reeves, a term which answers very well the Latin Saltuarius. The slave-guards of forests, in Crete, were called Ergatones.

Hesych. ap. Meurs. Cret. p. 190.

[3] Casaub. ad Theoph. Char. p. 223, seq. Theocrit. Eidyll. xxv. 27. Cf. Feith. Antiq. Hom. iv. i. 276, sqq. Vineyards in Athens still require guards. Speaking of his approach to Athens from the Peiræeus, Chandler observes : — " In a " tree was a kind of couch, shelter-" ed with boughs, belonging to a " man employed to watch there " during the vintage." ii. 27.

CHAPTER VI.

PASTORAL LIFE.

But within the circle of Hellenic country life [1] there was a kind of parenthetical existence, a remnant of the old nomadic habits, once common, perhaps, to the whole race, — I mean the pastoral life, of which we obtain so many glimpses through the leafy glades and grassy avenues of Greek poetry. No doubt, the fancy of imaginative men, thirsting for a degree of simplicity and happiness greater than they find around them in cities or villages, is apt to kindle and shed too glorious a light on approaching the tranquil solitudes, the pine forests, the mountain glens, the hidden lakes, the umbrageous streams that leap and frolic down the wild rocks of a country so rife with beauty as Greece. Nevertheless, adhering strictly to truth and reality, there is, in such regions, much about the pastoral life to delight the mind. In the first place, the occupations of an ancient shepherd left him great leisure, and he was generally, by habit no less than by inclination, led to prize that " dolce far niente " which, in all southern climates, constitutes the chief enjoyment of existence.

[1] The charm of that repose and freedom from care supposed to be tasted in the seclusion of the country, appears in all ages to have led to the belief, that there is something more natural in fields and forests than in cities, though it be quite as necessary that man should have dwellings as that he should cultivate the ground. The paradox, however, is thus expressed by Varro : Divina natura dedit agros, ars humana ædificavit urbes. De Re Rust. iii. 1, which Cowper, unconsciously perhaps, has thus translated,

God gave the country, but man made the town.

And indeed all the world over, repose, both of mind and body, is sweet. But not entire repose. Accordingly the Grecian shepherd, whose flocks fed tranquilly, whose condition, assured, and pinched by no necessities, left him at liberty to consult his own tastes in his recreations, took refuge from idleness in music and song.[1] At first, and perhaps always, their lays were rude ; but nature, their only teacher, infused into them originality and passion, such as we find in the only poet of antiquity, save Homer, in whose verses the fragrance of the woods still breathes. Whether like Paris and Anchises they kept their own flocks or undertook the care for others, they were still on the mountains perfectly free. Their education was peculiar. Abroad much after dark,[2] in a climate where the summer nights are soft and balmy beyond expression, and where the stars seem lovingly to crowd closer about the earth, they necessarily grew romantic and superstitious.[3] Events occurring early in their own lives or handed down to them by tradition, long meditated on, were in the end invested with supernatural attributes. Under similar circumstances their national religion had probably been first formed. They in the same way, in every canton, created a local re-

[1] Travellers find among the modern shepherds of the East much the same tastes and habits. " The hills," observed Dr. Chandler, speaking of Lydia, " were " enlivened by flocks of sheep and " goats, and resounded with the " rude music of the lyre and of " the pipe; the former a stringed " instrument resembling a guitar, " and held much in the same " manner, but usually played on " with a bow." Chandler, i. p. 85. Cf. Theocrit. Eidyll. i. 7. viii. 9.

[2] The same habits still prevail : " We could discern fires on Lesbos as before on several islands and capes, made chiefly by fishermen and shepherds, who live much abroad in the air, to burn the strong stalks of the Turkey wheat and the dry herbage on the mountains." Chandler, i. 11. Cf. p. 320.

[3] Among other things we find them putting the strongest faith in dreams—at least we may suppose the fishermen in Theocritus, who lay so much stress on the visions of the night, to hold a creed pretty nearly akin to that of shepherds. Eidyll. 21. v. 29. sqq.

ligion.[1] Their very creed was poetry. Tree, rock, mountain, spring, every thing was instinct with divinity, not mystically, as in certain philosophical systems, but literally; and, as they believed, the immortal race, their invisible companions at all hours, could when they pleased put on visibility, or rather remove from their eyes the film which prevented their habitually beholding them.

It is well known that, in the present day, among the nomadic nations of Asia, the sons of the chiefs still follow their flocks in the wilderness. And this in the heroic ages was likewise the case in Greece,[2] where youths of the noblest families watched over their fathers' sheep and cattle. Thus Bucolion, son of Laomedon, led to pasture the flocks of his sire, and, in the solitudes of the Phrygian mountains, was met and loved by a nymph.[3] Two sons also of Priam pursued the same occupation;[4] and thus among the Hebrews, David, the son of Jesse, passes his youth in the sheepfold, and his manhood on a throne. In this secluded and solitary life the sights and sounds of nature became familiar to them, the

[1] The gods they principally worshiped were Pan, the Muses, and the Nymphs. To the Nymphs and Pan they sacrificed as to gods presiding over mountains, where they themselves usually wandered. Pan, moreover, was skilled in the pipe, the instrument of their race. The Muses they adored as the goddesses of poetry and music. Schol. Theoc. i. 6. In verse 12 of the same Eidyll. the Nymphs are spoken of where the office of the Muses is in contemplation, which may easily be explained. For the Muses are properly the Nymphs of those fountains which inspire poets with their lays. Cf. Voss. ad Virg. Eclog. iii. 84.

By the Lydians the Muses were denominated Nymphs. Schol. Theoc. Eidyll. vii. 92. Cf. Eidyll. v. 140. Lyc. Cassand. 274. ibique Schol. et Potter. Kiessl. ad Theocrit.

[2] Lycoph. Cassand. 91, seq. in common with Homer and the other ancient poets, represent princes as shepherds. The guarding of flocks was then, in fact, a regal occupation. Didymos, ad Odyss. ν. 223, observes, that τὸ παλαιὸν καὶ οἱ τῶν βασιλέων παῖδες πανάπαλοι (l. παναίπολοι) ἐκαλοῦντο, καὶ ἐποίμαινον. Meurs. ad Lycoph. p. 1181. Varr. De Re Rust. ii. 1.

[3] Il. ζ. 25. Odyss. ο. 385, seq.

[4] Il. δ. 106.

voiçe of sudden torrents rushing from the mountains,[1]
the roar of lions springing on their folds, or the sweet
moonlight silvering both mountain and valley. It
is with the shepherd's life that Homer connects
that noble description of the night which Chap-
man has thus translated :

> As when about the silver moon, when air is free from wind,[2]
> And stars shine clear,[3] to whose sweet beams high prospects and
>   the brows
> Of all steep hills and pinnacles thrust up themselves for shows,
> And even the lonely valleys joy to glitter in their sight,
> When the unmeasured firmament bursts to disclose her light,
> And all the signs in heaven are seen, that glad the shepherd's
>   heart.

The glimpses of pastoral life, albeit too few, are
still frequent in Homer, who loves, whenever possible, to illustrate his subject by bringing before our
minds the image of a shepherd. Thus Hector, lifting a large rock, is compared to a shepherd bearing
a ram's fleece.[4]

> As when the fleece, though large yet light, the careful shepherd
>   rears,
> With both hands plunged within its folds, so he the rock uptears.

---

[1] Iliad. δ. 452, seq. ε. 137.
θ, 555.

[2] The following picture by
Milton almost seems to be designed to form a contrast to the
above :

As when from mountain-tops the
  dusky clouds
Ascending, while the north wind
  sleeps, o'erspread
Heaven's cheerful face, the low-
  ring element
Scowls o'er the darken'd landscape
  snow or shower ;
If chance the radiant sun, with
  farewell sweet,
Extend his evening beam, the
  fields revive,

The birds their notes renew, and
  bleating herds
Attest their joy, that hill and
  valley rings.
　　　Parad. Lost, ii. 488, sqq.

Iliad θ. 559, sqq. Here *shepherd,* observes the Scholiast, is
used for *herdsman.* Ποιμήν εἶπεν
ἀντὶ τοῦ βουκόλος διὰ νυκτὸς γὰρ
αἱ βόες νέμονται, in loc. i. 238.

[3] On this passage Ἀρίσταρχος
τὴν κατὰ φύσιν λαμπρὰν λέγει
κᾶν μὴ πλήθουσα ᾖ εἰ γὰρ πλη-
ροσέληνος ἦν, ἐκέκρυπτο ἄν μᾶλλον τὰ ἄστρα. Schol. Bekker.
t. i. 238. Cf. Eustath. in Iliad.
θ. t. i. p. 621.

[4] Iliad. μ. 451, seq.

Again, the Trojan forces following their leader,
Æneas, suggest to his mind the idea of innumerable flocks bounding after a ram to drink.[1]

The people followed, as the flock the shaggy ram succeeds,
Who to the cooling streamlet's bank the woolly nation leads
(While swells the shepherd's heart with joy) from pasture on the
　　meads.

Elsewhere, he describes a troop of hungry wolves
attacking the flocks on the mountains :—[2]

As when the hungry wolves, on folds forsaken by the watch,
Descend, the kids and tender lambs by thievish force to snatch ;
Or when the timid browsing crew are scattered far and wide,
And seized, by witless shepherds left upon the mountain side.

But, in another place, they are represented contending with a lion by night for the body of one
of their flock.[3]

Thus the night-watching shepherds strive, but vainly, to repel
The angry lion, whom the stings of want and rage impel,
Upon the carcase fastens he : his heart no fear can quell.

Where the number of the flock required the care
of several men a chief shepherd (ἐπιποιμήν) was appointed to overlook the rest.[4] Among the ancients
twenty sheep were thought to require the attention
of a man and a boy ;[5] but, in modern times, three

---

[1] Iliad. ν. 491, sqq.
[2] Iliad. π. 354, sqq.
[3] Iliad. σ. 161, seq.
[4] Odyss. μ. 131. The duties
of this servant are described by
Varro, who likewise states the
physical qualities required to
be found in shepherds. Con-
tra, pernoctare ad suum quem-
que gregem esse omnes sub
uno magistro pecoris cum esse
majorem natu potius quàm alios
et peritiorem quàm reliquos, quod
iis qui ætate, et scientia præstant animo æquiore reliquis parent. Ita tamen oportet ætate

præstare ut ne propter senectu-
tem minus sustinere possit labo-
res. Neque enim senes, neque
pueri callium difficultatem, ac
montium arduitatem, atque aspe-
ritatem facile ferunt : quod pa-
tiendum illis qui greges sequun-
tur præsertim armenticios, ac ca-
prinos quibus rupes ac silvæ ad
pabulandi cordi. De Re Rust.
ii. 10. Cf. Colum. ii. 1.
[5] Geop. xviii. 1. Yet we find
mention in Demosthenes of a
shepherd with a flock of fifty
sheep under his care. In Everg.
et Mnes. § 15.

men and a boy, with four or five dogs, are sometimes entrusted with a flock of five hundred, of
which two-thirds are ewes.[1] The proportion of rams
to ewes is at present as four to a hundred.

From very remote ages shepherds had learned
to avail themselves of the aid of dogs,[2] which in
farms were usually furnished with wooden collars.[3]
The breed generally employed in this service, in
later ages at least, was the Molossian,[4] which, though
exceedingly powerful and fierce towards strangers,
was by its masters found sufficiently gentle and
tractable. The shepherd's pipe,[5] frequently made
of the donax, or common river-reed,[6] likewise used
in thatching cottages, formed a no less necessary
accompaniment. Another of their instruments of
music was the flute crooked at the top, finely polished and rubbed with bees' wax.[7]

As the Arcadians, descendants of the Pelasgians,
derived one of their principal delights from music,[8]
it is reasonable to infer that the ancestral nation,
preëminently pastoral, was likewise addicted to this
science. The feeding of herds and flocks constituted the principal occupation of the Proselenoi,[9]
who were little devoted to agriculture, as may be
inferred from their acorn-eating habits; for no nation ever continued to feed on mast after they

[1] Leake, Travels in the Morea,
vol. i. p. 17.
[2] Plat. de Rep. iv. t. vi. p.
204. Columella describes with
poetical enthusiasm the character and qualities of the shepherd's dog, which he refuses to
class among dumb animals, its
bark being, according to him, full
of meaning: " Canis falso dicitur
" mutus custos nam quis homi-
" num clarius, aut tanta vocifera-
" tione bestiam vel furem præ-
" dicat quam iste latratu? quis
" famulus amantior domini ? quis
" fidelior comes? quis custos incor-

" ruptior ? quis excubitor inveniri
" potest vigilantior ? quis denique
" ultor aut vindex constantior?
" Quare vel in primis hoc animal
" mercari tuerique debet agricola,
" quod et villam et fructus fami-
" liamque, at pecora custodit."
De Re Rusticâ, 7. 12.
[3] Sch. Aristoph. Vesp. 897.
[4] Aristot. Hist. Animal. ix. 1.
[5] Luc. Bis Accus. § 11.
[6] Plat. Rep. iii. § 10. Stalb.
[7] Theocrit. i. 129. Plat. de
Rep. t. vi. p. 132. Mosch. Eidyll.
iii. 54.   [8] Athen. xiv. 22.
[9] Etym. Mag. 690. 11.

could obtain bread. A report prevailed in the ancient world that the Arcadians were of a poetical temperament, to which Virgil alludes in the well-known verses—

Arcades ambo,
Et cantare pares et respondere parati.

And as improvisatori they may possibly have excelled, though Greece knew nothing of an Arcadian literature. However, chiefly after the example of Virgil, the poets of modern times have always delighted to convert Arcadia into a kind of pastoral Utopia, which is done by Sannazaro, Tasso, Guarini, Sir Philip Sydney, Daniel, and many others. Palmerius à Grentmesnil[1] discovers something like the descendants of the Arcadians among the Irish, whose pastoral taste for music he conceives to be commemorated by the triangular harp in the national insignia.

Their usual clothing consisted of diptheræ, or dressed sheepskins,[2] just as at the present day among the Nubian shepherds, whom one may see thus clad, roaming through the sandy hollows of the Lybian desert. On the inside of these skins the traitor Hermion wrote the letters which betrayed the designs of his countrymen to the enemy in Laconia.[3]   Others wore goatskin cloaks, which they likewise used as a coverlet at night.[4] Euripides introduces his chorus of satyrs complaining of this miserable costume.[5]

[1] " Sic et hodie audio Hibernos, " qui pecuariam exercent, musicæ " deditos, et triangulari cithara " (quam vocamus *harpe*) plerum- " que se oblectare solere, unde " aiunt insignia regni Hiberniæ " fuisse olim et esse adhuc tale " musicum instrumentum." Desc. Græc. Ant. p. 61.

[2] Schol. Aristoph. Nub. 73.

Cf. Vesp. 442.   Küst.—Eq. 398. Bekk. Luc. Tim. § 8. We find mention also made of a cloak of wolfskin.   Philostrat. Vit. Sophist. ii. 6.

[3] Suidas. v. διφθέρα. t. i. p. 757. e.

[4] Harless. ad Theocrit. v. 2.

[5] Cyclop. 79, seq.

" Much loved Bacchos where dost thou
  Lonely dwell afar,
Shaking thy gold locks at eve
Like a blazing star ?
While I thy minister am fain
To serve this one-eyed Cyclop swain,
A slave borne down by fortune's stroke
In a wretched goatskin cloak."

And thus simple was ever their appearance in the East. But, as I have hinted above, their very great leisure,[1] the accidents of their occupation, and the grand and regular march of natural phenomena in those countries, often ripened their intellects beyond what the condition of a modern heath-trotter renders credible. Thus, in the mountains of Chaldæa, astronomy and all its parasitical sciences took birth among the shepherd race. From temperament and circumstances, the inhabitants of thinly-peopled tracts, if unvexed by wars, are profoundly meditative. What they behold in serene indistraction gradually rouses their thoughts, and presenting itself again and again, attended always, as the phenomena of the heavens are, by the same accidents, compels them to study.[2]

[1] Lord Bacon considers the pastoral state preferable in some respects to the agricultural : — " The two simplest and most " primitive trades of life ; that " of the shepherd (who by reason " of his leisure, rests in a place, " and living in view of heaven, " is a lively image of a contem- " plative life) and that of the " husbandman ; where we see the " favour of God went to the " shepherd and not to the tiller " of the ground."—Advancement of Learning, p. 64. Shepherds made libations of milk to the Muses.   Theocrit. i. 143, seq.

[2] Even yet we find the shepherds of Greece retain some smack of classical learning : " After dinner I walked out " with a shepherd's boy to her- " barise ; my pastoral botanist " surprised me not a little with " his nomenclature ; I traced the " names of Dioscorides, and Theo- " phrastus, corrupted, indeed, in " some degree by pronunciation, " and by the long *series annorum*, " which had elapsed since the " time of these philosophers, but " many of them were unmutila- " ted, and their virtues faithfully " handed down in the oral tradi- " tions of the country. My shep- " herd boy returned to his fold " not less satisfied with some " paras that I had given him, " than I was in finding in such " a rustic a repository of ancient " science."—Sibth. in Walp. i.

But solitude is less surely the nurse of science than of superstition. The leaven, which in populous cities scarcely swells visibly in the breast, ferments unrestrainedly in the depths of woods, in the high-piled recesses of mountains, in the gloom of caverns, where nature invests itself with attributes which address themselves powerfully to the heart, and appears almost to hold communion with its offspring. Hence the wild mythologies of Nomadic races, which are not loose-hanging creeds, to be put off and on like a cloak, but a belief inwrought into their souls, a part of themselves, and perhaps the best part, since it is from this that springs the whole dignity and poetry of their lives. In all

66, seq. There is in Sir John Fortescue, De Laudibus Legum Angliæ, translated by Robert Mulcaster, in the reign of Queen Elizabeth, a passage describing the pastoral habits of our ancestors, and the intellectual superiority they engendered, which appears to me so excellent, that I cannot resist the temptation to introduce it here :—" England " is so fertile and fruitefull, that " comparing quantity to quantity "it surmounteth all other landes " in fruitefulnesse. Yea, it bring-" eth forth fruite of itselfe, scant " provoked by mann's industrie "and labour. For there the " landes, the fieldes, the groves, " and the woodes, doe so aboun-" dantlye springe, that the same " untilled doe commonly yield to " their owners more profite then " tilled, though else they bee " most fruitefull of corne and "graine. There also are fieldes " of pasture inclosed with hedges " and ditches, with trees planted " and growing uppon the same, " which are a defence to their " heardes of sheepe and cattell, " against stormes and heate of " the sunne ; and the pastures are " commonly watered, so that cat-" tell shutte and closed therein " have no neede of keeping nei-"ther by day, nor by night. " For there bee no wolves, nor " beares, nor lyons, wherefore " their sheepe lye by night in " the fields, unkept within their " foldes wherewith their land is " manured. By the meanes " whereof, the men of that coun-" trie are scant troubled with "any painefull labour, wherefore " they live more spiritually, as " did the ancient fathers, which " did rather choose to keepe and " feede cattell, than to disturbe " the quietnesse of the minde with " care of husbandrie. And heere-" of it cometh, that menne of " this countrie are more apte and " fitte to discerne in doubtfull " causes of great examination "and triall, than are menne " whollye given to moyling in " the ground ; in whom that " rurall exercise engendereth " rudeness of witte and minde." chap. 29.

countries fables rise in the fields, to flow into and
be lost in the cities. Observe the wild picture
which Plato, in his Academic Dream, presents to
us of a group of Lydian shepherds. It has all the
poetical elements of an Arabian tale.

Tradition, he says, represented Gyges the ancestor
of Crœsus as a hired shepherd, who with many
others guarded the imperial flocks in the remoter
districts of the country. At this time happened a
great earthquake, attended by floods of rain, which,
in the parts where they were, opened up a vast
chasm in the earth. Gyges arriving alone at the
mouth of the gap stood amazed at its depth and
magnitude, but observing a practicable descent went
down, and roamed through its subterraneous passages. Many marvellous things, according to the
mythos, did he there see, and among the rest a
hollow brazen horse, with doors in its side, through
which looking in, he beheld a colossal naked corpse,
with a jewelled ring on its hand. Transferring this
to his own finger Gyges departed.

Shortly afterwards, still wearing the signet, he
went to the assembly of shepherds, which met
monthly, for the purpose of selecting a person to
bear the usual report of the flocks to the king.
Sitting down among the rest he happened to turn
the beavil of his ring towards himself, upon which
he became invisible to his companions,[1] as he clearly
discovered from their discourse, which proceeded as
if about an absent man. Smitten with much wonder
he returned the gem to its former position and
again became visible. He made the experiment
over and over and always with success; upon which,
like another Macbeth, a vast scheme of ambition
darkly shadowed itself upon his mind, and a crown

---

[1] The reader will in this place
perhaps remember the dream of
Rousseau, on the enjoyment
which the possession of such a
ring would have afforded him ;
when after pushing his speculations as far as they could go he
determines that he was much
better without it.—Rêveries du
Promeneur Solitaire,iii. 137.

tinged slightly with blood swam before him.   It
does not, however, appear that like the Thane of
Cawdor he was perplexed with scruples.   He does
not say,—

> " Why do I yield to that suggestion,
>   Whose horrid image doth unfix my hair,
>   And make my seated heart knock at my ribs,
>   Against the use of nature?   Present facts
>   Are less than horrible imaginings.
>   My thought whose murder's yet but phantasy,
>   Shakes so my single state of man, that function
>   Is smothered in surmise, and nothing is,
>   But what is not."

Gyges, with the ruthless resolution of an Oriental, forms his plan at once, and coolly works it out.
He procures himself to be elected one of the mis-
sion to the king, and on arriving at the capital,
dishonours the queen, murders his master, and as-
cends the throne.[1]

This may be regarded as a specimen of the shepherds' tales.[2]   But they moved for the most part in
an atmosphere of superstition, had ceremonies of
their own, a mythology of their own, and of the
whole the pervading spirit was love.   In communities highly civilised, this passion commonly degene-
rates into a plaything, despised when weak, and
mischievous when strong.   It is otherwise in the
early stages of society.   There, in proportion to
their freedom from the aspirations and anxieties of
ambition, men seek happiness in the cultivation of
the affections.   The society of women is to them
all in all.   And the evils that infest them, disturb

---

[1] Plat. Rep. ii. § 3. Cf. x.
§ 12. Stallb. Among the gods
similar powers were attributed to
the helmet of Hades. Thus, in
Homer, Athena is concealed from
Mars by the effect of this en-
chanted piece of armour.—Iliad.
ε. 845. Apollod. ii. 4. 2.

[2] To the same class belongs
that tradition of a brazen tablet
thrown up by a fountain in Lycia foretelling the overthrow of
the Persian monarchy by the
Greeks.—Plut. Alexand. § 17.

their quiet, and engender crime, spring, too, from
the same bitter-sweet fountain, which flows with
honey or gall according to the temper of those who
drink of it.   Consequently, in contemplating the
pastoral life of Greece, we must beware not to
overlook the shepherdesses,[1] those heroines of Bucolic poetry, whose freshness and nature still survive in Theocritus, and other fragments of antiquity, and may operate as an antidote to that insipid spawn whose loves and lamentations affect us
like ipecacuanha in modern pastorals.

In these latitudes of society, at least, women enjoyed their freedom, and the glimpses presented to
us of them as they there existed may be regarded
among the chief charms of Greek poetry.   Only,
for example, observe the picture which Chæremon
the Flower Poet, has delineated of a bevy of beautiful virgins sporting by moonlight :

" There one reclined apart I saw, within the moon's pale light,
With bosom through her parted robe appearing snowy white;
Another danced, and floating free her garments in the breeze
She seemed as buoyant as the wave that leaps o'er summer seas.
While dusky shadows all around shrunk backward from the place,
Chased by the beaming splendour shed like sunshine from her face :
Beside this living picture stood a maiden passing fair
With soft round arms exposed; a fourth with free and graceful air,
Like Dian when the bounding hart she tracks through morning dew,
Bared through the opening of her robes her lovely limbs to view.
And oh ! the image of her charms, as clouds in heaven above,
Mirrored by streams, left on my soul the stamp of hopeless love.
And slumbering near them others lay, on beds of sweetest flowers,
The dusky petaled violet, the rose of Paphian bowers.
The inula and saffron flower, which on their garments cast,
And veils, such hues as deck the sky when day is ebbing fast ;
While far and near tall marjoram bedecked the fairy ground,
Loading with sweets the vagrant winds that frolicked all around."[2]

In the ordinary bucolic poets women to be sure
are sketched with a rude pencil, though coquettish

[1] Cf. Varr. De Re Rust. ii. 10.   [2] Athen. xiii. 87.

as queens, of which we have an exemplification in
the picture on the shepherd's cup : [1]

> And there, by ivy shaded, sits a maid divinely wrought,
> With veil and circlet on her brows, by two fond lovers sought.
> Both beautiful with flowing hair, both sueing to be heard,
> On this side one, the other there, but neither is preferred.
> For now on this, on that anon, she pours her witching smile,
> Like sunshine on the buds of hope, in falsehood all and guile,
> Though ceaselessly, with swelling eyes, they seek her heart to
>   move,
> By every soft and touching art that wins a maiden's love.[2]

There is here no straining after the ideal. Like
Titian's beauties, these shepherdesses are all creatures of this earth, filled with robust health, dark-
eyed, warm, impassioned, and somewhat deficient in
reserve. They understand well how to act their
part in a dialogue. For every bolt shot at them
they can return another as keen. Each bower and
bosky bourne seems redolent of their smiles; their
laughter awakens the echoes; their ruddy lips and
pearly teeth hang like a vision over every bubbling
spring and love-hiding thicket which they were wont
to frequent. Hence the charm of Theocritus. And
a still stronger charm perhaps would have belonged
to the pages of him who should have painted the
shepherd's life of a remoter age,[3] when none were
above such an occupation, which therefore united
at once all the dignity of lofty independence with
the careless freedom of manners and unapprehensive
enjoyment in which consists the secret source of all
the pleasure which rustic pictures afford. Most of
his creations, though not all, are in this respect want-

[1] This was the κισσύβιον, a
goblet or cup turned of ivy wood.
It was usually rubbed with wax
and polished, for the purpose of
bringing out the beautiful carving
which adorned it. Cf. Etym.
Mag. 515. 33.

[2] Theocrit. i. 32, sqq.
[3] Though even here we detect
the presence of hirelings; for Homer observes, that, among the
Læstrigons, such shepherds as
could do with little sleep received
double wages. Odyss. κ. 84, seq.

ing. Ideas of penury[1] slip in, and, in the midst of
rich poetry, check the developement of pleasurable
feelings. For the musical swains, though apparently
ambitious of 'nought but the reputation of song, per-
mit us to discover, that they are but hirelings tending
flocks not their own. The contrast between persons
of this class and those who are owners of the sheep
they tend, is forcibly pointed out in the sacred language of Christ: " I am the good shepherd : the
" good shepherd giveth his life for the sheep. But
" he that is an hireling and not the shepherd and
" whose own the sheep are not, seeth the wolf
" coming, and leaveth the sheep and fleeth, and
" the wolf catcheth them and scattereth the sheep.
" The hireling fleeth because he is a hireling, and
" careth not for the sheep. I am the good shep-
" herd and know my sheep and am known of mine.
" As the Father knoweth me even so know I the
" Father; and I lay down my life for the sheep."[2]
The same affectionate tenderness is attributed to
shepherds in the prophetic writings : " he shall feed
" his flocks like a shepherd, he shall gather the
" lambs with his arm, and carry them in his bosom,
" and shall gently lead those that are with young."[3]

In the matter of virtues and vices, the shepherds
of antiquity were very much, no doubt, like other
men. Their habits were such as grew naturally out
of their position. Towards whatever their feelings led
them they proceeded vehemently, and with that sin-
gleness of purpose which belongs to men of simple
and decided character.[4] They were too commonly

---

[1] In fact black slaves, from
Africa, were sometimes employed
as shepherds, at least in Sicily.
Theoc. i. 24.

[2] John, x. 11, sqq.

[3] Isaiah, xl. 11.

[4] It has been observed by Gibbon, who had diligently studied
the pastoral nations of Asia in
their general habits and charac-

teristics, that ambition and the
spirit of conquest are powerfully
excited by the shepherd's manner
of life. " The thrones of Asia
" have been repeatedly overturned
" by the shepherds of the north,
" and their arms have spread ter-
" ror and devastation over the
" most fertile and warlike coun-
" tries of Europe. On this occa-

creatures of mere impulse. From the peculiar form of their communion with nature, which, like the masses of Egyptian architecture, was continued and monotonous, they acquired a peculiarity of mental temperament, warm, as it were, in parts, and cold in parts. Every circumstance around them tended to rouse, pique, and inflame the passion of desire and its concomitants ; the pairing of their flocks, of the birds, of the very wild beasts whose courage or ferocity they dreaded; their own leisure combined with the excess of health, the influence of climate, the solicitations of opportunity, impelled them into excess; and, accordingly, their morals in this respect sank to a low standard, and rendered them any thing but models of the golden age. The intellect of course was comparatively little cultivated; and there being no other check upon the feelings, suicides, murders of jealousy, and other evidences of ill-regulated passion would often occur.[1]

But, in proportion as we pierce further back into antiquity, these tragical incidents become fewer : not merely because our knowledge of those ages is more scanty, but that in ruder times morality is comparatively lax, and men's taste less fastidious. The rigid laws of marriage were then little observed. Women passed from husband to husband without losing character or caste ; and when they produced illegitimate offspring attributed the paternity to some

" sion, as well as on many others, " the sober historian is forcibly " awakened from a pleasing vision " and is compelled with some re- " luctance to confess, that the " pastoral manners which have " been adorned with the fairest " attributes of peace and inno- " cence are much better adapted " to the fierce and cruel habits of " a military life." Decline and Fall of the Roman Empire, iv. 348. Hippocrates in his brief but vigo-

rous manner has presented us with a picture of the Scythian shepherd's life in ancient times, (De Aër. et Loc. § 92, sqq.) and from modern travellers we find that it differed very little from that which they lead at the present day. See the travels of Rubriquis in Hakluyt, i. 101, sqq. See also the notes of Coray on Hippocrates, t. ii. 280, seq. [1] Theocritus describes Daphnis dying for love. Eidyll. i. 135.

god, and scarcely considered the circumstance a misfortune. Half the princes of the Homeric age were
illegitimate; for this is what is always meant by
saying they were descended from the gods. Æneas
was the son of some young woman whom Anchises
met on the mountains, where he pastured his father's flocks and pretended to have been loved by
Aphrodite.[1] Persons so circumstanced were, doubtless, capable of much romance. Nymphs and goddesses peopled their imagination, and their imagination let loose its brood upon the woods. Poets
afterwards, able to infuse a soul into these rustic
traditions, gave a local habitation and a name to
every beautiful legend they could collect. Hence
that sunny picture, the interview of Aphrodite and
Anchises amid the lofty recesses, the grassy slopes,
the sparkling leaping brooks, and old umbrageous
forests of Mount Ida. Already, however, the force
of dress was known, which Montaigne afterwards
celebrated; for the Homeric bard, about to record
an interview between the goddess and her shepherd-
lover, instead of supposing her to have been

" When unadorned, adorned the most,"

describes all the arts of a luxurious toilette.

The picture, however, of pastoral life which he
suggests rather than describes, is worked out with
strokes of great simplicity. All the other herdsmen disperse in the execution of their several duties, leaving Anchises alone in the cattle-sheds,[2]
spacious in dimensions, and tastefully erected, where
he amuses his solitary leisure with the music of the
cithara. While thus engaged he beholds the approach of the goddess,[3] and is at once struck with

[1] Hom. Hymn. ad Ven. 54,
sqq.
[2] Compare Trollope, Notes on
St. John, x. i.
[3] Aleuas, the Thessalian, is
said to have been favoured with

the visits of a very different mistress as he pastured his herds on
Mount Ossa, near the Hæmo-
nian spring; for a dragon of
enormous size, becoming enamoured of his beauty and golden

her beauty and the splendour of her raiment. At
the unearthly vision his love is kindled ; but the
poet, skilled in the mysteries of the heart, chastens
his passion by overmastering feelings of reverence,
such as necessarily belong to unsophisticated youth.
Anchises constitutes, indeed, the *beau idéal* of an
heroic shepherd, simple, high-minded, ingenuous,
venturous and fearless in contests with man or
beast, but in his intercourse with woman gentle, re-
verent,

> " And of his port as meek as is a maid."

In fact, the gallant knights of romance seem rather
to have been modelled after the heroic warriors of
Greece, than from any realities supplied by the chivalrous ages. The author of the Hymn is careful
in describing the shepherd's couch, to insinuate with
how great strength and courage he was endowed.
He reclines, we are told, on skins of bears and
lions slain by his own hand, though over these
there were cast, for show, garments of the softest
texture.[1]

Throughout this work it has been seen how the influence of climate and position concurred in the formation of the Greek character. We may ourselves
put the doctrine to the proof by observing the effect
upon our minds of those reflections of landscapes which
appear in language ; rude Boreal scenes exciting the
spirit of contention and energy ; while the soft valleys, groves, and odoriferous gardens of the South
produce a calm upon our thoughts favourable to the
more benevolent emotions. Hellenic shepherds,
therefore, no other causes preventing, may upon
the whole be supposed to have been humane.

hair, frequently approached the
shepherd with presents of game
of her own catching. Having
laid her gifts at his feet, she
would kiss his locks and lick his
face with her tongue, which, as

the fountain was so near it, may
be hoped was a work of super-
erogation. Ælian. De Nat. Animal. viii. 11.

[1] Hymn. ad Vener. 158, sqq.

Indeed, the very curious adventures of a sophist,[1]
in the mountains of Eubœa, preserved among the
literary wrecks of antiquity, open up to our view
a picture of pastoral life which, in spite of much
rudeness and indigence, exhibits the Greek character in its original roughness and simplicity, full of
kindness, full of gentleness, full of hospitable pro-
pensities, which would do honour to the noblest
Arab Sheikh. And the material scene itself, in
every feature Grecian, harmonises exactly with the
moral landscape.

The eastern shores of the island of Negropont,
beetled over by Mount Caphareus,[2] and indented by
no creeks or harbours, were in antiquity infamous
for shipwrecks, notwithstanding that they formed
the principal station of the purple fishers.[3] Cast
away on this coast, the sophist Dion, for his eloquence surnamed of the golden-mouth, fell in with
a pastoral hunter who, entertaining him generously,
furnished at the same time a complete idea of the
rude herdsman, who preserved in the vicinity of the
highest civilisation known to the old world the simplicity of the Homeric Abantes.[4] Nay, this wild
sportsman, pursuing with his huge dogs a stag along

---

[1] Dion Chrysostom. Orat. vii.
t. i. p. 219, sqq. Phot. 166. a. 24.

[2] On this mountain and the
mythological legends attached to
it, see Virg. Æn. xi. 260, with
the note of Servius. Ovid. Metamorph. xiv. 472. Cf. Propert.
v. 115, sqq. Jacobs. Plin. iv. 21.
An ancient scholiast, quoted by
Morell, thus relates the revenge
of Nauplios : Ναύπλιος τοῦ υἱέος
δὴ τοῦ Παλαμήδους τοῦ φόνου
ἀμυνόμενος τοὺς "Ελλήνας τοῦ
ἀνέμου αὐτοῖς ἐνστάντος· ἐπεὶ τοῦτον διὰ θαλάττης ἐγέλων. αὐτὸς
οὗτος τὸν Καφηρέα καταλαβὼν
εἶτα νυκτὸς πυρσεύων ἀπὸ τῶν
ἐκεῖσε πετρωδῶν πάγων, ἠπάτα

προσχεῖν, ὡς δή τινι εὐπροσόδῳ
ἀκτῇ τοῖς ἀποτόμοις κρημνοῖς εἰς
βάθος ἐρριζωμένοις καὶ χοιράσι
διειλημμένοις. καὶ οὕτως ἀπρό-
οπτως ἀπωλόντο.   Schediasm.
&c., in Dion. t. ii. p. 580, seq.
Cf. Strab. viii. 6. t. ii. p. 195.
Apollodor. ii. i. 5. Orph. Argo-
naut. 204, sqq.

[3] On the purple fisheries of
Eubœa, cf. Feder. Morell. Schediasm. &c., in Dion. ii. 576.
Reiske. and Aristot. Hist. Animal. v. 15.

[4] A life equally simple is led
by the Albanian shepherds of the
present day. " They live on the

the cliffs, powerful in limb, hale in colour, and with long hair streaming over his shoulders, appeared to be the natural descendant of those Heroic warriors.[1] Armed with his hunting-knife, he flays and cuts up the stag upon the spot, and taking along with him the skin and choicest pieces of venison abandons the remainder on the beach. As they go along he displays the knowledge wherewith experience stores the rustic mind. He understands the signs of the weather, and from the clouds which cap the summits of Caphareus foretells how long the sea will continue unnavigable.[2]

Rude as an American backwoodsman, he was precipitated, by the rare luck of meeting with a stranger, into equal inquisitiveness and garrulity. He put questions without waiting for an answer. He gossipped of his own concerns; explained without being asked the whole economy of his life; and exhibited all that enthusiasm of beneficence which belongs to human nature when uncorrupted by the thirst of gold. There is a rare truth in the description; far too much ever to have graced a sophist's tale, unless nature had supplied the model.

"There are two of us," says he, "who inhabit together the same rude nook, having married sisters, by whom we have both sons and daughters. We derive our subsistence principally from the chase, paying but little attention to agriculture, since we have no land of our own. Nor were our fathers better off in this respect than ourselves; for, though freeborn citizens, they were poor, and by their con-

"mountains, in the vale or the "plain, as the varying seasons "require, under arbours, or "sheds, covered with boughs, "tending their flocks abroad, or "milking the ewes and she-goats "at the fold, and making cheese "and butter to supply the city." Chandler, ii. p. 135.

[1] Iliad. β. 541. δ. 464. The

long hair of these ancient warriors is thus mentioned by the Homeric Scholiast : τὰ ὀπίσω μέρη τῆς κεφαλῆς κομῶντες ἀνδρείας χάριν. ἴδιον δὲ τοῦτο τῆς τῶν Εὐβοέων κουρᾶς, τὸ ὄπισθεν τὰς τρίχας βαθείας ἔχειν· t. i. p. 83. Bekker.

[2] Cf. Theoph. De Sign. Pluv. i. 22.

dition constrained to tend the herds of another, a man of great property, owning vast droves of cattle, numerous horses and sheep, several beautiful estates, with many other possessions, and all these mountains as far as you can see. This opulence, however, became his ruin. For the emperor, casting a covetous eye upon his domains, put him to death, that he might have a pretext for seizing on them. Our few beasts went along with our master's, and the wages due to us there was no one to pay.

" Here, therefore, of necessity we remained[1] where two or three huts were left us, with a slight wooden shed in which the calves had been housed in the summer nights.[2] For, during winter, we had been used to descend for pasture to the plains where, in the proper season, stores of hay were also laid up; but with the re-appearance of summer we returned again to the mountains. The spot which had formed our principal station now became our fixed dwelling. Branching off on either hand is a deep and shady valley, having in the middle a rivulet so shallow as to be easily traversed, both by cattle and their young. This stream, flowing from a spring hard by, is pure and perennial and cooled by the summer wind blowing perpetually up the ravine. The encircling forests of oak stretch forth their boughs far above, over a

---

[1] Had Bernardin de St. Pierre read this when he wrote his Indian Cottage ?

[2] An equal degree of contentment to that which in this recital we find exhibited by the Eubœan herdsmen, is still in our own times displayed by the rough peasants of the Lipari islands, in the midst of far greater privations :— " It is incredible at the same time " how contented these islanders " are amid all their poverty. U- " lysses perhaps cherished not a " greater love for his Ithaca than " they bear to their Eolian rocks " which, wretched as they may " appear, they would not ex- " change for the Fortunate islands. " Frequently have I entered their " huts which seem like the nests " of birds hung to the cliffs. They " are framed of pieces of lava ill- " joined together, equally desti- " tute of ornament within and " without, and scarcely admitting " a feeble uncertain light, like " some gloomy cavern." Spallanzani, Travels in the Two Sicilies, iv. 147.

carpet of soft verdure, which descends with a gentle slope into the stream, giving birth to a few gad-flies,[1] or any other insect hurtful to herds. Extending around are numerous lovely meadows, dotted with lofty trees, where the grass is green and luxuriant throughout the year."

The eloquence of this description, I mean in the original, is not unworthy to be compared with that in the Phædrus[2] which has given eternal bloom to the platane-tree and agnus castus on the banks of the Ilissos.

The conversion of these herdsmen into hunters is narrated by Dion with a patient simplicity worthy of Defoe. An air of solitude, snatched from Robinson Crusoe's island, seems to breathe at his bidding over Eubœa. The same education operates strange changes both in man and dog; and bringing them into hostile contact with wolves, wild boars, stags, and other large animals, gives the latter a taste for blood, and renders him fierce and destructive. Subsisting by the chase, they pursued it summer and winter, following both hares and fallow-deer by their tracks in the snow. In their intervals of leisure

[1] The absence of these tormentors of cattle was considered a matter of great importance by the ancients. Virgil, where he is giving directions respecting the best pastures suited to the youthful mothers of the herds, celebrates the exploits of the gadfly:

Saltibus in vacuis pascant, et plena secundum
Flumina: muscus ubi, et viridissima gramine ripa,
Speluncæque tegant, et saxea procubet umbra.
Est lucos Silari circa, ilicibusque virentem
Plurimus Alburnum volitans, cui nomen asilo
Romanum est, œstrum Graii vertere vocantes:

Asper, acerba sonans: quo tota exterrita sylvis
Diffugiunt armenta; furit mugitibus æther
Concussus, sylvæque et sicci ripa Tanagri.

Georg. iii. 143, sqq.

See the note of Philargyrius in loc. Aristot. Hist. Animal, iv. 4. v. 19.

[2] Plat. Opp. t. i. p. 9. To protect from pollution spots shaded by noble trees they were accustomed to consecrate them to some god, and to erect beneath the overhanging branches statues and altars. Id.ib. In Crete the fountains are often shaded still by majestic plane-trees. Pashley, ii. 31.

they strengthened and beautified their dwellings, saw their children intermarry and grow up to succeed them, without even once approaching any city or even village.

The style of hospitality prevalent among such men in antiquity differs very little from that which one would now find in the hut of a good-natured Albanian.[1] Their industry rendered them independent, and their independence rendered them generous. By degrees their rustic cottages were surrounded by a garden and fruit-trees, their court was walled in, and luxuriant vines hung their foliage and purple fruit over windows and porch. On the arrival of a stranger, the wife takes her station at table beside her husband. Their marriageable daughter, in the bloom and beauty of youth, aids her brothers in waiting at table, where host and guest recline on

---

[1] Or even in the shed of a Turkish shepherd in Asia Minor. Dr. Chandler has a passage illustrative of the hospitality of pastoral tribes, which is at once so picturesque and concise that I am tempted to transcribe it: "About "two in the morning our whole "attention was fixed by the "barking of dogs, which, as we "advanced, became exceedingly "furious. Deceived by the light "of the moon we now fancied we "could see a village, and were "much mortified to find only a "station of poor goatherds with- "out even a shed, and nothing "for our horses to eat. They "were lying wrapped in their "thick capotes or loose-coats by "some glimmering embers, among "the bushes in a dale under a "spreading tree by the fold. "They received us hospitably, "heaping on fresh fuel and pro- "ducing caimac or sour curds "and coarse bread which they "toasted for us on the coals. "We made a scanty meal, sitting "on the ground lighted by the "fire and by the moon, after "which sleep suddenly overpow- "ered me. On waking I found "my companions by my side, "sharing in the comfortable cover "of the Janizary's cloak which "he had carefully spread over us. "I was now much struck with "the wild appearance of the spot. "The tree was hung with rustic "utensils, the she-goats in a pen "sneezed and bleated and rustled "to and fro ; the shrubs, by which "our horses stood, were leafless, "and the earth bare ; a black "cauldron with milk was sim- "mering over the fire, and a "figure more than gaunt or sa- "vage close by us was struggling "on the ground with a kid whose "ears he had slit, and was en- "deavouring to cauterise with a "piece of red-hot iron." Chandler, vol. i. 180, seq.

highly raised divans of leaves covered with the skins of beasts. The young maiden, like a rustic Hebe, pours out the wine, dark and fragrant, while the youths served up the dishes and then laid out a table for themselves and dined together. And the sophist, versed in the courts of satraps and kings, conceived these rude hunters of the mountains the happiest and most enviable of mankind.

But a pastoral picture is incomplete without love. The youthful beauty of Caphareus, hidden, like another Nouronihar [1] from the world, is accordingly beloved by her cousin, an adventurous hunter like her sire, who joins the family circle in the evening, accompanied by his father, bringing in his hand a hare as a present to his mistress. The old man salutes the guest, the youth offers his present with a kiss, and immediately undertakes the office of the girl, who thereupon resumes her place beside her mother.

Observing this arrangement, the stranger inquires whether she is not soon to be married to some wealthy peasant, who might benefit the family, upon which the youth and maiden blush, and her father replies,

" Nay, but she will take a husband, humble in " rank, and like ourselves a hunter," glancing at the same time at the lover.

" How is it then that you wait? " inquired the stranger. " Do you expect him from the village? "

" No," answered the father, " he is not far off; " and so soon as we can fix upon a fortunate day " the nuptials will be celebrated."

" And by what do you judge of a fortunate day? "

" The moon must be approaching the full, the " weather fair, and the atmosphere transparent."

" And is the youth in reality an able hunter? "

" I am," said the young man, answering for himself, " in the chase of the stag or boar, as you " yourself, if you please, shall judge to-morrow "

---

[1] History of the Caliph Vathek. p. 102.

" And did you take this hare, my friend ? "

" I did," replied he with a smile, " having set a
" gin for him by night; [1] the weather being sur-
" passing beautiful, and the moon larger than it
" ever was before."

Upon this both the old men laughed, and the
lover abashed held his peace.

"But," observed the father of the maiden, " it
" is no fault of mine that the solemnity is deferred;
" we only wait at your father's desire, till a victim
" can be purchased ; for a sacrifice must be offered
" to the gods."

" With respect to the victim," interposed the
maiden's younger brother, " he has long provided
" one, and a noble one too, which is now feeding
" behind the cottage."

" And is it truly so ? " demanded the old man.

" It is," replied the lad.

" And where," addressing the youth, " did you
" procure it ? " inquired they.

" When we took the wild sow,[2] which was followed by her litter," answered he, " and the greater
" number, swifter than hares, made their escape ; I
" hit one with a stone, and my companions coming
" up threw a skin over him. This I secured, and
" exchanged in the village for a young domestic
" pig which has been fatted in a sty behind the
" house."

" I now understand," exclaimed the father, " the
" cause of your mother's mirth when I would won-
" der what that grunting could be, and how the
" barley was disappearing so fast."

" Nevertheless," observed the young man, " to be
" properly fatted our Euboean swine require acorns.[3]

---

[1] Cf. Philost. Icon. ii. 26, p.
851.

[2] The wild hog is still one of
the most common animals in the
forests of Greece and Asia Minor.
Chandler, i. 77. Even wild bulls

occasionally make their appearance in the latter country. 176.

[3] To this best and most economical food for hogs, Homer
makes allusion where he introduces the goddess Circe attending

"However, if you will just step this way I will "show her to you."

Upon which off they went, the boys quite at a run, and in vast glee.

In the meantime, the maiden going into the other cottage, brought forth a quantity of split ser-vice-berries,[1] medlars,[2] and winter apples, and bunches of superb grapes, bursting ripe,[3] and, brushing down the table, she spread them out there upon a layer of clean fern. Next moment the lads returned bringing in the pig, with much joking and shouts of laughter. Then came, too, the young man's mo-ther, with two of his little brothers, and they brought along with them nice white loaves, with boiled eggs in wooden salvers, with a quantity of parched peas. Having embraced her brother, with his wife and daughter, she sat down beside her husband, and said,

"Behold the victim, which my son has long fed "for his marriage, and the other things also are "ready; both the barley-meal and the flour. A "little wine, perhaps, may be wanting, but even "this we can easily procure from the village."

And her son standing near her, fixed his eyes wistfully upon his father-in-law.

The latter smilingly observed,—

"All delay now is on the lover's part, who, per-"haps, is anxious to fatten his pig."

---

to her sty, which she had filled with the transformed companions of Odysseus :

τοῖσι δὲ Κίρκη
Πὰρ ρ᾽ ἄκυλον, βάλανον τ᾽ ἔβαλεν,
καρπόν τε κρανείης
Ἔδμεναι, οἶα σύες χαμαιευνάδες
αἰὲν ἔδουσιν.
Od. κ. 241, sqq. Cf. ν. 409.

Ælian de Nat. Animal. v. 45, celebrates these Homeric dainties as the food of the hog to which

he elsewhere adds the fruit of the ash. viii. 9.

[1] Cf. Theoph. Hist. Plant. ii. 2. 10. ii. 7. 7—iii. 6. 5—vi. 3. 11. Ὄα, ἀκροδρύων εἶδος μήλοις μικ-ροῖς ἐμφερές.

Tim. Lec. Platon. in voce with the note of Ruhnken.

[2] On the three kinds of med-lars, Theoph. Hist. Plant. iii. 12. 5.

[3] Philost. Icon. i. 31, p. 809. ii. 26, p. 851.

" As to her," said the youth, " she is bursting with
" fat."

Upon this the sophist, willing to aid the lover,
interposed, and remarked, —

" But you must take care lest while the pig is
" fattening he himself grow thin."

" The stranger's remark is just," said his mother;
" for already he is more meagre than he used to be;
" and I have of late observed him to be wakeful at
" night, and to go forth from the cottage."

" Oh! that," said he, " was when the dogs barked,
" and I stepped out to see what was the matter."

" Not you!" said his mother, — " but went moping
" about. Let us, therefore," continued she, " put him
" to no further trial."

And throwing her arms about her sister, the maid-
en's mother, she kissed her; whereupon the latter,
addressing her husband, said, —

" Let us grant them their desire."

To which he agreed; and it was resolved, that the
marriage should be solemnized in three days, the
stranger being invited to remain and witness it, which
he did.

The above picture of an obscure herdsman's life
in its naked simplicity, void of all embellishment,
will probably be thought more trustworthy than the
elaborate descriptions of the poets, notwithstanding
that, even in these, it is easy to separate the real
from the fictitious.

In the estimation of the Greeks the herdsman [1]
commonly ranked before the shepherd, and the latter
before the goatherd, — for the dream of rank pursues
mankind even amid the quiet of the fields, — and
their manners are supposed to have corresponded.

---

[1] Robust persons, with loud voices, were ordinarily chosen for herdsmen, while goatherds were selected for their lightness and agility. Geop. ii. 1. Shepherds obtained among the Greeks the name of $\pi o\iota\mu\acute{e}\nu\epsilon\varsigma$; while the keepers of other flocks and herds were termed $a\iota\pi\acute{o}\lambda o\iota$. Schol. Theoc. i. 6.

Pollux,[1] however, reckons the goatherd next after the herdsman, and again inverts the order. Varro, on the other hand, gives precedence to the shepherd as the most ancient, the sheep, in his opinion, having been the animal earliest tamed.

In point of utility the goat, in some parts of the ancient world, rivalled the sheep, producing fine hair which was shorn like wool.[2] I may remark, too, in passing, that the large-tailed sheep still common in Asia Minor, as well as at the Cape, were anciently plentiful in Syria, where, according to the great naturalist,[3] their tails attained a cubit in breadth. In some parts of Arabia another more curious breed was found, with tails three cubits in length, to carry which they were supplied by the ingenuity of the shepherds with wooden carriages.[4]

In most parts of Greece, as well as in the East, it was customary to bring home the sheep from pasture towards evening, and shut them up for the night in warm and roomy cotes, which were surrounded by

---

[1] Onomast. i. 249.

[2] Arist. Hist. Anim. viii. 27. 3. Things manufactured from the hair of this animal were called κιλίκια. Etym. Mag. 513. 41.

[3] Arist. Hist. Anim. viii. 27. 3. Speaking of the neighbourhood of Smyrna,—The " sheep," observed Dr. Chandler, " have " broad tails, hanging down like " an apron, some weighing eight, " ten, or more pounds. These " are eaten as a dainty, and the " fat, before they are full-grown, " accounted as delicious as mar- " row." Travels, i. 77. Of the broad-tailed sheep mentioned by the ancients the most remarkable were those of India, where, according to Ctesios, of veracious memory, both they and the goats were larger than asses:—τὰ πρό-βατα τῶν Ἰνδῶν καὶ αἱ αἶγες μεί-

ζους ὄνων εἰσί, καὶ τίκτουσιν ἀνὰ τεσσάρων καὶ ἓξ ὡς ἐπὶ τὸ πολύ, ἔχουσι δὲ οὐρὰς μεγάλας· διὸ τῶν τοκάδων ἀποτέμνουσιν ἵνα δύνωνται ὀχεύεσθαι. Phot. Biblioth. Cod. 72. p. 46. b. Bekker. Ælian. de Nat. Animal. iv. 32, relates, without any symptoms of incredulity, precisely the same fact; and then adds a circumstance which may keep in countenance the Abyssinian story of Bruce respecting the carving of a rump-steak from a live cow, — for the Indians, observes Ælian, were in the habit of cutting open the tails of the rams, extracting all the fat, and then sowing them up again so dexterously that in a short time no trace of the incision remained visible.

[4] Herod. iii. 113. Ælian. Hist. Anim. x. 4.

wattled fences,[1] strong and high, both to prevent them from leaping over, and to exclude the wild beasts which, in remoter ages, abounded in the mountains. They were carefully roofed over, and every other precaution was taken to render them perfectly dry, the floor being usually pitched with stones, and slightly inclined. Their bedding[2] consisted of calaminth and asphodel and pennyroyal and polion (a sort of herb whose leaves appear white in the morning, of a purple colour at noon, and blue when the sun sets[3]) and fleabane and southernwood and origany,[4] all which repel vermin. The more completely to effect the same purpose, they were, likewise, in the habit of fumigating the cotes from time to time, by burning in them several locks of some shepherdess's hair,[5] together with gum ammoniac, hartshorn, the hoofs or hair of goats, bitumen, cassia, fleabane, or calaminth, for the smell of which serpents were thought to have a peculiar aversion.[6] Their ordinary food, while in the folds, consisted of green clover and cytisus, fenugreek, oaten and barley straw, and vegetable stalks,[7] which were supposed to be improved if sprinkled on the threshing-floor with brine, figs blown down by the wind, and dry leaves.

[1] Bound together, probably, by wild succory or cneoron, as in modern times by the withe-wind. Theoph. Hist. Plant. vii. 11. 3. vi. 2. 2.

[2] Geop. xviii. 2.

[3] Plin. xxi. 7.

[4] Dioscor. iii. 32.

[5] Geop. xviii. 2.

[6] Aristoph. Eccles. 644. Geop. xviii. 2.4.

[7] Geop. xviii. 2. Apropos of Cytisus, it is observed by Æschylides, in Ælian. de Nat. Animal. xvi. 32, that the rustics of Cios, on account of the aridity of the island, possessed few flocks. Those they had, however, were fed entirely on the leaves of the cytisus, the fig-tree, and the olive, mingled occasionally with the straw and halm of vegetables. The lambs reared on this island were of singular beauty, and sold at a higher price than those of most other parts. In Lydia and Macedonia sheep were sometimes fattened upon fish, which must have given the mutton of those countries a somewhat unsavoury odour. Ælian. De Nat. Animal. xv. 5. Another favourite food of sheep was the leaves of the white nymphæa, the tender shoots of which were eaten by swine, while men themselves fed upon the fruit. Theoph. Hist. Plant. iv. 10. 7. Children, too, it is

In the short and sharp days of winter,[1] they were not led forth to pasture till both the dew and the hoar frost had disappeared ; but in summer the shepherds were careful to be a-field with the dawn while the dew was still heavy on the grass. In Attica[2] and the environs of Miletus, where was produced the finest and costliest wool in the ancient world, the sheep[3] were protected from rain and dust and brambles and whatever else could damage their fleeces[4] by housings of purple leather.[5] The same practice prevailed also in the Megaris, where Diogenes beholding a flock of sheep[6] thus clad, while the children, like those of the Egyptian peasants were suffered to run about naked,

said, regarded as a delicacy the stalks of the phleos, the typha, and the butomos. The roots of this fruit were given as food to cattle. Id. ibid.

[1] Geop. xviii. 2.

[2] Cf. Athen, v. 60. Hom. Il. ε. 305, sqq.

[3] Those of the neighbouring country of Bœotia are now, however, more highly valued. " Flocks " of sheep whose fleeces were of a " remarkable blackness were feed- " ing on the plain ; the breed " was considerably superior in " beauty and size to that of Atti- " ca." Sibth. in Walp. i. 65. To dream of sheep of this colour was regarded by the ancients as unlucky. Artemid. Oneirocrit. ii. 12. p. 96. The finest black sheep in the ancient world were found in a district of Phrygia in the neighbourhood of the cities of Colossè and Laodicea, the wool of which not only exceeded that of Miletos in softness, but was of a glossy jet colour like that of the raven's wing. Φέρει δ' ὁ περὶ τὴν Λαοδίκειαν τόπος προβάτων ἀρετὰς, οὐκ εἰς μαλακότητας μό-

νον τῶν ἐρίων, ᾗ καὶ τῶν Μιλησί-ων διαφέρει, ἀλλὰ καὶ εἰς τὴν κο-ραξὴν χρόαν ὥστε καὶ προσοδεύον-ται λαμπρῶς ἀπ' αὐτῶν· ὥσπερ καὶ οἱ Κολοσσηνοὶ ἀπὸ τοῦ ὁμωνύμου χρώματος πλησίον οἰκοῦντες. Strab. xii. 8. t. iii. p. 74. Plin. Nat. Hist. viii. 73. Cf. Chandler, Travels in Greece and Asia Minor. i. 262. The country round Abydos also was celebrated for its black flocks among which not a single white sheep was to be discovered. Ælian de Nat. Animal. 3. 32.

[4] Varro. de Re Rust. ii. 2.

[5] Horace speaks of the " pel-lites oves Galesi." Od. ii. 6. 10.

[6] Diog. Laert. vi. 41. The practice is noticed also by Pliny who says, — " Ovium summa ge-" nera duo, tectum et colonicum ; " illiud mollius, hoc in pascuo " delicatius, quippe quum tectum " rubis vescatur. Operimenta ei " ex Arabicis præcipua." Nat. Hist. viii. 72. Columella also mentions these coverings : — " Molle " vero pecus, etiam velamen " quo protegitur, amittit atque " id non parvo sumptu reparatur. " vii. 3, seq.

said, " It is better to be a Megarean's ram
than his son." Ælian[1] alludes to this saying for
the purpose of noticing the ignorance and want of
education prevalent among the Megareans. We
find likewise in Plutarch[2] another version of the
anecdote taxing these Dorians with avarice and
meanness. Augustus imitated the saying of Diogenes and applied it to Herod, hearing of whose
cruelty to his family, he said, " It were better to be
Herod's hog than his son."[3] But if the Megareans
lived poorly they built grandly : so that of them it
was said, that they ate as if they were to die to-
morrow, and built as if they were to live for ever.[4]

Sheep, as most persons familiar with the country
will probably have observed, are wont in hot summer days to retire during the prevalence of the sun's
greatest heat beneath the shade of spreading trees,[5]
at which time a green sweep of uplands dotted
with antique oaks or beeches,[6] each with its stem
encircled by some portion of the flock reposing upon
their own fleeces, presents a picture of singular beauty and tranquillity. The picturesque features of the
scene were in old times enhanced by the addition
of several accompaniments now nowhere to be found,
consisting of statues, altars, or chapels, erected in
honour of the rural gods or nymphs.[7] Fountains,
moreover, of limpid water[8] in many places gushed
forth from beneath the trees, where there were usu-

---

[1] Var. Hist. xii. 56.

[2] De Cupiditate. § 7.

[3] Macrob. Sat. ii. 4.

[4] Tertull. in Apolog. ap. Menag. ad Laert. vi. 41. t. ii. p. 141.
b. c.

[5] Geop. xviii. 2.

[6] Nor in Asia Minor is the
shade of trees always deemed
sufficient. " We came," says Dr.
Chandler, " to a shed formed
" with boughs round a tree, to shel-
" ter the flocks and herds from the
" sun at noon." Travels, i. 25.

[7] Schol. Theoc. i. 21. Cf. Plat.
Phædr. t. i. p. 9.

[8] I cannot resist the temptation to introduce in this place
the picture in miniature of a
Greek landscape from the picturesque and beautiful journal of
Dr. Sibthorpe : " We dined under a rock, from whose side descended a purling spring among
violets, primroses, and the starry
hyacinth, mixed with black Si-
lyrium and different coloured or-
ches. The flowering ash hung
from the sides of the mountain,

ally a number of seats for the accommodation of
the shepherds and shepherdesses. In these retreats they generally passed the sultry hours of the
day, playing on the pastoral flute or the syrinx,
chanting their wild lays, or amusing each other
by the relation of those strange legends which inhabited the woods and lonely mountains of Greece.[1]
There prevailed among them a superstition against
disturbing by their music or otherwise that hushed
stillness which most persons must have observed
to characterise the summer noon. At this hour of
the day the God Pan,[2] in the opinion of Greek
shepherds, took his rest after the toils of the chase,
reclining under a tree in the solitary forest;[3] and,
as he was held to be of a hasty choleric disposition,
they abstained at that time from piping through
fear of provoking his anger. The other Gods likewise were believed to enjoy a short sleep at this
time, as we find in the case of the nymph Aura, in
the Dionysiacs.[4]

From a passage in St. John's gospel it would
appear, that the practice prevailed among the Oriental shepherds of distinguishing the several mem-

under the shade of which bloomed
saxifrages, and the snowy Isopy-
rum, with the Campanula Pyra-
midalis ; this latter plant is now
called χαρισονη ; it yields abundance of a sweet milky fluid, and
was said to promote a secretion
of milk, a quality first attributed
to it under the doctrine of sig-
natures. Our guide made nose-
gays of the fragrant leaves of the
Fraxinella ; the common nettle
was not forgotten as a pot-herb,
but the Imperatoria seemed to be
the favourite salad. Among the
shrubs I noticed our gooseberry-
tree, and the Cellis Australis grew
wild among the rocks." Walp.
Mem. i. 63.

[1] See Hesiod. Opp. et Dies,
582, sqq.

[2] To dream of this god was
considered auspicious by shepherds. Artemid. Oneirocrit. ii.
42. p. 133.

[3] Schol. Theoc. i. 15. Cal.
Hymn. in. Lav. Poll. 72. ibique
interp. Nem. Eclog. iii. 3. Cf.
Hom. Il. τ. 13. Od. ι. 9. The shepherd in the Anthology (Jacob. t.
ii. no. 227. p. 694) is not so religious as Theocritus' goatherd, for
he boldly pipes in the morn and
at noon χὼ ποιμὴν ἐν ὄρεσσι με-
σαμϐρινὸν ἀγχόθι παγᾶς συρίσ-
δων. Kiessling. ad Theoc. i. 15.

[4] Nonn. xlviii. 258, sqq. Cf.
Philost. Icon. ii. 11. et J. B. Carp-
zov. Disp. Phil. De Quiete Dei,
p. 16, sqq.

bers of their flocks by separate names: "The sheep
"hear his voice, and he calleth his own sheep by
" name and leadeth them out. And when he put-
" teth forth his own sheep he goeth before them,
"and the sheep follow him, for they know his voice."
We likewise find traces of the same custom in
Sicily, Crete, and various other parts of Greece,
where goats, and heifers, and sheep, enjoyed the
privilege of a name, as Cynœtha, Amalthea, and
others. In later times it was judged preferable,
that the flock should follow their shepherds by the
eye, for which reason they were accustomed to stuff
their ears with wool.[1] To prevent rams from but-
ting, they used to bore a hole[2] through their horns
near the roots. Sheep were generally shorn[3] during
the month of May, and after the wool had been
clipped, they were commonly anointed with wine,
oil, and the juice of bitter lupins.[4] In remoter ages
the practice prevailed of plucking off the wool instead of shearing it ; and this barbarous method, at
once so painful to the sheep and so laborious to
the shepherd, had not been entirely abandoned in
the age of Pliny.[5] It was a rule among the
pastoral tribes, that the number of their flocks
should be uneven.[6] The shepherds of Greece bestowed the name of Sekitai,[7] (from σηκος an enclosure) upon lambs taken early from the ewes, and

[1] Geop. xviii. 4.
[2] Ferocia ejus cohibetur cornu
juxta aurem terebrato. Plin. Nat.
Hist. viii. 72. Cf. Geopon. viii.
5. To the same purpose writes
also Columella :—Epicharmus Sy-
racusanus qui pecudum medici-
nas diligentissime conscripsit af-
firmat pugnacem arietem mitigari
terebra secundum auriculas fora-
tis cornibus qua curvantur in
flexu. Columell. vii. 3.
[3] It is observed by the ancients
that long lank wool indicated

strength in the sheep, curly wool
the contrary. Geop. xviii. 1, seq.
[4] Geop. xviii. 8.
[5] Duerat quibusdam in locis
vellendi mos. Plin. Nat. Hist.
vii. 73. Veliæ unde essent plures
accepi caussas inquies quod ibi
pastores palatim ex ovibus ante
tonsuram inventam vellere lanam
sint soliti, ex quo vellera dicuntur.
Varr. de Ling. Lat. iv. Cf. De
Re Rust. ii. 11. Isidor. xix. 27.
[6] Geop. xviii. 2.
[7] Schol. Theoc. i. 9.

fed by hand. They were usually kept in a cote apart from the other sheep.

As flocks, in most parts of Greece, were exposed to the rapacity of the wolf,[1] the shepherds had recourse to an extraordinary contrivance, to destroy this fierce animal; kindling large charcoal fires in open spaces in the woods, they cast thereon the powder of certain diminutive fish, caught in great numbers along the grassy shores of Greece, together with small slices of lamb and kid. Attracted by the savour which they could snuff from a distance, the wolves flocked in great numbers towards the fires, round which they prowled with loud howlings, in expectation of sharing the prey, the odour of which had drawn them thither. Stupified at length by the fumes of the charcoal, they would drop upon the earth in a lethargic sleep, when the shepherds coming up knocked them on the head.[2]

[1] From the relations of travellers it would appear that the method observed by the ancient Greeks in ridding themselves of the wolf is no longer known to their descendants, though the apprehension of their destructiveness and ferocity be as great as ever. Solon, it is well known set a price in his laws on the head of a wolf, which appears to have varied in different ages; (cf. Plut. Solon. § 23. Schol. Aristoph. Av. 369 ;) but could never have amounted to the sum of two talents. Whatever the ancient price may have been, however, it was paid by the magistrates; but "the peasant now produces "the skins in the bazaar or mar-"ket, and is recompensed by vo-"luntary contributions." Chandler, ii. p. 145. Close by a khan on mount Parnes, which is covered with pine trees, Sir George Wheler saw a very curious fountain, to which the wolves, bears, and wild boars commonly descend to drink. Id. p. 197.

[2] Geop. xviii. 14. Nevertheless, when a wolf bit a sheep without killing it, the flesh was supposed to be rendered more tender and delicate, an effect which Plutarch attributes to the hot and fiery breath of the beast. Sympos. ii. 9.